taste of home
BIG BOOK
OF
heartwarming
Soups

taste of home
BOOKS

REIMAN MEDIA GROUP, INC. • GREENDALE, WISCONSIN

taste of home Reader's Digest

A TASTE OF HOME/READER'S DIGEST BOOK

© 2010 Reiman Media Group, Inc.
5400 S. 60th St., Greendale WI 53129

Editor-in-Chief: Catherine Cassidy
Vice President, Executive Editor/Books: Heidi Reuter Lloyd
North American Chief Marketing Officer: Lisa Karpinski
Food Director: Diane Werner RD
Senior Editor/Books: Mark Hagen
Project Editor: Heidi Reuter Lloyd
Associate Editors: Julie Blume Benedict, Janet Briggs
Project Art Director: Chrissy Schuster
Associate Art Directors: Jessie Sharon, Courtney Lentz
Content Production Manager: Julie Wagner
Layout Designers: Kathy Crawford, Kathleen Bump
Proofreader: Vicki Soukup Jensen
Recipe Asset System Manager: Coleen Martin
Premedia Supervisor: Scott Berger
Recipe Testing & Editing: Taste of Home Test Kitchen
Food Photography: Taste of Home Photo Studio
Administrative Assistant: Barb Czysz

The Reader's Digest Association, Inc.
President and Chief Executive Officer: Mary G. Berner
President, North American Affinities: Suzanne M. Grimes

For other Taste of Home books and products, visit **shoptasteofhome.com.**

For more Reader's Digest products and information, visit **rd.com** (in the United States) or see **rd.ca** (in Canada).

International Standard Book Number (10): 0-89821-869-1
International Standard Book Number (13): 978-0-89821-869-5
Library of Congress Control Number: 2010937680

Cover Photography
Photographer: Dan Roberts
Food Stylists: Sarah Thompson, Sue Draheim
Set Stylist: Jennifer Bradley Vent

Pictured on the front cover (clockwise from top left):
Mexican Chicken Soup (p. 160), Chunky Chicken Noodle Soup (p. 163) and Broccoli & Cheese Soup (p. 201).

Printed in China
3 5 7 9 10 8 6 4 2

p. 99

p. 114

p. 26

table of contents

P. 20

P. 112

P. 68

P. 56

P. 104

P. 31

soothe the SOUL

SERVE UP A SPOONFUL OF COMFORT

CLAM CHOWDER, P. 222

There's something so comforting about curling up in a chair with a steaming bowl of soup on a dreary day. It was Mom's go-to food when she wanted to warm you up as the wind and rain blew noisily outside. She brought mugs full of hearty soup to ease your childhood colds and chase away other aches and pains, as well as to soothe bruised spirits.

Now you can be the one serving up a bowl of comfort with the 450+ fabulous soups in *Taste of Home Big Book of Heartwarming Soups*. With the impressive variety in this collection, you're sure to find dozens of recipes you'll be eager to make.

Browse through this cookbook, where the options are plentiful and delicious!

- Chicken and turkey soups with a range of flavorings, from classic Chicken Noodle Soup to spicy Hearty Chipotle Chicken Soup, are always family-pleasers.

- Economical beans & lentils help stretch your grocery dollars and serve up a satisfying meal.

- Beef and ground beef soups can be both filling and sophisticated. Just look at Meatball Tortellini Soup, Beef Barley Soup and Baked Beefy Onion Soup as yummy examples!

- Cream soups add a touch of elegance to any meal, and the ones showcased here are no exception, such as Roasted Garlic Potato Soup, Creamy Carrot Soup and Creamy Corn Crab Soup.

- Meatless soups are a delicious way to add more vegetables to your diet. Try Mushroom Barley Soup or Winter Harvest Vegetable Soup.

- Grilled cheese's favorite soup, tomato, has a section devoted just to it. Next time, pair your hot, creamy sandwich with Tomato Basil Soup, Tomato Soup with Herb Dumplings or Tomato Garlic Soup instead of plain canned tomato soup.

- Cooking for 2 will help you avoid leftovers. These tasty, small-yield soups make from 2 to 4 servings.

- Whether you like your chili mild or spicy, there are several that will tingle your palate, from White Chicken Chili to Zippy Three-Bean Chili. Yum!

You'll also find more than 150 tips from experienced cooks and our food editors to help you discover new ways to enhance and enjoy soup. As an added bonus, we have included a special section of fresh-baked breads to round out your meals.

Taste of Home Big Book of Heartwarming Soups is chock-full of tried-and-true favorites from home-style cooks just like you. And each one has been prepared and taste-tasted by our Test Kitchen home economists. That means you can make these recipes with confidence, enjoy the results and win raves from friends and family.

beef & ground beef

ASIAN VEGETABLE-BEEF SOUP, P. 14

beef and tortellini soup

BARBARA KEMMER
ROHNERT PARK, CALIFORNIA

This is my mom's recipe. My family loves it, and so does everyone else who tries it. With its great tomato flavor, so will you!

- 5 tablespoons all-purpose flour, *divided*
- 1/2 pound beef top sirloin steak, cut into 1/2-inch cubes
- 3 teaspoons butter, *divided*
- 1 medium onion, chopped
- 1 celery rib, chopped
- 1 medium carrot, chopped
- 2 garlic cloves, minced
- 1 can (28 ounces) diced tomatoes, undrained
- 2 cans (14-1/2 ounces *each*) reduced-sodium beef broth
- 1-1/2 cups water, *divided*
- 1 teaspoon dried thyme
- 1/2 teaspoon white pepper
- 1/4 teaspoon salt
- 2 cups frozen beef tortellini

1 Place 2 tablespoons flour in a large resealable plastic bag. Add beef, a few pieces at a time, and shake to coat. In a nonstick Dutch oven, brown beef in 2 teaspoons butter; remove and keep warm.

2 In the same pan, saute the onion, celery and carrot in remaining butter until tender. Add garlic; cook 1 minute longer. Add the tomatoes, broth, 1 cup water, thyme, pepper, salt and reserved beef. Bring to a boil. Reduce heat; cover and simmer for 20 minutes. Add tortellini; cook 5-10 minutes longer or until tender.

3 Combine remaining flour and water until smooth. Stir into the pan. Bring to a boil; cook and stir for 2 minutes or until thickened.

YIELD: 6 SERVINGS (2-1/4 QUARTS).

EDITOR'S NOTE: Top sirloin steak may be labeled as strip steak, Kansas City steak, New York strip, ambassador steak or boneless club steak in your region.

veggie meatball soup

CHARLA TINNEY | TYRONE, OKLAHOMA

It's a snap to put together this hearty soup before I leave for work. I just add cooked pasta when I get home, and I have a few minutes to relax before supper is ready.

- 3 cups beef broth
- 2 cups frozen mixed vegetables, thawed
- 1 can (14-1/2 ounces) stewed tomatoes
- 12 frozen fully cooked Italian meatballs (1/2 ounce *each*), thawed
- 3 bay leaves
- 1/4 teaspoon pepper
- 1 cup spiral pasta, cooked and drained

1 In a 3-qt. slow cooker, combine the first six ingredients. Cover and cook on low for 4-5 hours. Just before serving, stir in pasta; heat through. Discard bay leaves.

YIELD: 6 SERVINGS.

freezing celery for soup

When I have a bit of extra time, I chop a few stalks of celery or a few onions. After sauteing them in butter, I spoon them into ice cube trays, freeze, then pop the frozen "veggie cubes" into a labeled freezer bag to store. They are an invaluable addition to soups or casseroles when I'm in a hurry.

SALLY M., NELIGH, NEBRASKA

beef macaroni soup

DEBRA BAKER
GREENVILLE, NORTH CAROLINA

This is a quick version of delicious vegetable beef soup. With beef, veggies and pasta, it's just as good as the original with a lot less fuss.

- 1 pound ground beef
- 2 cups frozen mixed vegetables
- 1 can (14-1/2 ounces) diced tomatoes, undrained
- 1 can (14-1/2 ounces) beef broth
- 1/4 teaspoon pepper
- 1/2 cup uncooked elbow macaroni

1 In a large saucepan, cook beef over medium heat until no longer pink; drain. Stir in mixed vegetables, tomatoes, broth and pepper. Bring to a boil; add macaroni. Reduce heat; cover and simmer for 8-10 minutes or until macaroni and vegetables are tender.

YIELD: 5 SERVINGS.

leftover vegetable soup

There are just the two of us, so we sometimes end up with leftover vegetables after meals. I put them in a heavy-duty resealable plastic bag or freezer container and store in the freezer. When I have 3 to 4 cups, I make vegetable soup.

CAROLINE W., THERMOPOLIS, WYOMING

meatball mushroom soup

JOANN ABBOTT
KERHONKSON, NEW YORK

This creamy, super-thick soup is hearty with meatballs, mushrooms, barley, macaroni and rice. With dinner rolls or breadsticks, it's a simple and satisfying meal to eat on a rainy day. Leftovers easily reheat for a fast, filling lunch or dinner.

- 1/2 pound ground beef
- 2 cans (10-3/4 ounces *each*) condensed cream of mushroom soup, undiluted
- 1-1/3 cups milk
- 1-1/3 cups water
- 1 teaspoon Italian seasoning
- 1 teaspoon dried minced onion
- 1/2 teaspoon dried minced garlic
- 1/4 cup quick-cooking barley
- 1/4 cup uncooked elbow macaroni
- 1/4 cup uncooked long grain rice
- 1 medium carrot, shredded
- 1 jar (4-1/2 ounces) sliced mushrooms, drained
- 2 tablespoons grated Parmesan cheese

1 Shape the beef into 1-in. balls; set aside. In a large saucepan, combine soup, milk and water; bring to a boil. Add Italian seasoning, onion, garlic, barley, macaroni and rice. Reduce the heat; simmer, uncovered, for 15 minutes.

2 Meanwhile, brown meatballs in a nonstick skillet until no longer pink. Stir carrot into soup; cover and simmer for 5 minutes. Use a slotted spoon to transfer meatballs to soup. Stir in the mushrooms and Parmesan cheese; heat through.

YIELD: 6 SERVINGS.

beef barley soup

GINNY PERKINS | COLUMBIANA, OHIO

My husband doesn't usually consider a bowl of soup dinner, but this hearty, comforting soup got a thumbs up—even from him! Garnish with sweet potato chips.

- 1-1/2 pounds beef stew meat
- 1 tablespoon canola oil
- 1 can (14-1/2 ounces) diced tomatoes
- 1 cup *each* chopped onion, diced celery and sliced fresh carrots
- 1/2 cup chopped green pepper
- 4 cups beef broth
- 2 cups water
- 1 cup spaghetti sauce
- 2/3 cup medium pearl barley
- 1 tablespoon dried parsley flakes
- 2 teaspoons salt
- 1-1/2 teaspoons dried basil
- 3/4 teaspoon pepper

1 In a large skillet, brown meat in oil over medium heat; drain. Meanwhile, in a 5-qt. slow cooker, combine vegetables, broth, water, spaghetti sauce, barley and seasonings. Stir in beef. Cover and cook on low for 9-10 hours or until meat is tender. Skim fat from cooking juices.

YIELD: 8 SERVINGS (2-1/2 QUARTS).

wild rice and cheddar dumpling soup

TERESA CHRISTENSEN | OSCEOLA, WISCONSIN

I'm a homemaker and enjoy preparing hearty soups and stews for my husband and two daughters. This is one of their favorites.

- 10 cups water
- 1 pound sliced fresh mushrooms
- 2 cups diced potatoes
- 2 cups chopped carrots
- 1-1/2 cups chopped celery
- 1 medium onion, chopped
- 3 chicken bouillon cubes
- 3 to 4 cups cubed cooked roast beef
- 2 cups cooked wild rice
- 3/4 cup all-purpose flour
- 3 cups milk
- 1/4 cup butter
- 1 tablespoon minced fresh parsley
- 2 to 3 teaspoons salt
- 3/4 teaspoon dried basil
- 3/4 teaspoon pepper

DUMPLINGS:
- 2 cups biscuit/baking mix
- 1 cup (4 ounces) shredded cheddar cheese
- 2/3 cup milk

1 Place the first seven ingredients in a stockpot. Bring to a boil. Reduce heat; cover and simmer for 10-15 minutes or until vegetables are tender. Add beef and rice.

2 In a small bowl, combine flour and milk until smooth. Stir into the soup. Bring to a boil; cook and stir for 2 minutes or until thickened. Stir in the butter and seasonings.

3 Combine the baking mix, cheese and milk. Drop by tablespoonfuls onto simmering soup. Cover and simmer for 12 minutes or until a toothpick inserted in a dumpling comes out clean (do not lift the cover while simmering).

YIELD: 14 SERVINGS (ABOUT 5 QUARTS).

beefy vegetable soup

TERESA KING
CHAMBERSBURG, PENNSYLVANIA

I adapted this recipe from one I saw in a cookbook in an effort to add more vegetables to our diet. Our sons eat this up without hesitation.

- 1 pound ground beef
- 1 medium onion, chopped
- 1 garlic clove, minced
- 2 cans (8 ounces *each*) tomato sauce
- 2 cans (16 ounces *each*) kidney beans, rinsed and drained, optional
- 1 package (10 ounces) frozen corn
- 1 cup shredded carrots
- 1 cup chopped green pepper
- 1 cup chopped sweet red pepper
- 1 cup chopped fresh tomato
- 1 tablespoon chili powder
- 1/2 teaspoon dried basil
- 1/2 teaspoon salt
- 1/4 teaspoon pepper

Shredded cheddar cheese, sour cream and tortilla chips, optional

1 In a skillet, cook beef and onion over medium heat until the meat is no longer pink. Add garlic; cook 1 minute longer. Drain.

2 Transfer to a 5-qt. slow cooker. Stir in the tomato sauce, beans if desired, vegetables and seasonings. Cover and cook on low for 8 hours or until thick and bubbly, stirring occasionally. Serve with cheese, sour cream and chips if desired.

YIELD: 8-10 SERVINGS
(ABOUT 2-1/2 QUARTS).

EDITOR'S NOTE: Freeze Beefy Vegetable Soup in serving-size containers for quick, no-fuss lunches.

hearty split pea soup

BARBARA LINK
RANCHO CUCAMONGA, CALIFORNIA

For a different spin on traditional split pea soup, try this recipe. The flavor is peppery rather than smoky, and the corned beef is an unexpected, tasty change of pace.

- 1 package (16 ounces) dried split peas
- 8 cups water
- 2 medium potatoes, peeled and cubed
- 2 large onions, chopped
- 2 medium carrots, chopped
- 2 cups cubed cooked corned beef *or* ham
- 1/2 cup chopped celery
- 5 teaspoons chicken bouillon granules
- 1 teaspoon *each* dried marjoram, poultry seasoning and rubbed sage
- 1/2 to 1 teaspoon pepper
- 1/2 teaspoon dried basil
- 1/2 teaspoon salt, optional

1 In a Dutch oven, combine all the ingredients; bring to a boil. Reduce the heat; cover and simmer for 1-1/4 to 1-1/2 hours or until peas and vegetables are tender.

YIELD: 12 SERVINGS (3 QUARTS).

reuben chowder

TASTE OF HOME TEST KITCHEN

This dish contains all of your favorite Reuben sandwich ingredients in a delicious soup. If you don't have bread, simply cut the Swiss cheese into strips and place it on the broth.

- 1 small onion, sliced
- 1 tablespoon canola oil
- 2 cans (14-1/2 ounces *each*) vegetable broth
- 1 can (14-1/2 ounces) beef broth
- 2 teaspoons prepared horseradish
- 1 teaspoon Worcestershire sauce
- 1/2 teaspoon ground mustard
- 1/4 teaspoon celery salt
- 5 ounces deli corned beef, chopped
- 1 cup sauerkraut, rinsed and well drained
- 2 slices rye bread, cubed
- 4 slices Swiss cheese

1 In a small skillet, saute onion in oil until tender. Meanwhile, in a large saucepan, bring the vegetable and beef broth to a boil; stir in the horseradish, Worcestershire sauce, mustard and celery salt. Add the corned beef, sauerkraut and onion. Reduce heat to low; cover and simmer for 10 minutes.

2 Ladle soup into four ovenproof bowls; top with bread cubes and Swiss cheese. Broil 3-4 in. from the heat for 2-3 minutes or until cheese is melted.

YIELD: 4 SERVINGS.

zesty macaroni soup

JOAN HALLFORD
NORTH RICHLAND HILLS, TEXAS

The recipe for this thick, zippy soup first caught my attention for two reasons—it calls for convenience ingredients and it can be prepared in a jiffy. A chili macaroni mix gives this dish a little spice, but sometimes I jazz it up with chopped green chilies. It's a family favorite.

- 1 pound ground beef
- 1 medium onion, chopped
- 5 cups water
- 1 can (15 ounces) pinto beans, rinsed and drained
- 1 can (14-1/2 ounces) diced tomatoes, undrained
- 1 can (7 ounces) whole kernel corn, drained
- 1 can (4 ounces) chopped green chilies, optional
- 1/2 teaspoon ground mustard
- 1/2 teaspoon salt
- 1/8 teaspoon pepper
- 1 package (7-1/2 ounces) chili macaroni dinner mix

Salsa con queso dip

1 In a large saucepan, cook the beef and onion over medium heat until meat is no longer pink; drain. Stir in the water, beans, tomatoes, corn and chilies if desired. Stir in the mustard, salt, pepper and contents of the macaroni sauce mix. Bring to a boil. Reduce the heat; cover and simmer for 10 minutes.

2 Stir in contents of macaroni packet. Cover and simmer 10-14 minutes longer or until macaroni is tender, stirring occasionally. Serve with salsa con queso dip.

YIELD: 8-10 SERVINGS
(ABOUT 2-1/2 QUARTS).

EDITOR'S NOTE: This recipe was tested with Hamburger Helper brand chili macaroni. Salsa con queso dip can be found in the international food section or snack aisle of most grocery stores.

hungarian goulash soup

BETTY KENNEDY | ALEXANDRIA, VIRGINIA

I taught in Germany, where goulash soup is common. It was one of the first foods I tried overseas. When I got home, I pieced this recipe together so I could still enjoy this soup. I make it often. With two active boys, it's nice knowing that dinner is "under control!"

- 3 bacon strips, diced
- 1-1/2 pounds beef stew meat, cut into 1/2-inch cubes
- 1 small green pepper, seeded and chopped
- 2 medium onions, chopped
- 1 large garlic clove, minced
- 1 can (14-1/2 ounces) diced tomatoes
- 3 cups beef broth
- 2 tablespoons paprika
- 1-1/2 teaspoons salt

Pepper to taste

Dash sugar

- 2 large potatoes, peeled and diced
- 1/2 cup sour cream, optional

1 In a large kettle, cook bacon over medium heat until crisp. Remove to paper towels with a slotted spoon; drain, reserving 2 tablespoons drippings. Add beef cubes and brown on all sides. Add green pepper and onions; cook until tender. Add garlic; cook 1 minute longer. Stir in the tomatoes, broth, paprika, salt, pepper and sugar.

2 Cover and simmer for about 1-1/2 hours or until beef is tender. About a 1/2 hour before serving, add the potatoes and reserved bacon; cook until potatoes are tender. Garnish each serving with a dollop of sour cream if desired.

YIELD: 8 SERVINGS (ABOUT 2 QUARTS).

beef lentil soup

GUY TURNBULL
ARLINGTON, MASSACHUSETTS

You can prepare this soup as the main course for a hearty lunch or dinner. But, on cold winter evenings here in New England, I often pour a mugful and enjoy it as a snack.

- 1 pound ground beef (90% lean)
- 1 can (46 ounces) tomato or V8 juice
- 4 cups water
- 1 cup dried lentils, rinsed
- 2 cups chopped cabbage
- 1 cup sliced carrots
- 1 cup sliced celery
- 1 cup chopped onion
- 1/2 cup diced green pepper
- 1/2 teaspoon pepper
- 1/2 teaspoon dried thyme
- 1 bay leaf
- 1 teaspoon salt, optional
- 2 beef bouillon cubes, optional
- 1 package (10 ounces) frozen chopped spinach, thawed

1 In a large stockpot, cook beef over medium heat until no longer pink; drain. Add the tomato juice, water, lentils, cabbage, carrots, celery, onion, green pepper, pepper, thyme, bay leaf, salt and bouillon if desired.

2 Bring to a boil. Reduce heat; simmer, uncovered, for 1 to 1-1/2 hours or until the lentils and vegetables are tender. Add spinach and heat through. Remove bay leaf.

YIELD: 6 SERVINGS.

corny tomato dumpling soup

JACKIE FERRIS | TIVERTON, ONTARIO

In this savory tomato soup, corn stars in both the broth and dumplings. Ground beef makes it a hearty first course or satisfying light main dish.

- 1 pound ground beef
- 3 cups fresh *or* frozen corn
- 1 can (28 ounces) diced tomatoes, undrained
- 2 cans (14-1/2 ounces *each*) beef broth
- 1 cup chopped onion
- 1 garlic clove, minced
- 1-1/2 teaspoons *each* dried basil and dried thyme
- 1/2 teaspoon dried rosemary, crushed

Salt and pepper to taste

CORN DUMPLINGS:

- 1 cup all-purpose flour
- 1/2 cup cornmeal
- 2-1/2 teaspoons baking powder
- 1/2 teaspoon salt
- 1 egg
- 2/3 cup milk
- 1 cup fresh *or* frozen corn
- 1/2 cup shredded cheddar cheese
- 1 tablespoon minced fresh parsley

1 In a large saucepan over medium heat, cook beef until no longer pink; drain. Stir in the corn, tomatoes, broth, onion, garlic and seasonings. Bring to a boil. Reduce heat; cover and simmer for 30-45 minutes.

2 For dumplings, combine the flour, cornmeal, baking powder and salt in a large bowl. In another large bowl, beat egg; stir in milk, corn, cheese and parsley. Stir into dry ingredients just until moistened.

3 Drop by tablespoonfuls onto the simmering soup. Cover and simmer for 15 minutes or until a toothpick inserted in a dumpling comes out clean (do not lift cover while simmering).

YIELD: 8 SERVINGS (ABOUT 2 QUARTS).

taco bean soup

TONYA JONES | SUNDOWN, TEXAS

I have to admit that when a good friend gave me this recipe, I wasn't certain I'd like it. But, after one taste, I changed my mind! My husband loves it, too.

- 2 pounds lean ground beef (90% lean)
- 1 small onion, chopped
- 3 cans (14-1/2 ounces *each*) stewed tomatoes
- 1-1/2 cups water
- 1 can (16 ounces) lima beans, rinsed and drained
- 1 can (16 ounces) kidney beans, rinsed and drained
- 1 can (15 ounces) pinto beans, rinsed and drained
- 1 can (14-1/2 ounces) hominy, drained
- 3 cans (4 ounces *each*) chopped green chilies
- 1 envelope taco seasoning
- 1 envelope ranch salad dressing mix
- 1 teaspoon *each* salt and pepper

Shredded cheddar cheese, optional
Tortilla chips, optional

1 In a large Dutch oven, cook beef and onion over medium heat until meat is no longer pink; drain.

2 Stir in the next 11 ingredients; bring to a boil. Reduce heat; cover and simmer for 30 minutes. Garnish with cheese and serve with chips if desired.

YIELD: 10 SERVINGS.

spicy steak house soup

LISA RENSHAW | KANSAS CITY, MISSOURI

Think "steak dinner in a bowl" when eating this rich and hefty soup. It makes great cold-weather fare and packs a chili-powder nip of its own!

- 1/4 pound beef tenderloin, cut into 1/4-inch pieces
- 1/4 cup chopped onion
- 1/4 teaspoon salt
- 2 teaspoons olive oil
- 1-1/2 cups cubed peeled Yukon Gold potatoes
- 1 cup beef broth
- 1/4 cup steak sauce
- 3/4 teaspoon chili powder
- 1/4 teaspoon ground cumin
- 1/8 teaspoon cayenne pepper
- 2 tablespoons minced fresh parsley

1 In a large nonstick saucepan, saute the beef, onion and salt in oil for 4-5 minutes or until meat is no longer pink. Stir in the potatoes, broth, steak sauce, chili powder, cumin and cayenne. Bring to a boil. Reduce the heat; cover and simmer for 30-35 minutes or until the potatoes are tender. Garnish with parsley.

YIELD: 2 SERVINGS.

asian vegetable-beef soup

MOLLIE LEE | EUGENE, OREGON

My husband is Korean-American, and I enjoy working Asian flavors into our menu. This tasty soup was something I put together one night with what I found in our fridge. Everyone loved it!

- 1 pound beef stew meat, cut into 1-inch cubes
- 1 tablespoon canola oil
- 2 cups water
- 1 cup beef broth
- 1/4 cup sherry *or* additional beef broth
- 1/4 cup soy sauce
- 6 green onions, chopped
- 3 tablespoons brown sugar
- 2 garlic cloves, minced
- 1 tablespoon minced fresh gingerroot
- 2 teaspoons sesame oil
- 1/4 teaspoon cayenne pepper
- 1-1/2 cups sliced fresh mushrooms
- 1-1/2 cups julienned carrots
- 1 cup sliced bok choy
- 1-1/2 cups uncooked long grain rice
  Chive blossoms, optional

1 In a large saucepan, brown meat in oil on all sides; drain. Add the water, broth, sherry, soy sauce, onions, brown sugar, garlic, ginger, sesame oil and cayenne. Bring to a boil. Reduce heat; cover and simmer for 1 hour.

2 Stir in the mushrooms, carrots and bok choy; cover and simmer 20-30 minutes longer or until vegetables are tender. Meanwhile, cook rice according to the package directions.

3 Divide rice among six soup bowls, 3/4 cup in each; top each with 1 cup of soup. Garnish with chive blossoms if desired.

YIELD: 6 SERVINGS.

easy beef barley soup

CAROLE LANTHIER
COURTICE, ONTARIO

This soup takes very little time to make. You can serve it for a leftover lunch or for supper with homemade bread, which I do on occasion.

- 1/2 pound lean ground beef (90% lean)
- 2 large fresh mushrooms, sliced
- 1 celery rib, chopped
- 1 small onion, chopped
- 2 teaspoons all-purpose flour
- 3 cans (14-1/2 ounces *each*) reduced-sodium beef broth
- 2 medium carrots, sliced
- 1 large potato, peeled and cubed
- 1/2 teaspoon pepper
- 1/8 teaspoon salt
- 1/3 cup medium pearl barley
- 1 can (5 ounces) evaporated milk
- 2 tablespoons tomato paste

1 In a Dutch oven over medium heat, cook and stir the beef, mushrooms, celery and onion until meat is no longer pink; drain. Stir in the flour until blended; gradually add the broth. Stir in the carrots, potato, pepper and salt. Bring to a boil. Stir in the barley.

2 Reduce the heat; cover and simmer for 45-50 minutes or until the barley is tender. Whisk in milk and tomato paste; heat through.

YIELD: 4 SERVINGS.

thin out barley soup

Barley absorbs a lot of soup broth. If you like barley in your soup but the leftovers are too thick, add extra chicken, beef or vegetable broth to leftovers while reheating to achieve the desired consistency.

TASTE OF HOME TEST KITCHEN

swedish meatball soup

DEBORAH TAYLOR | INKOM, IDAHO

This is a very comforting, filling, homey soup. I especially like cooking it during winter months and serving it with hot rolls, bread or muffins.

- 1 egg
- 2 cups half-and-half cream, *divided*
- 1 cup soft bread crumbs
- 1 small onion, finely chopped
- 1-3/4 teaspoons salt, *divided*
- 1-1/2 pounds ground beef
- 1 tablespoon butter
- 3 tablespoons all-purpose flour
- 3/4 teaspoon beef bouillon granules
- 1/2 teaspoon pepper
- 1/8 to 1/4 teaspoon garlic salt
- 3 cups water
- 1 pound red potatoes, cubed
- 1 package (10 ounces) frozen peas, thawed

1 In a large bowl, beat the egg; add 1/3 cup cream, bread crumbs, onion and 1 teaspoon of salt. Crumble the beef over mixture and mix well. Shape into 1/2-in. balls.

2 In a Dutch oven, brown meatballs in butter in batches. Remove from the pan; set aside. Drain fat.

3 To pan, add the flour, bouillon, pepper, garlic salt and remaining salt; stir until smooth. Gradually stir in water; bring to a boil. Reduce heat; cook and stir for 2 minutes or until thickened. Add potatoes and meatballs.

4 Reduce the heat; cover and simmer for 25 minutes or until potatoes are tender. Stir in peas and remaining cream; heat through.

YIELD: 8 SERVINGS (ABOUT 2 QUARTS).

vegetable beef soup

MARIE CARLISLE | SUMRALL, MISSISSIPPI

Just brimming with veggies, this hearty soup will warm family and friends right to their toes! It's especially good served with corn bread, and it's even better the second day.

- 4 cups cubed peeled potatoes
- 6 cups water
- 1 pound ground beef
- 5 teaspoons beef bouillon granules
- 1 can (10-3/4 ounces) condensed tomato soup, undiluted
- 2 cups frozen corn, thawed
- 2 cups frozen sliced carrots, thawed
- 2 cups frozen cut green beans, thawed
- 2 cups frozen sliced okra, thawed
- 3 tablespoons dried minced onion

1 In a Dutch oven, bring the potatoes and water to a boil. Cover and cook for 10-15 minutes or until tender. Meanwhile, in a large skillet, cook beef over medium heat until no longer pink; drain.

2 Add the bouillon, soup, vegetables, dried minced onion and beef to the undrained potatoes. Bring to a boil. Reduce heat; simmer, uncovered, for 8-10 minutes or until heated through, stirring occasionally.

YIELD: 14 SERVINGS (3-1/2 QUARTS).

hearty taco soup

MARYLOU VON SCHEELE | UNIVERSITY PLACE, WASHINGTON

Savory and satisfying, this thick chili-like soup has a mild taco flavor and an appealing color. It comes together quickly and always brings compliments. The recipe can easily be doubled to make more servings.

- 1 pound lean ground beef (90% lean)
- 1 medium onion, chopped
- 1 medium green pepper, chopped
- 1 envelope taco seasoning
- 2/3 cup water
- 4 cups V8 juice
- 1 cup chunky salsa

TOPPINGS:
- 3/4 cup shredded lettuce
- 6 tablespoons chopped fresh tomatoes
- 6 tablespoons shredded cheddar cheese
- 1/4 cup chopped green onions
- 1/4 cup sour cream

Tortilla chips, optional

1 In a large saucepan coated with cooking spray, cook the beef, onion and pepper over medium heat until meat is no longer pink; drain. Stir in taco seasoning and water; cook and stir for 5 minutes or until liquid is reduced.

2 Add the V8 juice and salsa; bring to a boil. Reduce the heat; simmer, uncovered, for 5 minutes or until heated through. Top each serving with 2 tablespoons of lettuce, 1 tablespoon of tomato and cheese, and 2 teaspoons of green onions and sour cream. Serve with tortilla chips if desired.

YIELD: 6 SERVINGS.

beef and bacon chowder

NANCY SCHMIDT | CENTER, COLORADO

Rave reviews are sure to follow when this creamy chowder appears on the dinner table. Bacon makes it rich and hearty. It's a favorite with my entire family.

- 1 pound ground beef
- 2 cups chopped celery
- 1/2 cup chopped onion
- 4 cups milk
- 3 cups cubed peeled potatoes, cooked
- 2 cans (10-3/4 ounces *each*) condensed cream of mushroom soup, undiluted
- 2 cups chopped carrots, cooked
- Salt and pepper to taste
- 12 bacon strips, cooked and crumbled

1 In a Dutch oven, cook the beef, celery and onion over medium heat until meat is no longer pink; drain. Add the milk, potatoes, soup, carrots, salt and pepper; heat through. Stir in the bacon just before serving.

YIELD: 12 SERVINGS (3 QUARTS).

spicy cheeseburger soup

LISA MAST | WHITE CLOUD, MICHIGAN

This creamy soup brings my family to the table in a hurry. I love the warming zip of cayenne, but it also tastes terrific without it if you like milder flavor. With a few simple side dishes, this soup is a full meal.

- 1-1/2 cups water
- 2 cups cubed peeled potatoes
- 2 small carrots, grated
- 1 small onion, chopped
- 1/4 cup chopped green pepper
- 1 jalapeno pepper, seeded and chopped
- 1 garlic clove, minced
- 1 tablespoon beef bouillon granules
- 1/2 teaspoon salt
- 1 pound ground beef, cooked and drained
- 2-1/2 cups milk, *divided*
- 3 tablespoons all-purpose flour
- 8 ounces process American cheese (Velveeta), cubed
- 1/4 to 1 teaspoon cayenne pepper, optional
- 1/2 pound sliced bacon, cooked and crumbled

1 In a large saucepan, combine first nine ingredients; bring to a boil. Reduce heat. Cover; simmer for 15 minutes or until potatoes are tender.

2 Stir in the beef and 2 cups of milk; heat through. Combine the flour and remaining milk until smooth; gradually stir into soup. Bring to a boil; cook and stir for 2 minutes or until thickened and bubbly. Reduce heat; stir in cheese until melted. Add cayenne pepper if desired. Top with bacon just before serving.

YIELD: 6-8 SERVINGS (ABOUT 2 QUARTS).

EDITOR'S NOTE: When cutting hot peppers, disposable gloves are recommended. Avoid touching your face.

hearty hamburger soup

DIANE MROZINSKI | ESSEXVILLE, MICHIGAN

You'll get a thumbs-up when you serve this veggie-packed soup. You can substitute ground turkey for the beef, if you like, and easily double or triple the recipe to serve more people.

- 1/4 pound ground beef
- 1/4 cup chopped onion
- 1-1/2 cups water
- 1/4 cup thinly sliced carrot
- 1-1/2 teaspoons beef bouillon granules
- 1 can (5-1/2 ounces) V8 juice
- 1/4 cup frozen corn
- 1/4 cup frozen peas
- 1/4 cup sliced fresh mushrooms
- 1/4 cup sliced zucchini
- 1/8 teaspoon dried basil

Dash pepper

- 1/2 cup cooked elbow macaroni

1 In a small saucepan, cook beef and onion over medium heat until meat is no longer pink; drain. Add the water, carrot and bouillon. Bring to a boil. Reduce heat; simmer, uncovered, for 5 minutes.

2 Add the V8 juice, corn, peas, mushrooms, zucchini, basil and pepper. Simmer 6-8 minutes longer or until vegetables are tender. Add macaroni; heat through.

YIELD: 2 SERVINGS.

barley peasant soup

MARY SULLIVAN | SPOKANE, WASHINGTON

Barley brightens the broth of this soup that features a cornucopia of vegetables. The recipe makes a savory supper or lunch to chase away the chill of winter.

- 1 pound beef stew meat, cut into 1/2 – 3/4-inch cubes
- 1 tablespoon olive oil
- 2 cups chopped onions
- 1 cup sliced celery
- 2 garlic cloves, minced
- 5 cups water
- 5 cups beef broth
- 2 cups sliced carrots
- 1-1/2 cups medium pearl barley
- 1 can (15 ounces) garbanzo beans *or* chickpeas, rinsed and drained
- 1 can (15 ounces) kidney beans, rinsed and drained
- 4 cups sliced zucchini
- 3 cups diced plum tomatoes
- 2 cups chopped cabbage
- 1/4 cup minced fresh parsley
- 1 teaspoon dried thyme
- 1-1/2 teaspoons Italian seasoning

Salt and pepper to taste

Grated Parmesan cheese, optional

1 In a large saucepan, brown meat in oil. Add onions and celery. Cook until beef is no longer pink. Add garlic and cook 1 minute longer. Add water and broth; bring to a boil. Add carrots and barley. Reduce heat; cover and simmer for 45-60 minutes or until barley is tender.

2 Add the beans, zucchini, tomatoes, cabbage, parsley and seasonings; simmer 15-20 minutes or until the vegetables are tender. Top individual bowls with Parmesan cheese if desired.

YIELD: 16-20 SERVINGS.

colorful vegetable beef soup

RUBY WILLIAMS | BOGALUSA, LOUISIANA

Brimming with chunks of beef, potatoes, carrots, green beans and mushrooms, this satisfying soup is a meal in itself. When unexpected guests come to visit, this is one of my favorite recipes to prepare because it's ready in no time.

- 2 cans (14-1/2 ounces *each*) beef broth
- 1 tablespoon Worcestershire sauce
- 1 teaspoon ground mustard
- 1/2 teaspoon salt
- 1/4 teaspoon pepper
- 3 medium potatoes, peeled and cubed
- 6 medium carrots, cut into 1/2-inch slices
- 3 cups cubed cooked beef
- 2 cups frozen cut green beans, thawed
- 2 cups sliced fresh mushrooms
- 1 cup frozen peas, thawed
- 1 can (15 ounces) tomato sauce
- 2 tablespoons minced fresh parsley

1 In a Dutch oven, combine the broth, Worcestershire sauce, mustard, salt and pepper. Stir in potatoes and carrots. Bring to a boil. Reduce heat; cover and simmer for 12 minutes or until carrots are crisp-tender.

2 Stir in the remaining ingredients. Return to a boil. Reduce heat; simmer, uncovered, for 5 minutes or until the vegetables are tender.

YIELD: 12 SERVINGS (3 QUARTS).

savory winter soup

DANA SIMMONS | LANCASTER, OHIO

Even friends who don't particularly like soup enjoy this full-flavored version of traditional vegetable soup.

- 2 pounds ground beef
- 3 medium onions, chopped
- 1 garlic clove, minced
- 3 cans (10-1/2 ounces *each*) condensed beef broth, undiluted
- 1 can (28 ounces) diced tomatoes, undrained
- 3 cups water
- 1 cup *each* diced carrots and celery
- 1 cup fresh *or* frozen cut green beans
- 1 cup cubed peeled potatoes
- 2 tablespoons minced fresh parsley *or* 2 teaspoons dried parsley flakes
- 1 teaspoon dried basil
- 1/2 teaspoon dried thyme

Salt and pepper to taste

1 In a large skillet, cook beef and onions over medium heat until the meat is no longer pink. Add garlic; cook 1 minute longer. Drain.

2 Transfer skillet mixture into a 5-qt. slow cooker. Stir in the remaining ingredients. Cover and cook on high for 8 hours or until heated through.

YIELD: 14 SERVINGS (3-1/2 QUARTS).

EDITOR'S NOTE: To save chopping time, use frozen sliced carrots and cubed hash brown potatoes in Savory Winter Soup.

homemade beef broth

When I'm preparing a beef stir-fry, I cut the sirloin into thin strips. But some strips have more fat on them than we care to have. When I cut off the fat and there's still meat attached, I use those pieces to make beef broth. I put the fatty pieces in a hot pan with oil to brown them and add a cup or so of water. I simmer this for an hour and sometimes season the mixture with carrots, celery and onions. I strain and refrigerate the broth, then skim off the fat. This homemade broth allows me to control the amount of fat and sodium.

JEAN C., LAKEWOOD, COLORADO

hearty veggie meatball soup

PENNY FAGAN | MOBILE, ALABAMA

Loaded with veggies, meatballs and spices, this meal-in-one soup is hearty enough to warm up any cold winter day. It's a recipe you'll make again and again!

- 1 package (12 ounces) frozen fully cooked Italian meatballs
- 1 can (28 ounces) diced tomatoes, undrained
- 3 cups beef broth
- 2 cups shredded cabbage
- 1 can (16 ounces) kidney beans, rinsed and drained
- 1 medium zucchini, sliced
- 1 cup fresh green beans, cut into 1-inch pieces
- 1 cup water
- 2 medium carrots, sliced
- 1 teaspoon dried basil
- 1/2 teaspoon minced garlic
- 1/4 teaspoon salt
- 1/8 teaspoon dried oregano
- 1/8 teaspoon pepper
- 1 cup uncooked elbow macaroni
- 1/4 cup minced fresh parsley

Grated Parmesan cheese, optional

1. In a 5-qt. slow cooker, combine the first 14 ingredients. Cover and cook on low for 5-1/2 to 6 hours or until vegetables are almost tender.
2. Stir in the macaroni and parsley; cook 30 minutes longer or until macaroni is tender. Serve with cheese if desired.

YIELD: 6 SERVINGS (2-1/2 QUARTS).

meat and potato soup

TASTE OF HOME TEST KITCHEN

The satisfying combination of potatoes and roast beef come together to star in this rich and hearty soup. The result is a well-balanced, flavorful dish that's perfect for fall or any chilly day.

- 4 cups water
- 3 cups cubed cooked beef chuck roast
- 4 medium red potatoes, cubed
- 4 ounces sliced fresh mushrooms
- 1/2 cup chopped onion
- 1/4 cup ketchup
- 2 teaspoons beef bouillon granules
- 2 teaspoons cider vinegar
- 1 teaspoon brown sugar
- 1 teaspoon Worcestershire sauce
- 1/8 teaspoon ground mustard
- 1 cup coarsely chopped fresh spinach

1. In a Dutch oven, combine the first 11 ingredients. Bring to a boil. Reduce the heat; cover and simmer for 14-18 minutes or until the potatoes are tender. Stir in the spinach; cook 1-2 minutes longer or until tender.

YIELD: 6 SERVINGS (2 QUARTS).

freeze whole tomatoes

Put extra garden tomatoes in a plastic freezer bag and store in your freezer. To use in soup, stew or sauce, just hold the frozen tomatoes under warm water, and the skins will slip right off. Drop the whole skinless tomatoes into the pot—they'll break up during cooking, which also saves time chopping.

ELAINE T., PALMETTO, FLORIDA

quick beef barley soup

SHARON KOLENC | JASPER, ALBERTA

When making this versatile soup, I tend to clean out the refrigerator by adding leftovers I have on hand. My family says they have to watch out for the kitchen sink!

- 2 cups beef broth
- 8 cups water
- 2 cups chopped cooked roast beef
- 1/2 cup chopped carrots
- 3 celery ribs, chopped
- 1/2 cup chopped onion
- 1 can (14-1/2 ounces) diced tomatoes, undrained
- 1 cup quick-cooking barley
- 1 teaspoon dried oregano
- 1/2 teaspoon pepper
- 1 can (10-3/4 ounces) condensed tomato soup, undiluted
- 1/2 cup frozen *or* canned peas
- 1/2 cup frozen *or* canned cut green *or* wax beans

Seasoned salt to taste

1 In a stockpot, combine the first 10 ingredients; bring to a boil. Reduce heat; cover and simmer for 25 minutes, stirring occasionally. Add the soup, peas and beans. Simmer, uncovered, for 10 minutes. Add seasoned salt.

YIELD: 12-14 SERVINGS (ABOUT 3-1/2 QUARTS).

stuffed sweet pepper soup

JOSEPH KENDRA | CORAOPOLIS, PENNSYLVANIA

Tomatoes, peppers, garlic and onions are the mainstays of my garden. Being the oldest of seven children, I acquired a knack for cooking from my mom.

- 1 pound ground beef
- 8 cups water
- 4 cups tomato juice
- 3 medium sweet red pepper, diced
- 1-1/2 cups chili sauce
- 1 cup uncooked long grain rice
- 2 celery ribs, diced
- 1 large onion, diced
- 2 teaspoons browning sauce, optional
- 3 teaspoons chicken bouillon granules
- 2 garlic cloves, minced
- 1/2 teaspoon salt

1 In a Dutch oven, over medium heat, cook the beef until no longer pink; drain. Add the remaining ingredients; bring to a boil.

2 Reduce heat; simmer, uncovered, for 1 hour or until rice is tender.

YIELD: 16 SERVINGS (4 QUARTS).

chopping an onion

To quickly chop an onion, peel and cut in half from the root to the top. Leaving root attached, place flat side down on work surface. Cut vertically through the onion, leaving the root end uncut.

Cut across the onion, discarding root end. The closer the cuts, the finer the onion will be chopped. This method can also be used for shallots.

TASTE OF HOME TEST KITCHEN

meatball tortellini soup

SHERYL LITTLE | SHERWOOD, ARKANSAS

After our son left home, I had to learn to pare down recipes for just my husband and me. So I created this hearty soup with fast-cooking frozen meatballs.

- 1 can (14-1/2 ounces) reduced-sodium beef broth
- 12 frozen fully cooked Italian meatballs (1/2 ounce *each*)
- 3/4 cup fresh baby spinach
- 3/4 cup stewed tomatoes
- 1 can (11 ounces) Mexicorn, drained
- 3/4 cup frozen cheese tortellini (about 20)

Dash salt and pepper

1 In a large saucepan, bring the broth to a boil. Add the meatballs. Reduce heat; cover and simmer for 5 minutes.

2 Add the spinach, tomatoes and corn; cover and simmer for 5 minutes. Add the tortellini, salt and pepper; cover and simmer for 3 minutes or until the tortellini is tender.

YIELD: 4 SERVINGS.

beefy wild rice soup

MARILYN CHESBROUGH
WAUTOMA, WISCONSIN

Living in central Wisconsin, we experience many days of snow and cold temperatures. I like to prepare soup often, especially this one. My family loves it.

- 1 pound ground beef
- 1/2 teaspoon Italian seasoning
- 6 cups water, *divided*
- 2 large onions, chopped
- 3 celery ribs, chopped
- 1 cup uncooked wild rice
- 2 teaspoons beef bouillon granules
- 1/2 teaspoon pepper
- 1/4 teaspoon hot pepper sauce
- 3 cans (10-3/4 ounces *each*) condensed cream of mushroom soup, undiluted
- 1 can (4 ounces) mushroom stems and pieces, drained

1 In a Dutch oven, cook beef and Italian seasoning over medium heat until meat is no longer pink; drain. Add 2 cups water, onions, celery, rice, bouillon, pepper and hot pepper sauce; bring to a boil.

2 Reduce heat; cover and simmer for 45 minutes. Stir in the soup, mushrooms and remaining water. Cover and simmer for 30 minutes.

YIELD: 10-12 SERVINGS (3 QUARTS).

italian seasoning

Italian seasoning can be found in the spice aisle of most grocery stores. A basic blend might contain marjoram, thyme, rosemary, savory, sage, oregano and basil. If your grocery store does not carry Italian seasoning, ask the manager if it can be ordered. Or, mix up your own. If you don't have all the ingredients on your spice shelf, you can blend just a few of them with good results. Try substituting 1/4 teaspoon *each* of basil, thyme, rosemary and oregano for each teaspoon of Italian seasoning called for in a recipe.

TASTE OF HOME TEST KITCHEN

chicken & turkey

SPICED-UP HEALTHY SOUP, P. 30

basic turkey soup

KATIE KOZIOLEK | HARTLAND, MINNESOTA

To make this soup, I simmer a rich broth using the turkey carcass, then add my favorite vegetables and sometimes noodles.

TURKEY BROTH:

- 1 leftover turkey carcass
- 8 cups water
- 1 teaspoon chicken bouillon granules
- 1 celery rib with leaves
- 1 small onion, halved
- 1 carrot
- 3 whole peppercorns
- 1 garlic clove
- 1 teaspoon seasoned salt
- 1 teaspoon dried thyme

TURKEY VEGETABLE SOUP:

- 8 cups turkey broth
- 2 teaspoons chicken bouillon granules
- 1/2 to 3/4 teaspoon pepper
- 4 cups green beans, sliced carrots, corn *and/or* other vegetables
- 3/4 cup chopped onion
- 4 cups diced cooked turkey

1 Place all broth ingredients in a large stockpot; cover and bring to a boil. Reduce heat; simmer for 25 minutes. Strain broth; discard bones and vegetables. Cool; skim fat. Use immediately for turkey vegetable soup or refrigerate and use within 24 hours.

2 For soup, combine the broth, bouillon, pepper, vegetables and onion in a large stockpot. Cover and simmer for 15-20 minutes or until the vegetables are tender. Add turkey and heat through.

YIELD: 8-10 SERVINGS.

zippy chicken mushroom soup

JULIA THORNELY | LAYTON, UTAH

My sister-in-law telephoned me looking for a good cream of mushroom soup recipe. I gave her this hearty one. It gets its boost from a splash of hot pepper sauce.

- 1/2 pound fresh mushrooms, chopped
- 1/4 cup *each* chopped onion, celery and carrot
- 1/4 cup butter, cubed
- 1/2 cup all-purpose flour
- 5-1/2 cups chicken broth
- 1 teaspoon pepper
- 1/2 teaspoon white pepper
- 1/4 teaspoon dried thyme

Pinch dried tarragon

- 1/2 teaspoon hot pepper sauce
- 3 cups half-and-half cream
- 2-1/2 cups cubed cooked chicken
- 1 tablespoon minced fresh parsley
- 1-1/2 teaspoons lemon juice
- 1/2 teaspoon salt

1 In a Dutch oven, saute the mushrooms, onion, celery and carrot in butter until tender. Stir in flour until blended. Gradually add the broth and seasonings. Bring to a boil. Reduce heat; simmer, uncovered, for 10 minutes.

2 Stir in the cream, chicken, parsley, lemon juice and the salt; heat through (do not boil).

YIELD: 11 SERVINGS (2-3/4 QUARTS).

turkey vegetable soup

BONNIE SMITH | CLIFTON, VIRGINIA

This is one of my "tried-and-true" recipes that I always make after Thanksgiving when the turkey leftovers are just about used up. The carcass makes a wonderful broth, and it's amazing how much more meat is made available after boiling the bones!

- 6 cups turkey *or* chicken broth
- 3 medium potatoes, peeled and chopped
- 2 carrots, chopped
- 2 celery ribs, chopped
- 2 medium onions, chopped
- 2 cans (15 ounces *each*) cream-style corn
- 2 cans (8-1/2 ounces *each*) lima beans, drained
- 1 to 2 cups chopped cooked turkey
- 1/2 to 1 teaspoon chili powder

Salt and pepper to taste

1 In a large stockpot, combine the broth, potatoes, carrots, celery and onions. Bring to boil. Reduce heat; cover and simmer for 30 minutes or until the vegetables are tender.

2 Add the corn, lima beans, turkey, chili powder, salt and pepper. Cover and simmer 10 minutes longer.

YIELD: 12 SERVINGS
(ABOUT 3-1/2 QUARTS).

comforting chicken noodle soup

DIANE EDGECOMB
HUMBOLDT, SOUTH DAKOTA

I often add potatoes and corn to this soup. Rich soup served with slices of fresh homemade bread—that's great down-home food any time of the year.

- 1 broiler/fryer chicken (2 to 3 pounds)
- 2-1/2 quarts water
- 1/2 medium onion, chopped
- 3 teaspoons salt
- 2 teaspoons chicken bouillon granules
- 1/8 teaspoon pepper
- 1/4 teaspoon dried marjoram
- 1/4 teaspoon dried thyme
- 1 bay leaf
- 1-1/2 cups uncooked fine egg noodles
- 1 cup chopped celery
- 1 cup chopped carrots

1 In a stockpot, combine the first 9 ingredients; bring to a boil. Reduce the heat; cover and simmer for 1-1/2 hours. Remove chicken; allow to cool. Strain broth; discard bay leaf.

2 Skim fat. Debone the chicken and cut into chunks; return chicken and broth to pan. Add the noodles, celery and carrots; bring to a boil. Reduce the heat; cover and simmer for 25-30 minutes or until noodles and vegetables are tender.

YIELD: 8-10 SERVINGS.

noodle soup

When I make my favorite noodle soup, I find it tastes better if I refrigerate the soup without the noodles. When it's time to serve, I add the noodles and cook them until tender.

MARTHA D., NINEVEH, INDIANA

lemony chicken noodle soup

BILL HILBRICH | ST. CLOUD, MINNESOTA

This isn't Grandma's chicken soup, but it is comforting. The lemon juice gives this easy soup enough zip to make it interesting.

  1 small onion, chopped
  2 tablespoons olive oil
  1 tablespoon butter
1/4 pound boneless skinless chicken breast, cubed
  1 garlic clove, minced
  2 cans (14-1/2 ounces *each*) chicken broth
  1 medium carrot, cut into 1/4-inch slices
1/4 cup fresh *or* frozen peas
1/2 teaspoon dried basil
  2 cups uncooked medium egg noodles
  1 to 2 tablespoons lemon juice

1 In a small saucepan, saute onion in oil and butter until tender. Add chicken; cook and stir until chicken is lightly browned and meat is no longer pink. Add garlic; cook 1 minute longer.

2 Stir in the broth, carrot, peas and basil. Bring to a boil. Reduce heat; cover and simmer for 5 minutes. Add the noodles. Cover and simmer for 8-10 minutes or until noodles are tender. Stir in lemon juice.

YIELD: 2 SERVINGS.

chicken barley soup

DIANA COSTELLO | MARION, KANSAS

This is my favorite soup! It's so filling that I serve it as a main dish. I have shared the recipe many times.

  1 broiler/fryer chicken
     (2 to 3 pounds), cut up
  8 cups water
1-1/2 cups chopped carrots
  1 cup chopped celery
1/2 cup medium pearl barley
1/2 cup chopped onion
  1 teaspoon chicken bouillon granules
  1 teaspoon salt, optional
  1 bay leaf
1/2 teaspoon *each* poultry seasoning, pepper and rubbed sage

1 In a large stockpot, cook chicken in water until tender. Cool the broth and skim off fat. Set chicken aside until cool enough to handle. Remove the meat from bones; discard bones and cut meat into cubes. Return the meat to pan along with the remaining ingredients. Bring to a boil. Reduce the heat; cover and simmer for 1 hour or until vegetables and barley are tender. Discard bay leaf.

YIELD: 5 SERVINGS
(ABOUT 1-1/2 QUARTS).

freezing soup portions

I like to make a big batch of soup, then freeze individual servings. I line bowls with plastic wrap, pour in soup and freeze. Once frozen, the soup can be popped out of the bowls and stored in large freezer bags. These make nice gifts for someone living alone.

SHIRLEY P., REDMOND, WASHINGTON

chicken soup with potato dumplings

MARIE MCCONNELL
SHELBYVILLE, ILLINOIS

Our family calls this comforting, old-fashioned soup our "Sunday dinner soup" because it's almost a complete dinner in a bowl. You'll love the flavor!

- 1/4 cup chopped onion
- 1 tablespoon canola oil
- 2 garlic cloves, minced
- 6 cups chicken broth
- 2 cups cubed cooked chicken
- 2 celery ribs, chopped
- 2 medium carrots, sliced
- 1/4 teaspoon dried sage leaves

DUMPLINGS:

- 1-1/2 cups biscuit/baking mix
- 1 cup cold mashed potatoes (with added milk)
- 1/4 cup milk
- 1 tablespoon chopped green onion
- 1/8 teaspoon pepper

1 In a large saucepan, saute onion in oil for 3-4 minutes or until tender. Add garlic; cook 1 minute longer. Stir in the broth, chicken, celery, carrots and sage. Bring to a boil. Reduce heat; cover and simmer for 10-15 minutes or until vegetables are tender.

2 In a small bowl, combine the dumpling ingredients. Drop heaping tablespoonfuls of batter onto simmering soup. Cover and simmer for 20 minutes or until a toothpick inserted in a dumpling comes out clean (do not lift cover while simmering).

YIELD: 5 SERVINGS.

curry chicken pumpkin soup

PATTY D'AMORE
GLENDORA, CALIFORNIA

I made up this recipe and always serve it on Halloween. This fragrant, heart-warming soup hits the spot on a cool afternoon.

- 4 bacon strips, diced
- 1/4 cup chopped onion
- 2 cups cubed peeled pie pumpkin
- 2 cups chicken broth
- 1 can (14-1/2 ounces) diced tomatoes, undrained
- 1 teaspoon curry powder
- 3/4 cup cubed cooked chicken breast
- 1/3 cup frozen corn
- 1/3 cup cooked small pasta shells

1 In a large saucepan, cook the bacon and onion over medium heat until bacon is crisp; drain. Add the pumpkin, broth, tomatoes and curry; bring to a boil. Reduce heat; cover and simmer for 8-10 minutes or until pumpkin is tender. Stir in the chicken, corn and pasta; heat through.

YIELD: 4 SERVINGS.

roasted veggie and meatball soup

SANDY LUND
BROOKINGS, SOUTH DAKOTA

I fix this tasty soup almost every Sunday during our South Dakota winters. A variety of roasted vegetables and turkey meatballs perk up the broth. What a wonderful way to warm up!

- 5 medium red potatoes, cubed
- 4 large carrots, cut into 1/2-inch slices
- 1 large red onion, halved and cut into wedges
- 4 tablespoons canola oil, *divided*
- 1-1/4 teaspoons salt, *divided*
- 3 tablespoons minced fresh basil
- 3 garlic cloves, crushed
- 1 egg, lightly beaten
- 1/2 cup seasoned bread crumbs
- 1/4 cup grated Parmesan cheese
- 1/4 cup minced fresh parsley
- 1/2 teaspoon pepper
- 1 pound ground turkey
- 1 carton (32 ounces) chicken broth
- 2 cups water
- 1 can (14-1/2 ounces) diced tomatoes, undrained

1 In a large bowl, combine the potatoes, carrots, onion, 2 tablespoons oil and 1/2 teaspoon salt. Place in a single layer in two greased 15-in. x 10-in. x 1-in. baking pans.

2 Bake at 425° for 20 minutes. Add basil and garlic; toss to coat. Bake 10-15 minutes longer or until vegetables are tender.

3 In a large bowl, combine the egg, bread crumbs, cheese, parsley, 1/2 teaspoon salt and pepper. Crumble turkey over mixture and mix well. Shape into 1-in. balls.

4 In a Dutch oven, brown the meatballs in the remaining oil in batches; drain and set aside.

5 In the same pan, combine the broth, water, tomatoes, roasted vegetables and remaining salt. Return meatballs to pan. Bring to a boil. Reduce heat; cover and simmer for 45-55 minutes or until meatballs are no longer pink.

YIELD: 8 SERVINGS (3 QUARTS).

turkey noodle soup

DORIS NEHODA | COOS BAY, OREGON

My husband must eat a very low-fat diet, so I'm always experimenting to find recipes that will agree with his stomach, too. This easy, economical recipe makes two generous servings. Sometimes I substitute chicken, or a different pasta or vegetable.

- 2 cups water
- 3/4 cup cubed cooked turkey breast
- 1 celery rib with leaves, sliced
- 1/4 cup chopped onion
- 2 garlic cloves, minced
- 1/2 teaspoon salt
- 1/8 teaspoon dried marjoram
- 1/8 teaspoon pepper
- 1 bay leaf
- 1/2 cup cubed peeled potatoes
- 1/4 cup frozen peas
- 1/4 cup uncooked yolk-free wide noodles

Dash browning sauce, optional

1 In a large saucepan, combine the first nine ingredients; bring to a boil. Reduce heat; cover and simmer for 10 minutes or until celery is tender.

2 Add the potatos, peas and noodles; cover and simmer 15 minutes longer or until the potatoes are tender. Discard bay leaf. Stir in browning sauce if desired.

YIELD: 2 SERVINGS.

spiced-up healthy soup

**DIANE TAYMAN DIXON
GRAND DETOUR, ILLINOIS**

This has been a hit with family and friends. It's low-fat and filled with good-for-you ingredients.

        1 medium onion, chopped
    1/3 cup medium pearl barley
        2 tablespoons canola oil
        4 garlic cloves, minced
        5 cans (14-1/2 ounces *each*) reduced-sodium chicken broth
        2 boneless skinless chicken breast halves (4 ounces *each*)
        1 cup dried lentils, rinsed
        1 jar (16 ounces) picante sauce
        1 can (15 ounces) garbanzo beans *or* chickpeas, rinsed and drained
    1/2 cup minced fresh cilantro
        8 cups chopped fresh spinach

1 In a Dutch oven, saute onion and barley in oil until onion is tender. Add garlic; cook 1 minute longer. Add the broth, chicken and lentils; bring to a boil. Reduce heat; cover and simmer for 15 minutes or until chicken is no longer pink. Remove the chicken and set aside.

2 Add the picante sauce, garbanzo beans and cilantro to soup; cover and simmer 10 minutes longer or until barley and lentils are tender.

3 Shred chicken with two forks. Add spinach and chicken to soup. Simmer, uncovered, for 5 minutes or until spinach is wilted.

YIELD: 14 SERVINGS (3-1/2 QUARTS).

lemon-chicken velvet soup

**CELESTE BUCKLEY
REDDING, CALIFORNIA**

The lively flavor of lemon perks up this rich, brothy soup accented with sugar snap peas. I enjoy this soup with a green salad, sourdough bread and a glass of white wine.

        2 tablespoons butter
        2 tablespoons all-purpose flour
        1 can (14-1/2 ounces) chicken broth
        3 tablespoons lemon juice
    1-1/2 cups cubed cooked chicken breast
    10 fresh *or* frozen sugar snap peas
        2 tablespoons minced fresh parsley
        1 teaspoon grated lemon peel
        3 tablespoons heavy whipping cream

1 In a small saucepan, melt the butter. Stir in flour until smooth; gradually add broth and lemon juice. Bring to a boil; cook and stir for 1-2 minutes or until thickened.

2 Stir in the chicken, peas, parsley and lemon peel; cook 2-3 minutes longer or until chicken is heated through and peas are crisp-tender. Stir in cream; heat through (do not boil).

YIELD: 2 SERVINGS.

homemade turkey soup

JUNE SANGREY | MANHEIM, PENNSYLVANIA

With this recipe, you can make the most of even the smallest pieces of leftover holiday turkey. This soup has a wonderfully rich flavor. The hearty broth is creamy and full of rice and vegetables.

- 1 leftover turkey carcass (from a 10- to 12-pound turkey)
- 2 quarts water
- 1 medium onion, halved
- 1/2 teaspoon salt
- 2 bay leaves
- 1 cup chopped carrots
- 1 cup uncooked long grain rice
- 1/3 cup chopped celery
- 1/4 cup chopped onion
- 1 can (10-3/4 ounces) condensed cream of chicken *or* cream of mushroom soup, undiluted

1. Place the turkey carcass in a stockpot; add the water, onion, salt and bay leaves. Slowly bring to a boil over low heat; cover and simmer for 2 hours.

2. Remove carcass; cool. Strain broth and skim off fat. Discard onion and bay leaves. Return broth to the pan. Add the carrots, rice, celery and chopped onion; cover and simmer until rice and vegetables are tender.

3. Remove turkey from bones; discard bones and cut turkey into bite-size pieces. Add turkey and cream soup to broth; heat through.

YIELD: 8-10 SERVINGS (ABOUT 2 QUARTS).

cajun chicken & rice soup

LISA HAMMOND | HIGGINSVILLE, MISSOURI

We enjoy this comforting, spicy soup frequently in our household. It's really good served with corn bread fresh from the oven.

- 1 stewing chicken (about 6 pounds)
- 2 bay leaves
- 1 teaspoon salt
- 1 teaspoon poultry seasoning
- 1 teaspoon pepper
- 1 medium onion, chopped
- 2 celery ribs, chopped
- 1 tablespoon butter
- 12 garlic cloves, minced
- 1 can (10 ounces) diced tomatoes and green chilies, drained
- 3/4 cup orange juice
- 2 tablespoons minced fresh cilantro
- 2 teaspoons Cajun seasoning
- 1 teaspoon dried oregano
- 1/2 teaspoon *each* dried thyme, ground cumin and paprika
- 2 cups cooked rice
- 1 can (15 ounces) pinto beans, rinsed and drained

1. Place chicken in a large stockpot; cover with water. Add the bay leaves, salt, poultry seasoning and pepper. Bring to a boil. Reduce heat; cover and simmer for 1-1/2 hours or until chicken is tender.

2. Remove chicken from broth; set aside to cool. Strain broth, discarding seasonings. Set aside 6 cups broth for the soup; save remaining broth for another use. Skim fat from soup broth. When cool enough to handle, remove chicken from bones; discard bones. Shred and set aside 3 cups chicken (save remaining chicken for another use).

3. In a large stockpot, saute onion and celery in butter until onion is crisp-tender. Add garlic; cook 1 minute longer. Stir in the tomatoes, orange juice, cilantro, seasonings and reserved broth. Bring to a boil. Reduce heat; cover and simmer for 15 minutes or until vegetables are tender. Stir in the rice, beans and reserved chicken; heat through.

YIELD: 12 SERVINGS (3 QUARTS).

chicken tomato soup

CONNIE JOHNSON | SPRINGFIELD, MISSOURI

While creating this crowd-pleasing soup, I was trying to keep in mind a variety of textures, colors and flavors. Its sweet tomato base brims with chicken, broccoli, corn and a couple kinds of beans. It's especially tasty if you garnish it with shredded cheddar and crumbled bacon.

1-1/2 cups water
   3 cups frozen chopped broccoli
 3/4 cup chopped onion
   1 garlic clove, minced
 3/4 pound boneless skinless chicken breast, cut into 1-inch chunks
 1/2 teaspoon seasoned salt
 1/4 teaspoon pepper
   1 can (46 ounces) tomato juice
   1 can (15-1/2 ounces) great northern beans, rinsed and drained
   1 can (15 ounces) black beans, rinsed and drained
   1 can (11 ounces) whole kernel corn, drained
   1 tablespoon ketchup
   1 teaspoon brown sugar
Crumbled bacon and shredded cheddar cheese, optional

1 In a Dutch oven, combine the water, broccoli, onion and garlic. Bring to a boil; boil for 8-10 minutes, stirring frequently.

2 Meanwhile, in a nonstick skillet, cook the chicken until no longer pink, about 6 minutes. Sprinkle with seasoned salt and pepper. Add to broccoli mixture; stir in the tomato juice, beans, corn, ketchup and brown sugar; bring to a boil. Reduce heat; cover and simmer for 10-15 minutes, stirring occasionally. Garnish with bacon and cheese if desired.

YIELD: 12 SERVINGS (ABOUT 3 QUARTS).

chicken wild rice soup

GAYLE HOLDMAN | HIGHLAND, UTAH

Because this warming soup takes advantage of several convenience items, it's very quick to make. It's perfect for casual entertaining, because you can keep it warm in the slow cooker.

5-2/3 cups water
   1 package (4.3 ounces) long grain and wild rice mix
   1 envelope chicken noodle soup mix
   1 celery rib, chopped
   1 medium carrot, chopped
 1/3 cup chopped onion
   2 cans (10-3/4 ounces *each*) condensed cream of chicken soup, undiluted
   1 cup cubed cooked chicken

1 In a large saucepan, combine water, rice with the contents of seasoning packet and soup mix. Bring to a boil. Reduce the heat; cover and simmer for 10 minutes. Stir in the celery, carrot and onion.

2 Cover and simmer for 10 minutes. Stir in chicken soup and chicken. Cook 8 minutes longer or until rice and vegetables are tender.

YIELD: 5 SERVINGS.

cream of chicken noodle soup

DONNIE KINGMAN
SAN JACINTO, CALIFORNIA

When we were at a restaurant, my husband remarked that I could make a better soup than they could. A challenge! We began discussing what we'd add and take out, and soon came up with this comforting soup.

- 2 medium onions
- 2 celery ribs
- 4 cups water
- 3 boneless skinless chicken breast halves (6 ounces *each*)
- 1-1/2 teaspoons salt
- 1/4 teaspoon pepper
- 2 tablespoons butter
- 1 can (14-1/2 ounces) chicken broth
- 1 large carrot, chopped
- 1 medium potato, peeled and chopped
- 2 teaspoons chicken bouillon granules
- 1-1/2 teaspoons dried basil
- 2 cups uncooked wide egg noodles
- 1-3/4 cups milk, *divided*
- 1/3 cup all-purpose flour

1 Chop one onion and one celery rib; set aside. Cut remaining onion and celery into chunks; place in a Dutch oven. Add water, chicken, salt and pepper. Bring to a boil. Reduce heat; cover and simmer for 25-30 minutes or until a meat thermometer reads 170°. Remove chicken and strain broth; set both aside.

2 In the same pan, saute chopped onion and celery in butter until tender. Add the canned broth, carrot, potato, bouillon, basil and reserved broth. Bring to a boil. Reduce heat; cover and simmer for 20-30 minutes or until vegetables are tender.

3 Add the noodles. Return to a boil; cook for 6-8 minutes or until noodles are tender. Cut chicken into chunks; add to soup. Stir in 1-1/4 cups milk; heat through.

4 Combine flour and remaining milk until smooth; add to soup, stirring constantly. Bring to a boil; cook and stir for 2 minutes or until thickened.

YIELD: 8 SERVINGS.

macaroni 'n' cheese soup

TASTE OF HOME TEST KITCHEN

Chock-full of vegetables, chicken and pasta, this creamy creation is sure to become a favorite at your home. No one will suspect the sensational soup relies on leftover macaroni and cheese.

- 3-1/2 cups chicken broth
- 1-1/2 cups fresh broccoli florets
- 1 cup fresh cauliflowerets
- 1 cup sliced carrots
- 2 cups prepared macaroni and cheese
- 1 cup heavy whipping cream
- 1 cup cubed process cheese (Velveeta)
- 1 cup cubed cooked chicken

Pepper to taste

1 In a large saucepan, combine broth, broccoli, cauliflower and carrots. Bring to a boil. Reduce heat; simmer, uncovered, for 10 minutes or until vegetables are tender.

2 Add the macaroni and cheese, cream and process cheese. Cook and stir until cheese is melted. Add chicken and pepper; heat through.

YIELD: 8 SERVINGS.

freezing cubed cooked chicken

When chicken pieces are on sale, I buy several packages and bake all the chicken, skin side up, on foil-lined pans. When cool, I remove the skin and bones, cube the meat and freeze in measured portions to use in soups, casseroles and other quick suppers.

MARILYN W., DES MOINES, IOWA

turkey-tomato vegetable soup

BONNIE LEBARRON
FORESTVILLE, NEW YORK

Low-sodium ingredients don't diminish the full flavor of this brothy soup. The ground turkey gives the soup a heartiness everyone will welcome on a cold, blustery evening.

- 1 pound lean ground turkey
- 1 cup chopped celery
- 1/2 cup chopped onion
- 2 to 3 garlic cloves, minced
- 2 cans (14-1/2 ounces *each*) reduced-sodium beef broth
- 2-1/2 cups reduced-sodium tomato juice
- 1 can (14-1/2 ounces) diced tomatoes, drained
- 1 cup sliced fresh mushrooms
- 3/4 cup frozen French-style green beans
- 1/2 cup sliced carrots
- 1-1/2 teaspoons Worcestershire sauce
- 1 teaspoon *each* dried parsley flakes and dried thyme
- 1/2 teaspoon *each* sugar and dried basil
- 1/4 teaspoon pepper
- 1 bay leaf

1 In a Dutch oven coated with cooking spray, saute the turkey, celery and onion until meat is no longer pink. Add garlic; cook 1 minute longer. Drain.

2 Stir in remaining ingredients. Bring to a boil. Reduce heat; cover and simmer for 1 hour or until vegetables are tender. Discard bay leaf. Soup may be frozen for up to 3 months.

YIELD: 4 SERVINGS.

peanutty chicken soup

HEATHER EWALD | BOTHELL, WASHINGTON

Creamy peanut butter and pureed tomatoes flavor the tender chicken in this unusual soup. I got the recipe from my aunt who served as a missionary in Africa for 45 years. "Soup" is the Nigerian word for "gravy."

- 1 broiler/fryer chicken (3 to 4 pounds), cut up
- 4 tablespoons peanut oil, *divided*
- 2 tablespoons soy sauce

Dash salt

- 1 cup water
- 4 medium tomatoes, cut into wedges
- 3 large sweet red peppers, cut into wedges
- 1 large onion, cut into wedges
- 1 cup creamy peanut butter

1 In a Dutch oven, brown chicken in 2 tablespoons oil; drain. Brush chicken with soy sauce; sprinkle with salt. Add water. Bring to a boil. Reduce heat; cover and simmer for 30-35 minutes or until chicken juices run clear.

2 Meanwhile, in a food processor, combine the tomatoes, red peppers and onion. Cover and process until blended.

3 In a large saucepan, heat remaining oil over medium heat; add tomato mixture. Bring to a boil. Reduce heat; cook and stir for 5-7 minutes or until thickened. Remove from the heat; stir in peanut butter until blended. Add to the chicken mixture; heat through.

YIELD: 4 SERVINGS.

orzo chicken soup

BETTY RENCH | EATON, INDIANA

For a different twist on noodle soup, I add orzo, small rice-like grains of pasta. It cooks up nicely with tender chunks of chicken.

- 1/2 cup chopped onion
- 1 tablespoon butter
- 3 cans (14-1/2 ounces *each*) reduced-sodium chicken broth, *divided*
- 1/2 cup sliced carrot
- 1/2 cup chopped celery
- 1 cup cubed cooked chicken breast
- 1/2 cup uncooked orzo pasta
- 1/4 teaspoon pepper

Minced fresh parsley

1 In a large saucepan, saute the onion in butter until tender. Add 1 can broth, carrot and celery; bring to a boil. Reduce the heat; cover and simmer for 15 minutes. Add the chicken, orzo, pepper and remaining broth; return to a boil. Reduce the heat; cover and simmer for 25-30 minutes or until the orzo and vegetables are tender. Sprinkle with parsley.

YIELD: 4 SERVINGS.

chicken and dumpling soup

MORGAN BYERS | BERKLEY, MICHIGAN

Like a security blanket for the soul, this chicken and dumpling soup is a true classic. My husband is not very fond of leftovers, but he likes this so much, he says he could eat it every day of the week.

- 3/4 pound boneless skinless chicken breasts, cut into 1-inch cubes
- 1/4 teaspoon salt
- 1/8 teaspoon pepper
- 2 teaspoons olive oil
- 1/4 cup all-purpose flour
- 4 cups reduced-sodium chicken broth, *divided*
- 1 cup water
- 2 cups frozen French-cut green beans
- 1-1/2 cups sliced onions
- 1 cup coarsely shredded carrots
- 1/4 teaspoon dried marjoram
- 2/3 cup reduced-fat biscuit/baking mix
- 1/3 cup cornmeal
- 1/4 cup shredded reduced-fat cheddar cheese
- 1/3 cup fat-free milk

1 Sprinkle chicken with salt and pepper. In a nonstick skillet, saute chicken in oil until browned and no longer pink.

2 In a large saucepan, combine flour and 1/2 cup broth until smooth. Stir in water and remaining broth. Add the beans, onions, carrots, marjoram and chicken. Bring to a boil. Reduce heat; simmer, uncovered, for 10 minutes.

3 Meanwhile, in a small bowl, combine the biscuit mix, cornmeal and cheese. Stir in milk just until moistened. Drop batter in 12 mounds onto simmering soup. Cover and simmer for 15 minutes or until a toothpick inserted in a dumpling comes out clean (do not lift the cover while simmering).

YIELD: 4 SERVINGS.

chicken noodle soup

TERRY KUEHN | WAUNAKEE, WISCONSIN

I cook most of the weekend meals and share weekday cooking duties with my wife. I also like to take food to neighbors, coworkers and our parents. And I try to send things like this hearty soup to people I know are sick.

- 1 stewing chicken (about 4 pounds), cut up
- 3 quarts water
- 2 cans (14-1/2 ounces *each*) chicken broth
- 5 celery ribs, coarsely chopped, *divided*
- 4 medium carrots, coarsely chopped, *divided*
- 2 medium onions, quartered, *divided*
- 2/3 cup coarsely chopped green pepper, *divided*
- 1-1/4 teaspoons pepper, *divided*
- 1 bay leaf
- 2 teaspoons salt
- 8 ounces uncooked medium egg noodles

1 In a large stockpot, combine the chicken, water, broth, half of the celery, carrots, onions and green pepper, 1/2 teaspoon pepper and the bay leaf. Bring to a boil. Reduce the heat; cover and simmer for 2-1/2 hours or until chicken is tender. Chop the remaining onion; set aside.

2 Remove the chicken from broth. When cool enough to handle, remove meat from bones and cut into bite-size pieces. Discard bones and skin; set aside.

3 Strain broth and skim fat; return broth to stockpot. Add the salt, chopped onion and remaining celery, carrots, green pepper and pepper. Bring to a boil. Reduce heat; cover and simmer for 10-12 minutes or until vegetables are crisp-tender. Add noodles and chicken. Cover and simmer for 12-15 minutes or until noodles are tender.

YIELD: 16 SERVINGS.

zesty turkey tomato soup

KATHERINE PREISS
PENFIELD, PENNSYLVANIA

This chunky soup is full of flavor and zip! If you don't want as much heat, you can eliminate the jalapeno pepper. For a change of pace, I sometimes omit the turkey and add a small can of garbanzo beans in the last few minutes of cooking.

- 1/4 pound lean ground turkey
- 1 small zucchini, diced
- 1 small onion, chopped
- 1 can (14-1/2 ounces) reduced-sodium chicken broth
- 1 cup canned Mexican diced tomatoes
- 1/3 cup uncooked whole wheat spiral pasta
- 1/2 teaspoon minced fresh basil
- 1/4 teaspoon ground cumin
- 1/8 teaspoon pepper
- 1 tablespoon chopped jalapeno pepper, optional

Shredded fat-free cheddar cheese, optional

1 In a large saucepan, cook the turkey, zucchini and onion over medium heat until meat is no longer pink; drain.

2 Stir in the broth, tomatoes, pasta, basil, cumin, pepper and jalapeno if desired. Bring to a boil. Reduce heat; simmer, uncovered, for 13-15 minutes or until pasta is tender. Garnish with cheese if desired.

YIELD: 3 CUPS.

EDITOR'S NOTE: When cutting hot peppers, disposable gloves are recommended. Avoid touching your face.

chicken tortilla soup

KIM SEEGER | BROOKLYN PARK, MINNESOTA

I had tortilla soup at a restaurant and decided I could come up with an easy recipe to duplicate the flavor and enjoy the tasty dish at home.

- 1-1/4 pounds boneless skinless chicken breasts
- 1 cup chopped onion
- 1 teaspoon minced garlic
- 2 cans (14-1/2 ounces *each*) reduced-sodium chicken broth
- 1 can (28 ounces) crushed tomatoes
- 1 can (16 ounces) kidney beans, rinsed and drained
- 1 can (8 ounces) tomato sauce
- 1 can (6 ounces) tomato paste
- 1 can (4 ounces) chopped green chilies
- 2 teaspoons chili powder
- 1 teaspoon ground cumin
- 3/4 teaspoon dried oregano
- 1/2 teaspoon sugar
- 1/4 teaspoon salt
- 1/4 teaspoon pepper
- 3 corn tortillas (6 inches), cut into 1/2-inch strips

1 Broil chicken 3-4 in. from the heat for 5-6 minutes on each side or until a meat thermometer reads 170°.

2 In a Dutch oven coated with cooking spray, cook onion until tender. Add garlic; cook 1 minute longer. Stir in the broth, tomatoes, beans, tomato sauce, tomato paste, chilies and seasonings. Shred chicken with two forks; add to soup. Bring to a boil. Reduce heat; simmer, uncovered, for 10-15 minutes.

3 Meanwhile, place tortilla strips on an ungreased baking sheet. Bake at 350° for 12-15 minutes or until crisp. Serve with soup.

YIELD: 8 SERVINGS (3 QUARTS).

chicken cheese soup

LAVONNE LUNDGREN | SIOUX CITY, IOWA

Kids won't think twice about eating vegetables once they're incorporated into this creamy and cheesy soup.

- 4 cups cubed cooked chicken breast
- 3-1/2 cups water
- 2 cans (10-3/4 ounces *each*) condensed cream of chicken soup, undiluted
- 1 package (16 ounces) frozen mixed vegetables, thawed
- 1 can (14-1/2 ounces) diced potatoes, drained
- 1 package (16 ounces) process cheese (Velveeta), cubed

1 In a Dutch oven, combine the first five ingredients. Bring to a boil. Reduce the heat; cover and simmer for 8-10 minutes or until vegetables are tender. Stir in the cheese just until melted (do not boil).

YIELD: 7 SERVINGS.

garnishes for soup

Dress up a soup with a sprinkle of nuts, chopped fresh herbs, sliced green onions, slivers of fresh vegetables, croutons, tortilla strips, shredded cheese or crumbled bacon.

TASTE OF HOME TEST KITCHEN

chilly-day chicken soup

DEBORAH LOU MITCHELL
CLARKSVILLE, INDIANA

This was one of the things I ate on my healthy-heart diet, and I lost 67 pounds in 6 months. It's a very light and tasty chicken soup. I hope you like it as well as I do.

- 1/4 pound boneless skinless chicken breast, cut into small pieces
- 1/4 cup chopped onion
- 2 teaspoons butter
- 1 cup diced red potatoes
- 1 medium carrot, grated
- 1 can (14-1/2 ounces) reduced-sodium chicken broth
- 1/2 cup water
- 1/4 teaspoon pepper
- 2 tablespoons uncooked instant rice
- 1/8 teaspoon salt

1. In a small nonstick saucepan, saute chicken and onion in butter until chicken is no longer pink. Stir in the potatoes, carrot, broth, water and pepper. Bring to a boil. Reduce heat; cover and simmer for 10-12 minutes or until potatoes are tender.

2. Return to a boil; stir in rice and salt. Remove from heat. Cover and let stand for 5 minutes or until the rice is tender.

YIELD: 2 SERVINGS.

chunky chicken soup

NANCY CLOW
MALLORYTOWN, ONTARIO

I am a stay-at-home mom who relies on my slow cooker for fast, nutritious meals with minimal cleanup and prep time. I knew this recipe was a hit when I didn't have any leftovers, and my husband asked me to make it again.

- 1-1/2 pounds boneless skinless chicken breasts, cut into 2-inch strips
- 2 teaspoons canola oil
- 2/3 cup finely chopped onion
- 2 medium carrots, chopped
- 2 celery ribs, chopped
- 1 cup frozen corn
- 2 cans (10-3/4 ounces *each*) condensed cream of potato soup, undiluted
- 1-1/2 cups chicken broth
- 1 teaspoon dill weed
- 1 cup frozen peas
- 1/2 cup half-and-half cream

1. In a large skillet over medium-high heat, brown chicken in oil or until no longer pink. With a slotted spoon, transfer to a 5-qt. slow cooker. Add the onion, carrots, celery and corn. In a large bowl, whisk the soup, broth and dill until blended; stir into slow cooker. Cover and cook on low for 4 hours or until vegetables are tender. Stir in peas and cream.

2. Cover and cook 30 minutes longer or until heated through.

YIELD: 7 SERVINGS.

half-and-half substitute

To replace half-and-half in dishes that are cooked or baked, you can substitute 4-1/2 teaspoons melted butter plus enough whole milk to equal 1 cup. One cup of evaporated milk may also be used.

TASTE OF HOME TEST KITCHEN

hearty chipotle chicken soup

SONALI RUDER | NEW YORK, NEW YORK

Sweet corn and cool sour cream help tame the smoky hot flavors of chipotle pepper in this well-balanced soup that's perfect for chilly nights.

- 1 large onion, chopped
- 1 tablespoon canola oil
- 4 garlic cloves, minced
- 4 cups reduced-sodium chicken broth
- 2 cans (15 ounces *each*) pinto beans, rinsed and drained
- 2 cans (14-1/2 ounces *each*) fire-roasted diced tomatoes, undrained
- 3 cups frozen corn
- 2 chipotle peppers in adobo sauce, seeded and minced
- 2 teaspoons adobo sauce
- 1 teaspoon ground cumin
- 1/4 teaspoon pepper
- 2 cups cubed cooked chicken breast
- 1/2 cup fat-free sour cream
- 1/4 cup minced fresh cilantro

1 In a Dutch oven, saute onion in oil until tender. Add garlic; cook 1 minute longer. Add the broth, beans, tomatoes, corn, chipotle peppers, adobo sauce, cumin and pepper. Bring to a boil. Reduce heat; simmer, uncovered, for 20 minutes.

2 Stir in chicken; heat through. Garnish with sour cream; sprinkle with cilantro.

YIELD: 8 SERVINGS (3-1/4 QUARTS).

chicken vegetable soup

RUBY WILLIAMS | BOGALUSA, LOUISIANA

Every grandmother knows that nothing soothes a cold better than homemade soup. I find this recipe works nicely to accommodate my great-grandson and me.

- 1 medium onion, chopped
- 1 celery rib, chopped
- 2 teaspoons canola oil
- 1 garlic clove, minced
- 1-1/2 cups chicken broth
- 1 cup chopped tomatoes
- 1 cup cubed cooked chicken
- 1/4 teaspoon dried marjoram
- 1/4 teaspoon dried thyme
- 1/8 teaspoon pepper
- 1 bay leaf

1 In a large saucepan, saute onion and celery in oil until tender. Add garlic; cook 1 minute longer. Stir in the broth, tomatoes, chicken, marjoram, thyme, pepper and bay leaf. Bring to a boil. Reduce heat; cover and simmer for 30 minutes or until heated through. Discard bay leaf.

YIELD: 2 SERVINGS.

turkey soup

MYRNA SISEL | GREEN BAY, WISCONSIN

I make the most of my turkey by simmering the carcass to create this soup that's warm and comforting on a cold winter's day. The golden broth is full of rice, barley and colorful veggies.

- 1 leftover turkey breast carcass (from an 8-pound turkey breast)
- 3 quarts water
- 4 teaspoons chicken bouillon granules
- 2 bay leaves
- 1/2 cup uncooked instant rice
- 1/2 cup uncooked quick-cooking barley
- 1-1/2 cups sliced carrots
- 1 cup chopped onion
- 1 cup sliced celery
- 1 garlic clove, minced
- 1 teaspoon salt
- 1/4 teaspoon pepper
- 1 cup cubed cooked turkey
- 2 tablespoons minced fresh parsley *or* 2 teaspoons dried parsley flakes

1 Place carcass, water, bouillon and bay leaves in a Dutch oven; bring to a boil. Reduce heat; cover and simmer for 1-1/2 hours. Remove carcass; cool.

2 Remove meat from bones and cut into bite-size pieces; set meat aside. Discard bones. Strain broth and skim fat; discard bay leaves. Add rice and barley to broth; bring to a boil. Reduce heat; cover and simmer for 30 minutes.

3 Stir in the carrots, onion, celery, garlic, salt and pepper; cover and simmer 20-25 minutes longer or until the vegetables are tender. Add cubed turkey, parsley and reserved turkey; heat through.

YIELD: 12 SERVINGS.

salsa chicken soup

**BECKY CHRISTMAN
BRIDGETON, MISSOURI**

You wouldn't guess that this quick-and-easy soup is low in fat. Since my husband loves spicy foods, I sometimes use medium or hot salsa in this recipe for extra zip.

- 1/2 pound boneless skinless chicken breasts, cubed
- 1 can (14-1/2 ounces) chicken broth
- 1-3/4 cups water
- 1 to 2 teaspoons chili powder
- 1 cup frozen corn
- 1 cup salsa
- Shredded Monterey Jack cheese *or* pepper Jack cheese, optional

1 In a large saucepan, combine the chicken, broth, water and chili powder. Bring to a boil. Reduce heat; cover and simmer for 5 minutes. Add corn; return to a boil. Reduce heat; simmer, uncovered, for 5 minutes or until chicken is no longer pink and corn is tender. Add salsa and heat through. Garnish with cheese if desired.

YIELD: 6 SERVINGS.

vegetable soup

When my children say that their soup is too hot to eat, I add a few frozen vegetables to their bowls instead of adding ice cubes. The soup cools a bit as the veggies quickly thaw to a perfect tenderness, and the kids get some extra vitamins.

WENDEE B., DAYTONA BEACH, FLORIDA

curried chicken rice soup

REBECCA COOK | HELOTES, TEXAS

This lighter version of my family-favorite soup boasts all the hearty texture, warm comfort and delicious flavor of the original.

- 1/4 cup butter, cubed
- 2 large carrots, finely chopped
- 2 celery ribs, finely chopped
- 1 small onion, finely chopped
- 3/4 cup plus 2 tablespoons all-purpose flour
- 1 teaspoon seasoned salt
- 1 teaspoon curry powder
- 2 cans (12 ounces *each*) fat-free evaporated milk
- 1 cup half-and-half cream
- 4-1/2 cups reduced-sodium chicken broth
- 3 cups cubed cooked chicken breast
- 2 cups cooked brown rice

1 In a Dutch oven, melt butter. Add the carrots, celery and onion; saute for 2 minutes. Sprinkle with flour; stir until blended. Stir in seasoned salt and curry. Gradually add milk and cream. Bring to a boil; cook and stir for 2 minutes or until thickened.

2 Gradually add broth. Stir in chicken and rice; return to a boil. Reduce the heat; simmer, uncovered, for 10 minutes or until the vegetables are tender.

YIELD: 11 SERVINGS (2-3/4 QUARTS).

southwestern chicken black bean soup

EMILY FAST | LEAVENWORTH, KANSAS

This recipe was given to me by a good friend a couple of years ago, and I've been making it ever since. We love Mexican food, and bowls of this pack enough flavor to please even my husband.

- 1 pound boneless skinless chicken breasts, cubed
- 1 tablespoon canola oil
- 1 tablespoon chopped onion

- 1 jalapeno pepper, seeded and finely chopped
- 3 garlic cloves, minced
- 2 cans (14-1/2 ounces *each*) reduced-sodium chicken broth
- 3 cups fresh corn *or* frozen corn
- 1 can (15-1/2 ounces) black beans, rinsed and drained
- 2 tablespoons lime juice
- 1/2 teaspoon salt
- 1/2 teaspoon hot pepper sauce
- 1/4 teaspoon pepper
- 1/2 cup minced fresh cilantro
- 16 baked tortilla chip scoops, crumbled
- 1/2 cup shredded reduced-fat cheddar cheese

1 In a Dutch oven, saute chicken in oil until no longer pink. Remove with a slotted spoon and set aside. In the same pan, saute onion and jalapeno pepper until tender. Add garlic and saute; cook 1 minute longer.

2 Stir in the broth, corn, beans, lime juice, salt, hot pepper sauce, pepper and reserved chicken; bring to a boil. Reduce heat; simmer, uncovered, for 30 minutes.

3 Stir in cilantro. Top each serving with crumbled tortilla chips and cheese.

YIELD: 8 SERVINGS (2 QUARTS).

EDITOR'S NOTE: When cutting hot peppers, disposable gloves are recommended. Avoid touching your face.

pork, ham & sausage

ITALIAN SAUSAGE ORZO SOUP, P. 56

black-eyed pea soup

ERIN WALSTEAD | ORANGE, CALIFORNIA

This recipe is easy, delicious and can be made in very little time. Once you try it, this soup will become one of your favorite light meals.

- 3 bacon strips, diced
- 1 medium onion, finely chopped
- 1 garlic clove, minced
- 2 cans (14-1/2 ounces *each*) beef broth
- 1 can (10 ounces) diced tomatoes and green chilies, undrained
- 1/4 teaspoon salt
- 1/4 teaspoon pepper
- 2 cans (15-1/2 ounces *each*) black-eyed peas, rinsed and drained

1 In a large saucepan, cook bacon over medium heat until crisp. Using a slotted spoon, remove to paper towels to drain.

2 In the drippings, saute the onion until tender. Add the garlic; cook 1 minute longer. Stir in the broth, tomatoes, salt and pepper. Bring to a boil. Stir in the black-eyed peas and the bacon; heat through.

YIELD: 6 SERVINGS.

minestrone with italian sausage

LINDA REIS | SALEM, OREGON

I make this zippy, satisfying soup all the time, and it's my dad's favorite. The recipe makes a lot, and I have found that it freezes well and tastes just as great reheated.

- 1 pound bulk Italian sausage
- 1 large onion, chopped
- 2 large carrots, chopped
- 2 celery ribs, chopped
- 1 medium leek (white portion only), chopped
- 1 medium zucchini, cut into 1/2-inch pieces
- 1/4 pound fresh green beans, trimmed and cut into 1/2-inch pieces
- 3 garlic cloves, minced
- 6 cups beef broth
- 2 cans (14-1/2 ounces *each*) diced tomatoes with basil, oregano and garlic
- 3 cups shredded cabbage
- 1 teaspoon dried basil
- 1 teaspoon dried oregano
- 1/4 teaspoon pepper
- 1 can (15 ounces) garbanzo beans *or* chickpeas, rinsed and drained
- 1/2 cup uncooked small pasta shells
- 3 tablespoons minced fresh parsley
- 1/3 cup grated Parmesan cheese

1 In a Dutch oven, cook sausage and onion over medium heat until meat is no longer pink; drain. Stir in the carrots, celery and leek; cook for 3 minutes. Add the zucchini, green beans and garlic; cook 1 minute longer.

2 Stir in the broth, tomatoes, cabbage, basil, oregano and pepper. Bring to a boil. Reduce heat; cover and simmer for 45 minutes.

3 Return to a boil. Stir in the garbanzo beans, pasta and parsley. Cook for 6-9 minutes or until pasta is tender. Serve with cheese.

YIELD: 11 SERVINGS (ABOUT 3 QUARTS).

pizza soup

DONNA BRITSCH
TEGA CAY, SOUTH CAROLINA

Anyone who likes pizza will love this soup. My sons help themselves to a big bowl when they get home from school in the evening.

1-1/4 cups sliced fresh mushrooms
  1/2 cup finely chopped onion
    1 teaspoon canola oil
    2 cups water
    1 can (15 ounces) pizza sauce
    1 cup chopped pepperoni
    1 cup chopped fresh tomatoes
  1/2 cup cooked Italian sausage
  1/4 teaspoon Italian seasoning
  1/4 cup grated Parmesan cheese
Shredded part-skim mozzarella cheese

1 In a large saucepan, saute mushrooms and onion in oil for 2-3 minutes or until tender. Add the water, pizza sauce, pepperoni, tomatoes, sausage and Italian seasoning. Bring to a boil over medium heat. Reduce heat; cover and simmer for 20 minutes, stirring occasionally.

2 Before serving, stir in the Parmesan cheese. Garnish each bowl with the mozzarella cheese.

YIELD: 4 SERVINGS.

ham and corn chowder

SHARON PRICE | CALDWELL, IDAHO

I'm always on the lookout for easy soups because my husband and I love them, particularly in the winter months. This cream chowder gets a little kick from cayenne and chopped jalapeno pepper. Extra servings freeze very well.

    2 celery ribs, chopped
  1/4 cup chopped onion
    1 jalapeno pepper, seeded and chopped
    2 tablespoons butter
    2 tablespoons all-purpose flour
    3 cups whole milk
    2 cups cubed fully cooked ham
    2 cups cubed cooked potatoes
1-1/2 cups fresh or frozen corn
    1 can (14-3/4 ounces) cream-style corn
  3/4 teaspoon minced fresh thyme or 1/4 teaspoon dried thyme
  1/8 to 1/4 teaspoon cayenne pepper
  1/8 teaspoon salt

1 In a large saucepan, saute the celery, onion and jalapeno in butter until vegetables are tender. Stir in flour until blended; gradually add milk.

Bring to a boil; cook and stir for 2 minutes or until thickened. Stir in the remaining ingredients. Bring to a boil. Reduce the heat; cover and simmer for 10 minutes or until heated through.

YIELD: 8 SERVINGS (2 QUARTS).

EDITOR'S NOTE: When cutting hot peppers, disposable gloves are recommended. Avoid touching your face.

sausage potato soup

JENNIFER LEFEVRE | HESSTON, KANSAS

After a full day of teaching and coaching, I'm often too tired to spend a lot of time preparing dinner. So I rely on this thick, chunky blend that I can have on the table in about 30 minutes. The whole family enjoys the wonderful flavor of the smoked sausage.

- 1/2 pound smoked kielbasa, diced
- 6 medium potatoes, peeled and cubed
- 2 cups frozen corn
- 1-1/2 cups chicken broth
- 1 celery rib, sliced
- 1/4 cup sliced carrot
- 1/2 teaspoon garlic powder
- 1/2 teaspoon onion powder
- 1/2 teaspoon salt
- 1/4 teaspoon pepper
- 1-1/2 cups whole milk
- 2/3 cup shredded cheddar cheese
- 1 teaspoon minced fresh parsley

1. In a large saucepan, brown kielbasa; drain. Set kielbasa aside. In the same pan, combine the potatoes, corn, broth, celery, carrot and seasonings. Bring to a boil.
2. Reduce the heat; cover and simmer for 15 minutes or until vegetables are tender. Add the milk, cheese, parsley and sausage. Cook and stir over low heat until cheese is melted and the soup is heated through.

YIELD: 6 SERVINGS.

vegetable chowder

SHEENA HOFFMAN | NORTH VANCOUVER, BRITISH COLUMBIA

When the weather gets chilly, we enjoy comfort foods like this hearty chowder. It's easy to prepare, and the aroma makes my mouth water.

- 4 bacon strips, diced
- 1/2 cup chopped onion
- 2 medium red potatoes, cubed
- 2 small carrots, halved lengthwise and thinly sliced
- 1 cup water
- 1-1/2 teaspoons chicken bouillon granules
- 2 cups whole milk
- 1-1/3 cups frozen corn
- 1/4 teaspoon pepper
- 2 tablespoons all-purpose flour
- 1/4 cup cold water
- 1-1/4 cups shredded cheddar cheese

1. In a large saucepan, cook bacon over medium heat until crisp. Remove to paper towels with a slotted spoon; drain, reserving 2 teaspoons drippings. Saute onion in drippings until tender. Add the potatoes, carrots, water and bouillon. Bring to a boil. Reduce heat; cover and simmer for 15-20 minutes or until the vegetables are almost tender.
2. Stir in the milk, corn and pepper. Cook 5 minutes longer. Combine the flour and cold water until smooth; gradually stir into soup. Bring to a boil; cook and stir for 1-2 minutes or until thickened. Remove from the heat; stir in cheese until melted. Sprinkle with bacon.

YIELD: 4 SERVINGS.

creamy cauliflower and bacon soup

MILDRED CARUSO
BRIGHTON, TENNESSEE

This is such a rich dish, you don't need to serve a lot with it. For a simple garnish, I sometimes add a drop of hot sauce to the top and drag a butter knife through it.

- 1 medium head cauliflower (2 pounds), cut into florets
- 2 cups half-and-half cream, *divided*
- 1/2 cup shredded Asiago cheese
- 1/2 teaspoon salt
- 1/2 teaspoon ground nutmeg
- 1/8 teaspoon pepper
- 1/2 to 1 cup water
- 4 bacon strips, cooked and crumbled

1 Place cauliflower in a steamer basket; place in a large saucepan over 1 in. of water. Bring to a boil; cover and steam for 8-10 minutes or until tender. Cool slightly.

2 Place cauliflower and 1/2 cup cream in a food processor; cover and process until pureed. Transfer to a large saucepan.

3 Stir in the cheese, salt, nutmeg, pepper and remaining cream. Add enough water to reach desired consistency; heat through. Sprinkle each serving with bacon.

YIELD: 4 SERVINGS.

vegetable pork soup

DAVE BOCK | AUBURN, WASHINGTON

I concocted this hefty and full-flavored meal-in-a-bowl one cold winter day. Now it's a fast and fuss-free family favorite!

- 1 boneless pork loin chop (4 ounces), cut into 1/2-inch cubes
- 1/4 pound smoked kielbasa *or* Polish sausage, chopped
- 1/4 cup chopped onion
- 1 celery rib, chopped
- 1 small carrot, chopped
- 1 teaspoon butter
- 1 garlic clove, minced
- 1/4 teaspoon paprika
- 2 cups reduced-sodium chicken broth
- 1 small tart apple, chopped
- 1 small red potato, chopped
- 1/4 teaspoon Chinese five-spice powder
- 1 teaspoon honey

1 In a large saucepan, cook the pork, sausage, onion, celery and carrot in butter over medium-high heat for 5 minutes or until pork is no longer pink and vegetables are tender. Add garlic and paprika; cook 1 minute longer.

2 Stir in the broth, apple, potato and five-spice powder. Bring to a boil. Reduce heat; cover and simmer for 12-15 minutes or until pork is tender. Stir in honey; cook for 2 minutes or until heated through.

YIELD: 4 SERVINGS.

buying and storing cauliflower

When purchasing fresh cauliflower, look for a head with compact florets that are free from yellow or brown spots. The leaves should be crisp and green, not withered or discolored. Tightly wrap an unwashed head of cauliflower and refrigerate up to 5 days. Before using, wash and remove the leaves at the base and trim the stem.

TASTE OF HOME TEST KITCHEN

versatile ham and corn chowder

SHARON ROSE BRAND
STAYTON, OREGON

My mother is an excellent cook who rarely follows a recipe exactly. My two sisters and I do the same thing, adding something here, omitting something there. With this soup, I sometimes leave out the bacon and butter, and have used canned corn and creamed corn with good results. We like to eat this soup with big soft hot pretzels instead of crackers.

- 8 bacon strips, cut into 1-inch pieces
- 1 medium onion, finely chopped
- 1 cup sliced celery
- 1/2 cup diced green pepper
- 3 cups cubed peeled potatoes (about 3 medium)
- 3 cups chicken broth
- 4 cups whole milk, *divided*
- 4 cups fresh *or* frozen whole kernel corn, *divided*
- 2 cups cubed fully cooked ham
- 2 tablespoons butter
- 3 tablespoons minced fresh parsley
- 1 teaspoon salt
- 1/8 teaspoon pepper
- 1/8 teaspoon hot pepper sauce, optional

1 In a large saucepan, cook the bacon until crisp. Remove bacon to paper towel to drain, reserving 1/4 cup drippings in pan. Saute the onion, celery and green pepper in drippings for 5 minutes. Add potatoes and broth. Reduce heat; cover and simmer for 10 minutes.

2 Place 1/2 cup milk and 2 cups corn in a blender; cover and process until pureed. Pour into saucepan. Add ham and remaining corn; simmer for 10 minutes or until vegetables are tender. Stir in the butter, parsley, salt, pepper, pepper sauce if desired and remaining milk; heat through. Garnish with bacon.

YIELD: 10-12 SERVINGS (3 QUARTS).

hearty black-eyed pea soup

YVONNE PETERSON
MOUNTAIN VIEW, MISSOURI

This recipe for pea soup is so tasty, you'll find yourself going back for seconds and thirds.

- 1/4 cup sliced celery
- 1/4 cup chopped onion
- 1-1/2 teaspoons butter
- 1 can (15-1/2 ounces) black-eyed peas, rinsed and drained
- 1 cup water
- 3/4 cup Italian stewed tomatoes, cut up
- 1/2 cup cubed fully cooked ham
- 1/2 teaspoon Italian seasoning
- 1/8 teaspoon pepper
Pinch salt

1 In a large saucepan, saute celery and onion in butter until tender. Add the peas, water and tomatoes. Bring to a boil. Stir in the ham, Italian seasoning, pepper and salt. Reduce the heat; simmer, uncovered, for 20 minutes or until heated through.

YIELD: 2 SERVINGS.

slow-cooked sauerkraut soup

LINDA LOHR | LITITZ, PENNSYLVANIA

We live in Lancaster County, Pennsylvania, which has a rich heritage of German culture. Around here, many dishes include sauerkraut, potatoes and sausage. We enjoy this recipe on cold winter evenings, along with muffins and fruit.

- 1 medium potato, cut into 1/4-inch cubes
- 1 pound smoked kielbasa, cut into 1/2-inch cubes
- 1 can (32 ounces) sauerkraut, rinsed and well drained
- 4 cups chicken broth
- 1 can (10-3/4 ounces) condensed cream of mushroom soup, undiluted
- 1/2 pound fresh mushrooms, sliced
- 1 cup cubed cooked chicken
- 2 medium carrots, cut into 1/4-inch slices
- 2 celery ribs, sliced
- 2 tablespoons white vinegar
- 2 teaspoons dill weed
- 1/2 teaspoon pepper
- 3 to 4 bacon strips, cooked and crumbled

1 In a 5-qt. slow cooker, combine the first 12 ingredients. Cover and cook on high for 5-6 hours or until the vegetables are tender. Skim fat. Garnish with bacon.

YIELD: 10-12 SERVINGS (ABOUT 3 QUARTS).

ham and bean soup

MARY DETWEILER | MIDDLEFIELD, OHIO

When I was a cook in a restaurant years ago, this was our best-selling soup. One taste, and your family will agree it's a winner!

- 3/4 pound fully cooked ham, cubed
- 1 medium onion, chopped
- 2 garlic cloves, minced
- 2 tablespoons butter
- 2 cans (15-1/2 ounces *each*) great northern beans, rinsed and drained
- 3 cups chicken broth
- 2 cups water
- 1 cup diced peeled potatoes
- 3/4 cup diced carrots
- 3/4 cup diced celery
- 1/4 teaspoon pepper
- 1/2 cup frozen peas
- 2 tablespoons minced fresh parsley

1 In a large saucepan, saute the ham, onion and garlic in butter until onion is tender. Add the next seven ingredients; cover and simmer for 30 minutes or until vegetables are tender. Add peas and cook for 5 minutes longer or until heated through. Stir in parsley.

YIELD: 8 SERVINGS (ABOUT 2 QUARTS).

parmesan pointers

When a recipe calls for shredded Parmesan cheese, use the cheese found in bags in the grocery store dairy section. Shredded Parmesan is often used in salads or soups where the shreds make a pretty garnish. If grated Parmesan is called for, use the finely grated cheese sold in containers with shaker/pourer tops. (You can substitute either shredded or grated Parmesan in equal proportions in your favorite recipes.) If you decide to buy a chunk of Parmesan cheese and grate your own, be sure to use the finest section on your grating tool. You can also use a blender or food processor. Simply cut the cheese into 1-inch cubes and process 1 cup of cubes at a time on high until finely grated. TASTE OF HOME TEST KITCHEN

kielbasa potato chowder

MISTY CHANDLER
LAWTON, OKLAHOMA

There's just the right touch of comfort in this sensational sausage chowder. My husband and I make a meal of it with some warm bread.

- 1/2 pound smoked kielbasa *or* Polish sausage, cut into 1/2-inch pieces
- 3 bacon strips, diced
- 1 small onion, finely chopped
- 1 garlic clove, minced
- 1-1/2 cups reduced-sodium chicken broth
- 1-1/2 cups water
- 2 medium potatoes, peeled and cubed
- 1/2 teaspoon chicken bouillon granules
- 1/8 teaspoon pepper
- 2 kale leaves, torn *or* 1/3 cup chopped fresh spinach
- 1/2 cup heavy whipping cream *or* 2% milk

1 In a large nonstick skillet, brown the kielbasa and bacon; drain, reserving 1 teaspoon drippings. Add the onion; cook over medium heat for 2-3 minutes or until onion is tender. Add garlic; cook 1 minute longer.

2 In a large saucepan, bring the broth and water to a boil. Add the potatoes, bouillon and pepper. Cook for 10 minutes or until potatoes are tender.

3 Add the meat mixture and kale; cook over medium heat for 2 minutes or until kale is wilted. Reduce heat. Add the cream; cook 1 minute longer or until heated through.

YIELD: 4 CUPS.

onion soup with sausage

SUNDRA HAUCK
BOGALUSA, LOUISIANA

With a yummy slice of mozzarella cheese bread on top, this hearty broth makes an impressive lunch or light supper. It looks great and tastes wonderful.

- 1/2 pound pork sausage links, cut into 1/2-inch pieces
- 1 pound sliced fresh mushrooms
- 1 cup sliced onion
- 2 cans (14-1/2 ounces *each*) beef broth
- 4 slices Italian bread
- 1/2 cup shredded part-skim mozzarella cheese

1 In a large saucepan, cook sausage over medium heat until no longer pink; drain. Add mushrooms and onion; cook for 4-6 minutes or until tender. Stir in the broth. Bring to a boil. Reduce heat; simmer, uncovered, for 4-6 minutes or until heated through.

2 Ladle into four 2-cup ovenproof bowls. Top each with a slice of bread; sprinkle with cheese. Broil until cheese is melted.

YIELD: 4 SERVINGS.

skillet sausage

I stock my freezer with two easy main dishes. I buy two links of kielbasa or smoked sausage, cut them into 1/4-inch slices and fry them in a skillet. I find two large microwave-safe freezer containers and pour a large jar of sauerkraut into one and a large can of baked beans into the other. I divide the sausage slices between the two dishes, put the lids on and place them in the freezer. Each dish can be thawed in the fridge for a day before warming in the microwave.

KATIE W., TOPEKA, KANSAS

hot dog potato soup

JEANNIE KLUGH
LANCASTER, PENNSYLVANIA

You can use leftover meatballs instead of hot dogs, and leftover corn in place of frozen in this yummy soup. Feel free to use any shredded cheese blend you have on hand.

- 2 cans (18.8 ounces *each*) ready-to-serve chunky baked potato with cheddar and bacon bits soup
- 4 hot dogs, halved lengthwise and sliced
- 1 cup (4 ounces) shredded cheddar-Monterey Jack cheese
- 1 cup frozen corn
- 1 cup whole milk

1 In a large microwave-safe bowl, combine all the ingredients. Cover and microwave on high for 8-10 minutes or until heated through, stirring every 2 minutes.

YIELD: 5 SERVINGS.

EDITOR'S NOTE: This recipe was tested in a 1,100-watt microwave.

mexican leek soup

DONNA AHNERT | SCOTIA, NEW YORK

This soup is so satisfying. You can substitute other beans, kale or add leftover corn. For brunch, I add a fried egg on top; for dinner, my husband adds lots of hot sauce!

- 1 can (15 ounces) pinto beans, rinsed and drained
- 2 medium leeks (white portion only), chopped
- 1/2 cup water
- 3/4 cup coarsely chopped fresh spinach
- 1 cup (4 ounces) shredded cheddar cheese
- 2 tablespoons grated Parmesan cheese
- 2 tablespoons grated Romano cheese
- 1/2 teaspoon ground cumin
- 1/2 teaspoon coarsely ground pepper
- 1/4 teaspoon cayenne pepper
- 1/8 teaspoon salt
- 1/4 cup heavy whipping cream
- 1/4 cup french-fried onions
- 2 bacon strips, cooked and crumbled

1 Place the beans, leeks and water in a 1-qt. microwave-safe bowl. Cover and microwave on high for 4-5 minutes or until tender.

2 In a blender, process bean mixture and spinach until smooth. Return to the bowl; add cheeses and seasonings. Whisk in cream. Cover and cook for 2-3 minutes or until heated through, stirring once. Sprinkle with onions and bacon.

YIELD: 2 SERVINGS.

EDITOR'S NOTE: This recipe was tested in a 1,100-watt microwave.

creamed cabbage soup

LAURIE HARMS | GRINNELL, IOWA

Although we live in town, we have a big garden. I love planting vegetables, watching them grow, then using them in tasty recipes like this.

- 2 cans (14-1/2 ounces *each*) chicken broth
- 2 celery ribs, chopped
- 1 medium head cabbage (3 pounds), shredded
- 1 medium onion, chopped
- 1 medium carrot, chopped
- 1/4 cup butter
- 3 tablespoons all-purpose flour
- 1 teaspoon salt
- 1/4 teaspoon pepper
- 2 cups half-and-half cream
- 1 cup whole milk
- 2 cups cubed fully cooked ham
- 1/2 teaspoon dried thyme
- Minced fresh parsley

1 In a large Dutch oven, combine the broth, celery, cabbage, onion and carrot; bring to a boil. Reduce heat; cover and simmer for 15-20 minutes or until vegetables are tender.

2 Meanwhile, melt butter in a small saucepan. Stir in the flour, salt and pepper until blended. Combine cream and milk; gradually add to flour mixture. Bring to a boil; cook and stir for 2 minutes or until thickened. Gradually stir into vegetable mixture. Add ham and thyme and heat through. Garnish with parsley.

YIELD: 8-10 SERVINGS.

italian sausage tortellini soup

NANCY TAFOYA | FORT COLLINS, COLORADO

My husband is not a soup-for-dinner kind of guy, but he loves this chunky, stick-to-your-ribs soup. I always serve it with a warm loaf of homemade bread.

- 1/3 pound bulk hot Italian sausage
- 1/3 cup chopped onion
- 1 garlic clove, minced
- 1-3/4 cups beef broth
- 1-1/4 cups water
- 3/4 cup chopped tomatoes
- 1/2 cup chopped green pepper
- 1/3 cup sliced fresh carrot
- 1/3 cup dry red wine *or* additional beef broth
- 1/3 cup tomato sauce
- 1/4 cup tomato paste
- 1/4 teaspoon dried oregano
- 1/4 teaspoon dried basil
- 3/4 cup frozen cheese tortellini
- 1/2 cup sliced quartered zucchini
- 2 tablespoons minced fresh parsley

1 Crumble sausage into a large saucepan; cook over medium heat until no longer pink. Remove with a slotted spoon to paper towels. In the drippings, saute onion until tender. Add garlic; cook 1 minute longer.

2 Stir in the broth, water, tomatoes, green pepper, carrot, wine, tomato sauce, tomato paste, oregano and the basil. Bring to a boil. Reduce heat; simmer, uncovered, for 30 minutes.

3 Skim fat. Stir in the sausage, tortellini, zucchini and parsley. Cover and simmer 10-15 minutes longer or until tortellini is tender.

YIELD: 2 SERVINGS.

sausage tortellini soup

HEATHER PERSCH
HUDSONVILLE, MICHIGAN

Always searching for new and different soup recipes, I came across a similar one in an old church cookbook and changed a few ingredients to suit my family's tastes. Now it's one of our favorites, and I always get requests for the recipe.

- 1 pound bulk Italian sausage
- 2 cups water
- 2 cups chopped cabbage
- 1 can (14-1/2 ounces) Italian stewed tomatoes, undrained and cut up
- 1 can (14-1/2 ounces) beef broth
- 1 can (10-1/2 ounces) condensed French onion soup
- 1 package (9 ounces) refrigerated cheese tortellini
- 1/2 cup grated Parmesan cheese

1 In a large saucepan, cook the sausage over medium heat until no longer pink; drain. Stir in the water, cabbage, tomatoes, broth and soup. Bring to a boil. Reduce the heat; simmer, uncovered, for 8 minutes. Stir in tortellini; cook 7-9 minutes longer or until pasta is tender. Sprinkle with cheese.

YIELD: 10 SERVINGS (2-1/2 QUARTS).

ham 'n' swiss soup

TASTE OF HOME TEST KITCHEN

Loaded with ham and broccoli, this flavorful soup is sure to warm spirits. Add buttermilk biscuits and a spinach salad for a simple dinner.

- 4-1/2 teaspoons butter
- 4-1/2 teaspoons all-purpose flour
- 1 can (14-1/2 ounces) reduced-sodium chicken broth
- 1 cup chopped broccoli
- 2 tablespoons chopped onion
- 1 cup cubed fully cooked ham
- 1/2 cup heavy whipping cream
- 1/8 teaspoon dried thyme
- 3/4 cup shredded Swiss cheese

1 In a large saucepan, melt butter; stir in flour until smooth; gradually add broth. Bring to a boil; cook and stir for 2 minutes or until thickened. Add broccoli and onion; cook and stir until crisp-tender. Add the ham, cream and thyme; heat through. Stir in the cheese until melted.

YIELD: 2 SERVINGS.

home-canned tomatoes

Typically, Italian stewed tomatoes contain celery, onion, green pepper, sugar, Italian seasoning and salt. As a substitute for each 14-1/2-ounce can of stewed tomatoes, try adding 3 tablespoons finely chopped celery, 2 tablespoons finely chopped onion, 1 tablespoon finely chopped green pepper, 1/2 teaspoon sugar and 1/8 teaspoon salt to the same amount of home-canned tomatoes.

TASTE OF HOME TEST KITCHEN

broth substitute

You can use chicken or beef bouillon in place of broth if you don't have any broth on hand. One bouillon cube or 1 teaspoon of granules dissolved in 1 cup of boiling water may be substituted for 1 cup of broth in any recipe.

TASTE OF HOME TEST KITCHEN

italian zucchini soup

CLARA MAE CHAMBERS
SUPERIOR, NEBRASKA

This recipe was given to me by my neighbor. Nice and simple, it's a good way to use a lot of your zucchini and other garden vegetables. It freezes well and is great to have on hand on a cold winter day.

- 1 pound bulk Italian sausage
- 1 cup chopped onion
- 2 cups chopped celery
- 1 medium green pepper, chopped
- 2 to 4 tablespoons sugar
- 2 teaspoons salt
- 1/2 teaspoon dried basil
- 1/2 teaspoon dried oregano
- 1/2 teaspoon pepper
- 4 cups diced tomatoes, undrained
- 4 cups diced zucchini

Grated Parmesan cheese, optional

1 In a Dutch oven, brown sausage with onion; drain excess fat. Add the next eight ingredients; cover and simmer 1 hour. Stir in zucchini and simmer 10 minutes. Sprinkle with the cheese if desired.

YIELD: 2 QUARTS.

sausage cabbage soup

STELLA GARRETT | ORLANDO, FLORIDA

My family often requests this satisfying soup. I've served it to guests for lunch and as a cold-weather Sunday supper. It's really good with a tossed green salad and a crusty loaf of bread.

- 1 medium onion, chopped
- 1 tablespoon canola oil
- 1 tablespoon butter
- 2 medium carrots, thinly sliced and halved
- 1 celery rib, thinly sliced
- 1 teaspoon caraway seeds
- 2 cups water
- 2 cups chopped cabbage
- 1/2 pound fully cooked smoked kielbasa *or* Polish sausage, halved and cut into 1/4-inch slices
- 1 can (14-1/2 ounces) diced tomatoes, undrained
- 1 tablespoon brown sugar
- 1 can (15 ounces) white kidney beans, rinsed and drained
- 1 tablespoon white vinegar
- 1 teaspoon salt
- 1/4 teaspoon pepper

Minced fresh parsley

1 In a 3-qt. saucepan, saute onion in oil and butter until tender. Add carrots and celery; saute for 3 minutes. Add caraway; cook and stir 1 minute longer. Stir in the water, cabbage, sausage, tomatoes and brown sugar; bring to a boil. Reduce heat; cover and simmer for 15-20 minutes or until vegetables are tender.

2 Add the beans, vinegar, salt and pepper. Simmer, uncovered, for 5-10 minutes or until heated through. Sprinkle with parsley.

YIELD: 6 SERVINGS.

shaker bean soup

DEBORAH AMRINE
GRAND HAVEN, MICHIGAN

This soup tastes especially delicious and warming in cold weather.

- 1 pound dried great northern beans
- 1 meaty ham bone *or* 2 smoked ham hocks
- 8 cups water
- 1 large onion, chopped
- 3 celery ribs, diced
- 2 medium carrots, shredded

Salt to taste
- 1/2 teaspoon pepper
- 1/2 teaspoon dried thyme
- 1 can (28 ounces) crushed tomatoes in puree
- 2 tablespoons brown sugar
- 1-1/2 cups finely shredded fresh spinach

1 Sort and rinse beans. Place in a Dutch oven; cover with water and bring to a boil. Boil 2 minutes. Remove from heat; let stand 1 hour. Drain beans and discard liquid.

2 In the same pan, add the ham bone, water and beans. Bring to a boil. Reduce heat; cover and simmer for 1-1/2 hours or until meat easily falls from the bone.

3 Remove bone from broth; cool. Trim meat from the bone. Discard bone. Add the ham, onion, celery, carrots, salt, pepper and thyme to bean mixture. Cover and simmer for 1 hour or until beans are tender.

4 Add tomatoes and brown sugar. Cook for 10 minutes. Just before serving, add the spinach.

YIELD: 5 QUARTS.

sausage tortellini soup with spinach

JOYCE LULEWICZ | BRUNSWICK, OHIO

My husband's grandmother used to make this soup with her own homemade sausage and homemade tortellini. We don't hand-make those ingredients, but this soup is almost as good as hers. It's a great way to get the kids to eat spinach!

- 1/2 pound bulk Italian sausage
- 1 small onion, thinly sliced
- 1 garlic clove, minced
- 1 can (14-1/2 ounces) reduced-sodium chicken broth
- 1/2 cup water
- 1-1/2 cups torn fresh spinach
- 3/4 cup refrigerated cheese tortellini
- 2 tablespoons shredded Parmesan cheese

1 In a small saucepan, cook sausage over medium heat until no longer pink; drain. Add onion; cook and stir until tender. Add garlic; cook 1 minute longer. Stir in broth and water; bring to a boil. Reduce heat; simmer, uncovered, for 10 minutes.

2 Return to a boil. Reduce heat, add spinach and tortellini; cook for 7-9 minutes or until tortellini is tender. Sprinkle with cheese.

YIELD: 2 SERVINGS.

leftover meat miracle

When you have a variety of leftover meats, such as beef, turkey, Italian sausage, etc., cut them into small pieces and combine them in a stew pot. Add leftover gravy, frozen hash browns, shredded cabbage and leftover vegetables. Cook the mixture until the potatoes are tender. This delicious stew is great over biscuits or with a pan of corn bread.

TASTE OF HOME TEST KITCHEN

sausage wild rice soup

TONYA SCHAFFER | HURON, SOUTH DAKOTA

This recipe makes a big batch, so I often divide the leftovers into a few containers for handy "freezer meals."

- 9 cups water, *divided*
- 1 cup uncooked wild rice
- 2 pounds bulk Italian sausage
- 2 large onions, chopped
- 2 teaspoons olive oil
- 6 garlic cloves, minced
- 3 cartons (32 ounces *each*) chicken broth
- 1 can (28 ounces) diced tomatoes, undrained
- 1 can (6 ounces) tomato paste
- 2 teaspoons dried basil
- 2 teaspoons dried oregano
- 1 package (6 ounces) fresh baby spinach, coarsely chopped
- 1/2 teaspoon salt
- 1/2 teaspoon pepper

1 In a large saucepan, bring 3 cups water to a boil. Stir in rice. Reduce heat; cover and simmer for 55-60 minutes or until tender.

2 Meanwhile, in a stockpot, cook sausage over medium heat until no longer pink; drain. Remove and set aside. In the same pan, saute onions in oil until tender. Add garlic; cook 1 minute longer. Stir in the broth, tomatoes, tomato paste, basil, oregano and remaining water. Return sausage to the pan. Bring to a boil. Reduce heat; simmer, uncovered, for 20 minutes.

3 Stir in the spinach, salt, pepper and wild rice; heat through.

YIELD: 5 QUARTS (13 SERVINGS).

split pea soup

LAURIE TODD | COLUMBUS, MISSISSIPPI

This old-fashioned favorite is not only a snap to make, it's economical, too. Carrots, celery and onion accent the subtle flavor of the split peas, while a ham bone adds a meaty touch to this hearty soup. It's sure to chase away autumn's chill.

- 1 package (16 ounces) dried green split peas
- 1 meaty ham bone
- 1 large onion, chopped
- 1 teaspoon salt
- 1/2 teaspoon pepper
- 1/2 teaspoon dried thyme
- 1 bay leaf
- 1 cup chopped carrot
- 1 cup chopped celery

1 Sort peas and rinse with cold water. Place beans in a Dutch oven; add water to cover by 2 in. Bring to a boil; boil for 2 minutes. Remove from the heat; cover and let stand for 1 to 4 hours or until beans are softened. Drain and rinse beans, discarding liquid.

2 Return peas to Dutch oven. Add 2-1/2 qts. water, ham bone, onion, salt, pepper, thyme and bay leaf. Bring to a boil. Reduce heat; cover and simmer for 1-1/2 hours, stirring occasionally.

3 Remove the ham bone; when cool enough to handle, remove meat from bone. Discard bone; dice meat and return to soup. Add carrots and celery. Simmer, uncovered, for 45-60 minutes or until soup reaches desired thickness and vegetables are tender. Discard bay leaf.

YIELD: 10 SERVINGS (ABOUT 2-1/2 QUARTS).

italian sausage orzo soup

DEBORAH REDFIELD | BUENA PARK, CALIFORNIA

I always look for recipes high in taste and nutrition but low on prep time and fat. This thick, chunky soup fills the bill and is such a family favorite that I serve it at least once a month!

- 1/4 pound bulk Italian sausage
- 1/2 cup sliced fresh mushrooms
- 1/2 cup sliced zucchini
- 1/4 cup chopped onion
- 1 teaspoon olive oil
- 1 garlic clove, minced
- 1-1/4 cups chicken broth
- 1 cup canned diced tomatoes, undrained
- 1/2 teaspoon dried basil
- 1/8 teaspoon pepper
- 3 tablespoons uncooked orzo *or* small shell pasta
- 1 tablespoon minced fresh parsley

1 In a large saucepan, cook the sausage, mushrooms, zucchini and onion in oil over medium heat until the meat is no longer pink; drain. Add the garlic; cook 1 minute longer. Add the broth, tomatoes, basil and pepper. Bring to a boil. Stir in pasta. Reduce heat; cover and simmer for 15-20 minutes or until pasta is tender. Sprinkle with parsley.

YIELD: 2 SERVINGS.

ham 'n' chickpea soup

LINDA ARNOLD | EDMONTON, ALBERTA

Chock-full of ham, vegetables, chickpeas and orzo, this hearty soup is loaded with good-for-you flavor.

- 1/2 cup uncooked orzo pasta
- 1 small onion, chopped
- 2 teaspoons canola oil
- 1 cup cubed fully cooked lean ham
- 2 garlic cloves, minced
- 1 teaspoon dried rosemary, crushed
- 1 teaspoon rubbed sage
- 2 cups reduced-sodium beef broth
- 1 can (14-1/2 ounces) diced tomatoes, undrained
- 1 can (15 ounces) chickpeas *or* garbanzo beans, rinsed and drained
- 4 tablespoons shredded Parmesan cheese
- 1 tablespoon minced fresh parsley

1 Cook orzo according to package directions. Meanwhile, in a large saucepan, saute onion in oil for 3 minutes. Add the ham, garlic, rosemary and sage; saute 1 minute longer. Stir in broth and tomatoes. Bring to a boil. Reduce heat; simmer, uncovered, for 10 minutes.

2 Drain orzo; stir into soup. Add chickpeas; heat through. Sprinkle each serving with cheese and parsley.

YIELD: 4 SERVINGS.

kielbasa potato soup

BEVERLEE DEBERRY
HEMPSTEAD, TEXAS

This is a delicious and hearty soup. Combined with a nice loaf of French bread, it's a complete and satisfying meal. It has become an often-requested menu item at our house.

- 1 medium leek, (white portion only), halved and sliced
- 1 tablespoon butter
- 1-3/4 cups chicken broth
- 1 medium potato, peeled and diced
- 1/3 pound fully cooked kielbasa or Polish sausage, cut into bite-size pieces
- 1/4 cup heavy whipping cream
- 1/8 teaspoon *each* caraway and cumin seeds, toasted
- 1/3 cup thinly sliced fresh spinach

1 In a large saucepan, saute leek in butter until tender. Add broth and potato; bring to a boil. Reduce heat; cover and simmer for 15-20 minutes or until potato is tender.

2 Stir in sausage, cream, caraway and cumin; heat through (do not boil). Just before serving, add the spinach.

YIELD: 2 SERVINGS.

hearty corn chowder

MARK TWIEST | ALLENDALE, MICHIGAN

Everyone in my wife's family is a corn lover, so her mom came up with this wonderful recipe to satisfy their appetites. With the bacon, sausage and potatoes, it's hearty enough to be a one-pot meal. It's also really good made with chicken.

- 1/2 pound sliced bacon
- 1 cup chopped celery
- 1/2 cup chopped onion
- 2 cups cubed peeled potatoes
- 1 cup water
- 2 cups frozen corn
- 1 can (14-3/4 ounces) cream-style corn
- 1 can (12 ounces) evaporated milk
- 6 ounces smoked sausage links, cut into 1/4-inch slices
- 1 teaspoon dill weed

1 In a large saucepan, cook the bacon over medium heat until crisp. Remove to paper towels with a slotted spoon; drain, reserving 2 tablespoons drippings. Crumble the bacon and set aside.

2 Saute the celery and onion in drippings until the onion is lightly browned. Add the potatoes and water. Cover and cook over medium heat for 10 minutes. Stir in the corn, milk, sausage, dill and bacon. Cook until the potatoes are tender, about 30 minutes.

YIELD: 4-6 SERVINGS (1-1/2 QUARTS).

cream soups

CREAMY CARROT SOUP, P. 64

roasted garlic potato soup

MISTY BROWN | GLENDALE HEIGHTS, ILLINOIS

Roasting mellows and sweetens the blend of veggies in this hearty and heartwarming soup. It's perfect for a cozy night in.

        1   whole garlic bulb
1-1/2   teaspoons plus 2 tablespoons butter, *divided*
        2   pounds potatoes (about 6 medium), peeled and cubed
        2   medium onions, quartered
        2   tablespoons olive oil
    1/2   teaspoon salt
    1/4   teaspoon pepper
        6   cups vegetable broth, *divided*
4-1/2   teaspoons all-purpose flour
    1/2   cup milk

1   Remove the papery outer skin from garlic (do not peel or separate cloves); cut top off bulb. Melt 1-1/2 teaspoons butter; drizzle over garlic. Wrap in heavy-duty foil. Place in a 9-in. round baking pan; set aside.

2   Place the potatoes and onions in a single layer in an ungreased 15-in. x 10-in. x 1-in. baking pan. Drizzle with oil; sprinkle with salt and pepper. Toss to coat.

3   Bake garlic and potato mixture at 400° for 35-40 minutes or until tender, stirring vegetables once. Cool slightly.

4   In a blender, combine 2 cups broth and half of the vegetable mixture; cover and process until blended. Repeat with 2 cups broth and remaining vegetable mixture; set aside.

5   In a large saucepan, melt remaining butter. Stir in flour until smooth; gradually add remaining broth. Bring to a boil; cook and stir for 2 minutes or until thickened. Squeeze softened garlic into pan. Stir in milk and pureed vegetables; heat through.

YIELD: 8 SERVINGS.

asparagus brie soup

MELISSA PETREK-MYER | AUSTIN, TEXAS

This rich soup is wonderful when fresh asparagus is in season or any time of year. It's an elegant dish to serve to company or for a special occasion.

1/2   pound fresh asparagus, cut into 2-inch pieces
1/2   cup butter
1/4   cup all-purpose flour
    3   cups chicken *or* vegetable broth
    1   cup heavy whipping cream
1/2   cup white wine
    4   to 6 ounces Brie, rind removed
Dash salt and pepper

1   In a large saucepan, saute asparagus in butter until tender. Stir in flour until blended. Cook and stir for 2 minutes or until golden brown. Gradually add broth, cream and wine or additional broth. Bring to a boil. Reduce heat; simmer for 10-15 minutes.

2   In a blender; cover and process soup in batches until smooth. Return to the pan. Cube Brie and add to soup. Simmer, uncovered, for 5 minutes or until cheese is melted.

YIELD: 4 SERVINGS.

cordon bleu potato soup

NOELLE MYERS
GRAND FORKS, NORTH DAKOTA

I came up with this recipe when I was looking for a way to use up some leftover ingredients. It's so yummy! It's also an easy way to simmer up some hearty comfort in a hurry on chilly days.

- 2 cans (10-3/4 ounces *each*) condensed cream of potato soup, undiluted
- 1 can (14-1/2 ounces) chicken broth
- 1 cup (4 ounces) shredded Swiss cheese
- 1 cup diced fully cooked ham
- 1 cup whole milk
- 1 can (5 ounces) chunk white chicken, drained
- 2 teaspoons Dijon mustard

1 In a 2-qt. microwave-safe dish, combine all the ingredients. Cover and microwave on high for 5-8 minutes or until heated through, stirring twice.

YIELD: 4 SERVINGS.

EDITOR'S NOTE: This recipe was tested in a 1,100-watt microwave.

cream of mussel soup

DONNA NOEL | GRAY, MAINE

Every New England cook has a personal version of mussel soup, depending on the favored regional herbs and cooking customs. Feel free to start with my recipe, and develop your own luscious variation.

- 3 pounds fresh mussels (about 5 dozen), scrubbed and beards removed
- 2 medium onions, finely chopped
- 2 celery ribs, finely chopped
- 1 cup water
- 1 cup white wine *or* chicken broth
- 1 bottle (8 ounces) clam juice
- 1/4 cup minced fresh parsley
- 2 garlic cloves, minced
- 1/4 teaspoon salt
- 1/4 teaspoon pepper
- 1 cup half-and-half cream

1 Tap mussels; discard any that do not close. Set aside. In a stock pot, combine the onions, celery, water, wine or broth, clam juice, parsley, garlic, salt and pepper.

2 Bring to a boil. Reduce heat; add mussels. Cover and simmer for 5-6 minutes or until mussels have opened. Remove mussels with a slotted spoon, discarding any unopened mussels; set aside opened mussels and keep warm.

3 Cool cooking liquid slightly. In a blender, cover and process cooking liquid in batches until blended. Return all to pan. Add cream and the reserved mussels; heat through (do not boil).

YIELD: 5 SERVINGS.

white bean bisque

LINDA MIRANDA | WAKEFIELD, RHODE ISLAND

This is a meal that will leave you both satisfied and wanting more!

- 1/4 cup shredded Parmesan cheese
- Cayenne pepper
- 1/4 pound Italian turkey sausage links
- 2 tablespoons chopped onion
- 1 teaspoon olive oil
- 1 garlic clove, minced
- 1 can (15 ounces) white kidney *or* cannellini beans, rinsed and drained
- 1 cup reduced-sodium chicken broth
- 1/4 cup heavy whipping cream
- 2 teaspoons sherry, optional
- 1 teaspoon minced fresh parsley
- 1/8 teaspoon salt
- 1/8 teaspoon dried thyme

1 Spoon cheese into six mounds 3 in. apart on a parchment paper-lined baking sheet. Spread into 1-1/2-in. circles. Sprinkle with a dash of cayenne. Bake at 400° for 5-6 minutes or until light golden brown. Cool.

2 In a large saucepan, cook sausage and onion in oil over medium heat until meat is no longer pink; drain. Remove and keep warm.

3 In the same pan, saute garlic for 1 minute or until tender. Stir in the beans, broth, cream, sherry if desired, parsley, salt, thyme and a dash of cayenne. Bring to a boil. Reduce heat; simmer, uncovered, for 12-15 minutes or until heated through. Cool slightly.

4 Transfer to a blender; cover and process on high until almost blended. Pour into soup bowls; sprinkle with sausage mixture and Parmesan crisps.

YIELD: 2 SERVINGS.

enchilada chicken soup

CRISTIN FISCHER | BELLEVUE, NEBRASKA

Canned soups, bottled enchilada sauce and a few other convenience items make this recipe one of my fast-to-fix favorites. Use mild green chilies if they suit your tastes or try a spicier variety to give the soup more kick.

- 1 can (11 ounces) condensed fiesta nacho cheese soup, undiluted
- 1 can (10-3/4 ounces) condensed cream of chicken soup, undiluted
- 2-2/3 cups whole milk
- 1 can (10 ounces) chunk white chicken, drained
- 1 can (10 ounces) enchilada sauce
- 1 can (4 ounces) chopped green chilies
- Sour cream

1 In a large saucepan, combine the soups, milk, chicken, enchilada sauce and chilies. Cook until heated through. Serve with sour cream.

YIELD: 7 SERVINGS.

minced garlic

Minced garlic that you can buy, garlic that's been finely chopped by hand and garlic that's been put through a press, can all be used interchangeably in recipes. Choose whichever is easiest and most convenient for you.

TASTE OF HOME TEST KITCHEN

apple pumpkin soup

PAT HABIGER | SPEARVILLE, KANSAS

Relish autumn's colors and flavors with this creamy, golden soup. Just blend the ingredients and chill overnight. For a treat, serve in small hollowed-out pumpkins.

- 2 cups finely chopped peeled tart apples
- 1/2 cup finely chopped onion
- 2 tablespoons butter
- 1 tablespoon all-purpose flour
- 4 cups chicken broth
- 3 cups canned pumpkin
- 1/4 cup packed brown sugar
- 1/2 teaspoon *each* ground cinnamon, nutmeg and ginger
- 1 cup unsweetened apple juice
- 1/2 cup half-and-half cream
- 1/4 teaspoon salt
- 1/4 teaspoon pepper

1 In a large saucepan, saute apples and onion in butter for 3-5 minutes or until tender. Stir in flour until blended. Gradually whisk in broth. Stir in the pumpkin, brown sugar, cinnamon, nutmeg and ginger. Bring to a boil. Reduce heat; cover and simmer for 25 minutes. Cool slightly.

2 In a blender, cover and process the soup in batches until smooth. Pour into a bowl; cover and refrigerate for 8 hours or overnight.

3 Just before serving, transfer soup to a large saucepan. Cook over medium heat for 5-10 minutes. Stir in the apple juice, cream, salt and pepper; heat through.

YIELD: 12 SERVINGS (ABOUT 2 QUARTS).

lighter broccoli soup

CAROL COLVIN | DERBY, NEW YORK

My husband is diabetic, and I'm watching my weight, so this soup fits our diets perfectly. Friends and family will never guess it only takes 15 minutes to make!

- 1 can (10-3/4 ounces) reduced-fat reduced-sodium condensed cream of celery soup, undiluted
- 1 can (10-3/4 ounces) reduced-fat reduced-sodium condensed cream of chicken soup, undiluted
- 3 cups fat-free milk
- 1 tablespoon dried minced onion
- 1 teaspoon dried parsley flakes
- 1/2 teaspoon garlic powder
- 1/4 teaspoon pepper
- 3 cups frozen chopped broccoli, thawed
- 1 can (14-1/2 ounces) sliced potatoes, drained
- 1/2 cup shredded reduced-fat cheddar cheese

1 In a large saucepan, combine the soups, milk, onion, parsley, garlic powder and pepper. Stir in broccoli and potatoes; heat through. Just before serving, sprinkle with cheese.

YIELD: 8 SERVINGS.

mexican shrimp bisque

KAREN HARRIS
CASTLE ROCK, COLORADO

This bisque combines the perfect blend of seafood and Mexican spices. You'll want seconds for sure!

- 1 small onion, chopped
- 1 tablespoon olive oil
- 2 garlic cloves, minced
- 1 tablespoon all-purpose flour
- 1 cup water
- 1/2 cup heavy whipping cream
- 1 tablespoon chili powder
- 2 teaspoons chicken bouillon granules
- 1/2 teaspoon ground cumin
- 1/2 teaspoon ground coriander
- 1/2 pound uncooked medium shrimp, peeled and deveined
- 1/2 cup sour cream

Fresh cilantro and cubed avocado, optional

1 In a small saucepan, saute onion in oil until tender. Add garlic; cook 1 minute longer. Stir in flour until blended. Stir in the water, cream, chili powder, bouillon, cumin and coriander; bring to a boil. Reduce heat; cover and simmer for 5 minutes.

2 Cut shrimp into bite-size pieces; add to soup. Simmer 5 minutes longer or until shrimp turn pink. Gradually stir 1/2 cup hot soup into sour cream; return all to the pan, stirring constantly. Heat through (do not boil). Garnish with cilantro and avocado if desired.

YIELD: 3 CUPS.

creamy turkey vegetable soup

STEPHANIE MOON | BOISE, IDAHO

This is a satisfying soup that's great for a chilly night. This recipe also makes the best of leftover turkey!

- 1 cup chopped fresh carrots
- 1/2 cup chopped celery
- 1/3 cup chopped onion
- 2 tablespoons butter
- 2 cups diced cooked turkey
- 2 cups water
- 1-1/2 cups diced peeled potatoes
- 2 teaspoons chicken bouillon granules
- 1/2 teaspoon *each* salt and pepper
- 2-1/2 cups whole milk, *divided*
- 3 tablespoons all-purpose flour

1 In a large saucepan, saute the carrots, celery and onion in butter until tender. Stir in the turkey, water, potatoes, bouillon, salt and pepper. Bring to a boil. Reduce heat; cover and simmer for 10-12 minutes or until vegetables are tender.

2 Stir in 2 cups milk. Combine flour and remaining milk until smooth. Stir into soup. Bring to a boil; cook and stir for 2 minutes or until thickened.

YIELD: 4 SERVINGS.

storing celery

Remove celery from the store bag it comes in and wrap it in paper towel, then in aluminum foil. Store in the refrigerator. When you need some, break off what your recipe calls for, rewrap the rest and return to fridge. I find celery stored like this stays crisp longer.

LINDA J., MILNER, GEORGIA

creamy carrot soup

BERTHA MCCLUNG | SUMMERSVILLE, WEST VIRGINIA

This blended soup is loaded with vegetables, so it's delicious as well as good for you. Plus, its delightful golden color adds a special touch to your table.

- 3 cups thinly sliced carrots
- 1 cup chopped onion
- 2/3 cup chopped celery
- 1-1/2 cups diced peeled potatoes
- 1 garlic clove, minced
- 1/2 teaspoon sugar
- 2 teaspoons canola oil
- 4 cups reduced-sodium chicken broth

Dash ground nutmeg

Pepper to taste

1 In a Dutch oven or soup kettle over medium-low heat, saute carrots, onion, celery, potatoes, garlic and sugar in oil for 5 minutes. Add broth, nutmeg and pepper; bring to a boil. Reduce heat; cover and simmer for 30-40 minutes or until vegetables are tender. Remove from the heat and cool to room temperature. Puree in batches in a blender or food processor. Return to the kettle and heat through.

YIELD: 4 SERVINGS.

cream of crab soup

MARILYN SHAW | MIDDLETOWN, DELAWARE

A friend shared this soup at a potluck and I had to have the recipe. I love how it's so tasty and easy to make.

- 1 large onion, finely chopped
- 1 medium green pepper, finely chopped
- 2 tablespoons butter
- 2 garlic cloves, minced
- 3 pints half-and-half cream
- 2 cups frozen shredded hash brown potatoes, thawed
- 1 can (10-3/4 ounces) condensed cream of mushroom soup, undiluted
- 1 can (10-3/4 ounces) condensed cream of asparagus soup, undiluted
- 2 cans (6 ounces *each*) lump crabmeat, drained
- 1 package (8 ounces) imitation crabmeat, chopped
- 1-1/2 cups frozen corn, thawed
- 1 tablespoon dried parsley flakes
- 1-1/2 teaspoons dill weed
- 1-1/2 teaspoons seafood seasoning
- 1 teaspoon pepper

1 In a Dutch oven, saute onion and green pepper in butter until tender. Add garlic; saute 1 minute longer. Stir in the remaining ingredients. Cook and stir over medium-low heat until heated through (do not boil).

YIELD: 14 SERVINGS (3-1/2 QUARTS).

creamy reuben soup

JAY DAVIS | KNOXVILLE, TENNESSEE

I had a professor in college who loved Reuben sandwiches. When he got the flu, I came up with this creamy soup to share with him. He loved it!

- 1/2 cup chopped onion
- 1/4 cup chopped celery
- 1/4 cup chopped green pepper
- 1/4 cup butter, cubed
- 2 tablespoons all-purpose flour
- 1 cup beef broth
- 2 cups half-and-half cream
- 1/4 pound sliced deli corned beef, coarsely chopped
- 3/4 cup sauerkraut, rinsed and well drained
- 1/4 teaspoon salt
- 1/4 teaspoon pepper
- 1 cup (4 ounces) shredded Swiss cheese

1 In a large saucepan, saute the onion, celery and green pepper in butter until tender. Stir in flour until blended; gradually add broth. Bring to a boil; cook and stir for 2 minutes or until thickened.

2 Reduce heat to low. Add the cream, corned beef, sauerkraut, salt and pepper; heat through (do not boil). Stir in cheese until melted.

YIELD: 5 CUPS.

mincing and chopping

To mince or chop, hold the handle of a chef's knife with one hand, and rest the finger of your other hand on the top of the blade near the tip. Using the handle to guide and apply pressure, move knife in an arc across the food with a rocking motion until pieces of food are the desired size. Mincing results in pieces no larger than 1/8 in., and chopping can produce 1/4-in. to 1/2-in. pieces.

TASTE OF HOME TEST KITCHEN

summer squash soup

HEIDI WILCOX | LAPEER, MICHIGAN

Delicate and lemony, this squash soup would set the stage for a memorable ladies luncheon. It's the best of late summer in a bowl.

- 2 large sweet onions, chopped
- 1 medium leek (white portion only), chopped
- 2 tablespoons olive oil
- 6 garlic cloves, minced
- 6 medium yellow summer squash, seeded and cubed
- 4 cups reduced-sodium chicken broth
- 4 fresh thyme sprigs
- 1/4 teaspoon salt
- 2 tablespoons lemon juice
- 1/8 teaspoon hot pepper sauce
- 1 tablespoon shredded Parmesan cheese
- 2 teaspoons grated lemon peel

1 In a large saucepan, saute the onions and leek in oil until tender. Add garlic; cook 1 minute longer. Add squash; saute 5 minutes. Stir in the broth, thyme and salt. Bring to a boil. Reduce heat; cover and simmer for 15-20 minutes or until squash is tender.

2 Discard thyme sprigs. Cool slightly. In a blender, process soup in batches until smooth. Return all to the pan. Stir in lemon juice and hot pepper sauce; heat through. Sprinkle each serving with cheese and lemon peel.

YIELD: 8 SERVINGS (2 QUARTS).

to allow flavors to blend. Stir in cream; heat through (do not boil).

4 Meanwhile, for croutons, place bread on a baking sheet and brush with oil. Bake for 5-6 minutes or until golden brown. Spread with pesto and sprinkle with goat cheese and pepper. Bake 2 minutes longer. Ladle soup into bowls and top with croutons.

YIELD: 6 SERVINGS.

creamy wild rice soup

JOANNE EICKHOFF
PEQUOT LAKES, MINNESOTA

This is a quick way to add a homemade touch to canned soup. It is thick and creamy with added texture from crunchy wild rice and has a subtle smoky bacon flavor.

- 1/2 cup water
- 4-1/2 teaspoons dried minced onion
- 2/3 cup condensed cream of potato soup, undiluted
- 1/2 cup shredded Swiss cheese
- 1/2 cup cooked wild rice
- 1/2 cup half-and-half cream
- 2 bacon strips, cooked and crumbled

1 In a small saucepan, bring water and onion to a boil. Reduce heat. Stir in the potato soup, cheese, rice and cream; heat through (do not boil). Garnish with bacon.

YIELD: 2 SERVINGS.

yellow tomato soup with goat cheese croutons

PATTERSON WATKINS
PHILADELPHIA, PENNSYLVANIA

Get your next dinner party off to an impressive start with this savory cream soup. Guests will love the roasted tomato flavor and crispy bread slices. If you make it in summer, try grilling the tomatoes instead.

- 3 pounds yellow tomatoes, halved (about 9 medium)
- 2 tablespoons olive oil, *divided*
- 4 garlic cloves, minced, *divided*
- 1 teaspoon salt
- 1 teaspoon pepper
- 1 teaspoon minced fresh rosemary
- 1 teaspoon minced fresh thyme
- 1 large onion, chopped
- 1 cup vegetable broth
- 1/2 cup milk
- 1/2 cup heavy whipping cream

CROUTONS:
- 12 slices French bread baguette (1/2 inch thick)
- 1 tablespoon olive oil
- 2 tablespoons prepared pesto
- 1/2 cup crumbled goat cheese
- 1 teaspoon pepper

1 Place tomatoes, cut side down, in a greased 15-in. x 10-in. x 1-in. baking pan; brush with 1 tablespoon oil. Sprinkle with 2 teaspoons garlic and the salt, pepper, rosemary and thyme.

2 Bake at 400° for 25-30 minutes or until tomatoes are tender and skins are charred. Cool slightly. Discard tomato skins. In a blender, process tomatoes until blended.

3 In a large saucepan, saute the onion in remaining oil until tender. Add the remaining garlic; saute 1 minute longer. Add broth and milk; bring to a boil. Carefully stir in tomato puree. Simmer, uncovered, for 15 minutes

garlic fennel bisque

JANET ONDRICH | THAMESVILLE, ONTARIO

I usually serve this in the spring as a wonderful appetizer or side dish. The fennel in this bisque is so different and refreshing. The recipe makes a big batch of soup so you can easily serve a crowd.

- 4 cups water
- 2-1/2 cups half-and-half cream
- 24 garlic cloves, peeled and halved
- 3 medium fennel bulbs, cut into 1/2-inch pieces
- 2 tablespoons chopped fennel fronds
- 1/2 teaspoon salt
- 1/8 teaspoon pepper
- 1/2 cup pine nuts, toasted

1 In a Dutch oven, bring the water, cream and the garlic to a boil. Reduce the heat; cover and simmer for 15 minutes or until garlic is very soft. Add the fennel and fennel fronds; cover and simmer 15 minutes longer or until fennel is very soft.

2 Cool slightly. In a blender, process the soup in batches until blended. Return all to the pan. Season with salt and pepper; heat through. Sprinkle each serving with pine nuts.

YIELD: 14 SERVINGS.

veggie cheese soup

JEAN HALL | RAPID CITY, SOUTH DAKOTA

My niece makes this in a slow cooker by putting in all the ingredients but the cheese. When the veggies are tender, she adds the cubed cheese. Five minutes later, a nutritious meal is served.

- 1 medium onion, chopped
- 1 celery rib, chopped
- 2 small red potatoes, cut into 1/2-inch cubes
- 2-3/4 cups water
- 2 teaspoons reduced-sodium chicken bouillon granules
- 1 tablespoon cornstarch
- 1/4 cup cold water
- 1 can (10-3/4 ounces) reduced-fat reduced-sodium condensed cream of chicken soup, undiluted
- 3 cups frozen California-blend vegetables, thawed
- 1/2 cup chopped fully cooked lean ham
- 8 ounces reduced-fat process cheese (Velveeta), cubed

1 In a large nonstick saucepan coated with a cooking spray, cook onion and celery over medium heat until onion is tender. Stir in the potatoes, water and bouillon. Bring to a boil. Reduce heat; cover and simmer for 10 minutes.

2 Combine cornstarch and cold water until smooth; gradually stir into soup. Return to a boil; cook and stir for 1-2 minutes or until slightly thickened. Stir in condensed soup until blended.

3 Reduce heat; add vegetables and ham. Cook and stir until vegetables are tender. Stir in cheese until melted.

YIELD: 9 SERVINGS.

golden squash soup

BECKY RUFF | MCGREGOR, IOWA

This delectable soup feels like fall! Its golden color and rich, satisfying flavor have made it a favorite of mine for years.

- 5 medium leeks (white portion only), sliced
- 2 tablespoons butter
- 1-1/2 pounds butternut squash, peeled, seeded and cubed (about 4 cups)
- 4 cups chicken broth
- 1/4 teaspoon dried thyme
- 1/4 teaspoon pepper
- 1-3/4 cups shredded cheddar cheese
- 1/4 cup sour cream
- 2 tablespoons thinly sliced green onion

1 In a large saucepan, saute leeks in butter until tender. Stir in the squash, broth, thyme and pepper. Bring to a boil. Reduce heat; cover and simmer for 10-15 minutes or until squash is tender. Cool slightly.

2 In a blender, cover and process squash mixture in small batches until smooth; return all to the pan. Bring to a boil. Reduce heat to low. Add cheese; stir until soup is heated through and cheese is melted. Garnish with sour cream and onion.

YIELD: 6 SERVINGS.

spinach cheese soup

MARIA REGAKIS
SOMERVILLE, MASSACHUSETTS

Give yourself a delicious calcium boost with this creamy, cheesy soup. I like to serve it with a green salad. You can also add 2 cups of cubed cooked chicken, if you wish.

- 1 cup chicken broth
- 1 package (6 ounces) fresh baby spinach, chopped
- 1/2 teaspoon onion powder
- 1/8 teaspoon pepper
- 4 teaspoons all-purpose flour
- 1 can (5 ounces) evaporated milk
- 1 cup (4 ounces) shredded cheddar cheese

1 In a small saucepan, combine the broth, spinach, onion powder and pepper. Bring to a boil. Combine flour and milk until smooth; gradually add to soup. Return to a boil. Reduce heat; cook and stir for 2 minutes or until thickened. Stir in cheese until melted.

YIELD: 2 SERVINGS.

buying and storing winter squash

The most common varieties of winter squash are butternut, acorn, hubbard, spaghetti and turban. Look for squash that feel heavy for their size and have hard, deep-colored rinds that are free of blemishes. Unwashed winter squash can be stored in a dry, cool, well-ventilated place for up to 1 month.

TASTE OF HOME TEST KITCHEN

creamy clam chowder

LORI KIMBLE
MCDONALD, PENNSYLVANIA

At our Pittsburgh competition, my rich and satisfying chowder took top honors. This family favorite is perhaps the easiest recipe for clam chowder that I have ever made. Served with sourdough bread, it's especially delicious.

- 1 large onion, chopped
- 3 medium carrots, chopped
- 2 celery ribs, sliced
- 3/4 cup butter, cubed
- 2 cans (10-3/4 ounces *each*) condensed cream of potato soup, undiluted
- 3 cans (6-1/2 ounces *each*) minced clams
- 3 tablespoons cornstarch
- 1 quart half-and-half cream

1 In a large saucepan, saute the onion, carrots and celery in butter until tender. Stir in potato soup and two cans of undrained clams. Drain and discard juice from remaining can of clams; add clams to soup.

2 Combine cornstarch and a small amount of cream until smooth; stir into soup. Add remaining cream. Bring to a boil; cook and stir for 2 minutes or until thickened.

YIELD: 9 SERVINGS (ABOUT 2 QUARTS).

pretty autumn soup

MARGARET ALLEN
ABINGDON, VIRGINIA

Carrots, squash and sweet potato combine to make a healthy and colorful fall soup. This one's loaded with vitamin A!

- 2-1/2 cups cubed peeled butternut squash
- 1 large sweet potato, peeled and cubed
- 3 medium carrots, sliced
- 1/4 cup thawed orange juice concentrate
- 3 cups milk
- 1/4 teaspoon salt
- 1/4 teaspoon pepper
- 3 tablespoons sour cream
- 2 tablespoons minced chives
- 1 tablespoon sesame seeds, toasted

1 Place the squash, sweet potato and carrots in a steamer basket; place in a large saucepan over 1 in. of water. Bring to a boil; cover and steam for 12-16 minutes or until tender. Cool slightly. Transfer to a food processor; add juice concentrate. Cover and process until smooth.

2 Transfer to a large saucepan; stir in the milk, salt and pepper. Cook and stir over low heat until heated through (do not boil). Top each serving with 1-1/2 teaspoons sour cream, 1 teaspoon chives and 1/2 teaspoon sesame seeds.

YIELD: 6 SERVINGS.

tips for using blenders and food processors

Use a blender or food processor to make salad dressings and sauces and to puree soups. A food processor is best to mix and puree very thick mixtures such as cheese spreads, sandwich fillings and pesto sauces. Don't use a blender or food processor to mix cakes from scratch, whip cream or beat egg whites. **TASTE OF HOME TEST KITCHEN**

hearty cheese soup

SUZANNA SNADER
FREDERICKSBURG, PENNSYLVANIA

Thick and creamy, this soup is chock-full of rich cheese flavor. I came home with this recipe after an exchange at my church several years ago and I have shared it with many. I hope you enjoy it as much as we do.

1-1/2 cups cubed peeled potatoes
1/2 cup water
1/4 cup sliced celery
1/4 cup sliced fresh carrots
2 tablespoons chopped onion
1/2 teaspoon chicken bouillon granules
1/2 teaspoon dried parsley flakes
1/4 teaspoon salt
Dash pepper
1-1/2 teaspoons all-purpose flour
3/4 cup milk
1/4 pound process cheese (Velveeta), cubed

1 In a small saucepan, combine the first nine ingredients. Bring to a boil. Reduce the heat; cover and simmer for 10-12 minutes or until potatoes are tender.

2 In a small bowl, combine flour and milk until smooth. Stir into vegetable mixture. Bring to a boil; cook and stir for 2 minutes or until thickened. Reduce heat to low; stir in cheese until melted.

YIELD: 2 SERVINGS.

cream of mushroom soup

CAROLYN ZIMMERMAN
FAIRBURY, ILLINOIS

The earthy mushroom flavor shines in this tempting and hearty soup. It'll have you arguing over who gets the last serving!

1 teaspoon beef bouillon granules
1/4 cup boiling water
3 cups sliced fresh mushrooms
1/4 cup chopped onion
2 tablespoons butter
2 tablespoons all-purpose flour
1 cup 2% milk
6 ounces cream cheese, cubed

1 In a small bowl, dissolve bouillon in water; set aside. In a small saucepan, saute the mushrooms and onion in butter until tender. Stir in the flour.

2 Gradually add the milk and reserved broth. Bring to a boil over medium heat, stirring constantly; cook for 1-2 minutes or until thickened. Reduce the heat; stir in the cream cheese until melted and soup is heated through.

YIELD: 3 SERVINGS.

cream of broccoli soup

GAYLENE ANDERSON | SANDY, UTAH

This soup is a great meal starter, but I also serve it as the main course when I'm in need of a quick, nourishing lunch or dinner. Just add a green salad and biscuits or rolls.

- 2 cups water
- 4 teaspoons chicken bouillon granules
- 6 cups frozen chopped broccoli
- 2 tablespoons finely chopped onion
- 2 cans (10-3/4 ounces *each*) condensed cream of chicken soup, undiluted
- 2 cups evaporated milk
- 2 cups (16 ounces) sour cream
- 1 teaspoon dried parsley flakes
- 1/4 teaspoon pepper

1. In a large saucepan, combine the water and bouillon. Add the broccoli and onion. Bring to a boil; reduce the heat. Simmer for 10 minutes or until broccoli is crisp-tender.

2. In a large bowl, combine the soup, milk, sour cream, parsley and pepper; add to the broccoli mixture. Cook and stir for 3-5 minutes or until heated through.

YIELD: 6-8 SERVINGS.

hearty garlic potato soup

BETH ALLARD | BELMONT, NEW HAMPSHIRE

I started with a basic potato soup recipe and added my own touches to come up with this comforting recipe. I love the combination of potatoes and Italian sausage.

- 8 medium potatoes, peeled and cut into 1/2-inch cubes
- 1 large carrot, peeled and chopped
- 2 garlic cloves, peeled
- 1/2 pound bulk Italian sausage
- 1 small onion, chopped
- 1/4 cup butter, cubed
- 1/4 cup all-purpose flour
- 8 cups milk
- 2 teaspoons minced fresh parsley
- 1-1/2 teaspoons salt
- 1 teaspoon chicken bouillon granules
- 1/2 teaspoon seasoned salt
- 1/4 teaspoon pepper

1. Place potatoes, carrot and garlic in a Dutch oven and cover with water. Bring to a boil. Reduce heat; cover and simmer for 15-20 minutes or until tender. Drain. Place 3 cups potato mixture in a large bowl and mash. Set aside mashed potatoes and remaining potato mixture.

2. In a large skillet, cook the sausage and onion over medium heat until meat is no longer pink; drain and set aside. In a Dutch oven, melt the butter. Stir in the flour until smooth; gradually add the milk. Bring to a boil; cook and stir for 2 minutes or until soup is thickened.

3. Add the parsley, salt, bouillon, seasoned salt and pepper; mix well. Add mashed potato mixture; cook and stir until heated through. Add reserved potato and sausage mixtures. Heat through.

YIELD: 12 SERVINGS (ABOUT 3 QUARTS).

chowders

VEGGIE SALMON CHOWDER, P. 78

bacon tomato chowder

HEIDI SOLLINGER
BECHTELSVILLE, PENNSYLVANIA

This soup recipe is so warm and inviting for any occasion, but most of all, I like to cook it for just my husband and me. We love the combination of tomatoes and bacon.

    3 bacon strips, diced
  1/4 cup butter, cubed
  1/4 cup all-purpose flour
Dash ground nutmeg
    1 can (14-1/2 ounces) chicken broth
  3/4 cup canned diced tomatoes, undrained
  2/3 cup half-and-half cream

1 In a large saucepan, cook bacon over medium heat until crisp. Using a slotted spoon, remove to paper towels to drain. Discard drippings.

2 In the same pan, melt the butter. Stir in the flour and nutmeg until smooth. Gradually whisk in broth. Bring to a boil; cook and stir for 2 minutes or until thickened. Stir in tomatoes. Reduce the heat; stir in cream. Heat through (do not boil). Add the bacon.

YIELD: 2 SERVINGS.

winter chowder

BRENDA TURNER | SCHERERVILLE, INDIANA

As a mother of three, it goes without saying that time is short but precious to me. I whipped up this fast and nutritious chowder one night, and my 7-year-old son said it was awesome!

    3 medium potatoes, peeled and cut into 1/4-inch pieces
  1/2 cup chopped onion
    1 cup water
  3/4 teaspoon onion salt *or* onion powder
  1/2 teaspoon pepper
  1/8 teaspoon salt
    2 drops Louisiana-style hot sauce
  1/2 cup cubed fully cooked ham (1/4-inch pieces)
    1 cup fresh *or* frozen brussels sprouts, quartered
1-1/2 cups milk
  3/4 cup shredded Colby-Monterey Jack cheese, *divided*

1 In a large saucepan, bring the potatoes, onion and water to a boil. Reduce heat; cover and cook for 10-12 minutes or until tender. Do not drain. Mash potatoes (mixture will not be smooth). Stir in the onion salt, pepper, salt and hot sauce; set aside.

2 In a large nonstick skillet coated with cooking spray, saute ham and brussels sprouts for 5-6 minutes or until sprouts are tender. Stir into the potato mixture. Add milk. Bring to a boil. Reduce the heat; simmer, uncovered, for 5-6 minutes or until heated through, stirring occasionally.

3 Gradually stir in 1/2 cup cheese; cook for 2-3 minutes or until cheese is melted. Garnish with remaining cheese.

YIELD: 5 SERVINGS.

powders

Garlic and onion powders tend to absorb moisture from the air, especially during warm weather months. Store them in airtight spice jars to keep them as free from moisture and humidity as possible.

TASTE OF HOME TEST KITCHEN

potato chowder

ANNA MAYER | FORT BRANCH, INDIANA

One of the ladies in our church quilting group brought this savory potato soup to a meeting, and everyone loved how the cream cheese and bacon made this recipe so rich. It's easy to assemble in the morning then let it simmer on its own all day.

- 8 cups diced potatoes
- 1/3 cup chopped onion
- 3 cans (14-1/2 ounces *each*) chicken broth
- 1 can (10-3/4 ounces) condensed cream of chicken soup, undiluted
- 1/4 teaspoon pepper
- 1 package (8 ounces) cream cheese, cubed
- 1/2 pound sliced bacon, cooked and crumbled, optional

Minced chives, optional

1 In a 5-qt. slow cooker, combine the first five ingredients. Cover and cook on low for 8-10 hours or until potatoes are tender.

2 Add cream cheese; stir until blended. Garnish with bacon and chives if desired.

YIELD: 12 SERVINGS (3 QUARTS).

black bean corn chowder

SHELLY PLATTEN | AMHERST, WISCONSIN

This thick Southwestern-style chowder is delightfully seasoned with salsa, lime juice and cumin. I first made this for a special lunch with my daughter, and she immediately asked for the recipe. We like it with gourmet-style tortilla chips.

- 1/2 cup half-and-half cream
- 1 can (15 ounces) black beans, rinsed and drained, *divided*
- 1/2 cup chopped onion
- 1 teaspoon olive oil
- 2 garlic cloves, minced
- 1/2 cup salsa
- 1/3 cup fresh *or* frozen corn
- 1 tablespoon lime juice
- 3/4 teaspoon ground cumin
- 1/2 medium ripe avocado, peeled and chopped

Sour cream and shredded cheddar cheese, optional

1 In a blender, combine the cream and 3/4 cup black beans; cover and process until smooth. Set aside.

2 In a small saucepan, saute the onion in oil until tender. Add garlic; cook 1 minute longer. Stir in the salsa, corn, lime juice, cumin and remaining beans.

3 Reduce heat; stir in cream mixture. Cook, uncovered, for 2-3 minutes or until heated through. Stir in the avocado. Serve with sour cream and cheese if desired.

YIELD: 2 SERVINGS.

potato chowder

A tasty potato chowder recipe can be very versatile. I like to use my potato chowder as a hearty base when making clam chowder and corn chowder.

MARY JO E., CEDAR RAPIDS, IOWA

salmon chowder

VICKI THOMPSON | BRISTOL, NEW BRUNSWICK

This rich and hearty yet light chowder delivers many levels of flavor and is sure to add a little coziness to cold winter nights.

CHOWDERS

- 1 small onion, chopped
- 1 garlic clove, minced
- 1/4 teaspoon dried thyme
- 1/4 teaspoon dried basil
- 1 tablespoon butter
- 2 cups 1% milk
- 1 can (10-1/2 ounces) condensed chicken broth, undiluted
- 1/2 cup frozen corn
- 1/2 cup chopped carrot
- 1 medium red potato, cut into 1/2-inch cubes
- 3 tablespoons all-purpose flour
- 1/4 cup cold water
- 1/2 pound salmon fillet, cut into 1-inch pieces
- 1/2 cup chopped zucchini
- 1/2 teaspoon salt
- 1/4 teaspoon pepper
- 1/2 cup shredded reduced-fat cheddar cheese

1 In a large saucepan over medium heat, cook and stir the onion, garlic, thyme and basil in butter until onion is tender. Stir in the milk, broth, corn, carrot and potato. Bring to a boil. Reduce heat; cover and simmer for 6-8 minutes or until vegetables are tender.

2 Combine flour and water until smooth; stir into onion mixture. Bring to a boil; cook and stir for 2 minutes or until thickened. Reduce heat; add salmon and zucchini. Simmer, uncovered, for 3-5 minutes or until fish flakes easily with a fork. Stir in salt and pepper. Sprinkle with cheese before serving.

YIELD: 6 SERVINGS.

corn chowder

PHYLLIS WATSON
HAVELOCK, NORTH CAROLINA

My grandmother and mother made this dish to warm their families during the cold winter months. Nothing chased away a chill like this comforting chowder! Now when it's cold and damp outside, I make this dish and think of those days. Everyone in my household enjoys a steaming bowl of this soup.

- 6 potatoes, peeled and diced
- Water
- 1 can (16 ounces) whole kernel corn, drained
- 4 cups whole milk
- 1 large onion, diced
- 4 bacon strips, cooked and crumbled
- 1 teaspoon salt
- 1/4 teaspoon pepper
- 1/4 teaspoon dried thyme

1 Place the potatoes in a Dutch oven and cover with water. Bring to a boil. Reduce the heat; cover and cook for 10-15 minutes or until tender. Drain. Add the remaining ingredients; bring to a boil. Reduce heat and simmer for 15 minutes or until onion is soft.

YIELD: 4-6 SERVINGS.

cheesy chicken chowder

HAZEL FRITCHIE | PALESTINE, ILLINOIS

I like to serve this hearty mixture with garlic bread and a salad. It's a wonderful dish to prepare when company drops in. The mild, cheesy flavor and tender chicken and vegetables appeal to even children and picky eaters.

    3   cups chicken broth
    2   cups diced peeled potatoes
    1   cup diced carrots
    1   cup diced celery
  1/2   cup diced onion
  1-1/2 teaspoons salt
  1/4   teaspoon pepper
  1/4   cup butter, cubed
  1/3   cup all-purpose flour
    2   cups milk
    2   cups (about 8 ounces)
          shredded cheddar cheese
    2   cups diced cooked chicken

1 In a 4-quart saucepan, bring the chicken broth to a boil. Reduce the heat; add the potatoes, carrots, celery, onion, salt and pepper. Cover and simmer for 12-15 minutes or until the vegetables are tender.

2 Meanwhile, melt the butter in a medium saucepan; stir in flour until smooth. Gradually stir in the milk. Bring to a boil over medium heat; cook and stir for 2 minutes or until thickened. Reduce the heat; add cheese, stirring until melted. Add to broth along with the chicken. Cook and stir until heated through.

YIELD: 6-8 SERVINGS.

veggie chowder

VICKI KERR | PORTLAND, MAINE

This brothy soup features potatoes, carrots and corn for a delightful entree. Since it's not too heavy, this soup is also nice alongside sandwiches.

    2   cups chicken broth
    2   cups cubed peeled
          potatoes
    1   cup chopped carrots
  1/2   cup chopped onion
    1   can (14-3/4 ounces)
          cream-style corn
    1   can (12 ounces)
          evaporated milk
  3/4   cup shredded
          cheddar cheese
  1/2   cup sliced fresh mushrooms
  1/4   teaspoon pepper
    2   tablespoons real bacon bits

1 In a large saucepan, combine the broth, potatoes, carrots and onion. Bring to a boil. Reduce heat; simmer, uncovered, for 10-15 minutes or until vegetables are tender.

2 Add the corn, milk, cheese, mushrooms and pepper. Cook and stir 4-6 minutes longer or until heated through. Sprinkle with bacon.

YIELD: 7 SERVINGS.

new england clam chowder

SANDY LARSON
PORT ANGELES, WASHINGTON

In the Pacific Northwest, we dig our own razor clams and I grind them for the chowder! Since these aren't readily available, the canned clams are perfectly acceptable.

- 4 center-cut bacon strips
- 2 celery ribs, chopped
- 1 large onion, chopped
- 1 garlic clove, minced
- 3 small potatoes, peeled and cubed
- 1 cup water
- 1 bottle (8 ounces) clam juice
- 3 teaspoons chicken bouillon granules
- 1/4 teaspoon white pepper
- 1/4 teaspoon dried thyme
- 1/3 cup all-purpose flour
- 2 cups half-and-half cream, *divided*
- 2 cans (6-1/2 ounces *each*) chopped clams, undrained

1 In a Dutch oven, cook bacon over medium heat until crisp. Remove to paper towels to drain; set aside. Saute celery and onion in the drippings until tender. Add garlic; cook 1 minute longer. Stir in the potatoes, water, clam juice, bouillon, pepper and thyme. Bring to a boil. Reduce heat; simmer, uncovered, for 15-20 minutes or until potatoes are tender.

2 In a small bowl, combine flour and 1 cup half-and-half until smooth. Gradually stir into soup. Bring to a boil; cook and stir for 1-2 minutes or until thickened.

3 Stir in the clams and remaining half-and-half; heat through (do not boil). Crumble the reserved bacon; sprinkle over each serving.

YIELD: 5 SERVINGS.

grandmother's chowder

DULYSE MOLNAR | OSWEGO, NEW YORK

Nothing can compare to homemade soup, especially when this is the delicious result! Winter days seem a little warmer when I prepare this savory chowder.

- 1 pound ground beef
- 1 medium onion, chopped
- 12 medium potatoes, peeled and cubed
- 3 cups water

Salt and pepper to taste

- 2 cups whole milk
- 1 can (15-1/4 ounces) whole kernel corn, drained
- 2 teaspoons dried parsley flakes
- 1 cup (8 ounces) sour cream

1 In a Dutch oven, cook the beef and onion over medium heat until meat is no longer pink; drain. Add the potatoes, water, salt and pepper; bring to a boil. Reduce the heat; cover and simmer for 15-20 minutes or until the potatoes are tender.

2 Stir in the milk, corn and parsley; cook for 5 minutes or until heated through. Add a small amount of hot soup to sour cream. Gradually return all to pan, stirring constantly. Heat through but do not boil.

YIELD: 14 SERVINGS (3-1/2 QUARTS).

cooking utensils

As a general rule, do not use the utensil that was used to prepare uncooked meats to later stir or serve cooked foods. To avoid cross-contamination, wash utensils in hot, soapy water before reusing or simply use a different spoon.

TASTE OF HOME TEST KITCHEN

asparagus leek chowder

ELISABETH HARDERS
WEST ALLIS, WISCONSIN

To us, asparagus is the taste of spring, so we enjoy it in as many meals as we can. When this thick and creamy chowder is on the table, we know spring has arrived.

- 1 pound fresh asparagus, trimmed and cut into 1-inch pieces
- 3 cups sliced fresh mushrooms
- 3 large leeks (white portion only), sliced
- 6 tablespoons butter
- 1/4 cup all-purpose flour
- 1/2 teaspoon salt

Dash pepper

- 2 cups chicken broth
- 2 cups half-and-half cream
- 1 can (11 ounces) whole kernel corn, drained
- 1 tablespoon chopped pimientos

1 In a large saucepan, saute asparagus, mushrooms and leeks in butter for 10 minutes or until tender. Stir in the flour, salt and pepper until blended.

2 Gradually stir in broth and cream. Bring to a boil. Reduce heat; cook and stir for 2 minutes or until thickened. Stir in corn and pimientos; heat through.

YIELD: 7 SERVINGS.

veggie salmon chowder

LIV VORS | PETERBOROUGH, ONTARIO

This recipe came about as a way to use up odds and ends in my fridge. I thought other readers might enjoy a recipe that began as an experiment but became a mainstay for me.

- 1 medium sweet potato, peeled and cut into 1/2-inch cubes
- 1 cup chicken broth
- 1/2 cup fresh *or* frozen corn
- 1/2 small onion, chopped
- 2 garlic cloves, minced
- 1-1/2 cups fresh spinach, torn
- 1/2 cup flaked smoked salmon fillet
- 1 teaspoon pickled jalapeno slices, chopped
- 1 tablespoon cornstarch
- 1/2 cup 2% milk
- 1 tablespoon minced fresh cilantro

Dash pepper

1 In a large saucepan, combine the potato, broth, corn, onion and garlic. Bring to a boil. Reduce heat; cover and simmer for 8-10 minutes or until potato is tender.

2 Add the spinach, salmon and jalapeno; cook for 1-2 minutes or until spinach is wilted. Combine cornstarch and milk until smooth. Stir into chowder. Bring to a boil; cook and stir for 2 minutes or until thickened. Stir in cilantro and pepper.

YIELD: 2 SERVINGS.

south-of-the-border chowder

TONYA MICHELLE BURKHARD
ENGLEWOOD, FLORIDA

This filling soup comes together in no time. Loaded with potatoes, the combination of sweet corn and pearl onions, smoky bacon and lots of spice has a scrumptious Southwestern flavor.

- 1/2 cup chopped onion
- 4 bacon strips, diced
- 2 tablespoons all-purpose flour
- 1/2 teaspoon ground cumin
- 1/2 teaspoon chili powder
- 1/8 teaspoon garlic powder
- 1 package (32 ounces) frozen cubed hash brown potatoes
- 2 cans (14-1/2 ounces *each*) chicken broth
- 1 can (14-3/4 ounces) cream-style corn
- 1 can (11 ounces) Mexicorn, drained
- 1 can (4 ounces) chopped green chilies
- 1/4 cup pearl onions

Sour cream and minced fresh cilantro, optional

1 In a Dutch oven, saute onion and bacon until onion is tender and bacon is crisp. Stir in the flour, cumin, chili powder and garlic powder. Bring to a boil; cook and stir for 1 minute or until thickened.

2 Stir in the hash browns, broth, cream corn, Mexicorn, chilies and pearl onions. Bring to a boil. Reduce heat; simmer, uncovered, for 10 minutes or until heated through. Garnish with sour cream and cilantro if desired.

YIELD: 10 SERVINGS (2-1/2 QUARTS).

country potato chowder

SARA PHILLIPS | TOPEKA, KANSAS

This creamy, comforting chowder is thick with potatoes, carrots, green beans and corn. My mother served it on chilly evenings with warm French bread. Leftovers, if there are any, taste just as good and make a great lazy-day lunch.

- 6 bacon strips, diced
- 1 medium onion, chopped
- 3 celery ribs, chopped
- 1/4 cup all-purpose flour
- 4 cups half-and-half cream
- 4 medium potatoes, peeled and cut into 1/2-inch cubes
- 2 cans (10-3/4 ounces *each*) condensed cream of celery soup, undiluted
- 2 tablespoons dried parsley flakes
- 1 tablespoon Worcestershire sauce
- 1 teaspoon seasoned salt
- 1/2 teaspoon pepper
- 1 cup sliced carrots
- 1 cup fresh *or* frozen green beans, cut into 2-inch pieces
- 1 can (14-3/4 ounces) cream-style corn

1 In a Dutch oven, cook the bacon over medium heat until crisp; remove with a slotted spoon to paper towels. Drain, reserving 2 tablespoons drippings. In the drippings, saute the onion and celery until tender. Sprinkle with flour and stir until blended. Gradually add the cream. Stir in the potatoes, soup, parsley, Worcestershire sauce, seasoned salt and pepper. Bring to a boil; cook and stir for 1 minute. Reduce the heat; cover and simmer for 25 minutes, stirring occasionally.

2 Add carrots and beans. Cover and simmer 15 minutes longer or until vegetables are tender. Stir in corn and reserved bacon; heat through.

YIELD: 12 SERVINGS.

corn, mushrooms, chilies and onions. Bring to a boil. Add the tortilla strips. Reduce heat; simmer, uncovered, for 8-10 minutes or until heated through. Add cheese; stir just until melted. Serve immediately.

YIELD: 8-10 SERVINGS (2-1/2 QUARTS).

oyster corn chowder

LEWY OLFSON | MADISON, WISCONSIN

Chock-full of mushrooms, corn and oysters, this robust soup comes together easily with a can of cream-style corn and a little half-and-half cream.

- 2 cans (8 ounces *each*) whole oysters, undrained
- 1 can (14-3/4 ounces) cream-style corn
- 1 cup half-and-half cream
- 2 cans (4 ounces *each*) mushroom stems and pieces, drained
- 2 tablespoons butter
- 1/4 teaspoon Worcestershire sauce
- 1/8 teaspoon pepper

1 In a large saucepan, combine all the ingredients. Cook, uncovered, over medium-low heat until heated through (do not boil), stirring occasionally.

YIELD: 4 SERVINGS.

chicken tortilla chowder

JENNIFER GOUGE | LUBBOCK, TEXAS

As a student attending college full-time, I find my time in the kitchen is limited. This recipe helps me have a hot meal on the table when my husband gets home. He's a real meat-and-potatoes man, but he absolutely loves this thick, creamy chowder with tortilla strips that puff up like homemade noodles.

- 1 can (14-1/2 ounces) chicken broth
- 1 can (10-3/4 ounces) condensed cream of chicken soup, undiluted
- 1 can (10-3/4 ounces) condensed cream of potato soup, undiluted
- 1-1/2 cups milk
- 2 cups cubed cooked chicken
- 1 can (11 ounces) Mexicorn
- 1 jar (4-1/2 ounces) sliced mushrooms, drained
- 1 can (4 ounces) chopped green chilies
- 1/4 cup thinly sliced green onions
- 4 flour tortillas (6 to 7 inches), cut into 1/2-inch strips
- 1-1/2 cups (6 ounces) shredded cheddar cheese

1 In a Dutch oven, combine the broth, soups and milk. Stir in the chicken,

speedy cut green onions

When a recipe calls for sliced green onions, I find it easier and faster to cut them with a kitchen scissors than with a knife. If the recipe calls for quite a few, grab a bunch at one time and snip away. You're done before you know it, and this technique saves you from washing a cutting board.

LOUISE B., COLUMBIA, SOUTH CAROLINA

shrimp chowder

WILL ZUNIO | GRETNA, LOUISIANA

I simmer this rich and creamy creation in my slow cooker. Because the chowder is ready in less than 4 hours, it can be prepared in the afternoon and served to dinner guests that night.

- 1/2 cup chopped onion
- 2 teaspoons butter
- 2 cans (12 ounces *each*) evaporated milk
- 2 cans (10-3/4 ounces *each*) condensed cream of potato soup, undiluted
- 2 cans (10-3/4 ounces *each*) condensed cream of chicken soup, undiluted
- 1 can (11 ounces) white *or* shoepeg corn, drained
- 1 teaspoon Creole seasoning
- 1/2 teaspoon garlic powder
- 2 pounds cooked small shrimp, peeled and deveined
- 1 package (3 ounces) cream cheese, cubed

1 In a small skillet, saute the onion in butter until tender. In a 5-qt. slow cooker, combine the onion mixture, milk, soups, corn, Creole seasoning and garlic powder.

2 Cover and cook on low for 3 hours. Stir in the shrimp and cream cheese. Cook 30 minutes longer or until the shrimp are heated through and the cheese is melted. Stir to blend.

YIELD: 12 SERVINGS (3 QUARTS).

EDITOR'S NOTE: The following spices may be substituted for 1 teaspoon Creole seasoning: 1/4 teaspoon *each* salt, garlic powder and paprika; and a pinch *each* of dried thyme, ground cumin and cayenne pepper.

cheeseburger broccoli chowder

KAREN DAVIES | WANIPIGOW, MANITOBA

I invented this soup accidentally! Actually, it came about when I was new to cooking, and didn't know that chowder was a kind of soup.

- 1/2 pound ground beef
- 1/2 cup chopped onion
- 1/4 cup chopped green pepper
- 1 can (10-3/4 ounces) condensed cheddar cheese soup, undiluted
- 3/4 cup whole milk
- 1 teaspoon Worcestershire sauce
- 1 cup chopped broccoli
- 1 to 2 potatoes, peeled and diced

1 In a large saucepan, cook beef with onion and green pepper until the beef is no longer pink; drain. Stir in soup, milk and Worcestershire sauce. Add broccoli and potatoes. Bring to a boil, reduce the heat and simmer, covered, about 30 minutes or until potatoes are tender.

YIELD: 4 SERVINGS.

family-size ground beef

Although it's just the two of us, I buy family packs of ground beef on sale. I divide each pack into 1/4- or 1/2-pound portions to freeze for use in casseroles, hamburgers and meatballs.

KRISTIN M., MOULTRIE, GEORGIA

parmesan north pacific chowder

PAM WOOLGAR
QUALICUM BEACH, BRITISH COLUMBIA

This is so yummy and so fresh! Tender vegetables and tarragon add good flavor to this smooth fish soup.

- 8 bacon strips
- 1 small onion, chopped
- 1 celery rib, chopped
- 1 carton (32 ounces) chicken broth
- 4 medium red potatoes, cubed
- 2 tablespoons all-purpose flour
- 1 pint half-and-half cream
- 1 pound halibut fillets, cubed
- 1 tablespoon minced fresh tarragon *or* 1 teaspoon dried tarragon
- 1/2 teaspoon salt
- 1/4 teaspoon pepper

Tarragon sprigs, optional

1 In a large saucepan over medium heat, cook the bacon until crisp. Drain, reserving 1 teaspoon drippings. Crumble bacon and set aside. Saute onion and celery in the drippings. Add broth and potatoes. Bring to a boil. Reduce heat; cover and cook for 15-20 minutes or until potatoes are tender.

2 Combine flour and cream until smooth; gradually stir into soup. Bring to a boil; cook and stir for 2 minutes. Stir in halibut, tarragon, salt, pepper and reserved bacon. Reduce the heat; simmer, uncovered, for 5-10 minutes or until fish flakes easily with a fork. Garnish with tarragon sprigs if desired.

YIELD: 9 SERVINGS (2-1/4 QUARTS).

ramen corn chowder

DARLENE BRENDEN | SALEM, OREGON

This chowder tastes as good as if it simmered for hours, but it's ready in 15 minutes. I thought the original recipe was lacking in flavor, so I jazzed it up with extra corn and bacon bits.

- 2 cups water
- 1 package (3 ounces) chicken ramen noodles
- 1 can (15-1/4 ounces) whole kernel corn, drained
- 1 can (14-3/4 ounces) cream-style corn
- 1 cup 2% milk
- 1 teaspoon dried minced onion
- 1/4 teaspoon curry powder
- 3/4 cup shredded cheddar cheese
- 1 tablespoon crumbled, cooked bacon
- 1 tablespoon minced fresh parsley

1 In a small saucepan, bring the water to a boil. Break the noodles into large pieces. Add noodles and contents of seasoning packet to water. Reduce heat to medium. Cook, uncovered, for 2-3 minutes or until noodles are tender.

2 Stir in the corn, cream-style corn, milk, onion and curry; heat through. Stir in the cheese, bacon and parsley until blended.

YIELD: 4 SERVINGS.

ramen noodles add crunch

Inexpensive ramen noodles add quick crunch to recipes. In a skillet, you can brown the crushed noodles in a small amount of butter. Let them cool, then sprinkle on tossed salads or pastas in place of croutons or nuts.

EVELYN T., MARBLE, MINNESOTA

parmesan potato soup

MARY SHIVERS | ADA, OKLAHOMA

I decided to add some character to a basic potato chowder by adding roasted red peppers. The extra flavor gives a deliciously unique twist to an otherwise ordinary soup.

- 8 medium potatoes, peeled and cut into 1/2-inch cubes
- 6 cups chicken broth
- 1 large onion, chopped
- 1 jar (7 ounces) roasted sweet red peppers, drained and chopped
- 1 small celery rib, chopped
- 1/2 teaspoon garlic powder
- 1/2 teaspoon seasoned salt
- 1/2 teaspoon pepper
- 1/8 teaspoon rubbed sage
- 1/3 cup all-purpose flour
- 2 cups heavy whipping cream, *divided*
- 1 cup grated Parmesan cheese, *divided*
- 8 bacon strips, cooked and crumbled
- 2 tablespoons minced fresh cilantro

1 In a 5- or 6-qt. slow cooker, combine the first nine ingredients. Cover and cook on low for 5-6 hours or until vegetables are tender.

2 In a small bowl, combine flour and 1/2 cup cream until smooth; add to slow cooker. Stir in 3/4 cup cheese, bacon, cilantro and remaining cream. Cover and cook for 30 minutes or until slightly thickened. Ladle into bowls; sprinkle with remaining cheese.

YIELD: 12 SERVINGS (3 QUARTS).

ham cheddar chowder

RUTH PROTZ | OSHKOSH, WISCONSIN

Living in Wisconsin, I like to make dishes featuring cheese, and this chowder is one of my favorites. It makes a great meal served with salad greens and rye rolls.

- 3 cups water
- 3 cups cubed peeled potatoes
- 1 cup chopped carrots
- 1 cup chopped celery
- 1 medium onion, chopped
- 2 teaspoons salt
- 1/2 teaspoon pepper
- 6 tablespoons butter
- 6 tablespoons all-purpose flour
- 4 cups whole milk
- 3 cups (12 ounces) shredded cheddar cheese
- 1 cup cubed fully cooked ham

1 In a large saucepan, bring water to a boil. Add the potatoes, carrots, celery, onion, salt and pepper. Reduce heat. Cover and simmer for 20 minutes or until vegetables are tender; drain and set vegetables aside.

2 In same pan, melt butter. Stir in flour until smooth. Gradually add the milk. Bring to a boil; cook and stir for 2 minutes or until thickened. Remove from the heat; stir in cheese until melted. Add ham and reserved vegetables. Cook on low until heated through. Do not boil.

YIELD: 8 SERVINGS (ABOUT 2 QUARTS).

fish chowder

MARGARET JEAN
AYER, MASSACHUSETTS

A recipe book was included when we purchased a set of pots and pans years ago. Living in New England, we love fish in any dish, and this is something we especially enjoy when there's a chill in the air.

  1 bacon strip, diced
  2 tablespoons *each* chopped onion and chopped celery
2/3 cup condensed cream of potato soup, undiluted
1/2 cup water
1/8 teaspoon pepper
Dash salt
1/2 pound haddock fillets, cut into 1-inch pieces
1/2 cup milk
1-1/2 teaspoons butter
Oyster crackers, optional

1 In a small saucepan, saute the bacon, onion and celery until the vegetables are tender. Add soup, water, pepper and salt. Bring to a boil; reduce the heat. Add the haddock; cover and simmer for 8-12 minutes or until fish flakes easily with a fork. Stir in milk and butter; heat through. Serve with oyster crackers if desired.

YIELD: 2 SERVINGS.

curried chicken corn chowder

KENDRA DOSS | KANSAS CITY, MISSOURI

This recipe is close to one my mom used to make for us kids when the weather turned cold. Hers called for heavy cream, but I came up with a slimmer version that I think is pretty true to the original recipe!

  2 medium onions, chopped
  2 celery ribs, chopped
  1 tablespoon butter
  3 cans (14-1/2 ounces *each*) reduced-sodium chicken broth
  5 cups frozen corn
  2 teaspoons curry powder
1/4 teaspoon salt
1/4 teaspoon pepper
Dash cayenne pepper
1/2 cup all-purpose flour
1/2 cup 2% milk
  3 cups cubed cooked chicken breast
1/3 cup minced fresh cilantro

1 In a Dutch oven, saute the onions and celery in butter until tender. Stir in the broth, corn, curry, salt, pepper and cayenne. Bring to a boil. Reduce the heat; cover and simmer for 15 minutes.

2 In a small bowl, whisk the flour and milk until smooth. Whisk into the pan. Bring to a boil; cook and stir for 2 minutes or until thickened. Add chicken and cilantro; heat through.

YIELD: 9 SERVINGS (2-1/4 QUARTS).

salad bar servings

When I scale down a recipe that makes four or six servings to serve two, I usually need half of an onion or pepper, or just one rib of celery. The rest goes to waste. I solved this by visiting my local supermarket's salad bar. There, I can get as much sliced onion, pepper or celery as I need for my meal with no fuss or waste. At first, it seems more expensive, but not when compared to food that's not used and is eventually thrown away. It's time-saving, too, because I don't have to clean or chop the items.

BOB S., SILVER SPRING, MARYLAND

SWISS CHARD BEAN SOUP, P. 94

bart's black bean soup

SHARON ULLYOT | LONDON, ONTARIO

This soup is made in minutes yet tastes like you worked a lot harder on it since it's so flavorful. We enjoy this soup with rolls and a salad for a complete meal that's really tasty and easy!

- 1 can (15 ounces) black beans, rinsed and drained
- 1-1/2 cups chicken broth
- 3/4 cup chunky salsa
- 1/2 cup canned whole kernel corn, drained
- Dash hot pepper sauce
- 2 teaspoons lime juice
- 1 cup (4 ounces) shredded cheddar cheese
- 2 tablespoons chopped green onions

1 In a microwave-safe bowl, combine the black beans, broth, salsa, corn and hot pepper sauce. Cover and microwave on high for 2 minutes or until heated through. Pour the soup into four serving bowls; drizzle each with lime juice. Sprinkle with the cheese and green onions.

YIELD: 4 SERVINGS.

EDITOR'S NOTE: This recipe was tested in a 1,100-watt microwave.

three-bean soup

VALERIE LEE | SNELLVILLE, GEORGIA

When I was growing up, my mother prepared many different soups, each seasoned just right. She often made this colorful combination that's chock-full of harvest-fresh goodness. It showcases an appealing assortment of beans, potatoes, carrots and spinach.

- 1 medium onion, chopped
- 1 tablespoon canola oil
- 3 small potatoes, peeled and cubed
- 2 medium carrots, sliced
- 3 cans (14-1/2 ounces *each*) chicken *or* vegetable broth
- 3 cups water
- 2 tablespoons dried parsley flakes
- 2 teaspoons dried basil
- 1 teaspoon dried oregano
- 1 garlic clove, minced
- 1/2 teaspoon pepper
- 1 can (15-1/2 ounces) great northern beans, rinsed and drained
- 1 can (15 ounces) pinto beans, rinsed and drained
- 1 can (15 ounces) garbanzo beans *or* chickpeas, rinsed and drained
- 3 cups chopped fresh spinach

1 In a Dutch oven, saute the onion in oil. Add the next nine ingredients. Simmer, uncovered, until vegetables are tender. Add beans and spinach; heat through.

YIELD: 12 SERVINGS (ABOUT 3 QUARTS).

transporting soup

Whenever you're bringing a stew, soup or chili to a potluck dinner, you'll find it can be easily transported and kept hot in a 5-quart slow cooker.

CHARLENE S., APOLLO, PENNSYLVANIA

4 Bring to a boil. Reduce heat; stir in meatballs. Simmer, uncovered, for 15-20 minutes or until green beans are tender. Sprinkle with cheese.

YIELD: 6 SERVINGS.

peasant bean soup

BERTHA McCLUNG
SUMMERSVILLE, WEST VIRGINIA

This is an extra-good, hearty soup. I often multiply it and serve it to my church circle of over 100 members. I'm always asked for the recipe.

- 1 pound dried great northern beans, washed and sorted
- 2-1/2 quarts cold water, *divided*
- 3 medium carrots, sliced
- 3 celery ribs, sliced
- 2 medium onions, chopped
- 1 garlic clove, minced
- 1 can (16 ounces) stewed tomatoes, cut up
- 1 to 2 bay leaves
- 2 tablespoons olive oil

Salt and pepper to taste

1 Soak beans overnight in 2 qts. water.
2 Add remaining water to softened beans and bring to a boil; reduce heat and simmer 30 minutes.
3 Stir in the remaining ingredients; simmer 1 hour or until beans are tender. Discard bay leaves.

YIELD: 8 SERVINGS.

meatball soup

REBECCA PHIPPS
RURAL HALL, NORTH CAROLINA

My husband and I are both diabetics and like to find tasty recipes like this that are healthy and delicious. I serve this soup with baked wheat tortilla triangles and fresh fruit.

- 2-1/2 teaspoons Italian seasoning, *divided*
- 1/4 teaspoon paprika
- 1/4 teaspoon salt, *divided*
- 1/4 teaspoon coarsely ground pepper, *divided*
- 1 pound lean ground turkey
- 4 teaspoons olive oil, *divided*
- 2 celery ribs, chopped
- 15 fresh baby carrots, chopped
- 1 small onion, chopped
- 1 can (15 ounces) white kidney *or* cannellini beans, rinsed and drained
- 1 can (14-1/2 ounces) Italian diced tomatoes, undrained
- 1 can (14-1/2 ounces) reduced-sodium chicken broth
- 3/4 cup *each* chopped cabbage and cut fresh green beans
- 3 tablespoons shredded part-skim mozzarella cheese

1 In a large bowl, combine 1-1/2 teaspoons Italian seasoning, paprika, 1/8 teaspoon salt and 1/8 teaspoon pepper. Crumble turkey over mixture; mix well. Shape into 36 meatballs.
2 In a large nonstick skillet coated with cooking spray, brown meatballs in batches in 2 teaspoons oil until no longer pink. Remove and keep warm.
3 In a large saucepan coated with cooking spray, saute the celery, carrots and onion in remaining oil until tender. Stir in the white kidney beans, tomatoes, broth, cabbage, green beans and remaining Italian seasoning, salt and pepper.

black bean soup

ANGEE OWENS | LUFKIN, TEXAS

This is an awesome soup that is light and doesn't contain meat. The flavor does have a little kick. You could add lean beef or chicken for a variation.

- 3 cans (15 ounces *each*) black beans, rinsed and drained, *divided*
- 3 celery ribs with leaves, chopped
- 1 large onion, chopped
- 1 medium sweet red pepper, chopped
- 1 jalapeno pepper, seeded and chopped
- 2 tablespoons olive oil
- 4 garlic cloves, minced
- 2 cans (14-1/2 ounces *each*) reduced-sodium chicken broth *or* vegetable broth
- 1 can (14-1/2 ounces) diced tomatoes with green peppers and onions, undrained
- 3 teaspoons ground cumin
- 1-1/2 teaspoons ground coriander
- 1 teaspoon Louisiana-style hot sauce
- 1/4 teaspoon pepper
- 1 bay leaf
- 1 teaspoon lime juice
- 1/2 cup reduced-fat sour cream
- 1/4 cup chopped green onions

1 In a small bowl, mash one can black beans; set aside. In a large saucepan, saute the celery, onion, red pepper and jalapeno in oil until tender. Add the garlic; cook 1 minute longer.

2 Stir in the broth, tomatoes, cumin, coriander, hot sauce, pepper, bay leaf, remaining beans and reserved mashed beans. Bring to a boil. Reduce heat; cover and simmer for 15 minutes.

3 Discard bay leaf. Stir in lime juice. Garnish each serving with 1 tablespoon sour cream and 1-1/2 teaspoons green onion.

YIELD: 8 SERVINGS (2 QUARTS).

EDITOR'S NOTE: When cutting hot peppers, disposable gloves are recommended. Avoid touching your face.

chicken lima bean soup

CAROL ANN KAISER
PENDLETON, OREGON

When I was little, my father could be found in the kitchen during his free time. This soup is one of his most memorable dishes...and one of my most treasured recipes.

- 1 pound dried large lima beans
- 1 broiler/fryer chicken (3 to 3-1/2 pounds)
- 3 quarts water
- 2 celery ribs with leaves, sliced
- 4 chicken bouillon cubes
- 2-1/2 teaspoon salt
- 1/2 teaspoon pepper
- 3 medium carrots, chopped
- 4 cups chopped fresh spinach
- 2 tablespoons minced fresh parsley

1 In a Dutch oven, combine the beans, chicken, water, celery, bouillon, salt and pepper; bring to a boil. Reduce heat; cover and simmer for 2 hours or until beans are tender.

2 Remove the chicken. When cool enough to handle, remove meat from bones; discard bones. Cut meat into bite-size pieces; return to pan. Add carrots; simmer for 30 minutes or until tender. Stir in spinach and parsley; heat through.

YIELD: 12-14 SERVINGS (3-1/2 QUARTS).

sportsman's bean soup

HOWELL VINCENT
GEORGETOWN, KENTUCKY

I've been cooking and freezing soups and stews for 45 years. This hearty, wholesome soup is one of my wife's favorites. The way to a woman's heart is through her stomach, too.

2 pounds dried navy beans
3 large onions, chopped
2 tablespoons butter
4 medium carrots, chopped
2 smoked ham hocks
1 tablespoon marinade for chicken
12 orange peel strips (1 to 3 inches)
1 teaspoon salt
1/2 teaspoon dried thyme
2 bay leaves
3 cups cubed fully cooked ham
1 can (28 ounces) diced tomatoes, undrained
1/4 cup cider vinegar

1 Sort beans and rinse with cold water. Place in a stock pot; add water to cover by 2 in. Bring to a boil; boil for 2 minutes. Remove from the heat; cover and let stand for 1-4 hours or until beans are softened.

2 Drain and rinse beans; discard liquid and set beans aside. In the same pan, saute onions in butter until tender. Add carrots; saute 4-5 minutes longer.

3 Add the ham hocks, marinade for chicken, orange peel, salt, thyme, bay leaves, beans and enough water to cover by 2 in. Bring to a boil. Reduce heat; cover and simmer for 2 hours or until beans are tender.

4 Remove ham hocks; when cool enough to handle, remove meat from bones. Discard bones and cut meat into cubes; return to the soup. Add the additional ham, tomatoes and vinegar; heat through. Discard bay leaves and orange peel before serving.

YIELD: 27 SERVINGS (6-3/4 QUARTS).

EDITOR'S NOTE: This recipe was tested with Lea & Perrins Marinade for Chicken.

veggie bean soup

LOIS DEAN | WILLIAMSON, WEST VIRGINIA

I wanted to make a meatless soup for a Lenten lunch. I came up with this colorful vegetable recipe and got rave reviews.

1/2 cup chopped onion
1/2 cup *each* sliced celery and sliced fresh carrots
1 tablespoon olive oil
1/2 teaspoon minced garlic
2 cups water
1 can (15-1/2 ounces) great northern beans, rinsed and drained
3/4 cup chicken broth
3/4 cup Italian stewed tomatoes
1/2 cup cubed peeled potato
1/2 cup frozen cut green beans
1 bay leaf
1/2 teaspoon salt, optional
1/4 teaspoon pepper

1 In a large saucepan, saute the onion, celery and carrots in oil until tender. Add garlic; cook 1 minute longer. Stir in the remaining ingredients. Bring to a boil. Reduce heat; simmer, uncovered, for 15 minutes or until heated through. Discard bay leaf.

YIELD: 4 SERVINGS.

zuppa di fagioli

MARY CARON
EDENTON, NORTH CAROLINA

I like to welcome family home with steaming bowls of this hearty white bean soup. It features plenty of healthy vegetables as well as tender Italian meatballs.

- 2 tablespoons dry bread crumbs
- 1 tablespoon grated Parmesan cheese
- 1/4 pound bulk Italian sausage
- 1 cup sliced leeks (white portion only)
- 1 medium carrot, chopped
- 1 celery rib, chopped
- 1 tablespoon canola oil
- 1 garlic clove, minced
- 2 cans (15-1/2 ounces *each*) great northern beans, rinsed and drained
- 2 cans (14-1/2 ounces *each*) reduced-sodium chicken broth
- 1 can (14-1/2 ounces) reduced-sodium beef broth
- 1 can (14-1/2 ounces) diced tomatoes in sauce
- 1 package (6 ounces) fresh baby spinach
- 3 tablespoons minced fresh basil
- 2 tablespoons minced fresh parsley
- 1/2 teaspoon salt
- 1/4 teaspoon pepper

1 In a large bowl, combine the bread crumbs and the cheese. Crumble the sausage over mixture and mix well. Shape into 1/2-in. balls.

2 Place in a greased 15-in. x 10-in. x 1-in. baking pan. Bake at 350° for 8-10 minutes or until the juices run clear; drain and set aside.

3 In a Dutch oven, saute the leeks, carrot and celery in oil until tender. Add the garlic; cook 1 minute longer. Stir in the beans, broths, tomatoes, spinach, basil, parsley, salt, pepper and reserved meatballs. Cover and cook until the spinach is tender and the meatballs are heated through.

YIELD: 10 SERVINGS (2-1/4 QUARTS).

how to make dry bread crumbs

Soft bread crumbs are made from fresh or slightly stale bread. Tear the bread apart with a fork or use a blender or food processor to break it into fluffy crumbs. Pile gently into a measuring cup and do not pack. Dry bread crumbs may be purchased or made from very dry bread or zwieback crackers. Place dry bread or crackers in a plastic bag and crush with a rolling pin. Spoon into a measuring cup.

TASTE OF HOME TEST KITCHEN

split pea vegetable soup

MAUREEN YLITALO
WAHNAPITAE, ONTARIO

This recipe originated with the master chef of our family—my father-in-law. It freezes so well that frequently I'll cook up a double batch of soup.

- 1-1/2 cups dried green split peas, rinsed
- 2-1/2 quarts water
- 7 to 8 whole allspice, tied in a cheesecloth bag
- 2 teaspoons salt
- 1/2 teaspoon pepper
- 6 large potatoes, peeled and cut into 1/2-inch cubes
- 6 medium carrots, chopped
- 2 medium onions, chopped
- 2 cups cubed cooked ham
- 1/2 medium head cabbage, shredded

1 In a Dutch oven, combine the peas, water, allspice, salt and pepper; bring to a boil. Reduce heat; cover and simmer for 1 hour.

2 Stir in the potatoes, carrots, onions, ham and cabbage; return to a boil. Reduce heat; cover and simmer for about 30 minutes or until vegetables are tender, stirring occasionally. Discard allspice.

YIELD: 16-20 SERVINGS (ABOUT 5 QUARTS).

stacy's black bean soup

STACY MARTI | JENKS, OKLAHOMA

We love this low-fat black bean soup—and you will too! It's packed with good-for-you vegetables and beans. To make it completely vegetarian, substitute vegetable broth for the chicken broth.

- 1-1/2 cups dried black beans
- 3 celery ribs, chopped
- 3 medium carrots, chopped
- 1 large onion, chopped
- 2 teaspoons olive oil
- 2 garlic cloves, minced
- 6-1/2 cups reduced-sodium chicken broth
- 1 teaspoon dried oregano
- 1/2 teaspoon dried thyme
- 1/2 teaspoon salt
- 1/4 teaspoon cayenne pepper
- 1 bay leaf
- 3 tablespoons lime juice
- 1/2 cup reduced-fat sour cream
- 1/4 cup minced fresh cilantro

1 Place beans in a large saucepan; add water to cover by 2 in. Bring to a boil; boil for 2 minutes. Remove from the heat; cover and let stand for 1 to 4 hours or until beans are softened. Drain and rinse beans, discarding liquid.

2 In a Dutch oven coated with cooking spray, saute the celery, carrots and onion in oil until vegetables are tender. Add garlic; cook 1 minute longer. Add the beans, broth, oregano, thyme, salt, cayenne and bay leaf. Bring to a boil. Reduce heat; cover and simmer for 1 to 1-1/4 hours or until beans are tender. Discard bay leaf. Cool slightly.

3 In a blender, cover and process soup in batches until smooth. Return to pan; heat though. Stir in lime juice. Garnish each serving with sour cream and cilantro.

YIELD: 8 SERVINGS (2 QUARTS).

kielbasa split pea soup

SANDRA BONDE | BRAINERD, MINNESOTA

Turkey kielbasa brings great flavor to this simple split pea soup. It's been a hit with my entire family.

- 2 celery ribs, thinly sliced
- 1 medium onion, chopped
- 1 package (16 ounces) dried green split peas
- 9 cups water, *divided*
- 1 package (14 ounces) smoked turkey kielbasa, halved and sliced
- 4 medium carrots, halved and thinly sliced
- 2 medium potatoes, peeled and cubed
- 1 tablespoon minced fresh parsley
- 1 teaspoon dried basil
- 1-1/2 teaspoons salt
- 1/2 teaspoon pepper

1 In a Dutch oven coated with cooking spray, cook celery and onion until tender. Stir in split peas and 6 cups water. Bring to a boil. Reduce heat; cover and simmer for 25 minutes.

2 Stir in the kielbasa, carrots, potatoes, parsley, basil, salt, pepper and remaining water. Return to a boil. Reduce heat; cover and simmer for 20-25 minutes or until peas and vegetables are tender.

YIELD: 12 SERVINGS (3 QUARTS).

bean soup with cheddar cornmeal dumplings

SHANNON KOHN
SIMPSONVILLE, SOUTH CAROLINA

I created my own easy-to-prepare bean soup based on one we liked at a local Mexican restaurant. I added dumplings to make it a more complete meal.

- 1/4 cup chopped onion
- 1/4 cup fresh baby carrots, cut into 1/4-inch slices
- 1 can (15 ounces) pinto beans, rinsed and drained
- 1 cup chicken broth
- 1 cup chunky salsa
- 1/3 cup self-rising flour
- 2 tablespoons cornmeal
- 1/8 teaspoon salt
- 1/4 cup 2% milk
- 2 tablespoons shredded cheddar cheese

1 In a large saucepan coated with cooking spray, saute onion and carrots until tender. Stir in the beans, broth and salsa. Bring to a boil. Reduce the heat; simmer, uncovered, for 3-5 minutes or until reduced slightly.

2 For dumplings, in a small bowl, combine the flour, cornmeal and salt. Stir in milk and cheese just until moistened. Drop by tablespoonfuls onto simmering soup.

3 Cover and simmer for 15 minutes or until a toothpick inserted near the center of a dumpling comes out clean (do not lift cover while simmering).

YIELD: 2 SERVINGS.

EDITOR'S NOTE: As a substitute for 1/3 cup of self-rising flour, place 1/2 teaspoon baking powder and 1/8 teaspoon salt in a measuring cup. Add all-purpose flour to measure 1/3 cup.

hearty minestrone soup

BONNIE HOSMAN | **YOUNG, ARIZONA**

I picked up this recipe in California in the 80's and have been making it ever since. I love it partly because it's simple to put together and partly because the flavor is so wonderful!

- 2 cans (one 28 ounces, one 14-1/2 ounces) diced tomatoes, undrained
- 2 cups water
- 2 medium carrots, sliced
- 1 medium onion, chopped
- 1 medium zucchini, chopped
- 1 package (3-1/2 ounces) sliced pepperoni
- 2 teaspoons minced garlic
- 2 teaspoons chicken bouillon granules
- 1/2 teaspoon dried basil
- 1/2 teaspoon dried oregano
- 2 cans (16 ounces *each*) kidney beans, rinsed and drained
- 1 package (10 ounces) frozen chopped spinach, thawed and squeezed dry
- 1-1/4 cups cooked elbow macaroni
  Shredded Parmesan cheese

1 In a 5-qt. slow cooker, combine the first 10 ingredients. Cover and cook on low for 6-7 hours or until the vegetables are tender.

2 Stir in the beans, spinach and the macaroni. Cover and cook 15 minutes longer or until heated through. Sprinkle with cheese.

YIELD: 7 SERVINGS (2-3/4 QUARTS).

bean, chicken and sausage soup

LINDA JOHNSON
SEVIERVILLE, TENNESSEE

I found this recipe in a magazine and have tried different ingredients through the years. My husband thinks this is the best version yet. I hope you enjoy it, too!

- 1-1/2 pounds bulk Italian sausage
- 2 cups chopped onion
- 6 bacon strips, diced
- 2 quarts water
- 2 cans (14-1/2 ounces *each*) tomatoes with liquid, cut up
- 2 bay leaves
- 2 teaspoons garlic powder
- 1 teaspoon *each* dried thyme, savory and salt
- 1/2 teaspoon *each* dried basil, oregano and pepper
- 4 cups cubed cooked chicken
- 2 cans (15 to 16 ounces *each*) great northern beans, rinsed and drained

1 In a heavy 8-qt. Dutch oven, cook the sausage, onion and bacon over medium-high heat until sausage is no longer pink; drain. Add the water, tomatoes and seasonings. Cover and simmer for 30 minutes.

2 Add chicken and beans. Simmer, uncovered, for 30-45 minutes. Discard bay leaves.

YIELD: 18 SERVINGS (4-1/2 QUARTS).

swiss chard bean soup

TASTE OF HOME TEST KITCHEN

This hearty soup combines nutritious Swiss chard with other garden favorites. Its light broth is surprisingly rich in flavor, and the grated Parmesan packs an additional punch.

- 1 medium carrot, coarsely chopped
- 1 small zucchini, coarsely chopped
- 1 small yellow summer squash, coarsely chopped
- 1 small red onion, chopped
- 2 tablespoons olive oil
- 2 garlic cloves, minced
- 3 cans (14-1/2 ounces *each*) reduced-sodium chicken broth
- 4 cups chopped Swiss chard
- 1 can (15-1/2 ounces) great northern beans, rinsed and drained
- 1 can (14-1/2 ounces) diced tomatoes, undrained
- 1 teaspoon dried thyme
- 1/2 teaspoon salt
- 1/2 teaspoon dried oregano
- 1/4 teaspoon pepper
- 1/4 cup grated Parmesan cheese

1 In a Dutch oven, saute the carrot, zucchini, yellow squash and onion in oil until tender. Add the garlic; saute 1 minute longer. Add the broth, Swiss chard, beans, tomatoes, thyme, salt, oregano and pepper.

2 Bring to a boil. Reduce heat; simmer, uncovered, for 15 minutes or until chard is tender. Just before serving, sprinkle with cheese.

YIELD: 10 SERVINGS (2-1/2 QUARTS).

shrimp and black bean soup

ELIZABETH LEWIS | HAYDEN, ALABAMA

Packed with tomatoes, beans, corn and, of course, shrimp, this is a bold and spicy soup. My family likes spicy foods and everyone really enjoys this soup. It's especially good during cold weather.

- 1 large onion, chopped
- 1 tablespoon olive oil
- 2 cans (14-1/2 ounces *each*) reduced-sodium chicken broth
- 2 cans (10 ounces *each*) diced tomatoes and green chilies, undrained
- 2 cups frozen corn
- 1 can (15 ounces) black beans, rinsed and drained
- 1 can (14-1/2 ounces) diced tomatoes, undrained
- 4-1/2 teaspoons chili powder
- 1 teaspoon sugar
- 1/2 teaspoon salt
- 1 pound uncooked medium shrimp, peeled and deveined
- 1/4 cup minced fresh parsley

1 In a Dutch oven, saute onion in oil for 3-4 minutes or until tender. Add the broth, tomatoes and green chilies, corn, black beans, tomatoes, chili powder, sugar and salt. Bring to a boil, stirring occasionally. Reduce heat; cover and simmer for 20 minutes.

2 Stir in the shrimp; cook 5-6 minutes longer or until the shrimp turn pink. Stir in the parsley.

YIELD: 8 SERVINGS (3 QUARTS).

yankee bean soup

ANN NACE | PERKASIE, PENNSYLVANIA

My family really enjoys this hearty soup, which is perfect for a wintry day. Bacon, molasses and onion add great flavor. A friend from Massachusetts gave me the recipe years ago, and I've made it countless times since then.

- 1-1/2 cups dried navy beans
- 1/2 pound sliced bacon, diced
- 3/4 cup chopped onion
- 1/2 cup chopped carrot
- 1/3 cup chopped celery leaves
- 4 cups water
- 2 cups milk
- 2 teaspoons molasses
- 1-1/2 teaspoons salt

1 Place the beans in a Dutch oven; add water to cover by 2 in. Bring to a boil; boil for 2 minutes. Remove from the heat; cover and let stand for 1 hour.

2 Drain and rinse beans, discarding liquid. Set beans aside. In the same pan, cook the bacon over medium heat until crisp. Using a slotted spoon, remove to paper towels; drain, reserving 2 tablespoons drippings.

3 In the drippings, saute onion until tender. Stir in carrot and celery leaves. Return beans to the pan. Add water. Bring to a boil. Reduce heat; cover and simmer for 1-3/4 to 2 hours or until beans are tender.

4 Stir in the milk, molasses, salt and bacon. Remove about 2-1/2 cups of soup; cool slightly. Place in a blender or food processor; cover and process until pureed. Return to the pan; heat through.

YIELD: 6 SERVINGS.

spice up bean soup

Spice up bean soup with a couple whole cloves. Remove the cloves just before serving. People notice the special taste but usually can't identify the source.

SARAH H., MUNCIE, INDIANA

zesty italian soup

MYRNA SIPPEL | THOMPSON, ILLINOIS

While visiting my sister-in-law, we had a delicious Italian soup at a restaurant. We decided to duplicate it at home and came up with this recipe.

- 1 pound bulk Italian sausage
- 3 cans (14-1/2 ounces *each*) reduced-sodium chicken broth
- 1 can (15 ounces) black beans, rinsed and drained
- 1 can (15 ounces) pinto beans, rinsed and drained
- 1 can (14-1/2 ounces) diced tomatoes and green chilies, undrained
- 1 can (14-1/2 ounces) Italian diced tomatoes
- 1 large carrot, chopped
- 1 jalapeno pepper, seeded and chopped
- 1-1/2 teaspoons Italian seasoning
- 1 teaspoon dried minced garlic
- 1-1/2 cups cooked elbow macaroni

1 In a large skillet, cook sausage over medium heat until no longer pink; drain.

2 Transfer to a 5-qt. slow cooker. Stir in the broth, beans, tomatoes, carrot, jalapeno, Italian seasoning and garlic. Cover and cook on low for 7-8 hours or until heated through. Just before serving, stir in macaroni.

YIELD: 10 SERVINGS (3-1/2 QUARTS).

EDITOR'S NOTE: When cutting hot peppers, disposable gloves are recommended. Avoid touching your face.

beefy bean soup

CAROLYN BURBIDGE | BOUNTIFUL, UTAH

This quick and filling soup makes a bunch, but it won't last long! Any leftovers you have are even better the next day.

- 1 can (29 ounces) tomato puree
- 1 can (14-1/2 ounces) diced tomatoes, undrained
- 1 cup water
- 1 cup beef broth
- 4-1/2 teaspoons chicken bouillon granules
- 3/4 teaspoon *each* salt, dried basil and dried oregano
- 3/4 cup uncooked elbow macaroni
- 1/2 pound ground beef
- 1 cup chopped celery
- 1/2 cup chopped onion
- 1/2 teaspoon dried minced garlic
- 1 can (16 ounces) kidney beans, rinsed and drained
- 1 can (15-1/2 ounces) great northern beans, rinsed and drained

1 In a Dutch oven, combine the first eight ingredients. Bring to a boil. Stir in macaroni. Reduce heat; simmer, uncovered, for 10-15 minutes or until macaroni is tender.

2 Meanwhile, in a large skillet, cook the beef, celery and onion over medium heat until meat is no longer pink. Add garlic; cook 1 minute longer. Drain. Add to tomato mixture. Stir in beans; heat through.

YIELD: 8 SERVINGS (3 QUARTS).

lighter soup secrets

Keep these secrets in mind when you're lightening up your soup du jour:

Stir additional herbs or a salt-free seasoning blend into your soup instead of salt. When recipes call for canned chicken broth, substitute the reduced-sodium kind.

Use "thin thickeners." Watching your weight doesn't mean writing off creamy soups. Puree a cooked peeled potato and reduced-fat milk or fat-free half-and-half to a creamy consistency. Slowly stir the mixture into boiling soup to thicken it. To thicken Southwestern soups and chili, add pureed cooked beans.

Cut back on beef. Try preparing a recipe with additional vegetables or pasta in place of beef. Or, consider periodically replacing beef with cooked poultry.

TASTE OF HOME TEST KITCHEN

flavorful taco soup

SANDI LEE | HOUSTON, TEXAS

You'll get a kick out of this hearty, Southwest-inspired soup. Feel free to dunk your tortilla chips right into it and enjoy!

- 1/2 pound lean ground beef (90% lean)
- 1 can (15 ounces) pinto beans, rinsed and drained
- 1 can (10 ounces) diced tomatoes with mild green chilies, undrained
- 1 can (8-3/4 ounces) whole kernel corn, drained
- 1-1/2 cups water
- 2 tablespoons taco seasoning
- 4-1/2 teaspoons ranch salad dressing mix

TOPPINGS:
- 1/2 medium ripe avocado, peeled and cubed
- 2 tablespoons shredded cheddar cheese
- 2 teaspoons minced fresh cilantro

Tortilla chips

1 In a large saucepan, cook beef over medium heat until no longer pink; drain. Stir in the beans, tomatoes, corn, water, taco seasoning and salad dressing mix. Bring to a boil. Reduce heat; cover and simmer for 30-35 minutes or until heated through.

2 Spoon into bowls; top with avocado, cheese and cilantro. Serve with tortilla chips.

YIELD: 4 CUPS.

ham and lentil soup

ANDI HAUG | HENDRUM, MINNESOTA

This is a combination of two soup recipes I came across and adapted. I often serve it for Sunday dinner, making enough so there are leftovers for my husband's lunch. He's a bricklayer and regularly works outside during winter.

- 1 meaty ham bone
- 6 cups water
- 1-1/4 cups dried lentils, rinsed
- 1 can (28 ounces) diced tomatoes, undrained
- 2 to 3 carrots, sliced
- 2 celery ribs, sliced
- 1/4 cup chopped green onions
- 1/2 teaspoon salt
- 1/2 teaspoon garlic powder
- 1/2 teaspoon dried oregano
- 1/8 teaspoon pepper
- 12 ounces bulk pork sausage, cooked and drained
- 2 tablespoons chopped fresh parsley

1 In a Dutch oven, bring ham bone and water to a boil. Reduce heat; cover and simmer for 1-1/2 hours.

2 Remove ham bone. To broth, add the lentils, tomatoes, carrots, celery, onions and seasonings; bring to a boil. Reduce heat; cover and simmer for 30-40 minutes or until lentils and vegetables are tender.

3 Meanwhile, remove the ham from the bone; coarsely chop. Add the ham, sausage and parsley to soup; heat through.

YIELD: 10-12 SERVINGS (3 QUARTS).

nutritional value of onions

Onions are low in calories but high in taste—they're an excellent way to boost the flavor in light and savory dishes. Onions contain only a trace amount of calcium and iron but are a good source of potassium. Comparatively speaking, 1/2 cup of chopped onion yields about 240 mg of potassium (similar to 1/2 banana or 1/2 cup of orange juice).

TASTE OF HOME TEST KITCHEN

chili

SPICED CHILI, P. 102

chunky chipotle pork chili

PETER HALFERTY | CORPUS CHRISTI, TEXAS

Perfect for using leftover pork roast, this tasty, easy recipe can be made ahead and reheated.

- 1 medium green pepper, chopped
- 1 small onion, chopped
- 1 chipotle pepper in adobo sauce, finely chopped
- 1 tablespoon canola oil
- 3 garlic cloves, minced
- 1 can (16 ounces) red beans, rinsed and drained
- 1 cup beef broth
- 1/2 cup salsa
- 2 teaspoons ground cumin
- 2 teaspoons chili powder
- 2 cups cubed cooked pork
- 1/4 cup sour cream

1 In a large saucepan, saute the green pepper, onion and chipotle pepper in oil until tender. Add garlic; saute 1 minute longer.

2 Add the beans, broth, salsa, cumin and chili powder. Bring to a boil. Reduce heat; simmer, uncovered, for 10 minutes or until thickened. Add pork; heat through. Serve with sour cream.

YIELD: 4 SERVINGS.

white chicken chili

TASTE OF HOME COOKING SCHOOL

Folks will enjoy a change from the traditional when they spoon into this flavorful blend of tender chunks of chicken, white beans and just enough zip.

- 1 medium onion, chopped
- 1 tablespoon olive oil
- 2 cloves garlic, minced
- 4 boneless skinless chicken breast halves (4 ounces *each*), chopped
- 2 cans (14 ounces *each*) chicken broth
- 1 can (4 ounces) chopped green chilies
- 2 teaspoons ground cumin
- 2 teaspoons dried oregano
- 1-1/2 teaspoons cayenne pepper
- 3 cans (14-1/2 ounces *each*) great northern beans, drained, *divided*
- 1 cup (4 ounces) shredded Monterey Jack cheese

Chopped jalapeno pepper, optional

1 In a large saucepan over medium heat, cook onion in oil for 10 minutes or until tender. Add garlic; cook 1 minute longer. Add the chicken, chicken broth, green chilies, cumin, oregano and cayenne pepper; bring to a boil.

2 Reduce heat to low. With a potato masher, mash one can of beans until smooth. Add to saucepan. Add remaining beans to saucepan. Simmer for 20-30 minutes or until heated thoroughly.

3 Top each serving with cheese and jalapeno pepper if desired.

YIELD: 10 SERVINGS (2-1/2 QUARTS).

2 Stir in the water, tomato sauce, beans, cocoa, hot sauce and seasonings. Bring to a boil. Reduce heat; cover and simmer for 30 minutes.

3 Garnish each serving with 1 tablespoon each of sour cream, crushed chips and cheese.

YIELD: 8 SERVINGS (2 QUARTS).

elk meat chili

JO MAASBERG | FARSON, WYOMING

The longer this hearty chili simmers, the better it tastes! It's a cold-weather favorite at our ranch.

- 2 pounds ground elk *or* buffalo meat
- 1/2 cup chopped onion
- 3 garlic cloves, minced
- 2 cans (14-1/2 ounces *each*) diced tomatoes, undrained
- 1 can (28 ounces) pork and beans, undrained
- 3 tablespoons salsa
- 1 tablespoon brown sugar
- 1 tablespoon chili powder
- 1/2 teaspoon garlic salt
- 1/2 teaspoon pepper

1 In a Dutch oven, cook elk and onion over medium heat until meat is no longer pink. Add garlic; cook 1 minute longer. Drain. Stir in the remaining ingredients; bring to a boil. Reduce heat; cover and simmer for 2 hours.

YIELD: 6-8 SERVINGS.

fully loaded chili

CYNTHIA BACA
CRANBERRY TOWNSHIP, PENNSYLVANIA

With lean ground beef, four types of beans and lots of seasonings and toppings, this chili is truly "fully-loaded." But those aren't the only heavyweights in here—every serving provides a hefty 26 g protein and 11 g fiber.

- 1 pound lean ground beef (90% lean)
- 1 medium onion, chopped
- 1 medium green pepper, chopped
- 1-3/4 cups water
- 2 cans (8 ounces *each*) tomato sauce
- 1 can (16 ounces) kidney beans, rinsed and drained
- 1 can (15-1/2 ounces) great northern beans, rinsed and drained
- 1 can (15 ounces) garbanzo beans *or* chickpeas, rinsed and drained
- 1 can (15 ounces) black beans, rinsed and drained
- 1 tablespoon baking cocoa
- 2 teaspoons Louisiana-style hot sauce
- 1/2 teaspoon pepper
- 1/2 teaspoon chili powder
- 1/4 teaspoon garlic powder
- 1/8 teaspoon cayenne pepper

GARNISHES:
- 1/2 cup reduced-fat sour cream
- 1/2 cup crushed baked tortilla chip scoops
- 1/2 cup shredded reduced-fat cheddar cheese

1 In a Dutch oven over medium heat, cook the beef, onion and pepper until meat is no longer pink; drain.

roasted vegetable chili

HANNAH BARRINGER | LOUDON, TENNESSEE

I suggest serving this delicious and satisfying recipe with corn chips, cheese, sour cream and a small salad. To save time, purchase vegetables that have already been cut up.

- 1 medium butternut squash, peeled and cut into 1-inch pieces
- 3 large carrots, sliced
- 2 medium zucchini, cut into 1-inch pieces
- 2 tablespoons olive oil, *divided*
- 1-1/2 teaspoons ground cumin
- 2 medium green peppers, diced
- 1 large onion, chopped
- 3 cans (14-1/2 ounces *each*) reduced-sodium chicken broth
- 3 cans (14-1/2 ounces *each*) diced tomatoes, undrained
- 2 cans (15 ounces *each*) cannellini *or* white kidney beans, rinsed and drained
- 1 cup water
- 1 cup salsa
- 3 teaspoons chili powder
- 6 garlic cloves, minced

1 Place the squash, carrots and zucchini in a 15-in. x 10-in. x 1-in. baking pan. Combine 1 tablespoon oil and cumin; drizzle over vegetables and toss to coat. Bake, uncovered, at 450° for 25-30 minutes or until tender, stirring once.

2 Meanwhile, in a stockpot, saute green peppers and onion in remaining oil for 3-4 minutes or until tender. Stir in the broth, tomatoes, beans, water, salsa, chili powder and garlic. Bring to a boil. Reduce heat; simmer, uncovered, for 10 minutes.

3 Stir in roasted vegetables. Return to a boil. Reduce heat; simmer, uncovered, for 5-10 minutes or until heated through.

YIELD: 13 SERVINGS (5 QUARTS).

chuck wagon chili

ELAINE PETERS | OSLER, SASKATCHEWAN

While planning a chili supper a few years ago, I came across this recipe. I decided to try it and was showered with compliments. This chunky chili has been a much-requested dish ever since.

- 1-1/2 pounds ground beef
- 1 can (16 ounces) kidney beans, undrained
- 1 can (10-3/4 ounces) condensed tomato soup, undiluted
- 1 can (8 ounces) sliced mushrooms, undrained
- 6 hot dogs, halved and cut into bite-size pieces
- 2 medium carrots, sliced
- 1 medium onion, chopped
- 1 teaspoon salt
- 1 teaspoon chili powder
- 1/4 teaspoon pepper

1 In a large saucepan, cook beef over medium heat until no longer pink; drain. Add the remaining ingredients and bring to a boil. Reduce heat; cover and simmer for 1 hour or until thick and bubbly.

YIELD: 6-8 SERVINGS.

spiced chili

JULIE BRENDT | GOLD RIVER, CALIFORNIA

My father was a cook in the Army and taught me the basics in the kitchen. My childhood babysitter inspired my love of cooking, too—in fact, she gave me this recipe.

- 1-1/2 pounds ground beef
- 1/2 cup chopped onion
- 4 garlic cloves, minced
- 2 cans (16 ounces *each*) kidney beans, rinsed and drained
- 2 cans (15 ounces *each*) tomato sauce
- 2 cans (14-1/2 ounces *each*) stewed tomatoes, cut up
- 1 cup water
- 2 bay leaves
- 1/4 cup chili powder
- 1 tablespoon salt
- 1 tablespoon brown sugar
- 1 tablespoon *each* dried basil, Italian seasoning and dried thyme
- 1 tablespoon pepper
- 1 teaspoon *each* dried oregano and dried marjoram

Shredded cheddar cheese, optional

1 In a large skillet, cook beef and onion over medium heat until the meat is no longer pink. Add the garlic; cook 1 minute longer. Drain.

2 Transfer to a 5-qt. slow cooker. Stir in the beans, tomato sauce, tomatoes, water and seasonings. Cover and cook on low for 4-5 hours. Discard bay leaves. Garnish with cheese if desired.

YIELD: 12 SERVINGS (ABOUT 3 QUARTS).

spicy vegetable chili

**NANCY ZIMMERMAN
CAPE MAY COURT HOUSE, NEW JERSEY**

This chili makes a great comforting meal on cool autumn nights. I love dipping oat bran bread into it.

- 1 medium onion, chopped
- 1 medium carrot, thinly sliced
- 1 medium green pepper, chopped
- 1/2 pound sliced fresh mushrooms
- 1 small zucchini, sliced
- 1 tablespoon olive oil
- 4 garlic cloves, minced
- 1 can (28 ounces) diced tomatoes, undrained
- 2 cans (16 ounces *each*) kidney beans, rinsed and drained
- 2 cans (8 ounces *each*) no-salt-added tomato sauce
- 1 can (4 ounces) chopped green chilies
- 3 tablespoons chili powder
- 3 teaspoons dried oregano
- 2 teaspoons ground cumin
- 2 teaspoons paprika
- 1/4 teaspoon crushed red pepper flakes
- 1 tablespoon white wine vinegar

Minced fresh cilantro and fat-free sour cream, optional

1 In a Dutch oven, saute the onion, carrot, pepper, mushrooms and zucchini in oil until tender. Add garlic; cook 1 minute longer. Add the tomatoes, beans, tomato sauce, green chilies and seasonings. Bring to a boil. Reduce heat; simmer, uncovered, for 35 minutes, stirring occasionally.

2 Stir in vinegar. Serve in soup bowls; garnish each with cilantro and sour cream if desired.

YIELD: 8 SERVINGS (2 QUARTS).

two-bean chili

RONALD JOHNSON | ELMHURST, ILLINOIS

The first time I had this chili was at a football party, I was on my second bowl before I realized it had no meat! It's so chock-full of ingredients and flavor that it's hard to believe this is a low-fat recipe. Enjoy!

- 1/2 pound sliced fresh mushrooms
- 1 large green pepper, chopped
- 1 large sweet red pepper, chopped
- 2 celery ribs, chopped
- 1 medium onion, chopped
- 1 jalapeno pepper, seeded and chopped
- 1 tablespoon olive oil
- 4 garlic cloves, minced
- 2 teaspoons ground cumin
- 1 teaspoon dried oregano
- 1 can (28 ounces) diced tomatoes, undrained
- 1 can (16 ounces) red beans, rinsed and drained
- 1 can (15 ounces) black beans, rinsed and drained
- 1 large carrot, chopped
- 1/2 cup water
- 1/2 cup barbecue sauce
- 1/4 cup chili powder
- 1 teaspoon Liquid Smoke, optional

OPTIONAL TOPPINGS:
Reduced-fat sour cream, hot pepper sauce, shredded cheddar cheese, chopped onion *and/or* crushed baked tortilla chip scoops

1 In a large skillet over medium heat, cook and stir the mushrooms, peppers, celery, onion and jalapeno in oil until onion is lightly browned. Add the garlic, cumin and oregano; cook and stir 1 minute longer.

2 Transfer to a 5-qt. slow cooker. Stir in the tomatoes, beans, carrot, water, barbecue sauce, chili powder and Liquid Smoke if desired. Cover and cook on low for 8 hours or until vegetables are tender. Serve with sour cream, pepper sauce, cheese, onion and/or chips if desired.

YIELD: 6 SERVINGS (2 QUARTS).

EDITOR'S NOTE: When cutting hot peppers, disposable gloves are recommended. Avoid touching your face.

chili con carne

KARLEEN WARKENTIN | MCALLEN, TEXAS

I love to cook, but meals at my house have to be ready in a hurry because we're always on the go. I found this recipe years ago and use it often because it preps so easily.

- 1/2 pound ground beef
- 1/2 cup chopped onion
- 1 garlic clove, minced
- 1 can (10 ounces) diced tomatoes and green chilies
- 1 can (8 ounces) tomato sauce
- 3/4 cup canned pinto beans, rinsed and drained
- 2-1/2 teaspoons chili powder
- 1/2 teaspoon dried oregano
- 1/4 teaspoon salt, optional
- 1/4 teaspoon ground cumin
- 1/4 teaspoon pepper

1 In a large saucepan, cook beef and onion over medium heat until meat is no longer pink. Add garlic; cook 1 minute longer; drain. Stir in the tomatoes, tomato sauce, beans, chili powder, oregano, salt if desired, cumin and pepper. Bring to a boil. Reduce the heat; cover and simmer for 1 hour.

YIELD: 2 SERVINGS.

30-minute chili

JANICE WESTMORELAND
BROOKSVILLE, FLORIDA

A dear neighbor gave me a pot of this delicious chili, and I asked for the recipe. The pork sausage is a nice change from the ground beef called for in many chili recipes.

- 1 pound bulk pork sausage
- 1 large onion, chopped
- 1 can (28 ounces) crushed tomatoes
- 2 cans (16 ounces *each*) chili beans, undrained
- 3 cups water
- 1 can (4 ounces) chopped green chilies
- 1 envelope chili seasoning mix
- 2 tablespoons sugar

1 In a Dutch oven, cook sausage and onion over medium heat until meat is no longer pink; drain. Add remaining ingredients; cover and simmer for 20 minutes, stirring often.

YIELD: 12 SERVINGS (3 QUARTS).

cincinnati chili

JOYCE ALM | THORP, WASHINGTON

The chocolate in this recipe threw me off at first, but now it's the only way I make chili. You'll find layers of delicious flavor in this heartwarming dish. Its slow cooker preparation makes it a convenient dish to serve.

- 3 pounds ground beef
- 1-1/2 cups chopped onions
- 1-1/2 teaspoons minced garlic
- 2 cans (16 ounces *each*) kidney beans, rinsed and drained
- 2 cans (15 ounces *each*) tomato sauce
- 2 cups beef broth
- 1/4 cup chili powder
- 1/4 cup red wine vinegar
- 1/4 cup Worcestershire sauce
- 1 ounce unsweetened chocolate, coarsely chopped
- 1-1/2 teaspoons ground cinnamon
- 1-1/2 teaspoons ground cumin
- 1 teaspoon salt
- 1 teaspoon dried oregano
- 1/2 teaspoon pepper
- 1/8 teaspoon ground cloves

Hot cooked spaghetti
Shredded cheddar cheese and sliced green onions, optional

1 In a Dutch oven, cook the beef and onions over medium heat until meat is no longer pink. Add garlic; cook 1 minute longer. Drain.

2 In a 5-qt. slow cooker, combine the beans, tomato sauce, broth, chili powder, vinegar, Worcestershire sauce, chocolate, cinnamon, cumin, salt, oregano, pepper and cloves. Stir in beef mixture. Cover and cook on low for 5-1/2 to 6 hours or until heated through.

3 Serve with spaghetti. Garnish with cheese and green onions if desired.

YIELD: 10 SERVINGS.

four-star chili

FRANK FENTI | HORNELL, NEW YORK

This spicy chili features traditional ingredients like ground beef, green peppers and tomatoes, but the addition of carrots and white beans makes it deliciously different.

- 1-1/2 pounds ground beef
- 2 large green peppers, diced
- 1 medium onion, diced
- 4 garlic cloves, minced
- 1 can (28 ounces) crushed tomatoes
- 1 can (15-1/2 ounces) great northern beans, rinsed and drained
- 1 can (14-1/2 ounces) chicken broth
- 1 medium carrot, chopped
- 1 celery rib, chopped
- 2 jalapeno peppers, finely chopped
- 2-1/2 teaspoons pepper blend
- 1 teaspoon paprika
- 1/2 teaspoon crushed red pepper flakes
- Hot cooked rice
- Sour cream
- Shredded Colby cheese

1 In a stockpot, cook the beef, green peppers and onion over medium heat until the meat is no longer pink. Add the garlic; cook 1 minute longer. Drain. Add the tomatoes, beans, broth, carrot, celery, jalapenos and seasonings; bring to a boil. Reduce the heat; cover and simmer for 1-1/2 hours or until thick and bubbly.

2 Serve with rice, sour cream and cheese.

YIELD: 18 SERVINGS (4-1/4 QUARTS).

EDITOR'S NOTE: When cutting hot peppers, disposable gloves are recommended. Avoid touching your face.

scalloped potato chili

SHERRY HULVA | DECATUR, ILLINOIS

Potatoes add a unique layer to ordinary chili. My mother used to serve this when I was growing up. My husband loves spicy food, so I put the chili powder on the table for him to add more.

- 1-1/2 pounds ground beef
- 3/4 cup chopped onion
- 1/2 cup chopped green pepper
- 2 cans (16 ounces each) kidney beans, rinsed and drained
- 2 cans (14-1/2 ounces each) stewed tomatoes
- 1 package (5-1/4 ounces) scalloped potatoes
- 1 can (8 ounces) sliced mushrooms, drained
- 1 cup water
- 1 teaspoon salt
- 3/4 teaspoon chili powder
- Shredded Parmesan cheese

1 In a large saucepan, cook beef, onion and green pepper over medium heat until meat is no longer pink; drain. Stir in the beans, tomatoes, contents of potato package, mushrooms, water, salt and chili powder; bring to a boil. Reduce heat; cover and simmer for 40-45 minutes or until potatoes are tender. Sprinkle with cheese.

YIELD: 10 SERVINGS (2-1/2 QUARTS).

EDITOR'S NOTE: If you're making Scalloped Potato Chili for a potluck, prepare it at home on the stove, then take it to the gathering in a slow cooker.

freeze extra pasta & rice

To cut down on side dish preparation time, I always cook whole packages of rice or noodles and freeze the extra portions in resealable plastic bags. Later it's easy to take them out of the bag, pop in the microwave and have fresh hot rice or noodles in a snap!
JEAN B., OCONOMOWOC, WISCONSIN

spicy two-bean chili

LESLEY PEW | LYNN, MASSACHUSETTS

Chili fans will get a kick out of this nontraditional recipe. Tomatoes with green chilies, lime juice and kidney and black beans give it an original twist. It's wonderful ladled over rice and topped with cheese.

        2 pounds ground beef
        3 large onions, chopped
        6 garlic cloves, minced
        2 cans (16 ounces *each*) kidney beans, rinsed and drained
        2 cans (15 ounces *each*) black beans, rinsed and drained
        2 cans (10 ounces *each*) diced tomatoes and green chilies, undrained
        1 can (14-1/2 ounces) chicken broth
      1/2 cup lime juice
        6 tablespoons cornmeal
      1/4 cup chili powder
        4 teaspoons dried oregano
        3 teaspoons ground cumin
        2 teaspoons salt
        2 teaspoons rubbed sage
      1/2 teaspoon white pepper
      1/2 teaspoon paprika
      1/2 teaspoon pepper
    Hot cooked rice
    Shredded cheddar cheese

1 In a Dutch oven, cook beef and onions over medium heat until meat is no longer pink. Add garlic; cook 1 minute longer; drain.
2 Transfer to a 5-qt. slow cooker. Stir in the beans, tomatoes, broth, lime juice, cornmeal and seasonings. Cover and cook on low for 8 hours or until heated through. Serve with rice; sprinkle with cheese.

YIELD: 11 SERVINGS.

black bean 'n' pumpkin chili

DEBORAH VLIET | HOLLAND, MICHIGAN

Our family loves this slow-cooked recipe, especially on cold days. It's a wonderful variation on standard chili that freezes well and even tastes great as leftovers.

        1 medium onion, chopped
        1 medium sweet yellow pepper, chopped
        2 tablespoons olive oil
        3 garlic cloves, minced
        3 cups chicken broth
        2 cans (15 ounces *each*) black beans, rinsed and drained
    2-1/2 cups cubed cooked turkey
        1 can (15 ounces) solid-pack pumpkin
        1 can (14-1/2 ounces) diced tomatoes, undrained
        2 teaspoons dried parsley flakes
        2 teaspoons chili powder
    1-1/2 teaspoons dried oregano
    1-1/2 teaspoons ground cumin
      1/2 teaspoon salt

1 In a large skillet, saute the onion and yellow pepper in oil until tender. Add garlic; cook 1 minute longer. Transfer to a 5-qt. slow cooker; stir in the remaining ingredients. Cover and cook on low for 4-5 hours or until heated through.

YIELD: 10 SERVINGS (2-1/2 QUARTS).

hearty turkey chili

JUDY NIEMEYER | BRENHAM, TEXAS

My mother-in-law introduced our family to this chili a few years ago, and we can't seem to get enough of it! It makes a lot, so why not freeze extra portions for convenient lunches or dinners on hectic nights?

- 2 pounds lean ground turkey
- 1 large onion, chopped
- 2 celery ribs, chopped
- 4 garlic cloves, minced
- 2 cans (16 ounces *each*) kidney beans, rinsed and drained
- 6 cans (5-1/2 ounces *each*) reduced-sodium V8 juice
- 1 cup reduced-sodium beef broth
- 1 can (6 ounces) tomato paste
- 3 teaspoons ground cumin
- 1 teaspoon salt
- 1/2 teaspoon crushed red pepper flakes
- 2 bay leaves

1 In a Dutch oven, cook the turkey, onion and celery over medium heat or until the meat is no longer pink. Add garlic; cook 1 minute longer. Drain. Stir in the remaining ingredients. Bring to a boil.

2 Reduce heat; simmer, uncovered, for 15 minutes to allow flavors to blend. Discard bay leaves.

YIELD: 8 SERVINGS (2-1/2 QUARTS).

spicy chicken chili

NATALIE HUGHES | JOPLIN, MISSOURI

My recipe was inspired when I was on a low-calorie, low-fat, high-fiber diet. I entered it in a chili cook-off and had several people say that it was the best chili they'd ever had!

- 1 small onion, chopped
- 1 small green pepper, chopped
- 1 small sweet red pepper, chopped
- 2 jalapeno peppers, seeded and chopped
- 1 serrano pepper, seeded and chopped
- 1 tablespoon olive oil
- 3 garlic cloves, minced
- 1 can (28 ounces) crushed tomatoes
- 1 can (14-1/2 ounces) stewed tomatoes, cut up
- 1 can (14-1/2 ounces) diced tomatoes with mild green chilies
- 1 can (16 ounces) kidney beans, rinsed and drained
- 1 can (15 ounces) black beans, rinsed and drained
- 1 carton (32 ounces) reduced-sodium chicken broth
- 3 tablespoons chili powder
- 1 tablespoon ground cumin
- 1 to 2 teaspoons crushed red pepper flakes
- 2 to 4 tablespoons Louisiana-style hot sauce
- 2-1/2 cups cubed cooked chicken breast
- 2 cups frozen corn
- 3/4 cup reduced-fat sour cream
- 3/4 cup shredded reduced-fat cheddar cheese

1 In a Dutch oven, saute the first five ingredients in oil until tender. Add garlic, cook 1 minute longer. Add the tomatoes, beans, broth, seasonings and hot sauce. Bring to a boil. Reduce heat; simmer, uncovered, for 15 minutes. Stir in chicken and corn; heat through. Garnish each serving with 1 tablespoon each of sour cream and cheese.

YIELD: 12 SERVINGS (4 QUARTS).

EDITOR'S NOTE: When cutting hot peppers, disposable gloves are recommended. Avoid touching your face.

meatless

TOMATO SPINACH SOUP, P. 112

winter harvest vegetable soup

BARBARA MARAKOWSKI | LOYSVILLE, PENNSYLVANIA

Rich, earthy root vegetables blend with savory spices and the tartness of apples in this wonderful soup. A friend gave me this low-fat recipe after my husband's cardiac surgery and now it's our favorite. It gets even better with reheating!

- 3 medium carrots, halved and thinly sliced
- 3/4 cup chopped celery
- 1 medium onion, chopped
- 2 green onions, thinly sliced
- 1 tablespoon butter
- 1 tablespoon olive oil
- 1 garlic clove, minced
- 7 cups reduced-sodium chicken broth *or* vegetable broth
- 3 cups cubed peeled potatoes
- 2 cups cubed peeled butternut squash
- 2 large tart apples, peeled and chopped
- 2 medium turnips, peeled and chopped
- 2 parsnips, peeled and sliced
- 1 bay leaf
- 1/2 teaspoon dried basil
- 1/4 teaspoon dried thyme
- 1/4 teaspoon pepper

Additional thinly sliced green onions, optional

1 In a Dutch oven over medium heat, cook and stir the carrots, celery and onions in butter and oil until tender. Add garlic; cook 1 minute longer.

2 Add the broth, potatoes, squash, apples, turnips, parsnips and bay leaf. Bring to a boil. Reduce heat; simmer, uncovered, for 20 minutes.

3 Stir in the basil, thyme and pepper; simmer 15 minutes longer or until vegetables are tender. Discard bay leaf before serving. Garnish with additional green onions if desired.

YIELD: 12 SERVINGS (3 QUARTS).

basil tomato soup

SARAH TRAVIS | EDINA, MINNESOTA

Fresh basil perks up the flavor in this creamy, from-scratch tomato soup. My aunt gave me this recipe years ago, and it's been one of my favorites ever since.

- 1 medium onion, chopped
- 1 medium carrot, shredded
- 1-1/2 teaspoons butter
- 4 medium tomatoes, peeled and seeded
- 1/4 teaspoon sugar
- 1/4 teaspoon salt
- 1/8 teaspoon coarsely ground pepper
- 1/4 cup loosely packed fresh basil leaves
- 1 cup reduced-sodium chicken broth *or* vegetable broth

1 In a small saucepan, saute onion and carrot in butter until tender. Stir in the tomatoes, sugar, salt and pepper. Bring to a boil. Reduce heat; cover and simmer for 10 minutes. Cool slightly.

2 Transfer to a blender; add basil. Cover and process until smooth. Return to the pan; stir in broth and heat through.

YIELD: 2 SERVINGS.

MEATLESS

cream of lentil soup

KIM RUSSELL
NORTH WALES, PENNSYLVANIA

Lentil lovers will want a second bowl of this nourishing soup with a subtle touch of curry. It looks particularly appealing thanks to the color the fresh spinach adds.

- 6 cups reduced-sodium chicken broth *or* vegetable broth
- 2 cups dried lentils, rinsed
- 1 bay leaf
- 1 whole clove
- 1 medium red onion, chopped
- 2 celery ribs, chopped
- 2 tablespoons butter
- 2 medium carrots, chopped
- 1 teaspoon salt
- 1 teaspoon sugar
- 1/2 teaspoon curry powder
- 1/8 teaspoon pepper
- 2 garlic cloves, minced
- 3 cups coarsely chopped fresh spinach
- 1-1/2 cups heavy whipping cream
- 1 tablespoon lemon juice
- 1/3 cup minced fresh parsley

1 In a large saucepan, combine the broth, lentils, bay leaf and clove. Bring to a boil. Reduce heat; cover and simmer for 25-30 minutes or until lentils are tender.

2 Meanwhile, in a Dutch oven, saute the onion and celery in butter until crisp-tender. Add the carrots, salt, sugar, curry powder and pepper;

saute 2-3 minutes longer or until vegetables are tender. Add garlic; cook for 1 minute.

3 Drain lentils; discard bay leaf and clove. Add to vegetable mixture. Stir in the spinach, cream, lemon juice and parsley; cook over low heat until heated through and spinach is wilted.

YIELD: 9 SERVINGS (2-1/4 QUARTS).

cream of vegetable soup

VICKI KAMSTRA | SPOKANE, WASHINGTON

I belong to an RV club and have passed this recipe on to 30 other women. It's special and delicious.

- 2 cups chopped sweet onions
- 1-1/2 cups chopped carrots
- 1 cup chopped celery
- 2 tablespoons canola oil
- 4 cups cubed peeled potatoes
- 1 large head cauliflower, broken into florets
- 3 cans (14-1/2 ounces *each*) reduced-sodium chicken broth *or* vegetable broth
- 2 teaspoons *each* salt and white pepper
- 1/2 cup half-and-half cream

Fresh basil

1 In Dutch oven, saute the onions, carrots and celery in oil until onions are tender. Add potatoes and cauliflower; saute 5-6 minutes longer. Add the broth, salt and pepper. Bring to a boil. Reduce heat; cover and simmer for 10-12 minutes or until vegetables are tender. Let stand until cool.

2 Puree vegetable mixture in a blender or food processor in batches. Return to pan. Stir in cream; heat through. (Do not boil.) Garnish with basil.

YIELD: 11 SERVINGS.

quick chopped carrots

To chop carrots coarsely for soup, I peel, remove the ends and cut the carrots into quarters. Then I let the food processor do the chopping!
MARION K., WATERLOO, IOWA

pear squash bisque with cinnamon cream

ELAINE SWEET | DALLAS, TEXAS

This lightly sweet and fruity squash soup makes a lovely first course for Thanksgiving. The texture is creamy and smooth.

- 3/4 cup sour cream
- 1-1/2 teaspoons maple syrup
- 1/2 teaspoon ground cinnamon
- 2 medium butternut squash (3 pounds *each*)
- 1 tablespoon butter, melted
- 1-1/2 teaspoons Caribbean jerk seasoning
- 4-1/2 cups vegetable broth
- 4 medium pears, peeled and chopped
- 1/2 cup packed brown sugar
- 1-1/2 teaspoons ground cinnamon
- 1/2 teaspoon salt
- 1/2 teaspoon ground ginger
- 1/4 teaspoon ground nutmeg
- 1/4 teaspoon ground cloves
- 3/4 cup heavy whipping cream

1 For cinnamon cream, in a small bowl, combine the sour cream, maple syrup and cinnamon. Cover and refrigerate until serving.

2 Peel squash. Scoop out seeds and pulp; rinse and pat seeds dry. In a small bowl, combine the squash seeds, butter and jerk seasoning. Spread onto a greased 15-in. x 10-in. x 1-in. baking pan. Bake at 375° for 12-15 minutes or until lightly browned, stirring once. Cool on a wire rack.

3 Meanwhile, cut the squash into cubes. In a large saucepan, combine the squash, broth and pears; bring to a boil. Reduce the heat; cover and simmer for 10-15 minutes or until squash is tender. Cool slightly.

4 In a blender, process squash mixture in batches until smooth. Return all to the pan. Add brown sugar and seasonings. Gradually stir in whipping cream. Garnish soup with cinnamon cream and spiced seeds.

YIELD: 12 SERVINGS (3 QUARTS).

parmesan corn chowder

MICHELLE KAISER | BOZEMAN, MONTANA

My mom made this thick soup when I was young. She shared the recipe by giving me a "Favorite Recipes Box" she created when I started college. This dish remains one of my favorites.

- 2 cups water
- 2 cups cubed peeled potatoes
- 1/2 cup sliced carrots
- 1/2 cup sliced celery
- 1/4 cup chopped onion
- 1/4 cup butter
- 1/4 cup all-purpose flour
- 1 teaspoon salt
- 1/2 teaspoon pepper
- 2 cups whole milk
- 1 can (14-3/4 ounces) cream-style corn
- 1-1/2 cups (6 ounces) shredded Parmesan cheese

1 In a large saucepan, combine the first five ingredients; bring to a boil. Reduce heat; cover and simmer for 12-15 minutes or until vegetables are tender (do not drain).

2 Meanwhile, in a small saucepan, melt butter. Stir in the flour, salt and pepper until smooth; gradually stir in milk. Bring to a boil; cook and stir for 2 minutes or until thickened. Stir into the vegetable mixture. Add corn and cheese. Cook 10 minutes longer or until heated through.

YIELD: 7 SERVINGS.

tomato spinach soup

ERNA KETCHUM | SAN JOSE, CALIFORNIA

I first sampled this soup in a local restaurant. After some experimenting with ingredients and seasonings, I finally found a combination my family preferred to the original.

- 2 large yellow onions, cubed
- 2 tablespoons olive oil
- 1 can (28 ounces) diced tomatoes, undrained
- 1 quart water
- 4 beef bouillon cubes
- 1 cup sliced fresh mushrooms
- 3/4 teaspoon Italian seasoning
- 1/2 teaspoon dried basil
- 1/2 teaspoon salt
- 1/8 teaspoon pepper
- 4 cups loosely packed spinach leaves

Grated Parmesan *or* shredded cheddar cheese, optional

1 In a Dutch oven or soup kettle, saute onions in oil over medium heat for 10 minutes or until tender. Add the next eight ingredients; bring to a boil. Reduce heat; cover and simmer for 30 minutes. Stir in spinach; simmer for 3-5 minutes or until tender. Garnish individual servings with cheese if desired.

YIELD: 8-10 SERVINGS (2-1/2 QUARTS).

spinach bean soup

MELISSA GRIFFIN | LANSING, MICHIGAN

This easy soup is so good. Chock-full of pasta, beans and spinach, it makes a fresh-tasting and satisfying first course or a light meal in itself.

- 1/2 cup chopped onion
- 1 tablespoon olive oil
- 3 garlic cloves, minced
- 2 cups water
- 1 can (15 ounces) tomato puree
- 1 can (14-1/2 ounces) reduced-sodium chicken broth *or* vegetable broth
- 1 teaspoon dried oregano
- 1/2 teaspoon *each* sugar and salt
- 1/4 teaspoon pepper
- 5 cups packed torn fresh spinach
- 1 can (16 ounces) navy beans, rinsed and drained
- 1-1/2 cups cooked small tube pasta *or* other small pasta
- 1/2 to 1 teaspoon hot pepper sauce
- 8 teaspoons shredded Parmesan cheese

1 In a large saucepan, saute onion in oil until tender. Add garlic; cook 1 minute longer. Stir in the water, tomato puree, broth, oregano, sugar, salt and pepper. Bring to a boil.

2 Reduce heat; cover and simmer for 20 minutes. Add the spinach, beans, cooked pasta and hot pepper sauce, heat through. Sprinkle with cheese.

YIELD: 5 SERVINGS.

have a huge tomato supply?

To quickly use a huge supply of garden tomatoes, I wash and core them, then puree in the blender with lemon juice, onion and celery to taste. This makes a great vegetable juice. I simmer several batches until slightly thickened for spaghetti sauce or until very thick for pizza sauce. I store it in the freezer.

MARION W., GREENFIELD, WISCONSIN

 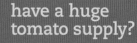

chunky vegetarian chili

SUSAN WRIGHT | YARMOUTH, MAINE

I downsized the yield but not the flavor of my favorite vegetarian chili. Use leftovers to spice up some tacos or burritos.

- 1 cup chopped onion
- 3/4 cup chopped green pepper
- 1 tablespoon canola oil
- 1 can (16 ounces) kidney beans, rinsed and drained
- 1 cup canned diced tomatoes
- 2/3 cup water
- 2 tablespoons tomato paste
- 1-1/2 teaspoons *each* mustard seed and chili powder
- 1/2 teaspoon *each* cumin seeds and baking cocoa
- 1/8 teaspoon ground cinnamon

ONION TOPPING:

- 1 cup water
- 2 teaspoons white vinegar, *divided*
- 1/2 large red onion, thinly sliced
- 1 teaspoon canola oil
- 1/4 teaspoon mustard seed
- 1/8 teaspoon ground cumin

Dash salt

1 In a large saucepan, saute onion and green pepper in oil for 5 minutes. Stir in the beans, tomatoes, water, tomato paste, mustard seed, chili powder, cumin seeds, cocoa and cinnamon. Bring to a boil. Reduce the heat; simmer, uncovered, for 40 minutes or until heated through.

2 Meanwhile, in a small saucepan, bring water and 1 teaspoon vinegar to a boil. Add onion; cook, uncovered, over medium heat for 2 minutes. Drain and cool. In a bowl, combine the oil, mustard seed, cumin, salt and remaining vinegar; stir in onion. Serve over chili.

YIELD: 3 SERVINGS.

butternut squash soup

LINDA ROSE PROUDFOOT
HUNTINGTON, CONNECTICUT

This deep golden soup is as pretty as it is yummy. If you like, you can intensify the garlic flavor by adding an extra bulb. The garlic is what really flavors this soup.

- 3 pounds unpeeled butternut squash, halved and seeded
- 2 large unpeeled onions
- 1 small garlic bulb
- 1/4 cup olive oil
- 2 tablespoons minced fresh thyme *or* 2 teaspoons dried thyme
- 3 to 3-1/2 cups chicken *or* vegetable broth
- 1/2 cup heavy whipping cream
- 3 tablespoons minced fresh parsley
- 1/2 teaspoon salt
- 1/4 teaspoon pepper

Sprigs fresh thyme, optional

1 Cut squash into eight large pieces. Place cut side up in a 15-in. x 10-in. x 1-in. baking pan. Cut 1/4 in. off tops of onion and garlic bulbs (the end that comes to a closed point).

2 Place cut side up in baking pans. Brush with oil; sprinkle with thyme. Cover tightly and bake at 350° for 1-1/2 to 2 hours or until vegetables are very tender. Uncover and let stand until lukewarm.

3 Remove peel from squash and onions; remove soft garlic from skins. In a large bowl, combine the vegetables, broth and cream. Puree in small batches in a blender until smooth; transfer to a large saucepan. Add the parsley, salt and pepper; heat through (do not boil). Garnish with thyme if desired.

YIELD: 8 SERVINGS (2 QUARTS).

baked potato soup

JOANN GOETZ | GENOA, OHIO

My husband and I enjoyed a delicious potato soup at a restaurant while on vacation, and I came home determined to duplicate it. It took me 5 years to get the taste just right! I know you'll like this recipe.

- 4 large baking potatoes (about 2-3/4 pounds)
- 2/3 cup butter
- 2/3 cup all-purpose flour
- 3/4 teaspoon salt
- 1/4 teaspoon white pepper
- 6 cups milk
- 1 cup (8 ounces) sour cream
- 1/4 cup thinly sliced green onions
- 10 bacon strips, cooked and crumbled
- 1 cup (4 ounces) shredded cheddar cheese

1 Bake potatoes at 350° for 65-75 minutes or until tender; cool completely. Peel and cube potatoes.

2 In a large saucepan, melt butter; stir in flour, salt and pepper until smooth. Gradually add milk. Bring to a boil; cook and stir for 2 minutes or until thickened. Remove from the heat; whisk in sour cream. Add potatoes and green onions. Garnish with bacon and cheese.

YIELD: 10 SERVINGS.

carrot broccoli soup

SANDY SMITH | LONDON, ONTARIO

This soup is a staple at my house. It's easy, fast, nutritious and so yummy!

- 1 medium onion, chopped
- 2 medium carrots, chopped
- 2 celery ribs, chopped
- 1 tablespoon butter
- 3 cups fresh broccoli florets
- 3 cups fat-free milk, *divided*
- 3/4 teaspoon salt
- 1/2 teaspoon dried thyme
- 1/8 teaspoon pepper
- 3 tablespoons all-purpose flour

1 In a large saucepan coated with cooking spray, cook the onion, carrots and celery in butter for 3 minutes. Add the broccoli; cook 3 minutes longer. Stir in 2-3/4 cups milk, salt, thyme and pepper.

2 Bring to a boil. Reduce heat; cover and simmer for 5-10 minutes or until vegetables are tender. Combine the flour and remaining milk until smooth; gradually stir into the soup. Bring to a boil; cook 2 minutes longer or until thickened.

YIELD: 4 SERVINGS.

zucchini tomato soup

NANCY JOHNSON
LAVERNE, OKLAHOMA

There's garden-fresh flavor in every spoonful of this easy-to-make soup. I like it for a low-calorie lunch, along with a roll and fruit for dessert. It serves just two, so you don't end up with leftovers.

  2 small zucchini, coarsely chopped
1/4 cup chopped red onion
1-1/2 teaspoons olive oil
1/8 teaspoon salt
  1 cup spicy hot V8 juice
  1 small tomato, cut into thin wedges
Dash *each* pepper and dried basil
  2 tablespoons shredded cheddar cheese, optional
  1 to 2 tablespoons crumbled cooked bacon, optional

1 In a large skillet, saute zucchini and onion in oil until crisp-tender. Sprinkle with salt. Add the V8 juice, tomato, pepper and basil; cook until heated through. Sprinkle with cheese and bacon if desired.

YIELD: 2 SERVINGS.

hearty lentil soup

JOY MAYNARD | ST. IGNATIUS, MONTANA

Chock-full of veggies, this delicious lentil soup is really simple to fix. I often double the recipe and freeze half for later. This hearty soup packs a full 15g of fiber per serving!

  3 cups water
  3 cups vegetable broth
  3 medium carrots, sliced
  1 medium onion, chopped
  1 cup dried lentils, rinsed
  2 celery ribs, sliced
  1 small green pepper, chopped
1/4 cup uncooked brown rice
  1 teaspoon dried basil
  1 garlic clove, minced
  1 bay leaf
3/4 cup tomato paste
1/2 cup frozen corn
1/2 cup frozen peas

1 In a large saucepan, combine the first 11 ingredients. Bring to a boil. Reduce heat; cover and simmer for 1 to 1-1/2 hours or until lentils and rice are tender.
2 Add the tomato paste, corn and peas; stir until blended. Cook, uncovered, for 15-20 minutes or until corn and peas are tender. Discard bay leaf.

YIELD: 6 SERVINGS.

2 Stir in the refried beans; simmer 10 minutes longer. Garnish each serving with 2 teaspoons each of cheese and green onions.

YIELD: 8 SERVINGS (2-1/2 QUARTS).

EDITOR'S NOTE: When cutting hot peppers, disposable gloves are recommended. Avoid touching your face.

garlic-basil tortellini soup

LINDA KEES | BOISE, IDAHO

This soup is so tasty and filling, it can be served as a main dish.

- 2 garlic cloves, minced
- 1 teaspoon butter
- 2 cans (14-1/2 ounces *each*) reduced-sodium chicken broth *or* vegetable broth
- 1/2 cup water
- 1/3 cup minced fresh basil
- 1/4 teaspoon pepper
- 2-1/2 cups frozen cheese tortellini
- 1 can (19 ounces) white kidney beans *or* cannellini beans, rinsed and drained
- 2 tablespoons balsamic vinegar
- 1/4 cup shredded Parmesan cheese

1 In a large saucepan, saute garlic in butter until tender. Stir in the broth, water, basil and pepper. Bring to a boil. Stir in tortellini. Reduce heat; simmer, uncovered, for about 3 minutes or until tortellini begins to float. Stir in beans and vinegar; heat through. Sprinkle with Parmesan cheese.

YIELD: 4 SERVINGS.

spicy three-bean chili

MELISSA MENDEZ | GILBERT, MINNESOTA

Even my meat-loving family devours this hearty meatless chili. We find that it's fun to scoop it up with tortilla chips! It's fast, simple to make and freezes well.

- 1 medium green pepper, chopped
- 1 medium sweet yellow pepper, chopped
- 1 jalapeno pepper, seeded and chopped
- 1 medium onion, chopped
- 1 tablespoon olive oil
- 3 garlic cloves, minced
- 2 cans (14-1/2 ounces *each*) diced tomatoes with mild green chilies, undrained
- 1 can (10 ounces) diced tomatoes and green chilies, undrained
- 1 can (16 ounces) kidney beans, rinsed and drained
- 1 can (15 ounces) black beans, rinsed and drained
- 1 cup vegetable broth
- 1 teaspoon chili powder
- 3/4 teaspoon ground cumin
- 1/2 teaspoon cayenne pepper
- 1 can (16 ounces) spicy fat-free refried beans
- 1/3 cup shredded reduced-fat cheddar cheese
- 1/3 cup thinly sliced green onions

1 In a Dutch oven coated with cooking spray, saute the peppers and onion in oil until tender. Add garlic; cook 1 minute longer. Stir in the tomatoes, kidney beans, black beans, broth, chili powder, cumin and cayenne. Bring to a boil. Reduce heat; simmer, uncovered for 10 minutes.

broccoli cheese soup

MARGE HILL | GLENSIDE, PENNSYLVANIA

When my husband and I visit fresh-food stands, we often come home with more vegetables than we can eat. I lightened up this tarragon-flavored soup to use up the broccoli we buy. I like it with crusty bread, a salad or a sandwich.

- 1/2 cup chopped sweet onion
- 3 garlic cloves, minced
- 2 tablespoons all-purpose flour
- 1 can (14-1/2 ounces) reduced-sodium chicken broth *or* vegetable broth
- 4 cups fresh broccoli florets
- 1/4 to 1/2 teaspoon dried tarragon
- 1/4 teaspoon dried thyme
- 1/8 teaspoon pepper
- 1-1/2 cups 1% milk
- 1-1/4 cups shredded reduced-fat cheddar cheese, *divided*

1 In a large nonstick saucepan coated with cooking spray, saute onion until tender. Add garlic; cook 1 minute longer. Stir in flour until blended.

Gradually whisk in broth. Bring to a boil; cook and stir for 1-2 minutes or until slightly thickened.

2 Add the broccoli, tarragon, thyme and pepper; return to a boil. Reduce heat; cover and simmer for 10 minutes or until broccoli is tender. Add milk; cook, uncovered, 5 minutes longer. Remove from the heat; cool to room temperature.

3 In a blender, process soup in batches until smooth. Return all to the pan; heat through. Reduce the heat. Add 1 cup of cheese; stir just until melted. Serve immediately. Garnish with remaining cheese.

YIELD: 4 SERVINGS.

garden chowder

DARLENE BRENDEN | SALEM, OREGON

This creamy chowder is chock-full of savory ingredients straight from the garden.

- 1/2 cup chopped green pepper
- 1/2 cup chopped onion
- 1/4 cup butter

- 1 cup *each* diced potato, celery, cauliflower, carrot and broccoli
- 3 cups water
- 3 chicken bouillon cubes
- 1 teaspoon salt
- 1/4 teaspoon pepper
- 1/2 cup all-purpose flour
- 2 cups whole milk
- 1 tablespoon minced fresh parsley
- 3 cups (12 ounces) shredded cheddar cheese

1 In a Dutch oven, saute green pepper and onion in butter until tender. Add the vegetables, water, bouillon, salt and pepper; bring to a boil. Reduce heat; cover and simmer for 20 minutes or until the vegetables are tender.

2 Combine flour and milk until smooth; stir into pan. Bring to a boil; cook and stir for 2 minutes. Add parsley. Just before serving, stir in cheese until melted.

YIELD: 6-8 SERVINGS (2 QUARTS).

fresh broccoli stalks

When cleaning fresh broccoli, I don't throw away the stalks like many people do. After washing the broccoli, I use a vegetable peeler to remove the tough outer layer from the stalks. I chop the florets and peeled stalks, then drop them into boiling water for just 5 minutes. I drain them and immediately run them under cold water to stop the cooking process. Then I place meal-size portions in freezer bags and store them in the freezer. This way, I always have broccoli ready for almost any recipe, or just to heat and enjoy as a side dish. The peeled stalks are as tender as the florets once they're cooked.

STEPHEN H., READING, PENNSYLVANIA

roasted red pepper soup

TASTE OF HOME TEST KITCHEN

If you like cream of tomato soup, try making it with purchased roasted red peppers instead. Using jarred roasted red peppers makes it extra easy, and pureeing the soup in a blender gives it a nice smooth texture.

- 1 large sweet onion, chopped
- 2 teaspoons butter
- 2 garlic cloves, minced
- 2 jars (15-1/2 ounces *each*) roasted sweet red peppers, drained
- 2 cups vegetable broth
- 1/2 teaspoon dried basil
- 1/4 teaspoon salt
- 1 cup half-and-half cream

1 In a large saucepan, saute onion in butter for 2-3 minutes or until tender. Add garlic; cook 1 minute longer. Stir in the red peppers, broth, basil and salt. Bring to a boil. Reduce heat; cover and simmer for 20 minutes. Cool slightly.

2 In a blender, cover and process soup in batches until smooth. Remove 1 cup to a small bowl; stir in cream. Return remaining puree to pan. Stir in the cream mixture; heat through (do not boil).

YIELD: 6 SERVINGS.

cream of potato soup

RUTH ANN STELFOX | RAYMOND, ALBERTA

This soup is comfort food, especially when the temperatures take a plunge. I serve this often. It's a simple supper that can be prepared in a short amount of time.

- 2 medium potatoes, peeled and diced
- 1 cup water
- 2 tablespoons chopped onion
- 2 tablespoons butter
- 2 tablespoons all-purpose flour
- 3 cups whole milk
- 1/2 teaspoon salt
- 1/8 teaspoon celery salt

Dash pepper

Paprika and minced fresh parsley

1 Place the potatoes and water in a saucepan; bring to a boil over medium-high heat. Cover and cook until tender; drain and set aside.

2 In the same pan, saute the onion in butter until tender. Stir in flour until blended. Gradually stir in milk. Bring to a boil; cook and stir for 2 minutes or until thickened. Reduce the heat; add the potatoes, salt, celery salt and pepper. Cook for 2-3 minutes or until heated through. Sprinkle with the paprika and parsley.

YIELD: 2 SERVINGS.

fast vegetable soup

JENNIFER SHIELDS
CHESNEE, SOUTH CAROLINA

I dress up canned minestrone to make this shortcut soup that's loaded with colorful vegetables. Serve bowls with a sandwich or salad for a satisfying yet fast meal.

- 1 can (19 ounces) ready-to-serve minestrone soup
- 1 package (16 ounces) frozen mixed vegetables
- 1 can (14-3/4 ounces) whole kernel corn, drained
- 1 can (15 ounces) black beans, rinsed and drained
- 1 can (14-1/2 ounces) Italian diced tomatoes, undrained

1 In a 2-1/2 quart microwave-safe bowl, combine all the ingredients. Cover and microwave on high for 8-10 minutes, stirring twice.

YIELD: 9 SERVINGS.

EDITOR'S NOTE: This recipe was tested in a 1,100-watt microwave.

super soups

To make a delicious, hearty meal out of canned tomato or vegetable soup, I dilute the concentrate with V8 vegetable juice instead of water. Then top the bubbling mixture with your favorite homemade dumplings.

ESTHER T., PORTALES, NEW MEXICO

cheese-topped vegetable soup

ANNA MINEGAR | ZOLFO SPRINGS, FLORIDA

Just-picked garden flavor makes this hearty vegetable soup a summer and harvesttime staple. It warms the soul.

- 1 can (28 ounces) Italian stewed tomatoes
- 1-1/2 cups water
- 1 can (8-3/4 ounces) whole kernel corn, drained
- 3/4 cup chopped sweet red pepper
- 2/3 cup chopped red onion
- 2/3 cup chopped green pepper
- 1/4 cup minced fresh basil
- 1 garlic clove, minced
- 1/2 teaspoon salt
- 1/4 teaspoon pepper
- 1/2 cup salad croutons
- 1/4 cup shredded part-skim mozzarella cheese

1 In a large saucepan, combine the first 10 ingredients. Bring to a boil. Reduce heat; simmer, uncovered, for 20-25 minutes or until heated through and vegetables are tender.

2 Ladle the soup into ovenproof bowls. Top each with croutons and cheese. Broil 6 in. from the heat until cheese is melted.

YIELD: 4 SERVINGS.

harvest sweet potato soup

GAYLE BECKER | MT. CLEMENS, MICHIGAN

I always double this recipe whenever I prepare it, since we love leftovers. This is the easiest soup I've ever made. Little children can really dig in. The thick, nutritious mixture clings to their spoons. We prefer to eat it warm, but it can also be served chilled.

- 1 cup chopped celery
- 1/2 cup chopped onion
- 1 tablespoon canola oil
- 3 medium sweet potatoes (about 1 pound), peeled and cubed
- 3 cups chicken *or* vegetable broth
- 1 bay leaf
- 1/2 teaspoon dried basil
- 1/4 teaspoon salt, optional

1 In a Dutch oven, saute celery and onion in oil until tender. Add remaining ingredients; bring to a boil over medium heat. Reduce heat; simmer for 25-30 minutes or until tender.

2 Discard bay leaf. Cool slightly. In a blender, process soup in batches until smooth. Return all to the pan and heat through.

YIELD: 4 SERVINGS.

cheesy floret soup

JANICE RUSSELL | KINGFISHER, OKLAHOMA

Talk about comfort food! I received this recipe from my mom, and my family requests it often. It's especially good with crusty French bread.

- 3 cups fresh broccoli florets
- 3 cups fresh cauliflowerets
- 3 celery ribs, sliced
- 1 small onion, chopped
- 2 cups water
- 1/2 teaspoon celery salt
- 3 tablespoons butter
- 3 tablespoons all-purpose flour
- 2-1/3 cups whole milk
- 1 pound process cheese (Velveeta), cubed

1 In a large saucepan, combine the first six ingredients. Bring to a boil. Reduce heat; cover and simmer for 12-15 minutes or until vegetables are tender.

2 Meanwhile, in a small saucepan, melt butter; stir in flour until smooth. Gradually stir in milk. Bring to a boil; cook and stir for 2 minutes or until thickened. Reduce heat; add cheese. Cook and stir until cheese is melted. Drain vegetables; add cheese sauce and heat through.

YIELD: 4-6 SERVINGS.

what is process cheese?

Process cheese is a blend of different cheeses and emulsifiers. It is stable at room temperature and stays smooth and creamy when it is heated. The most common brand name of process cheese is Velveeta. In the past, our recipes called for "process American cheese" when Velveeta was used. But recently, Velveeta's packaging changed, and the label now reads "pasteurized prepared cheese product" instead. To avoid confusion, we are now listing this ingredient as "process cheese (Velveeta)."

TASTE OF HOME TEST KITCHEN

spill-the-beans minestrone

REUBEN TSUJIMURA
WALLA WALLA, WASHINGTON

A meal in itself, here's a hearty soup that's chock-full of good-for-you veggies and vitamins. Serve with crunchy breadsticks, and no one will even miss the meat!

- 1 medium onion, chopped
- 1 tablespoon olive oil
- 2 garlic cloves, minced
- 2 cans (14-1/2 ounces *each*) reduced-sodium chicken broth *or* vegetable broth
- 1 can (16 ounces) kidney beans, rinsed and drained
- 1 can (15 ounces) garbanzo beans *or* chickpeas, rinsed and drained
- 1 can (14-1/2 ounces) stewed tomatoes, cut up
- 2 cups chopped fresh kale
- 1/2 cup water
- 1/2 cup uncooked small pasta shells
- 1 teaspoon Italian seasoning
- 1/4 teaspoon crushed red pepper flakes
- 6 teaspoons shredded Parmesan cheese

1 In a large saucepan, saute onion in oil until onion is tender. Add garlic; cook 1 minute longer. Add the broth, beans, tomatoes, kale, water, pasta, Italian seasoning and pepper flakes. Bring to a boil. Reduce heat; cover and simmer for 10-15 minutes or until pasta is tender. Sprinkle each serving with cheese.

YIELD: 6 SERVINGS.

vegetable barley soup

MARY TALLMAN
ARBOR VITAE, WISCONSIN

You'll love this delicious vegetarian soup brimming with veggies and barley. And the great news? It's good for you, too!

- 1 large sweet potato, peeled and cubed
- 1-1/2 cups fresh baby carrots, halved
- 1-1/2 cups frozen cut green beans
- 1-1/2 cups frozen corn
- 3 celery ribs, thinly sliced
- 1 small onion, chopped
- 1/2 cup chopped green pepper
- 2 garlic cloves, minced
- 6 cups water
- 2 cans (14-1/2 ounces *each*) vegetable broth
- 1 cup medium pearl barley
- 1 bay leaf
- 1-3/4 teaspoons salt
- 1/2 teaspoon fennel seed, crushed
- 1/4 teaspoon pepper
- 1 can (14-1/2 ounces) Italian diced tomatoes, undrained

1 In a 5-qt. slow cooker, combine the first eight ingredients. Stir in the water, broth, barley, bay leaf and seasonings. Cover and cook on low for 8-9 hours or until barley and vegetables are tender.

2 Stir in tomatoes; cover and cook on high for 10-20 minutes or until heated through. Discard bay leaf before serving.

YIELD: 12 SERVINGS (ABOUT 3-1/2 QUARTS).

vegetable yields

Freezing peppers and onions is a great way to enjoy garden produce when summer days are long gone. A medium green pepper, chopped, will yield about 1 cup. A large green pepper, chopped, will yield about 1-1/3 to 1-1/2 cups. A medium onion, chopped, will equal about 1/2 cup; a large onion, about 1 cup. Store both green peppers and onions in heavy-duty resealable plastic bags. Green peppers can be frozen for up to 6 months, and onions can be frozen for up to 1 year.

TASTE OF HOME TEST KITCHEN

chilled veggie & fruit soups

WATERMELON GAZPACHO, P. 127

herbed gazpacho

CAROLE BENSON
CABAZON, CALIFORNIA

For a unique first course, serve this colorful soup. Chilled V8 juice is the base for this soup that's chock-full of generous chunks of chopped tomatoes, green pepper and cucumber. Garnish each bowl with shrimp for a fancy finish.

1	can (46 ounces) V8 juice, chilled
1	can (14-1/2 ounces) Italian stewed tomatoes
3	medium tomatoes, chopped
1	medium green pepper, chopped
1	medium cucumber, chopped
1/2	cup Italian salad dressing
1/4	cup minced fresh parsley
4	to 6 garlic cloves, minced
1	teaspoon Italian seasoning
1	teaspoon salt
1/4	teaspoon pepper

Cooked chopped shrimp, optional

1 In a large bowl, combine the first 11 ingredients. Cover and refrigerate for at least 1 hour. Garnish with the shrimp if desired.

YIELD: 10-12 SERVINGS (ABOUT 3 QUARTS).

strawberry dessert soup

SHARON DELANEY-CHRONIS | SOUTH MILWAUKEE, WISCONSIN

When I first prepared this change-of-pace soup for a party, everyone called it a hit! My husband always likes it warmed up, but I prefer my soup chilled. Any leftovers are drizzled over frozen custard for a fresh, fruity topping. What a treat!

1	cup water, *divided*
1	cup unsweetened apple juice
2/3	cup sugar
1/2	teaspoon ground cinnamon
1/8	teaspoon ground cloves
2	cups fresh strawberries, hulled
2	cups strawberry yogurt
2	to 3 drops red food coloring, optional
1/4	cup sour cream
2	tablespoons milk

1 In a large saucepan, combine 3/4 cup water, apple juice, sugar, cinnamon and cloves. Bring to a boil, stirring occasionally. Remove from the heat.

2 Place strawberries and remaining water in a blender; cover and process until smooth. Pour into apple juice mixture. Stir in yogurt and food coloring if desired. Cover and refrigerate for at least 2 hours or until chilled.

3 Ladle soup into bowls. Combine sour cream and milk; spoon about 2-1/2 teaspoons into the center of each bowl. Using a toothpick, pull mixture out, forming a flower or design of your choice.

YIELD: 7 SERVINGS.

cool tomato soup

WENDY NICKEL | KIESTER, MINNESOTA

It's easy to crave soup—even on a hot day—when it's chilled and filled with fresh summery flavors. Serve a tomatoey batch as an appetizer or a side for a main dish salad.

- 4 cups tomato juice, *divided*
- 5 medium tomatoes, peeled, seeded and chopped
- 2 medium cucumbers, peeled, seeded and cut into chunks
- 1 medium green pepper, quartered
- 1 medium sweet red pepper, quartered
- 1 medium onion, peeled and quartered
- 2 garlic cloves, peeled
- 1 tablespoon minced fresh thyme
- 1/4 cup white balsamic vinegar
- 4 cups cubed bread, crusts removed
- 2 tablespoons olive oil
- 1/4 teaspoon pepper

Fat-free sour cream, fat-free croutons and parsley, optional

1 In a blender, cover and process 1 cup tomato juice and half of the tomatoes, cucumbers, peppers, onion, garlic and thyme until chopped. Transfer to a large bowl. Repeat.

2 Place the vinegar and remaining tomato juice in the blender. Add the bread; cover and process until smooth. Add to vegetable mixture; stir in oil and pepper.

3 Cover and refrigerate for 1-2 hours before serving. Garnish with the sour cream, croutons and parsley if desired.

YIELD: 9 SERVINGS.

fresh fruit soup

**BEULAH GOODENOUGH
BELLEVILLE, NEW JERSEY**

On a hot summer day, nothing can top the flavor of the season's finest fruits. This recipe is a fun, fast and delicious change of pace.

- 2 cups water
- 2 tablespoons quick-cooking tapioca
- 1 can (6 ounces) frozen orange juice concentrate, thawed
- 1 to 2 tablespoons sugar
- 1 tablespoon honey
- 1/8 teaspoon almond extract

Pinch salt

2-1/2 cups fresh fruit of your choice

1 In a large saucepan, combine water and tapioca; let stand for 10 minutes. Bring to a boil; cook and stir for 2 minutes or until thickened. Remove from the heat; stir in orange juice concentrate, sugar, honey, extract and salt. Chill. Add fruit; refrigerate until ready to serve.

YIELD: 4 SERVINGS.

gazpacho

TASTE OF HOME TEST KITCHEN

Healthy vegetables are the basis of this cold, tasty soup. We recommend using spicy V8 juice for a version with more heat.

- 2 medium tomatoes, seeded and chopped
- 1/2 small green pepper, chopped
- 1/3 cup chopped peeled cucumber
- 1/3 cup chopped red onion
- 1-1/3 cups reduced-sodium tomato juice
- 1/4 teaspoon dried oregano
- 1/4 teaspoon dried basil
- 1/8 teaspoon salt
- 1 small garlic clove, minced

Dash pepper

Dash hot pepper sauce

- 1 tablespoon minced chives

Chopped sweet yellow pepper, optional

1 In a large bowl, combine the tomatoes, green pepper, cucumber and onion. In another bowl, combine the tomato juice, oregano, basil, salt, garlic, pepper and pepper sauce; pour over vegetables.

2 Cover and refrigerate for at least 4 hours or overnight. Just before serving, sprinkle with chives and yellow pepper if desired.

YIELD: 2 SERVINGS.

raspberry-cranberry soup for two

SUSAN STULL | CHILLICOTHE, MISSOURI

Looking for a fabulous recipe for two? Look no further!

- 1 cup fresh *or* frozen cranberries
- 1 cup unsweetened apple juice
- 1/2 cup fresh *or* frozen raspberries, thawed
- 1/4 to 1/2 cup sugar
- 1-1/2 teaspoons lemon juice
- 1/8 teaspoon ground cinnamon
- 1 cup half-and-half cream, *divided*
- 1-1/2 teaspoons cornstarch

Whipped cream and additional raspberries, optional

1 In a large saucepan, bring cranberries and apple juice to a boil. Reduce the heat and simmer, uncovered, for 10 minutes. Press through a sieve; return to the pan. Press the raspberries through the sieve; discard the skins and seeds. Add to the cranberry mixture; bring to a boil. Stir in the sugar, lemon juice and cinnamon; remove from the heat.

2 Cool for 4 minutes. Stir 1/2 cup soup into 3/4 cup cream. Return all to pan; bring to a gentle boil. Mix cornstarch with the remaining cream until smooth; gradually stir into soup. Cook and stir for 2 minutes or until thickened. Serve hot or chilled. Serve with whipped cream and additional raspberries if desired.

YIELD: 2 SERVINGS.

chilled avocado soup

EDITH HERRING
GRAND CANE, LOUISIANA

No cooking is necessary for this rich and creamy soup with a kick! I like to line the bowl with crumbled corn chips and pour the soup on top.

- 1 medium ripe avocado, peeled, halved and pitted
- 1 can (14-1/2 ounces) reduced-sodium chicken broth
- 1/2 cup reduced-fat sour cream
- 1 green onion, chopped
- 1-1/2 teaspoons minced fresh cilantro
- 1/8 teaspoon salt
- 1/8 teaspoon ground cumin
- Dash cayenne pepper
- Dash pepper

1 Place avocado in a blender, cover and process until smooth. While processing, gradually add broth; process until smooth. Add the remaining ingredients; cover and process until blended. Refrigerate for 1 hour or until chilled.

YIELD: 3 SERVINGS.

chilled peach soup

LANE MCLOUD
SILOAM SPRINGS, ARKANSAS

Welcome summer with the fresh, creamy taste of this chilled soup. It's very simple to prepare. Topped with toasted almonds, enjoy a crunchy kick with your light, tasty soup.

- 1-1/2 cups chopped peeled fresh peaches
- 1/2 cup plain yogurt
- 1/2 teaspoon lemon juice
- 1/8 teaspoon almond extract
- 2 tablespoons sliced almonds, toasted

1 In a blender, combine the peaches, yogurt, lemon juice and extract; cover and process until smooth. Refrigerate until chilled. Sprinkle with almonds just before serving.

YIELD: 2 SERVINGS.

how much is "a dash?"

Traditionally, a dash is a very small amount of seasoning added with a quick downward stroke of the hand. A pinch is thought to be the amount of a dry ingredient that can be held between your thumb and forefinger. If recipes call for a dash of an ingredient, use somewhere between 1/16 and a scant 1/8 teaspoon. Sometimes you might have to experiment with amounts to get delicious results that suit your taste.

TASTE OF HOME TEST KITCHEN

watermelon gazpacho

NICOLE DEELAH
NASHVILLE, TENNESSEE

This is a delightfully simple, elegant dish. Serve as a side or with pita and hummus as a meal. It's so refreshing!

- 4 cups cubed watermelon, seeded, *divided*
- 2 tablespoons lime juice
- 1 tablespoon grated lime peel
- 1 teaspoon minced fresh gingerroot
- 1 teaspoon salt
- 1 cup chopped tomato
- 1/2 cup chopped cucumber
- 1/2 cup chopped green pepper
- 1/4 cup minced fresh cilantro
- 2 tablespoons chopped green onion
- 1 tablespoon finely chopped seeded jalapeno pepper

1 Puree 3 cups watermelon in a blender. Cut remaining watermelon into 1/2-inch pieces; set aside.

2 In a large bowl, combine the watermelon puree, lime juice, lime peel, ginger and salt. Stir in the tomato, cucumber, green pepper, cilantro, onion, jalapeno and cubed watermelon. Chill until serving.

YIELD: 4 SERVINGS.

EDITOR'S NOTE: When cutting hot peppers, disposable gloves are recommended. Avoid touching your face.

cool raspberry soup

JANET MOOBERRY | PEORIA, ILLINOIS

An exquisite combination of spices and a rich berry flavor make this beautiful soup so irresistible. It's a lovely and tasty way to begin a luncheon. Your guests will rave about the special treat.

- 1 package (20 ounces) frozen unsweetened raspberries, thawed

- 1-1/4 cups water
- 1/4 cup white wine, optional
- 1 cup cran-raspberry juice
- 1/2 cup sugar
- 1-1/2 teaspoons ground cinnamon
- 3 whole cloves
- 1 tablespoon lemon juice
- 1 cup (8 ounces) raspberry yogurt
- 1/2 cup sour cream

1 In a blender, puree the raspberries, water and wine if desired. Transfer to a large saucepan; add cran-raspberry juice, sugar, cinnamon and cloves. Bring just to a boil over medium heat. Remove from the heat; strain and allow to cool.

2 Whisk in lemon juice and yogurt. Refrigerate. To serve, pour soup into small bowls and top each with a dollop of sour cream.

YIELD: 4-6 SERVINGS.

straining berries

It takes time and patience to make a good sauce from strained berries, but the results are typically a great reward. Here's how you can speed up the process a bit: After pureeing fruit in a food processor or blender, use the back of a wooden spoon or a rubber spatula to firmly push the pulp through a fine meshed sieve. If the holes are too large, line the sieve with several layers of cheesecloth that have been moistened with water and squeezed dry.

TASTE OF HOME TEST KITCHEN

black bean gazpacho

SHELLEY GRAFF | PHILO, ILLINOIS

I first tried this colorful chilled soup at my best friend's house during one of the hottest summers I can remember. Its garden-fresh flavor really hit the spot and was so memorable!

- 3 cans (11-1/2 ounces *each*) spicy hot V8 juice
- 4 medium tomatoes, seeded and chopped
- 1 can (15 ounces) black beans, rinsed and drained
- 1 cup cubed fully cooked ham
- 1/2 cup *each* chopped green, sweet yellow and red pepper
- 1/2 cup chopped cucumber
- 1/2 cup chopped zucchini
- 1/4 cup finely chopped green onions
- 2 tablespoons Italian salad dressing
- 3/4 teaspoon salt
- 1/8 to 1/4 teaspoon hot pepper sauce

1 Combine all of the ingredients in a large bowl. Cover and refrigerate for at least 2 hours.

YIELD: 10 SERVINGS.

EDITOR'S NOTE: Two 14-1/2-ounce cans of diced tomatoes, drained, can be substituted for the fresh tomatoes.

summer strawberry soup

VERNA BOLLIN | POWELL, TENNESSEE

You'll be amazed that just five ingredients can create something so spectacular! This fruity cold soup is certain to become a new summertime favorite for you.

- 2 cups vanilla yogurt
- 1/2 cup orange juice
- 2 pounds fresh strawberries, halved (8 cups)
- 1/2 cup sugar

Additional vanilla yogurt and fresh mint leaves, optional

1 In a blender, combine the yogurt, orange juice, strawberries and sugar in batches; cover and process until blended. Refrigerate for at least 2 hours. Garnish with additional yogurt and mint leaves if desired.

YIELD: 6 SERVINGS.

chilled melon soup

MARY LOU TIMPSON | COLORADO CITY, ARIZONA

Looking for something to put pizazz in a summer luncheon? Try this pretty, refreshing soup with a kick of cayenne pepper to get the conversation going.

3/4 cup orange juice
1 cup (8 ounces) plain yogurt
1 medium cantaloupe, peeled, seeded and cubed
1 tablespoon honey
1/4 teaspoon salt
1/4 teaspoon ground nutmeg
1/8 teaspoon cayenne pepper
6 mint sprigs

1 Place the orange juice, yogurt and cantaloupe in a blender; cover and process until pureed. Add the honey, salt, nutmeg and cayenne; cover and process until smooth. Refrigerate for at least 1 hour before serving. Garnish with mint sprigs.

YIELD: 6 SERVINGS.

crystallized honey

I'm a beekeeper and have found it is helpful to freeze honey to keep it from crystallizing. It will never freeze solid since the moisture content is low. It will, however, become thick and sludgy until thawed to room temperature, when it should return to its original consistency. When buying a large amount of honey, divide it into freezer-proof containers and freeze. When needed, defrost at room temperature for about 30 minutes.

J. M., WEST BEND, WISCONSIN

strawberry orange soup

SHERRI CYR | CANTON, MAINE

Chill out with this fun, fruity soup that has a smooth, glossy texture and sweet-tart taste. Its cheerful, pink color makes it the perfect menu item for a bridal or baby shower, or when having friends over for lunch or dinner. You can make it ahead, store it in the fridge, then garnish and serve later without last-minute fuss.

1 cup orange juice
2 cups fresh strawberries, hulled
2 teaspoons cornstarch
3/4 cup white grape juice
2 tablespoons seedless strawberry jam
2 teaspoons honey
Whipped topping and orange peel strips, optional

1 In a blender, combine orange juice and strawberries; cover and process until blended. Press mixture through a fine meshed sieve; discard seeds.

2 In a large saucepan; combine cornstarch and grape juice until smooth. Stir in strawberry puree and jam. Bring to a boil over medium heat; cook and stir for 2 minutes or until thickened. Reduce heat; add honey. Simmer, uncovered, for 10 minutes.

3 Transfer to a bowl; cover and refrigerate until chilled. Garnish with the whipped topping and orange peel if desired.

YIELD: 3 SERVINGS.

CHILLED VEGGIE & FRUIT SOUPS

BIG BOOK OF HEARTWARMING SOUPS 129

soup mixes & easy breads

BAZAAR SOUP MIX, P. 136

homemade cream-style soup mix

DEANN ALLEVA | WORTHINGTON, OHIO

This easy soup mix is a wonderful substitute for canned cream soup in a recipe. It's great to have on hand for those nights when you need to whip up supper in a hurry.

- 2 cups nonfat dry milk powder
- 1/2 cup plus 2 tablespoons cornstarch
- 1/2 cup mashed potato flakes
- 1/4 cup chicken bouillon granules
- 2 teaspoons dried parsley flakes
- 2 teaspoons dried minced onion
- 1 teaspoon dried celery flakes
- 1 teaspoon dried minced garlic
- 1 teaspoon onion powder
- 1/2 teaspoon dried marjoram
- 1/4 teaspoon garlic powder
- 1/8 teaspoon white pepper

1 In a small bowl, combine all ingredients. Store in an airtight container in a cool dry place for up to 1 year.

YIELD: 3 CUPS (16 BATCHES).

2 **To use as a substitute for condensed cream of mushroom or celery soup:** In a microwave-safe bowl, whisk 2/3 cup water and 3 tablespoons soup mix. Microwave, uncovered, on high for 2 to 2-1/2 minutes or until thickened and bubbly, whisking occasionally. For mushroom soup, add 1/4 to 1/2 cup sauteed sliced mushrooms. For celery soup, add 1/8 teaspoon celery salt or one sauteed sliced or chopped celery rib.

YIELD: HALF OF A 10-3/4-OZ. CAN OF CONDENSED CREAM SOUP.

paradise buns

LIZ LAZENBY
VICTORIA, BRITISH COLUMBIA

I think frozen bread dough should be called magic dough because there is so much you can do with it. These flavorful knots are delicious with soup or salad.

- 1 loaf (1 pound) frozen bread dough, thawed
- 1 cup (4 ounces) shredded cheddar cheese
- 1/4 cup diced mushrooms
- 1/4 cup broccoli
- 1/4 cup sweet red pepper
- 1/4 cup yellow pepper
- 1 tablespoon chopped green onion
- 1 garlic clove, minced
- 1/2 teaspoon garlic powder

1 Divide the bread dough into eight pieces. In a shallow bowl, combine the cheese, vegetables, garlic and garlic powder. Roll each piece of dough into an 8-in. rope. Roll in the cheese mixture, pressing mixture into dough. Tie into a knot and press the vegetables into dough; tuck the ends under.

2 Place 2 in. apart on greased baking sheets. Cover and let rise until doubled about 30 minutes.

3 Bake at 375° for 15-20 minutes or until golden brown.

YIELD: 8 SERVINGS.

pull-apart bacon bread

TRACI COLLINS | CHEYENNE, WYOMING

I stumbled across this recipe while looking for something different to take to a brunch. Boy, am I glad I did! Everyone asked for the recipe and could not believe it only called for five ingredients. It's the perfect item to bake for an informal get-together.

- 12 bacon strips, diced
- 1 loaf (1 pound) frozen bread dough, thawed
- 2 tablespoons olive oil, *divided*
- 1 cup (4 ounces) shredded part-skim mozzarella cheese
- 1 envelope (1 ounce) ranch salad dressing mix

1 In a large skillet, cook the bacon over medium heat for 5 minutes or until partially cooked; drain on paper towels. Roll out the dough to 1/2-in. thickness; brush with 1 tablespoon of oil. Cut into 1-in. pieces; place in a large bowl. Add the bacon, cheese, dressing mix and remaining oil; toss to coat.

2 Arrange pieces in a 9-in. x 5-in. oval on a greased baking sheet, layering as needed. Cover and let rise in a warm place for 30 minutes or until doubled.

3 Bake at 350° for 15 minutes. Cover with foil; bake 5-10 minutes longer or until golden brown.

YIELD: 1 LOAF.

spice mix for chili

VIVIAN HUIZINGA
SHALLOW LAKE, ONTARIO

This spice mix comes from my mother's chili recipe, which is fantastic. It'll make a great gift for the hearty eaters you know, especially if you pair it with a loaf of bread.

- 3-1/2 teaspoons garlic salt
- 3-1/2 teaspoons chili powder
- 2 teaspoons *each* salt, onion powder, pepper, ground cumin, paprika and dried parsley flakes
- 1/2 teaspoon cayenne pepper

ADDITIONAL INGREDIENTS (FOR EACH BATCH):
- 1 pound ground beef
- 1 medium onion, chopped
- 1 cup sliced fresh mushrooms, optional
- 1 can (28 ounces) diced tomatoes, undrained
- 1 can (16 ounces) kidney beans, rinsed and drained
- 1 can (16 ounces) hot chili beans, undrained
- 1 can (10-3/4 ounces) condensed tomato soup, undiluted
- 1 teaspoon Worcestershire sauce
- 2 garlic cloves, minced
Shredded cheddar cheese

1 In a small bowl, combine all of the seasonings. Store in an airtight container in a cool dry place for up to 6 months.

YIELD: 3 BATCHES
(ABOUT 6 TABLESPOONS TOTAL).

2 **To prepare chili:** In a large saucepan or Dutch oven, cook the beef, onion and mushrooms if desired over medium heat until the meat is no longer pink; drain.

3 Stir in the tomatoes, beans, soup, 2 tablespoons spice mix, Worcestershire sauce and garlic. Bring to a boil. Reduce heat; cover and simmer for 20 minutes, stirring occasionally. Garnish with cheese.

YIELD: 8-10 SERVINGS.

hearty pasta soup mix

TASTE OF HOME TEST KITCHEN

Warm up loved ones on frosty winter nights with a gift of this hearty, stick-to-the-ribs soup mix. Layered in pretty bow-tied jars, it looks just as good as it tastes! Be sure to include preparation instructions and a list of any additional ingredients needed with your gift card.

- 1/2 cup dried split peas
- 2 tablespoons chicken bouillon granules
- 1/2 cup dried lentils
- 2 tablespoons dried minced onion
- 1 teaspoon dried basil
- 1 teaspoon dried parsley flakes
- 1 envelope savory herb with garlic soup mix *or* vegetable soup mix
- 2 cups uncooked tricolor spiral pasta

ADDITIONAL INGREDIENTS:

- 10 cups water
- 3 cups cubed cooked chicken
- 1 can (28 ounces) diced tomatoes, undrained

1 In a 1-qt. glass container, layer the first seven ingredients in the order listed. Place the pasta in a 1-qt. resealable plastic bag; add to the jar. Seal tightly.

YIELD: 1 BATCH (4 CUPS).

2 **To prepare soup:** Remove pasta from top of jar and set aside. Place water in a Dutch oven; stir in soup mix. Bring to a boil. Reduce heat; cover and simmer for 45 minutes. Add the chicken, tomatoes and pasta. Cover and simmer for 15-20 minutes longer or until pasta, peas and lentils are tender.

YIELD: 14 SERVINGS (3-1/2 QUARTS).

herb bubble bread

JOAN ANDERSON | WEST COVINA, CALIFORNIA

This bread is an absolute must! I never have leftovers. Fun to eat and delicious to enjoy, this recipe will be a hit with any crowd.

- 1/2 cup grated Parmesan cheese
- 3/4 teaspoon dried parsley flakes
- 1/4 teaspoon dill weed
- 1/8 teaspoon *each* dried thyme, basil and rosemary, crushed
- 1/4 cup butter, melted
- 2 teaspoons minced garlic
- 1 loaf (1 pound) frozen bread dough, thawed

1 In a small bowl, combine cheese and seasonings. In another bowl, combine butter and garlic; set aside.

2 Divide dough into 16 pieces. Roll into balls. Coat balls in butter mixture, then dip in cheese mixture. Place in a greased 9-in. x 5-in. loaf pan.

3 Cover and let rise in a warm place until doubled, about 1 hour. Bake at 350° for 22-26 minutes or until golden brown. (Cover loosely with foil if top browns too quickly.) Cool for 10 minutes before removing from the pan to a wire rack. Serve warm.

YIELD: 16 SERVINGS.

savory biscuit bites

WENDY CHILTON | BROOKELAND, TEXAS

These light, golden puffs are super simple to make, and their flavor is oh-so-good. Their small size makes them easy to munch, and they're wonderful warm or cold.

- 1/4 cup butter, melted
- 2 tablespoons grated Parmesan cheese
- 1 tablespoon dried minced onion
- 1-1/2 teaspoons dried parsley flakes
- 1 tube (12 ounces) refrigerated biscuits

1 In a small bowl, combine the butter, cheese, onion and parsley. Cut biscuits into quarters; roll in butter mixture. Place in a greased 15-in. x 10-in. x 1-in. baking pan; let stand for 25 minutes.

2 Bake at 400° for 8 minutes or until lightly browned.

YIELD: 40 PIECES.

homemade onion soup mix

I am on a very low-salt diet and struggle when making some of the old recipes my husband likes. For example, several casseroles call for very high-sodium ingredients like onion soup mix. So I came up with a handy substitute. I use two packets of very low-sodium beef bouillon powder and 2 tablespoons of dried minced onion. This doesn't significantly change the taste or texture of the dish. But because it now has only 10-15 mg of sodium instead of 400-500 mg, we both can enjoy it.

SUE T., PASADENA, CALIFORNIA

keep dried herbs fresh

Dried herbs don't spoil, but they do lose flavor and potency over time. For maximum flavor in your cooking, you may want to replace herbs that are over a year old. Store dried herbs in airtight containers and keep them away from heat and light. Don't put them in the cupboard above the stove.

TASTE OF HOME TEST KITCHEN

making soup mix a gift

To make a soup mix into a gift, put the assembled mix in a decorated jar, then into a larger basket along with a couple other items. Things you might consider are cans of additional ingredients needed to prepare a batch of the soup, a baked loaf of homemade bread, a package of purchased bread sticks or a large mug. Don't forget to include the recipe for preparing the soup from the mix!

TASTE OF HOME TEST KITCHEN

decorative jar covers

Here's an easy way to put pretty cloth toppers and a bow on jars of homemade soup mix, jelly etc.: Cut a circular piece of cloth to fit over the lid of the jar with a little extra to fold over the top. Put the cloth over the jar and use a rubber band to hold it in place. Tie a ribbon around the jar, then carefully snip off the rubber band.

CHARLOTTE S., HARRISONBURG, VIRGINIA

cheese flatbread

SHARON DELANEY-CHRONIS
SOUTH MILWAUKEE, WISCONSIN

The convenience of frozen bread dough and dried herbs makes this treat about as easy as it gets. To boost fiber, you can also use frozen whole wheat bread dough.

- 1 loaf (1 pound) frozen bread dough, thawed
- 2 tablespoons butter, softened
- 2 teaspoons paprika
- 1/2 teaspoon garlic powder
- 1/2 teaspoon dried oregano
- 1/2 teaspoon dried basil
- 1 cup (4 ounces) shredded part-skim mozzarella cheese

1 On a lightly floured surface, roll dough into a 16-in. x 11-in. rectangle. Transfer to a 15-in. x 10-in. x 1-in. baking pan coated with cooking spray; build up edges slightly. Spread with butter. Sprinkle with paprika, garlic powder, oregano and basil. Prick the dough several times with a fork; sprinkle with cheese. Cover and let rise for 30 minutes.

2 Bake at 375° for 20-25 minutes or until crust is golden brown and cheese is melted. Serve warm.

YIELD: 16 SERVINGS.

pasta fagioli soup mix

TAMRA DUNCAN | CASTLE, OKLAHOMA

This meatless soup is both economical and flavorful. Church groups could buy the ingredients in bulk and assemble mixes to give to shut-ins or other community groups.

- 1 cup small pasta shells
- 3/4 cup dried great northern beans
- 3/4 cup dried pinto beans
- 3/4 cup dried kidney beans
- 1/4 cup dried minced onion
- 3 tablespoons dried parsley flakes
- 1 teaspoon dried basil
- 1 teaspoon dried oregano
- 1/2 teaspoon dried rosemary, crushed
- 1/4 teaspoon dried minced garlic
- 1 bay leaf

Dash crushed red pepper flakes

ADDITIONAL INGREDIENTS:

- 14 cups water, *divided*
- 1 can (28 ounces) diced tomatoes, undrained
- 3 medium carrots, chopped
- 1 celery rib, chopped
- 1 teaspoon salt

Grated Parmesan cheese, optional

1 Place pasta in a small resealable plastic bag; place in a 1-qt. glass jar. Layer with beans. Place seasonings in another plastic bag; place in jar. Cover and store in a cool dry place for up to 3 months.

YIELD: 1 BATCH.

2 **To prepare soup:** Remove seasoning packet from jar. Remove beans; sort and rinse. Set pasta aside.

3 Place beans in a Dutch oven; add 6 cups water. Bring to a boil; boil for 2 minutes. Remove from the heat; cover and let stand for 1 to 4 hours or until beans are softened. Drain and discard liquid.

4 Return beans to the pan. Add contents of seasoning packet and remaining water. Bring to a boil. Reduce heat; cover and simmer for 1 hour or until beans are tender. Add the tomatoes, carrots, celery and salt; cover and simmer 30 minutes longer, stirring occasionally.

5 Stir in the pasta. Cover and simmer for 5-10 minutes or until pasta and carrots are tender, stirring occasionally. Remove bay leaf before serving. Garnish with cheese if desired.

YIELD: 14 SERVINGS (3-1/2 QUARTS).

bazaar soup mix

PEARL BROCK | COUDERSPORT, PENNSYLVANIA

Our women's group assembles this soup mix to give to visitors and to sell at our annual bazaar. Each container is labeled with the directions to make it and additional ingredients needed.

- 1/4 cup dried lentils, sorted
- 1/4 cup dried green split peas, sorted
- 1/4 cup uncooked long grain rice
- 2 tablespoons medium pearl barley
- 4 teaspoons beef *or* chicken bouillon granules
- 2 tablespoons dried minced onion
- 1 teaspoon celery salt
- 1/2 teaspoon Italian seasoning
- 3 tablespoons dried parsley flakes
- 1/2 cup uncooked small pasta shells

ADDITIONAL INGREDIENTS:

- 1/2 pound ground beef
- 8 cups water
- 1 can (14-1/2 ounces) diced tomatoes, undrained

1 In a 1-pint jar or container with a tight-fitting lid, layer the first nine ingredients in the order listed. Wrap pasta in a small piece of plastic wrap; add to jar. Seal tightly. Store in a cool dry place for up to 3 months.

YIELD: 1 BATCH (1-1/2 CUPS).

2 **To prepare soup:** Remove pasta from top of jar and set aside. In a Dutch oven, cook beef over medium heat until no longer pink; drain. Add the water, tomatoes and soup mix; bring to a boil. Reduce heat; cover and simmer for 45 minutes.

3 Stir in reserved pasta; cover and simmer 15-20 minutes longer or until pasta, lentils, peas and barley are tender.

YIELD: 8 SERVINGS (2 QUARTS).

three-cheese twists

JUNE POEPPING | QUINCY, ILLINOIS

My daughter has given me many great recipes, but this is one of my favorites. Although these tasty twists look like you fussed, convenient frozen dinner rolls hurry along the preparation. I usually serve them with chili, but they're great with a salad, too.

- 1/2 cup butter, melted
- 1/4 teaspoon garlic salt
- 1-1/2 cups (6 ounces) finely shredded cheddar cheese
- 1-1/2 cups (6 ounces) finely shredded part-skim mozzarella cheese
- 3/4 cup grated Parmesan cheese
- 1 tablespoon dried parsley flakes
- 24 frozen bread dough dinner rolls, thawed

1 In a shallow bowl, combine butter and garlic salt. In another shallow bowl, combine cheeses and parsley. On a lightly floured surface, roll each dinner roll into a 10-in. rope. Dip in butter mixture, then in cheese mixture.

2 Fold each rope in half and twist twice; pinch the ends together to seal. Place 2-in. apart on greased baking sheets. Cover and let rise in a warm place until almost doubled, about 30 minutes.

3 Bake at 350° for 15 minutes or until golden brown.

YIELD: 2 DOZEN.

italian garlic breadsticks

TASTE OF HOME TEST KITCHEN

A seasoned Parmesan cheese coating gives refrigerated breadsticks a terrific taste twist. The wonderful aroma of these breadsticks baking is so irresistible you just may need to make another batch!

- 1/2 cup grated Parmesan cheese
- 2 teaspoons Italian seasoning
- 1 teaspoon garlic powder
- 1/4 cup butter, melted
- 1 tube (11 ounces) refrigerated breadsticks

1 In a shallow bowl, combine the cheese, Italian seasoning and the garlic powder. Place the butter in another shallow bowl. Separate the dough into individual breadsticks. Dip in butter, then in cheese mixture. Twist 2-3 times and place on an ungreased baking sheet.

2 Bake at 375° for 12-14 minutes or until golden brown. Serve immediately.

YIELD: 1 DOZEN.

savory pull apart bread

JANNE ROWE | WICHITA, KANSAS

This yummy pull apart bread is perfect for any gathering. Give it a try!

- 1/4 cup grated Parmesan cheese
- 3 tablespoons sesame seeds
- 1/2 teaspoon dried basil
- 1 package (30 ounces) frozen roll dough (24 rolls)
- 1/4 cup butter, melted
- 2 tablespoons bacon bits, optional

1 In a small bowl, combine the Parmesan cheese, sesame seeds and basil; sprinkle one-third in the bottom and up the sides of a greased 12-cup fluted tube pan.

2 Place half of the thawed rolls in pan; drizzle with half of the butter. Sprinkle with half of the remaining cheese mixture and bacon bits if desired. Arrange remaining rolls on top; drizzle with remaining butter. Sprinkle with remaining cheese mixture. Cover and refrigerate overnight.

3 Remove from the refrigerator 30 minutes before baking. Bake at 350° for 20 minutes. Cover loosely with foil; bake 10-15 minutes longer.

YIELD: 10-12 SERVINGS.

butter alternative

Our Test Kitchen home economists use butter in recipes for a variety of reasons. In some recipes, we felt that butter adds a rich flavor that margarine would not achieve. Also, because labeling laws have changed, there's some confusion on the part of consumers as to how margarine is defined. Both butter and margarine contain 80% fat. Margarine is a butter substitute made with vegetable oils. Margarine in stick form can generally be used in place of butter unless the distinct flavor of butter is key to the recipe, as with butter cookies.

TASTE OF HOME TEST KITCHEN

cutting & chopping techniques

MINCING AND CHOPPING

Holding the handle of a chef's knife with one hand, rest the fingers of your other hand on the top of the blade near the tip. Using the handle to guide and apply pressure, move knife in an arc across the food with a rocking motion until pieces of food are the desired size. Mincing results in pieces no larger than 1/8 in., and chopping can produce 1/4-in. to 1/2-in. pieces.

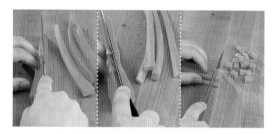

DICING AND CUBING VEGETABLES

1) Using a utility knife, trim each side of the vegetable, squaring it off. Cut lengthwise into evenly spaced strips. The narrower the strips, the smaller the pieces will be. Dicing results in 1/8-in. to 1/4-in. uniform pieces, and cubing yields 1/2-in. to 1-in. uniform pieces.

2) Stack the strips and cut lengthwise into uniform-sized strips.

3) Arrange the square-shaped strips into a pile and cut widthwise into cubes.

SLICING OR CHOPPING A SWEET PEPPER

1) To slice or chop, cut each side from pepper by cutting close to the stem and down. Discard top and scrape out seeds. Cut away any ribs.

2) Place cut side down on work surface and flatten slightly with your hand. Cut lengthwise into strips, then widthwise into pieces if desired.

CHOPPING AN ONION

1) To quickly chop an onion, peel and cut in half from the root to the top. Leaving the root attached, place flat side down on work surface. Cut vertically through the onion, leaving the root end uncut.

2) Cut across the onion, discarding root end. The closer the cuts, the finer the onion will be chopped. This method can also be used for shallots.

PEELING AND MINCING FRESH GARLIC

Using the blade of a chef's knife, crush garlic clove. Peel away skin. Mince as directed at top left.

SNIPPING FRESH HERBS

Hold herbs over a small bowl and make 1/8-in. to 1/4-in. cuts with a kitchen shears.

FREEZING HERBS

You can freeze chopped herbs in freezer containers or bags and just use the amount you need directly from the freezer.

p. 153

p. 161

p. 187

TABLE OF CONTENTS

PAGE 144
pasta pizza soup

PAGE 184
pasta fagioli soup

PAGE 236
heartwarming chili

MAKING HOMEMADE BROTH

Remove the excess fat from meat. In a kettle or Dutch oven, combine meat, vegetables, cold water and seasonings.

Bring to a boil over low heat. Skim foam as it rises to the top of the water. Reduce heat; cover and simmer until the meat is tender, about 1 hour.

Start making a stock with cold water. Just cover the bones, meat and/or vegetables with water. Add seasonings but do not add salt. Bring slowly to a boil over low heat. Using a ladle, skim foam from the top of liquid. If water evaporates, add enough additional water to cover the bones, meat and/or vegetables. Skim fat or remove solidified fat after chilling. Strain stock; divide among several containers. Place containers in an ice bath to cool quickly. When chilled, refrigerate or freeze.

Add little or no salt, as well as other flavors, when making stock since it concentrates as it simmers and the liquid evaporates. Taste the soup when it is just about ready to be served and add enough salt to suit your family's preferences.

Add a pinch of turmeric or simmer an unpeeled whole yellow onion in the cooking liquid for golden homemade chicken and turkey broths.

Store soups in the refrigerator for up to 3 days. If there is rice or pasta in the soup, you may want to cook and store them separately, since they may continue to absorb the liquid.

Many broth-based soups freeze well for up to 3 months. Thaw in the refrigerator before reheating. It's best not to freeze soups prepared with potatoes, fruit, cheese, sour cream, yogurt, eggs, milk or cream.

homemade beef broth

TASTE OF HOME TEST KITCHEN

Roasting the soup bones brings out delicious beefy flavors for this soup base. It refrigerates and freezes well to use as needed.

- 4 pounds meaty beef soup bones (beef shanks or short ribs)
- 3 medium carrots, cut into chunks
- 3 celery ribs, cut into chunks
- 2 medium onions, quartered
- 1/2 cup warm water
- 3 bay leaves
- 3 garlic cloves
- 8 to 10 whole peppercorns
- 3 to 4 sprigs fresh parsley
- 1 teaspoon each dried thyme, marjoram and oregano
- 3 quarts cold water

- Place soup bones in a large roasting pan. Bake, uncovered, at 450° for 30 minutes. Add the carrots, celery and onions. Bake 30 minutes longer; drain fat.

- Using a slotted spoon, transfer bones and vegetables to a large Dutch oven. Add warm water to the roasting pan; stir to loosen browned bits from pan. Transfer pan juices to kettle. Add seasonings and enough cold water just to cover.

- Slowly bring to a boil, about 30 minutes. Reduce heat; simmer, uncovered, for 4-5 hours, skimming the surface as foam rises. If necessary, add hot water during the first 2 hours to keep ingredients covered.

- Remove beef bones and set aside until cool enough to handle. If desired, remove meat from bones; discard bones and save meat for another use. Strain broth through a cheesecloth-lined colander, discarding vegetables and seasonings.

Remove the fat

Remove meat; let stand until cool enough to handle. Remove meat from bones; discard bones. Dice meat; use immediately or cover and refrigerate. Chill broth several hours or overnight; lift fat from surface of broth and discard.

Strain the broth

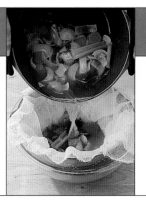

Remove meat and bones from stock. Line a colander with a double thickness of cheesecloth; place in a large heat-resistant bowl. Pour stock into colander. Discard vegetables, seasonings and cheesecloth. For a clear stock or broth, do not press liquid from vegetables and seasonings in the colander.

- If using immediately, skim fat or refrigerate for 8 hours or overnight, then remove fat from surface. Broth can be covered and refrigerated for up to 3 days or frozen for 4 to 6 months.

Yield: about 2-1/2 quarts.

homemade chicken broth

NILA GRAHL, GURNEE, ILLINOIS

Whether you're making a chicken soup or just a broth to use in other dishes, this recipe makes a tasty base for most anything.

- 1 broiler/fryer chicken (3 to 4 pounds), cut up
- 10 cups water
- 1 large carrot, sliced
- 1 large onion, sliced
- 1 celery rib, sliced
- 1 garlic clove, minced
- 1 bay leaf
- 1 teaspoon each dried thyme and salt
- 1/4 teaspoon pepper

- In a large soup kettle or Dutch oven, combine all the ingredients. Slowly bring to a boil over low heat. Cover and simmer for 45-60 minutes or until the meat is tender, skimming the surface as foam rises.

- Remove chicken and set aside until cool enough to handle. Remove and discard skin and bones. Chop chicken; set aside for soup or save for another use.

- Strain broth through a cheesecloth-lined colander, discarding vegetables and bay leaf. If using immediately, skim fat or refrigerate for 8 hours or overnight, then remove fat from surface. Broth can be covered and refrigerated for up to 3 days or frozen for 4 to 6 months.

Yield: about 2 quarts.

homemade vegetable broth

TASTE OF HOME TEST KITCHEN

The flavors of celery and mushrooms come through in this homemade vegetable broth. You can use it in place of chicken or beef broth.

- 2 tablespoons olive oil
- 2 medium onions, cut into wedges
- 2 celery ribs, cut into 1-inch pieces
- 1 whole garlic bulb, separated into cloves and peeled
- 3 medium leeks, white and light green parts only, cleaned and cut into 1-inch pieces
- 3 medium carrots, cut into 1-inch pieces
- 8 cups water
- 1/2 pound fresh mushrooms, quartered
- 1 cup packed fresh parsley sprigs
- 4 sprigs fresh thyme
- 1 teaspoon salt
- 1/2 teaspoon whole peppercorns
- 1 bay leaf

- Heat oil in a stockpot over medium heat until hot. Add the onions, celery and garlic. Cook and stir for 5 minutes or until tender. Add leeks and carrots; cook and stir 5 minutes longer. Add the water, mushrooms, parsley, thyme, salt, peppercorns and bay leaf; bring to a boil. Reduce heat; simmer, uncovered, for 1 hour.

- Remove from the heat. Strain through a cheesecloth-lined colander; discard vegetables. If using immediately, skim fat or refrigerate for 8 hours or overnight, then remove fat from surface. Broth can be covered and refrigerated for up to 3 days or frozen for up to 4 to 6 months.

Yield: 5-1/2 cups.

BEEF & GROUND BEEF

You will find a surprising number of ways to "beef up" your soup recipe collection in this chapter. Stir up kettles that include ground beef, leftover roast, stew meat and even steak that partner with nutritious veggies, pasta, rice or tortilla chips to create combinations that your family will savor. Be prepared for compliments to the cook!

italian wedding soup

italian wedding soup

NOELLE MYERS, GRAND FORKS, NORTH DAKOTA

I enjoyed a similar soup for lunch at work one day and decided to re-create it at home. I love the combination of meatballs, vegetables and pasta.

      2   eggs, lightly beaten
   1/2   cup seasoned bread crumbs
      1   pound ground beef
      1   pound bulk Italian sausage
      3   medium carrots, sliced
      3   celery ribs, diced
      1   large onion, chopped
      3   garlic cloves, minced
  4-1/2 teaspoons olive oil
      4   cans (14-1/2 ounces each) reduced-sodium chicken broth
      2   cans (14-1/2 ounces each) beef broth
      1   package (10 ounces) frozen chopped spinach, thawed and squeezed dry
   1/4   cup minced fresh basil
      1   envelope onion soup mix
  4-1/2 teaspoons ketchup
   1/2   teaspoon dried thyme
      3   bay leaves
  1-1/2 cups uncooked penne pasta

- In a large bowl, combine eggs and bread crumbs. Crumble beef and sausage over mixture; mix well. Shape into 3/4-in. balls.

- Place meatballs on a greased rack in a foil-lined 15-in. x 10-in. x 1-in. baking pan. Bake at 350° for 15-18 minutes or until meatballs are no longer pink.

- Meanwhile, in a soup kettle or Dutch oven, saute carrots, celery, onion and garlic in oil until tender. Stir in the broth, spinach, basil, soup mix, ketchup, thyme and bay leaves.

- Drain meatballs on paper towels. Bring soup to a boil; add meatballs. Reduce heat; simmer, uncovered, for 30 minutes. Add pasta; cook 13-15 minutes longer or until pasta is tender, stirring occasionally. Discard bay leaves before serving.

Yield: 10 servings.

baked beefy onion soup

JEANNE ROBINSON, CINNAMINSON, NEW JERSEY

This is the only onion soup recipe I know of that is baked in a casserole, making it easy to serve to a crowd as a first course. I love this recipe for dinner parties because it can be made ahead. The rich soup can also be a meal in itself.

  1-1/2 pounds meaty beef soup bones
      2   quarts water
      1   medium carrot, quartered
      4   black peppercorns
      3   teaspoons beef bouillon granules
      2   sprigs fresh parsley
      2   large onions, thinly sliced
   1/4   cup butter
      6   slices French bread (1/2 inch thick)
      6   slices Swiss cheese

- In a soup kettle, combine the first six ingredients. Bring to a boil over medium-high heat. Reduce heat; cover and simmer for 3 hours. Strain the broth, discarding soup bones, carrot and seasoning; skim fat.

- Meanwhile, in a large skillet, saute the onions in butter over medium heat for 30 minutes or until golden brown. Divide the onions among six ovenproof bowls. Ladle about 1 cup broth onto each. Top each with a slice of bread and Swiss cheese. Bake at 350° for 50-55 minutes or until golden brown.

Yield: 6 servings.

baked beefy onion soup

pasta pizza soup

pasta pizza soup

LINDA FOX, SOLDOTNA, ALASKA

A steaming bowl of this soup hits the spot on a cold rainy or snowy day, which we have in abundance here. Oregano adds fast flavor to the pleasant combination of tender vegetables, pasta spirals and ground beef.

1   pound ground beef
4   ounces sliced fresh mushrooms
1   medium onion, chopped
1   celery rib, thinly sliced
1   garlic clove, minced
4   cups water
1   can (14-1/2 ounces) Italian diced tomatoes, undrained
2   medium carrots, sliced
4   teaspoons beef bouillon granules
1   bay leaf
1-1/2 teaspoons dried oregano
1-1/2 cups cooked tricolor spiral pasta

■ In a large saucepan over medium heat, cook beef, mushrooms, onion, celery and garlic until meat is no longer pink and vegetables are tender; drain. Stir in water, tomatoes, carrots, bouillon, bay leaf and oregano. Bring to a boil. Reduce heat; cover and simmer for 20-25 minutes or until carrots are tender. Stir in pasta; heat through. Discard bay leaf.

Yield: 8 servings.

To chop carrots coarsely for soup, I peel, remove the ends and cut the carrots into quarters. Then I let the food processor do the chopping!
—Marion K., Waterloo, Iowa

steak 'n' vegetable soup

EDIE DESPAIN, LOGAN, UTAH

This tasty soup calls for a lot of fresh herbs to enhance the flavor of the other ingredients. The aroma while it is cooking is absolutely wonderful. I like to serve steaming bowls alongside a green salad and baking powder biscuits.

1   pound boneless beef sirloin steak, cut into 1/2-inch cubes
1   cup chopped onion
2   teaspoons canola oil
2   cups cubed red potatoes
1   cup chopped carrots
1   cup frozen peas
1   can (14-1/2 ounces) beef broth
1   cup water
2   tablespoons balsamic vinegar
1   tablespoon minced fresh parsley
1   tablespoon minced chives
1-1/2 teaspoons minced fresh basil or 1/2 teaspoon dried basil
1   teaspoon minced fresh thyme or 1/4 teaspoon dried thyme
3/4 teaspoon salt
1/4 teaspoon pepper

■ In a large saucepan, cook beef and onion in oil until meat is no longer pink; drain. Stir

steak 'n' vegetable soup

beef vegetable soup

in the potatoes, carrots and peas. Add the broth, water, vinegar, parsley, chives, basil, thyme, salt and pepper. Bring to a boil. Reduce heat; cover and simmer for 20-30 minutes or until the meat and vegetables are tender.

Yield: 6 servings.

beef vegetable soup

COLLEEN JUBL, DAYTON, OHIO

Here's a slow-cooked meal-in-one just perfect for chilly winter nights. It's nice to come home to a dinner that's ready to eat. It goes well with a fruit salad and bread.

- 1 **pound ground beef**
- 1 **medium onion, chopped**
- 2 **garlic cloves, minced**
- 4 **cups picante V8 juice**
- 2 **cups coleslaw mix**
- 1 **can (14-1/2 ounces) Italian stewed tomatoes**
- 1 **package (10 ounces) frozen corn**
- 1 **package (9 ounces) frozen cut green beans**
- 2 **tablespoons Worcestershire sauce**
- 1 **teaspoon dried basil**
- 1/4 **teaspoon pepper**

■ In a large nonstick skillet, cook the beef, onion and garlic over medium heat until meat is no longer pink; drain. Transfer to a 5-qt. slow cooker. Stir in the remaining ingredients. Cover and cook on high for 4-5 hours or until heated through.

Yield: 9 servings.

stuffed pepper soup

TRACY THOMPSON, CRANESVILLE, PENNSYLVANIA

This is an excellent example of how convenience foods can be combined for a tasty entree. Ready in minutes when I get home from work, this soup becomes part of a balanced meal with a tossed salad, rolls or fruit. For variation, try chicken, turkey or even venison instead of ground beef.

- 1 **pouch (8.8 ounces) ready-to-serve long grain and wild rice**
- 1 **pound ground beef**
- 2 **cups frozen chopped green peppers, thawed**
- 1 **cup chopped onion**
- 1 **jar (26 ounces) chunky tomato pasta sauce**
- 1 **can (14-1/2 ounces) Italian diced tomatoes, undrained**
- 1 **can (14 ounces) beef broth**

■ Prepare rice according to package directions. Meanwhile, in a large saucepan, cook the beef, green peppers and onion until meat is no longer pink; drain. Stir in the pasta sauce, tomatoes, broth and prepared rice; heat through.

Yield: 6-8 servings.

stuffed pepper soup

vegetable steak soup

BRIGITTE SCHULTZ, BARSTOW, CALIFORNIA

Your crew will chase away winter's chill with a spoon when you cook up this soup. It has such a rich flavor, and it's packed with chunks of tender steak to curb big appetites.

- 1 pound boneless beef sirloin steak, cut into 1/2-inch cubes
- 1/4 teaspoon pepper, divided
- 2 teaspoons olive oil
- 2 cans (14-1/2 ounces each) beef broth
- 2 cups cubed peeled potatoes
- 1-1/4 cups water
- 2 medium carrots, sliced
- 1 tablespoon onion soup mix
- 1 tablespoon dried basil
- 1/2 teaspoon dried tarragon
- 2 tablespoons cornstarch
- 1/2 cup white wine or additional beef broth

- Sprinkle steak with 1/8 teaspoon pepper. In a Dutch oven, brown steak in batches in oil over medium heat. Add the broth, potatoes, water, carrots, onion soup mix, basil, tarragon and remaining pepper; bring to a boil. Reduce heat; cover and simmer for 20-25 minutes or until vegetables are tender.

- In a small bowl, combine the cornstarch and

pasta beef soup

wine or additional broth until smooth; stir into soup. Bring to a boil; cook and stir for 2 minutes or until thickened.

Yield: 7 servings.

pasta beef soup

BRENDA JACKSON, GARDEN CITY, KANSAS

You'll be thankful for this simple-to-prepare soup when you have a busy day and need to prepare dinner in a hurry. It's chock-full of nutritious veggies, too!

- 1 pound ground beef
- 2 cans (14-1/2 ounces each) beef broth
- 1 package (16 ounces) frozen pasta with broccoli, corn and carrots in garlic-seasoned sauce
- 1-1/2 cups tomato juice
- 1 can (14-1/2 ounces) diced tomatoes, undrained
- 2 teaspoons Italian seasoning
- 1/4 cup shredded Parmesan cheese, optional

- In a large saucepan, cook beef over medium heat until no longer pink; drain. Add the broth, pasta with vegetables, tomato juice, tomatoes and Italian seasoning; bring to a boil. Reduce heat; cover and simmer for 10 minutes or until vegetables are tender. Serve with Parmesan cheese if desired.

Yield: 6 servings.

vegetable steak soup

beef 'n' black bean soup

VICKIE GIBSON, GARDENDALE, ALABAMA

I lead a busy life, so I'm always trying to come up with time-saving recipes. This zippy and colorful soup is one of my husband's favorites. It has been a hit at family gatherings, too.

- 1 pound ground beef
- 2 cans (14-1/2 ounces each) chicken broth
- 1 can (14-1/2 ounces) diced tomatoes, undrained
- 8 green onions, thinly sliced
- 3 medium carrots, thinly sliced
- 2 celery ribs, thinly sliced
- 2 garlic cloves, minced
- 1 tablespoon sugar
- 1-1/2 teaspoons dried basil
- 1/2 teaspoon salt
- 1/2 teaspoon dried oregano
- 1/2 teaspoon ground cumin
- 1/2 teaspoon chili powder
- 2 cans (15 ounces each) black beans, rinsed and drained
- 1-1/2 cups cooked rice

- In a skillet over medium heat, cook beef until no longer pink; drain. Transfer to a 5-qt. slow cooker. Add the next 12 ingredients. Cover and cook on high for 1 hour. Reduce heat to low; cook for 4-5 hours or until vegetables are tender. Add the beans and rice; cook 1 hour longer or until heated through.

Yield: 10 servings.

Having leftover cooked rice in the refrigerator is quite a time-saver. I can quickly make fried rice, Spanish rice, rice pilaf, rice pudding and even add it to soups.
—Grace R., Wrightwood, California

easy hamburger soup

easy hamburger soup

MARY PRIOR, RUSH CITY, MINNESOTA

Lunches on the run will be a little tastier with this hot and satisfying beef and barley soup. The recipe is very simple to prepare.

- 1-1/2 pounds ground beef
- 1 medium onion, chopped
- 1 can (28 ounces) diced tomatoes, undrained
- 2 cans (14-1/2 ounces each) beef broth
- 1 cup water
- 4 celery ribs, thinly sliced
- 4 large carrots, halved and thinly sliced
- 10 whole peppercorns
- 1 teaspoon dried thyme
- 1/2 teaspoon salt
- 1/2 cup quick-cooking barley
- 1/4 cup minced fresh parsley

- In a large saucepan, cook beef and onion over medium heat until meat is no longer pink; drain. Stir in the tomatoes, broth and water. Add celery and carrots.

- Place peppercorns on a double thickness of cheesecloth; bring up corners of cloth and tie with kitchen string to form a bag. Add to beef mixture. Stir in thyme and salt. Bring to a boil. Reduce heat; cover and simmer for 45 minutes or until vegetables are tender.

- Return to a boil. Stir in barley. Reduce heat; cover and simmer for 10-12 minutes or until barley is tender. Remove from the heat; stir in parsley. Let stand for 5 minutes. Discard spice bag.

Yield: 8 servings.

beef 'n' black bean soup

beef goulash soup

beef goulash soup

SHARON BICKETT, CHESTER, SOUTH CAROLINA

Paprika, cayenne pepper and caraway spice up tender chunks of beef, potatoes and carrots in this tantalizing tomato-based soup. I garnish each bowl with a dollop of sour cream.

- 2 **pounds boneless beef sirloin steak, cut into 1/2-inch cubes**
- 1 **large onion, chopped**
- 1 **large green pepper, chopped**
- 2 **tablespoons olive oil**
- 3 **medium potatoes, peeled and cubed**
- 3 **medium carrots, chopped**
- 4 **cups beef broth**
- 1 **cup water**
- 2 **tablespoons paprika**
- 1 **tablespoon sugar**
- 1 **to 2 teaspoons salt**
- 1/2 **teaspoon pepper**
- 1/4 **teaspoon cayenne pepper**
- 2 **bay leaves**
- 1 **can (28 ounces) crushed tomatoes**
- 1 **can (6 ounces) tomato paste**
- 2 **tablespoons caraway seeds**

Sour cream

- In a Dutch oven over medium-high heat, cook and stir the beef, onion and green pepper in oil until meat is browned on all sides; drain. Stir in the next 10 ingredients.

I wash and core my garden tomatoes, then puree in the blender with lemon juice, onion and celery to taste. This makes a great vegetable juice that we can drink or use in soups.
—Marion W., Greenfield, Wisconsin

Bring to a boil. Reduce heat; cover and simmer for 25-30 minutes or until the potatoes are tender.

- Stir in the tomatoes, tomato paste and caraway seeds. Cover and simmer 25-30 minutes longer or until meat is tender. Discard the bay leaves. Top each serving with a dollop of sour cream.

Yield: 16 servings.

beef noodle soup

ARLENE LYNN, LINCOLN, NEBRASKA

I take advantage of convenience items to prepare this yummy soup in a hurry. Bowls of the chunky mixture are chock-full of ground beef, noodles and vegetables.

- 1 **pound ground beef**
- 1 **can (46 ounces) V8 juice**
- 1 **envelope onion soup mix**
- 1 **package (3 ounces) beef ramen noodles**
- 1 **package (16 ounces) frozen mixed vegetables**

- In a large saucepan, cook beef over medium heat until no longer pink; drain. Stir in the V8 juice, soup mix, contents of noodle seasoning packet and mixed vegetables.

- Bring to a boil. Reduce heat and simmer, uncovered, for 6 minutes or until vegetables are tender. Return to a boil; stir in noodles. Cook for 3 minutes or until the noodles are tender.

Yield: 8 servings.

beef noodle soup

taco soup

thyme for meatball soup

Jennie Freeman, Long Creek, Oregon

Thyme is one of my favorite herbs to grow. It adds a fresh spark to this veggie-packed soup.

- 1 egg
- 1/4 cup dry bread crumbs
- 2 tablespoons minced fresh thyme or 2 teaspoons dried thyme, divided
- 1/2 teaspoon salt
- 1-1/2 pounds ground beef
- 1 small onion, chopped
- 2 medium carrots, chopped
- 3/4 pound fresh mushrooms, sliced
- 1 tablespoon olive oil
- 1-1/2 pounds red potatoes, cubed
- 2 cans (14-1/2 ounces each) beef broth
- 1 can (14-1/2 ounces) stewed tomatoes

- In a large bowl, combine egg, bread crumbs, half of the thyme and salt. Crumble beef over mixture and mix well. Shape into 1-in. balls. In a Dutch oven or soup kettle, brown meatballs; drain and set aside.

- In the same pan, saute onion, carrots and mushrooms in oil until onion is tender. Stir in the potatoes, broth, tomatoes, meatballs and remaining thyme. Bring to a boil. Reduce heat; cover and simmer for 25-30 minutes or until potatoes are tender.

Yield: 12 servings.

taco soup

Sue Burton, Frankfort, Kansas

This is a quick-and-easy recipe to make, and it's one of our favorite meals for cold winter nights.

- 1-1/2 pounds ground beef
- 1 large onion, chopped
- 1 can (15 ounces) pinto beans, rinsed and drained
- 1 can (14-1/2 ounces) stewed tomatoes
- 1 can (10 ounces) diced tomatoes and green chilies
- 1 can (10 ounces) chili without beans
- 1 pound process cheese (Velveeta), cubed

Salt, pepper and garlic powder to taste
- 2 cups (16 ounces) sour cream, divided

- In a Dutch oven or soup kettle, cook beef and onion over medium heat until meat is no longer pink; drain. Add the beans, tomatoes, chili, cheese and seasonings. Reduce heat to low; cook and stir until cheese is melted. Stir in 1 cup sour cream; heat through (do not boil). Garnish with remaining sour cream.

Yield: 3-1/4 quarts.

thyme for meatball soup

chunky taco soup

EVELYN BUFORD, BELTON, MISSOURI

I've gotten great responses at our church dinners and senior groups whenever I bring this thick, easy-to-fix soup. I usually take home an empty pot and often get requests for the recipe. The flavor seems to improve with leftovers—if there are any!

1-1/2	pounds boneless beef sirloin or round steak, cut into 3/4-inch cubes
1	medium onion, chopped
1	tablespoon olive oil
2	cans (15 ounces each) pinto beans, rinsed and drained
2	cans (14-1/2 ounces each) diced tomatoes and green chilies, undrained
2	cups water
1	can (15 ounces) black beans, rinsed and drained
1	can (14-3/4 ounces) cream-style corn
1	envelope ranch salad dressing mix
1	envelope taco seasoning
1/4	cup minced fresh cilantro

■ In a large kettle or Dutch oven, brown beef and onion in oil. Add the pinto beans, tomatoes, water, black beans, corn, salad dressing mix and taco seasoning. Bring to a boil. Reduce heat; cover and simmer for 20-30 minutes or until the meat is tender. Sprinkle with cilantro.

Yield: 12 servings.

spicy chuck-wagon soup

spicy chuck-wagon soup

KELLY WILLIAMS, LA PORTE, INDIANA

Chunks of potatoes and carrots mix with pieces of beef roast to make this special soup. Cayenne gives it a little zip.

2	tablespoons all-purpose flour
1	tablespoon paprika
1	teaspoon plus 1 tablespoon chili powder, divided
2	teaspoons salt
1	teaspoon garlic powder
1	boneless beef chuck roast (3 pounds), cut into 1-inch pieces
1/4	cup canola oil
2	medium onions, chopped
1	can (28 ounces) stewed tomatoes, undrained
1	can (10-1/2 ounces) condensed beef broth, undiluted
1	bay leaf
1/4	to 1/2 teaspoon cayenne pepper
5	medium red potatoes, cubed
4	medium carrots, sliced
1	can (11 ounces) whole kernel corn, drained

■ In a large resealable plastic bag, combine the flour, paprika, 1 teaspoon chili powder, salt and garlic powder. Add beef, a few pieces at a time, and shake to coat.

■ In a large soup kettle, brown beef in oil in batches. Stir in the onions, tomatoes, broth, bay leaf, cayenne and remaining chili powder. Bring to a boil. Reduce heat; cover and simmer for 30 minutes, stirring occasionally.

chunky taco soup

- Add potatoes and carrots. Cover and simmer 35-40 minutes longer or until meat and vegetables are tender. Add corn and heat through. Discard bay leaf before serving.

Yield: 10 servings.

ground beef noodle soup

JUDY BRANDER, TWO HARBORS, MINNESOTA

This savory specialty combines ground beef with onions, celery and carrots. This is a wonderful fast soup to make any day of the week.

1-1/2	pounds ground beef
1/2	cup each chopped onion, celery and carrot
7	cups water
1	envelope au jus mix
2	tablespoons beef bouillon granules
2	bay leaves
1/8	teaspoon pepper
1-1/2	cups uncooked egg noodles

- In a large saucepan or Dutch oven, cook the beef, onion, celery and carrot over medium heat until meat is no longer pink and vegetables are tender; drain.

- Add the water, au jus mix, bouillon, bay leaves and pepper; bring to a boil. Stir in the noodles. Return to a boil. Cook, uncovered, for 15 minutes or until noodles are tender, stirring occasionally. Discard bay leaves before serving.

Yield: 8 servings.

hamburger minestrone

hamburger minestrone

MAUDIE BREEN, SALT LAKE CITY, UTAH

This hearty soup is filled with Italian seasoning, vegetables, ground beef and macaroni.

1	pound ground beef
1/2	cup chopped onion
1	garlic clove, minced
6	cups water
1	can (28 ounces) diced tomatoes, undrained
1-1/2	cups sliced zucchini
1	can (16 ounces) kidney beans, rinsed and drained
1-1/2	cups frozen whole kernel corn, thawed
1	cup shredded cabbage
1	celery rib with leaves, chopped
2	teaspoons beef bouillon granules
2	teaspoons Italian seasoning
3/4	teaspoon salt
1/2	cup uncooked elbow macaroni

- In a Dutch oven, cook the beef, onion and garlic over medium heat until meat is no longer pink; drain. Add the water, tomatoes, zucchini, beans, corn, cabbage, celery, bouillon, Italian seasoning and salt. Add macaroni. Bring to a boil. Reduce heat; cover and simmer for 15 minutes or until macaroni is tender.

Yield: 9 servings.

ground beef noodle soup

dumpling vegetable soup

dumpling vegetable soup

PEGGY LINTON, COBOURG, ONTARIO

Delicious rice dumplings give a homemade touch to this soup that takes advantage of canned goods, frozen vegetables and dry soup mix. My mom found this to be a quick, nourishing all-in-one-pot meal, and so do I.

  1/2 **pound ground beef**
    4 **cups water**
    1 **can (28 ounces) diced tomatoes, undrained**
    1 **package (10 ounces) frozen mixed vegetables**
    1 **envelope dry onion soup mix**
  1/2 **teaspoon dried oregano**
  1/4 **teaspoon pepper**

RICE DUMPLINGS:

1-1/4 **cups all-purpose flour**
    1 **teaspoon baking powder**
  1/2 **teaspoon salt**
    1 **tablespoon shortening**
  1/3 **cup cooked rice, room temperature**
    1 **tablespoon minced fresh parsley**
    1 **egg, lightly beaten**
  1/2 **cup milk**

■ In a Dutch oven, cook beef over medium heat until no longer pink; drain. Add the water, tomatoes, vegetables, soup mix, oregano and pepper; bring to a boil. Reduce heat; cover and simmer for 30-40 minutes or until the vegetables are tender.

■ For dumplings, combine the flour, baking powder and salt in a bowl. Cut in shortening until the mixture resembles coarse crumbs. Add rice and parsley; toss. In a small bowl, combine egg and milk. Add to rice mixture; stir just until moistened. Drop by teaspoonfuls onto simmering soup. Cover and simmer for 15 minutes or until a toothpick inserted in a dumpling comes out clean (do not lift the cover while simmering). Serve immediately.

Yield: 6-8 servings.

beef soup in a hurry

LOELLEN HOLLEY, TOPOCK, ARIZONA

I need just a few canned goods to stir up this comforting microwave mixture. I call this "throw-together soup." Serve it with a green salad and hot bread or rolls. You can also simmer this soup in a slow cooker.

    1 **can (24 ounces) beef stew**
    1 **can (14-1/2 ounces) stewed tomatoes, cut up**
    1 **can (10-3/4 ounces) condensed vegetable beef soup, undiluted**
    1 **can (8-3/4 ounces) whole kernel corn, drained**
  1/8 **teaspoon hot pepper sauce**

■ Combine all ingredients in a microwave-safe bowl. Cover and microwave on high for 2-3 minutes or until heated through, stirring once.

Yield: 6 servings.

Editor's Note: This recipe was tested in a 1,100-watt microwave.

beef soup in a hurry

beefy barley soup

wintertime beef soup

CAROL TUPPER, JOPLIN, MISSOURI

Kidney beans, ground beef, green pepper and chopped cabbage make this thick and hearty soup very satisfying.

- 1 pound ground beef
- 4 celery ribs, coarsely chopped
- 1 medium onion, coarsely chopped
- 1 medium green pepper, coarsely chopped
- 1 garlic clove, minced
- 2 cups water
- 2 cups reduced-sodium tomato juice
- 1 can (14-1/2 ounces) diced tomatoes, undrained
- 1 can (8 ounces) tomato sauce
- 2 teaspoons reduced-sodium beef bouillon granules
- 2 teaspoons chili powder
- 1/2 teaspoon salt
- 2 cans (16 ounces each) kidney beans, rinsed and drained
- 2 cups coarsely chopped cabbage

- ■ In a large saucepan or Dutch oven, cook the beef, celery, onion, green pepper and garlic over medium heat until meat is no longer pink; drain. Stir in the water, tomato juice, tomatoes, tomato sauce, bouillon, chili powder and salt. Bring to a boil. Reduce heat; cover and simmer for 30 minutes.

- ■ Stir in kidney beans; return to a boil. Stir in cabbage. Reduce heat; cover and cook 12 minutes longer or until cabbage is tender.

Yield: 8 servings.

beefy barley soup

ELIZABETH KENDALL

CAROLINA BEACH, NORTH CAROLINA

This filling barley soup is a favorite menu item in our house throughout the year. Everyone savors the flavor.

- 1 pound boneless beef top round steak, cut into 1/2-inch cubes
- 1 tablespoon canola oil
- 3 cans (14-1/2 ounces each) beef broth
- 2 cups water
- 1/3 cup medium pearl barley
- 1 teaspoon salt
- 1/8 teaspoon pepper
- 1 cup chopped carrots
- 1/2 cup chopped celery
- 1/4 cup chopped onion
- 3 tablespoons minced fresh parsley
- 1 cup frozen peas

- ■ In a Dutch oven or soup kettle, brown beef in oil; drain. Stir in the broth, water, barley, salt and pepper. Bring to a boil. Reduce heat; cover and simmer for 1 hour.

- ■ Add the carrots, celery, onion and parsley; cover and simmer for 45 minutes or until vegetables are tender. Stir in the peas; And heat through.

Yield: 9 servings.

You can purchase jarred minced garlic at the grocery store. One garlic clove equals a half teaspoon of the pre-minced variety. The flavor may be a little milder if you substitute jarred garlic for the minced fresh variety.

wintertime beef soup

CHICKEN & TURKEY

Your family will rave about these warming soups. There's an endless variety of ingredients, from noodles, rice and barley to carrots, beans and celery, to pique the appetites of your loved ones. As a double bonus, you can even use leftover chicken, turkey and vegetables and your family will love the results!

old-fashioned turkey noodle soup

old-fashioned turkey noodle soup

TASTE OF HOME TEST KITCHEN

We created this down-home soup to make the most of leftover turkey. Roasting the turkey bones, garlic and vegetables adds richness and depth to the flavor without additional fats.

BROTH:

- 1 leftover turkey carcass (from a 12- to 14-pound turkey)
- 2 cooked turkey wings, meat removed
- 2 cooked turkey drumsticks, meat removed
- 1 turkey neck bone
- 1 medium unpeeled onion, cut into wedges
- 2 small unpeeled carrots, cut into chunks
- 6 to 8 garlic cloves, peeled
- 4 quarts plus 1 cup cold water, divided

SOUP:

- 3 quarts water
- 5 cups uncooked egg noodles
- 2 cups diced carrots
- 2 cups diced celery
- 3 cups cubed cooked turkey
- 1/4 cup minced fresh parsley
- 2-1/2 teaspoons salt
- 2 teaspoons dried thyme
- 1 teaspoon pepper

- Place the turkey carcass, bones from wings and drumsticks, neck bone, onion, carrots and garlic in a 15-in. x 10-in. x 1-in. baking pan coated with cooking spray. Bake, uncovered, at 400° for 1 hour, turning once.

- Transfer the carcass, bones and vegetables to an 8-qt. soup kettle. Add 4 qts. cold water; set aside. Pour remaining cold water into baking pan, stirring to loosen browned bits. Add to kettle. Bring to a boil. Reduce heat; cover and simmer for 3-4 hours.

- Cool slightly. Strain broth; discard bones and vegetables. Set soup kettle in an ice-water bath until cooled, stirring occasionally. Cover and refrigerate overnight.

- Skim fat from broth. Cover and bring to a boil. Reduce heat to a simmer. Meanwhile, in a Dutch oven, bring 3 qts. water to a boil. Add noodles and carrots; cook for 4 minutes. Add celery; cook 5-7 minutes longer or until noodles and vegetables are tender. Drain; add to simmering broth. Add cubed turkey; heat through. Stir in the parsley, salt, thyme and pepper.

Yield: 10 servings.

southwestern chicken soup

HAROLD TARTAR, WEST PALM BEACH, FLORIDA

This slow cooker recipe brings people back for seconds. Chock-full of chicken, corn, tomatoes, peppers and chilies, the savory soup is sure to put a little zip in mealtime.

- 1-1/4 pounds boneless skinless chicken breasts, cut into thin strips
- 1 to 2 tablespoons vegetable oil
- 2 cans (14-1/2 ounces each) chicken broth
- 1 package (16 ounces) frozen corn, thawed
- 1 can (14-1/2 ounces) diced tomatoes, undrained
- 1 medium onion, chopped
- 1 medium green pepper, chopped
- 1 medium sweet red pepper, chopped
- 1 can (4 ounces) chopped green chilies
- 1-1/2 teaspoons seasoned salt
- 1 teaspoon ground cumin
- 1/2 teaspoon garlic powder

- In a large skillet, saute the chicken in oil until lightly browned. Transfer to a 5-qt. slow cooker with a slotted spoon. Stir in the remaining ingredients. Cover and cook on low for 7-8 hours. Stir before serving.

Yield: 10 servings.

southwestern chicken soup

vegetable chicken soup

vegetable chicken soup

Betty Kline, Panorama Village, Texas

I need to eat low-fat and my husband loves a good, satisfying soup, so this recipe fits the bill for both of us. My friends have raved over this soup, and all our grandchildren gobble up their vegetables this way.

      3 quarts water
      2 large carrots, sliced
      1 cup chopped onion
      3 celery ribs, sliced
      2 cups fresh broccoli florets
      2 cups fresh cauliflowerets
      2 garlic cloves, minced
      3 tablespoons chicken bouillon granules
      3 tablespoons picante sauce
  2-1/4 teaspoons minced fresh thyme
         or 3/4 teaspoon dried thyme
  2-1/4 teaspoons minced fresh basil
         or 3/4 teaspoon dried basil
      1 teaspoon minced fresh rosemary
         or 1/2 teaspoon dried rosemary,
         crushed
    1/4 teaspoon cayenne pepper, optional
      2 cups cubed cooked chicken breast
  3-1/2 cups egg noodles, cooked and
         drained

- In a large soup kettle, combine the water, carrots, onion and celery. Bring to a boil. Reduce heat; cover and simmer for 20 minutes or until the vegetables are tender.

- Add the broccoli, cauliflower, garlic, bouillon, picante sauce and seasonings. Cover and

When I make my chicken noodle soup, I find it tastes better if I refrigerate the soup without the noodles. When it's time to serve, I add the noodles to the amount of soup I'm going to use and cook until tender.
—Martha D.,
Nineveh,
Indiana

simmer for 20 minutes or until broccoli and cauliflower are tender.

- Add chicken and noodles. Cover and simmer for 5 minutes or until heated through.

Yield: 12 servings.

turkey rice soup

Taste of Home Test Kitchen

This tasty soup has a surprisingly short prep time. Leftover turkey has never tasted so good! If you don't have frozen mixed vegetables, stir in extra veggies from your Thanksgiving meal until heated through.

    1/2 cup sliced fresh mushrooms
    1/2 cup chopped onion
      2 teaspoons vegetable oil
      2 cans (14-1/2 ounces each) chicken
         broth
      2 cups water
    1/2 cup apple juice, optional
      1 package (6 ounces) long grain
         and wild rice mix
  2-1/2 cups cubed cooked turkey
      2 cups frozen mixed vegetables

- In a large saucepan, saute mushrooms and onion in oil for 3 minutes. Stir in the broth, water and apple juice if desired. Bring to a boil. Stir in rice mix. Reduce heat; cover and simmer for 20 minutes. Stir in turkey and vegetables; cook 5 minutes longer or until rice and vegetables are tender.

Yield: 6 servings.

turkey rice soup

zesty chicken soup

Cook and stir until onion is tender. Add broth and potatoes. Bring to a boil. Reduce heat; cover and simmer for 10 minutes. Add the corn, chilies, cilantro and pepper. Cook until heated through. Stir in lime juice. Garnish with tortilla strips.

Yield: 6 servings.

chunky chicken rice soup

Jacquie Olson, West Linn, Oregon

This is a simple and delicious soup that my family has always enjoyed. It goes great with a grilled sandwich.

- 2 cans (14-1/2 ounces each) chicken broth
- 1 cup water
- 1 package (16 ounces) frozen mixed vegetables, thawed
- 1 package (6 ounces) grilled chicken strips, cut into 1/2-inch cubes
- 1/2 teaspoon poultry seasoning
- 1/4 teaspoon pepper
- 2 cups uncooked instant rice
- 1 tablespoon minced fresh parsley

■ In a large saucepan, combine the first six ingredients; bring to a boil over medium heat. Reduce heat; cover and simmer for 5 minutes. Stir in rice and parsley. Remove from heat; cover and let stand for 5 minutes.

Yield: 6 servings.

zesty chicken soup

Marianne Morgan, Traverse City, Michigan

The fresh lime and cilantro in this zesty treat remind me of warmer climates—a nice bonus on chilly days here in northern Michigan. I lightened up the original recipe by baking the tortilla strips rather than frying them.

- 3 corn tortillas (6 inches), cut into 1/4-inch strips
- 4 teaspoons olive oil, divided
- 1/4 teaspoon salt
- 3/4 pound boneless skinless chicken breasts, cut into 1/2-inch chunks
- 1 large onion, chopped
- 5 cups reduced-sodium chicken broth
- 1 pound red potatoes, cut into 1/2-inch cubes
- 1 cup frozen corn
- 1 can (4-1/2 ounces) chopped green chilies
- 1/4 cup minced fresh cilantro
- 1/4 teaspoon pepper
- 3 tablespoons lime juice

■ In a large resealable plastic bag, combine tortilla strips, 1 teaspoon oil and salt. Seal bag and shake to coat. Arrange tortilla strips on an ungreased baking sheet. Bake at 400° for 8-10 minutes or until crisp, stirring once. Remove to paper towels to cool.

■ In a large saucepan, saute chicken in remaining oil until lightly browned. Add the onion.

chunky chicken rice soup

turkey pasta soup

MARIE EWERT, RICHMOND, MICHIGAN

This quick soup has such great flavor that every friend I've shared it with has added the recipe to her collection.

- 1 cup uncooked small pasta shells
- 1 pound lean ground turkey
- 2 medium onions, chopped
- 2 garlic cloves, minced
- 3 cans (14-1/2 ounces each) reduced-sodium chicken broth
- 2 cans (15 ounces each) white kidney or cannellini beans, rinsed and drained
- 2 cans (14-1/2 ounces each) Italian stewed tomatoes
- 2 teaspoons dried oregano
- 2 teaspoons dried basil
- 1 teaspoon fennel seed, crushed
- 1 teaspoon pepper
- 1/2 teaspoon salt
- 1/4 teaspoon crushed red pepper flakes

- Cook pasta according to package directions. Meanwhile, in a large soup kettle, cook the turkey, onions and garlic over medium heat until meat is no longer pink; drain. Stir in the broth, beans, tomatoes and seasonings. Bring to a boil. Reduce heat; simmer, uncovered, for 10 minutes.

- Drain pasta and add to the soup. Cook 5 minutes longer or until heated through.

Yield: 10 servings.

tortilla chicken soup

turkey pasta soup

tortilla chicken soup

TASTE OF HOME TEST KITCHEN

Bring a bit of the Southwest to your table with this spirit-warming soup. Loaded with tender chicken, diced tomatoes and plenty of seasonings, it's sure to be requested again and again.

- 1 cup chopped onion
- 1 teaspoon minced garlic
- 3 cups chicken broth
- 1 can (14-1/2 ounces) Mexican diced tomatoes
- 1/2 teaspoon chili powder
- 1/4 teaspoon ground cumin
- 1-1/2 pounds boneless skinless chicken breast, cubed
- 2 tablespoons cornstarch
- 1/4 cup cold water
- 1/4 cup shredded Mexican cheese blend
- 1 tablespoon minced fresh cilantro

Tortilla chips, optional

- In a large saucepan, combine the first six ingredients; bring to a boil. Add chicken. Reduce heat; cover and simmer for 4-6 minutes or until chicken is no longer pink. Combine cornstarch and water until smooth; gradually stir into soup.

- Bring to a boil; cook and stir for 1 minute or until thickened. Top servings with cheese and cilantro. Serve with tortilla chips if desired.

Yield: 6 servings.

turkey barley tomato soup

DENISE KILGORE, LINO LAKES, MINNESOTA

This low-calorie soup is so quick to prepare and tastes so good. It's a real stomach-filler and warms us up on cold winter days.

- 1 pound lean ground turkey
- 3/4 cup sliced or baby carrots
- 1 medium onion, chopped
- 1 celery rib, chopped
- 1 garlic clove, minced
- 1 envelope reduced-sodium taco seasoning, divided
- 3-1/2 cups water
- 1 can (28 ounces) Italian diced tomatoes, undrained
- 3/4 cup quick-cooking barley
- 1/2 teaspoon minced fresh oregano or 1/8 teaspoon dried oregano

- In a Dutch oven, cook the turkey, carrots, onion, celery, garlic and 1 tablespoon taco seasoning over medium heat until meat is no longer pink. Stir in the water, tomatoes and remaining taco seasoning; bring to a boil.

- Reduce heat; cover and simmer for 20 minutes. Add barley; cover and simmer for 15-20 minutes longer or until barley is tender. Stir in oregano.

Yield: 6 servings.

I shred carrots and freeze them in plastic bags in 1-cup portions. When a recipe calls for shredded carrots, I just pull a bag out of the freezer.
—Candace Z., Eagar, Arizona

amish chicken corn soup

amish chicken corn soup

BEVERLY HOFFMAN, SANDY LAKE, PENNSYLVANIA

Cream corn and butter add richness to this homey chicken noodle soup. It makes a big batch and freezes well for future meals. That's one reason why soups are my favorite thing to make.

- 12 cups water
- 2 pounds boneless skinless chicken breasts, cubed
- 1 cup chopped onion
- 1 cup chopped celery
- 1 cup shredded carrots
- 3 chicken bouillon cubes
- 2 cans (14-3/4 ounces each) cream-style corn
- 2 cups uncooked egg noodles
- 1/4 cup butter
- 1 teaspoon salt
- 1/4 teaspoon pepper

- In a Dutch oven or soup kettle, combine the water, chicken, onion, celery, carrots and bouillon. Bring to a boil. Reduce heat; simmer, uncovered, for 30 minutes or until chicken is no longer pink and the vegetables are tender.

- Stir in the corn, noodles and butter; cook 10 minutes longer or until noodles are tender. Season with salt and pepper.

Yield: 16 servings.

turkey barley tomato soup

mulligatawny soup

parsley; return to a boil. Reduce heat; cover and simmer for 20-30 minutes. Add the rice; simmer for 5 minutes or until heated through. Remove cloves before serving.

Yield: 6-8 servings.

mexican chicken soup

MARLENE KANE, LAINESBURG, MICHIGAN

This zesty dish is loaded with chicken, corn and black beans in a mildly spicy red broth. As a busy mom, I'm always looking for dinner recipes that can be prepared in the morning. The kids love the taco-like taste of this easy soup.

1-1/2	pounds boneless skinless chicken breasts, cubed
2	teaspoons canola oil
1/2	cup water
1	envelope taco seasoning
1	can (32 ounces) V8 juice
1	jar (16 ounces) salsa
1	can (15 ounces) black beans, rinsed and drained
1	package (10 ounces) frozen corn, thawed
6	tablespoons cheddar cheese
6	tablespoons sour cream
2	tablespoons chopped fresh cilantro

- In a large nonstick skillet, saute chicken in oil until no longer pink. Add water and taco seasoning; simmer until chicken is well coated.

mulligatawny soup

ESTHER NAFZIGER, LA JUNTA, COLORADO

One taste of this traditional curry-flavored soup, and folks will know it didn't come from a can! This soup fills the kitchen with a wonderful aroma while it's simmering.

1	medium tart apple, peeled and diced
1/4	cup each chopped carrot, celery and onion
1/4	cup butter
1/3	cup all-purpose flour
1	teaspoon curry powder
1/2	teaspoon sugar
1/2	teaspoon salt
1/8	teaspoon pepper
1/8	teaspoon ground mace
6	cups chicken or turkey broth
1	cup cubed cooked chicken or turkey
1	medium tomato, peeled, seeded and chopped
1/2	cup chopped green pepper
2	whole cloves
1	tablespoon minced fresh parsley
1	cup cooked rice

- In a Dutch oven or soup kettle, saute apple, carrot, celery and onion in butter for 5 minutes or until tender. Add flour, curry, sugar, salt, pepper and mace; stir until smooth. Gradually add broth. Bring to a boil; boil for 2 minutes, stirring constantly. Add the chicken, tomato, green pepper, cloves and

mexican chicken soup

basil turkey soup

turkey bean soup

TASTE OF HOME TEST KITCHEN

Substitute your favorite beans if cannellini and lima beans are not to your family's taste or they just don't happen to be in your pantry when you make this soup.

- 1 pound ground turkey
- 1 cup chopped onion
- 1 cup chopped celery
- 1 tablespoon olive oil
- 1 can (49-1/2 ounces) chicken broth
- 2 cups frozen corn
- 1 can (15 ounces) cannellini or white kidney beans, rinsed and drained
- 1 cup frozen lima beans
- 1 can (4 ounces) chopped green chilies
- 1 teaspoon dried oregano
- 1 teaspoon ground cumin
- 1 teaspoon chili powder
- 1/2 teaspoon salt

Shredded cheddar cheese, optional

- ■ In a Dutch oven, cook the turkey, onion and celery in oil over medium heat until meat is no longer pink. Add the broth, corn, beans, chilies, oregano, cumin, chili powder and salt. Bring to a boil. Reduce heat; cover and simmer for 30 minutes or until heated through. Serve with cheese if desired.

Yield: 8 servings.

- ■ Transfer to a 5-qt. slow cooker. Add V8 juice, salsa, beans and corn; mix well. Cover and cook on low for 3-4 hours or until heated through. Serve with cheese, sour cream and cilantro.

Yield: 6 servings.

basil turkey soup

TASTE OF HOME TEST KITCHEN

After a busy day, it's easy to put together this soup with leftover turkey and frozen vegetables. It tastes like it simmered all day!

- 2 cups beef broth
- 2-1/2 cups frozen mixed vegetables
- 1 can (14-1/2 ounces) diced tomatoes, undrained
- 3/4 cup uncooked small shell pasta
- 3/4 teaspoon dried basil
- 3/4 teaspoon pepper
- 2-1/2 cups cubed cooked turkey
- 2-1/2 teaspoons dried parsley flakes

- ■ In a large saucepan, combine the first six ingredients. Bring to a boil. Reduce heat; cover and simmer for 7-10 minutes or until the pasta and vegetables are tender. Stir in the turkey and parsley; heat through.

Yield: 6 servings.

turkey bean soup

hearty turkey vegetable soup

JULIE ANDERSON, BLOOMINGTON, ILLINOIS

I found this recipe on the Internet, but it was too high in fat. After experimenting, I created a more nutritious version. I often double this chili-like soup to freeze or to share with friends.

- 1 pound lean ground turkey
- 1 medium onion, chopped
- 2 small zucchini, quartered lengthwise and sliced
- 1 large carrot, cut into 1-inch julienne strips
- 3 cans (14 ounces each) reduced-sodium beef broth
- 1 jar (26 ounces) garden-style pasta sauce or meatless spaghetti sauce
- 1 can (16 ounces) kidney beans, rinsed and drained
- 1 can (15-1/2 ounces) great northern beans, rinsed and drained
- 1 can (14-1/2 ounces) Italian diced tomatoes, undrained
- 1 tablespoon dried parsley flakes
- 2 teaspoons dried oregano
- 1 teaspoon pepper
- 1 teaspoon hot pepper sauce
- 1 cup uncooked small shell pasta

- In a Dutch oven coated with cooking spray, cook turkey and onion over medium heat until meat is no longer pink; drain. Add zucchini and carrot; cook and stir 1 minute longer. Stir in the broth, pasta sauce, beans, tomatoes, parsley, oregano, pepper and hot pepper sauce.

chicken corn soup with rivels

- Bring to a boil. Reduce heat; cover and simmer for 45 minutes. Meanwhile, cook pasta according to package directions. Just before serving, stir in pasta.

Yield: 10 servings.

chicken corn soup with rivels

ELISSA ARMBRUSTER, MEDFORD, NEW JERSEY

Traditional chicken soup gets an interesting twist from a dumpling-like broth-stretcher called rivels. This recipe is chock-full of chicken, vegetables and herbs. You won't be able to resist it.

- 1 cup chopped carrots
- 1 celery rib, chopped
- 1 medium onion, chopped
- 2 teaspoons canola oil
- 2 cans (14-1/2 ounces each) chicken broth
- 2 cups fresh or frozen corn
- 2 cups cubed cooked chicken breast
- 1/2 teaspoon minced fresh parsley
- 1/4 teaspoon salt
- 1/4 teaspoon dried tarragon
- 1/4 teaspoon pepper
- 3/4 cup all-purpose flour
- 1 egg, beaten

- In a large saucepan, saute the carrots, celery and onion in oil until tender. Add the broth, corn, chicken, parsley, salt, tarragon and pepper. Bring to a boil.

- Meanwhile, for rivels, place flour in a bowl; cut in egg with a fork until crumbly. Drop dough

hearty turkey vegetable soup

by teaspoonfuls into boiling soup, stirring constantly. Cook and stir for 1-2 minutes or until rivels are cooked through.

Yield: 7 servings.

southwestern chicken barley soup

chunky chicken noodle soup

COLEEN MARTIN, BROOKFIELD, WISCONSIN

Marjoram and thyme come through nicely in this old-fashioned soup that tastes just like Grandma used to make. You can modify the recipe to include vegetables your family enjoys. My kids love carrots, so I always toss in extra.

1/2	cup diced carrot
1/4	cup diced celery
1/4	cup chopped onion
1	teaspoon butter
6	cups chicken broth
1-1/2	cups diced cooked chicken
1	teaspoon salt
1/2	teaspoon dried marjoram
1/2	teaspoon dried thyme
1/8	teaspoon pepper
1-1/4	cups uncooked medium egg noodles
1	tablespoon minced fresh parsley

■ In a large saucepan, saute the carrot, celery and onion in butter until tender. Stir in the broth, chicken and seasonings; bring to a boil. Reduce heat. Add noodles; cook for 10 minutes or until noodles are tender. Sprinkle with parsley.

Yield: 6 servings.

After chopping onions, sprinkle your hands with table salt, rub together for a few moments, then wash them. No more smelly hands!
—Connie S., Amherst, Ohio

southwestern chicken barley soup

KELL FERRELL, ALAMO, NORTH DAKOTA

I need quick, healthy dishes to fix for my family. This is a huge favorite. If I don't have leftover chicken, I simply boil or poach some chicken breasts. I use the cooking liquid to replace part of the water in the recipe to add even more flavor.

1	medium onion, chopped
1	garlic clove, minced
1	tablespoon olive oil
3	cups water
1	can (15-1/4 ounces) whole kernel corn, drained
1	can (15 ounces) black beans, rinsed and drained
1	can (15 ounces) tomato sauce
1	can (14-1/2 ounces) diced tomatoes, undrained
1	can (14-1/2 ounces) chicken broth
1/2	cup medium pearl barley
1	can (4 ounces) chopped green chilies, drained
1	tablespoon chili powder
1/2 to 1	teaspoon ground cumin
3	cups cubed cooked chicken

■ In a Dutch oven or soup kettle, saute onion and garlic in oil until tender. Add the next 10 ingredients. Bring to a boil. Reduce heat; cover and simmer for 45 minutes.

■ Stir in the chicken; cook 15 minutes longer or until chicken is heated through and barley is tender.

Yield: 12 servings.

chunky chicken noodle soup

turkey dumpling soup

turkey dumpling soup

DEBBIE WOLF, MISSION VIEJO, CALIFORNIA

Simmering up a big pot of this soup is one of my favorite holiday traditions. This is a variation on a recipe my mom made while I was growing up. My husband and children can't get enough of the tender dumplings.

1 meaty leftover turkey carcass (from an 11-pound turkey)
6 cups chicken broth
6 cups water
2 celery ribs, cut into 1-inch slices
1 medium carrot, cut into 1-inch slices
1 tablespoon poultry seasoning
1 bay leaf
1/2 teaspoon salt
1/2 teaspoon pepper

SOUP INGREDIENTS:
1 medium onion, chopped
2 celery ribs, chopped
2 medium carrots, sliced
1 cup fresh or frozen cut green beans
1 package (10 ounces) frozen corn
1 package (10 ounces) frozen peas
2 cups biscuit/baking mix
2/3 cup milk

- In a large soup kettle or Dutch oven, combine the first nine ingredients. Bring to a boil. Reduce heat; cover and simmer for 3 hours.

- Remove carcass and allow to cool. Remove meat and set aside 4 cups for soup (refrigerate any remaining meat for another use); discard bones. Strain broth, discarding vegetables and bay leaf.

- Return broth to kettle; add onion, celery, carrots and beans. Bring to a boil. Reduce heat; cover and simmer for 10 minutes or until the vegetables are tender. Add the corn, peas and reserved turkey. Bring to a boil; reduce heat.

- Combine biscuit mix and milk. Drop by teaspoonfuls onto simmering broth. Cover and simmer for 10 minutes or until a toothpick inserted in a dumpling comes out clean (do not lift the cover while simmering).

Yield: 16 servings.

Combine leftover turkey and 1-1/2 cups rice with 1/2 cup each of diced green onions, celery, tomato, and green, red and yellow peppers. Add a small can of vegetarian baked beans and toss with a dressing made with mayonnaise and barbecue sauce. Chill. —Rachel P., Fisher, Arkansas

italian chicken rice soup

WENDY SORENSEN, LOGAN, UTAH

I created this soup so my family and I could enjoy a satisfying sit-down meal on busy nights. It's ready in no time but tastes like it simmered all day. Try adding fresh zucchini or using leftover turkey instead of chicken.

1 can (49-1/2 ounces) chicken broth
1 jar (26 ounces) meatless spaghetti sauce
1-1/2 cups cubed cooked chicken
2 tablespoons minced fresh parsley
1/2 to 1 teaspoon dried thyme
3 cups cooked rice
1 teaspoon sugar

- In a soup kettle or Dutch oven, combine the broth, spaghetti sauce, chicken, parsley and thyme. Bring to a boil. Reduce heat; simmer, uncovered, for 10 minutes. Stir in rice and sugar. Simmer, uncovered, for 10 minutes or until heated through.

Yield: 10 servings.

italian chicken rice soup

chunky chicken veggie soup

until vegetables are crisp-tender. Stir in the remaining ingredients; heat through.

Yield: 20 servings.

Editor's Note: The following spices may be substituted for 1 teaspoon Creole seasoning: 1/4 teaspoon each salt, garlic powder and paprika; and a pinch each of dried thyme, ground cumin and cayenne pepper.

turkey meatball soup

TASTE OF HOME TEST KITCHEN

Cooked Italian turkey meatballs can be found in the refrigerated section of your local grocery stores. You can also substitute frozen beef meatballs.

  1 package (12 ounces) refrigerated fully cooked Italian turkey meatballs
  1 can (49-1/2 ounces) chicken broth
  2 cups uncooked egg noodles
  2 cups cut fresh green beans
  1 cup sliced fresh carrots
  1 cup chopped celery
  1 cup chopped onion
  1 tablespoon dried parsley flakes
  1 teaspoon garlic powder
  1 teaspoon dried oregano
  1 teaspoon dried basil
1/4 teaspoon pepper

■ In a Dutch oven, combine all ingredients. Bring to a boil. Reduce heat; simmer, uncovered, for 20-25 minutes or until the noodles are tender.

Yield: 6 servings.

chunky chicken veggie soup

SUNDRA HAUCK, BOGALUSA, LOUISIANA

Catering to a holiday crowd or a huddle of hungry Super Bowl fans? Try this hot, savory soup loaded with veggies, chicken and seasonings. Ladle it up with warm bread for a stick-to-your-ribs meal in a bowl.

  8 cups chicken broth
  6 medium carrots, sliced
  2 medium onions, chopped
  2 small zucchini, chopped
  4 garlic cloves, minced
  6 cups cubed cooked chicken
  2 cans (28 ounces each) crushed tomatoes
  1 can (14-1/2 ounces) diced tomatoes, undrained
  1 can (10 ounces) diced tomatoes with green chilies, undrained
  1 can (8 ounces) tomato sauce
  4 teaspoons sugar
  1 teaspoon salt
  1 teaspoon celery salt
  1 teaspoon Creole seasoning
1/2 teaspoon pepper

■ In a large soup kettle, bring the broth, carrots and onions to a boil. Reduce heat; simmer, uncovered, for 5 minutes. Add the zucchini and garlic; simmer 5 minutes longer or

turkey meatball soup

PORK, HAM & SAUSAGE

Sausage, meatballs, ham, pork loin and even breakfast sausage links—you'll find a variety of delicious soups that feature pork in this chapter. When your family sees a steaming pot of soup on the stove, they'll thank you for the tasty comfort, and you'll also be grateful for the convenient ingredients and simple preparation.

sauerkraut sausage soup

sauerkraut sausage soup

YVONNE KETT, APPLETON, WISCONSIN

My husband and I make our own sauerkraut and grow many of the vegetables in this easy slow cooker soup. It cooks all day and smells delicious when we come home from work.

- 4 cups chicken broth
- 1 pound smoked Polish sausage, cut into 1/2-inch slices
- 1 can (16 ounces) sauerkraut, rinsed and well drained
- 2 cups sliced fresh mushrooms
- 1-1/2 cups cubed peeled potatoes
- 1 can (10-3/4 ounces) condensed cream of mushroom soup, undiluted
- 1-1/4 cups chopped onions
- 2 large carrots, sliced
- 2 celery ribs, chopped
- 2 tablespoons white vinegar
- 2 teaspoons dill weed
- 1 teaspoon sugar
- 1/4 teaspoon pepper

- In a 5-qt. slow cooker, combine all ingredients. Cover and cook on low for 5-6 hours or until vegetables are tender.

Yield: 10 servings.

hearty meatball soup

JANICE THOMPSON, LANSING, MICHIGAN

A little bit of this thick and hearty soup goes a long way, so it's terrific to take to potlucks. My husband, Patrick, and I enjoy this on cold winter nights.

- 2 eggs
- 1 cup soft bread crumbs
- 1 teaspoon salt
- 1/2 teaspoon pepper
- 1 pound lean ground beef
- 1 pound ground pork
- 1/2 pound ground turkey
- 4 cups beef broth
- 1 can (46 ounces) tomato juice
- 2 cans (14-1/2 ounces each) stewed tomatoes

- 8 cups shredded cabbage
- 1 cup thinly sliced celery
- 1 cup thinly sliced carrots
- 8 green onions, sliced
- 3/4 cup uncooked long grain rice
- 2 teaspoons dried basil
- 3 tablespoons minced fresh parsley
- 2 tablespoons soy sauce

- In a large bowl, combine the eggs, bread crumbs, salt and pepper. Crumble meat over mixture and mix well. Shape into 1-in. balls.

- In a soup kettle, bring broth to a boil. Carefully add the meatballs. Add the tomato juice, tomatoes, vegetables, rice and basil. Bring to a boil. Reduce heat; cover and simmer for 30 minutes.

- Add the parsley and soy sauce. Simmer, uncovered, for 10 minutes or until meatballs are no longer pink and vegetables are tender.

Yield: 22 servings.

hearty meatball soup

corn and sausage soup

corn and sausage soup

Rebecca Clark, Hammond, Louisiana

I created this recipe years ago when I received an abundance of fresh sweet corn from friends. The soup is easy to make and has always been a big hit with family and friends. I usually serve it with bread and a tossed salad.

2-1/2 cups chopped onions
1/2 cup each chopped green pepper, sweet red pepper and celery
6 tablespoons butter
1-1/2 pounds fully cooked smoked sausage, cut into 1/4-inch pieces
3 garlic cloves, minced
4 cans (15 ounces each) Italian-style tomato sauce
3 packages (16 ounces each) frozen corn
2 cans (14-1/2 ounces each) Italian diced tomatoes, undrained
2 cups water
3 bay leaves
1-1/2 teaspoons each dried basil, oregano and thyme
1/2 teaspoon pepper
1/4 teaspoon dried marjoram
1/4 teaspoon hot pepper sauce, optional

- In a Dutch oven or soup kettle, saute onions, peppers and celery in butter until tender. Add sausage and garlic; cook for 8-10 minutes or until heated.
- Stir in the remaining ingredients. Bring to a boil. Reduce heat; simmer, uncovered, for 1 hour, stirring occasionally. Discard bay leaves before serving.

Yield: 16-18 servings.

spinach sausage soup

Bonita Krugler, Anderson, Indiana

Chock-full of potatoes, Italian sausage and spinach, this hearty soup is sure to disappear fast. Not only is it delicious and quick, but it freezes well. Adjust the amount of broth to suit your family's preference.

1 pound bulk Italian sausage
4 cans (14-1/2 ounces each) chicken broth
8 small red potatoes, quartered and thinly sliced
1 envelope Italian salad dressing mix
2 cups fresh spinach or frozen chopped spinach

- In a large skillet, brown sausage over medium heat. Meanwhile, in a Dutch oven, combine the broth, potatoes and salad dressing mix. Bring to a boil; cover and simmer for 10 minutes or until potatoes are tender.
- Drain sausage. Add sausage and spinach to broth mixture; heat through.

Yield: 10 servings.

spinach sausage soup

stir-fried pork soup

smoked sausage soup
RACHEL LYN GRASMICK, ROCKY FORD, COLORADO

This rich soup is packed with vegetables, sausage and chicken. I guarantee it's unlike any other soup you've ever tasted.

- 2 cups chopped onions
- 2 tablespoons butter
- 2 cups cubed cooked chicken
- 1 pound smoked sausage, cut into bite-size pieces
- 3 cups sliced celery
- 3 cups sliced summer squash
- 2 cups chicken broth
- 1 can (8 ounces) tomato sauce
- 1/4 cup minced fresh parsley
- 2 tablespoons cornstarch
- 2 tablespoons poultry seasoning
- 1 teaspoon dried oregano
- 1 teaspoon ground cumin
- 1 teaspoon Liquid Smoke, optional
- 1/2 teaspoon pepper

■ In a small skillet, saute onions in butter until tender. Transfer to a 3-qt. slow cooker. Stir in the remaining ingredients. Cook on high for 5-8 hours or until the vegetables are tender.

Yield: 6-8 servings.

stir-fried pork soup
LOUISE JOHNSON, HARRIMAN, TENNESSEE

Especially to guests who enjoy the variety of Chinese cooking, this is a treat. I like serving it with fried noodles or rice as a side dish.

- 2/3 pound boneless pork loin, cut into thin strips
- 1 cup sliced fresh mushrooms
- 1 cup chopped celery
- 1/2 cup diced carrots
- 2 tablespoons vegetable oil
- 6 cups chicken broth
- 1/2 cup chopped fresh spinach
- 2 tablespoons cornstarch
- 3 tablespoons cold water
- 1 egg, lightly beaten

Pepper to taste

■ In a 3-qt. saucepan, stir-fry pork, mushrooms, celery and carrots in oil until pork is browned and vegetables are tender. Add broth and spinach.

■ Combine cornstarch and water to make a thin paste; stir into soup. Return to a boil; boil for 1 minute. Quickly stir in egg. Add pepper. Serve immediately.

Yield: 4-6 servings.

smoked sausage soup

pork noodle soup

ELEANOR NISKA, TWIN FALLS, IDAHO

My daughter created this soup when she needed to use up some leftover pork. More water can be used for a thinner soup or less water for a noodle dish. It's good with mushroom-flavored ramen noodles, too.

- 1/2 cup chopped celery
- 1/2 cup chopped onion
- 1/2 teaspoon minced garlic
- 1 tablespoon olive oil
- 7 cups water
- 1-1/2 cups cut fresh asparagus (1-inch pieces)
- 1/2 cup chopped cabbage
- 1-1/2 teaspoons minced fresh parsley
- 3/4 teaspoon dried tarragon

Dash cayenne pepper, optional

- 2 packages (3 ounces each) pork ramen noodles
- 2 cups cubed cooked pork

- In a Dutch oven, saute the celery, onion and garlic in oil until tender. Stir in the water, asparagus, cabbage, parsley, tarragon and cayenne if desired. Bring to a boil.

- Coarsely crush the noodles. Add the noodles with the contents of the seasoning packets to the kettle. Bring to a boil. Reduce heat; simmer, uncovered, for 3-5 minutes or until the noodles and vegetables are tender. Add the pork; heat through.

Yield: 10 servings.

tortellini soup

pork noodle soup

tortellini soup

KAREN SHIVELEY, SPRINGFIELD, MINNESOTA

This rich and spicy soup brings a little Italian flair to your table. It's a nice recipe I invented after trying a similar version in a local restaurant.

- 2 packages (7 ounces each) pork breakfast sausage links
- 2 cans (14-1/2 ounces each) Italian stewed tomatoes
- 2 cups water
- 1 cup chopped onion
- 1/2 cup chopped celery
- 1 garlic clove, minced
- 1 teaspoon dried oregano
- 1/8 to 1/4 teaspoon cayenne pepper
- 1/8 to 1/4 teaspoon hot pepper sauce
- 1 bay leaf
- 3/4 cup refrigerated tortellini

- In a 3-qt. saucepan, brown sausage; drain and cut into bite-size pieces. Return to pan; stir in the next nine ingredients.

- Bring to a boil. Reduce heat; simmer, uncovered, for 15 minutes. Add tortellini. Bring to a boil. Reduce heat; simmer, uncovered, for 5 minutes or until pasta is tender. Discard bay leaf.

Yield: 8 servings.

kielbasa cabbage soup

MARCIA WOLFF, ROLLING PRAIRIE, INDIANA

A friend brought samples of this recipe to a soup-tasting class sponsored by our extension homemakers club. It was a great hit with my family. The mix of sausage, apples and vegetables makes a different and flavorful combination.

- 3 cups coleslaw mix
- 2 medium carrots, chopped
- 1/2 cup chopped onion
- 1/2 cup chopped celery
- 1/2 teaspoon caraway seeds
- 2 tablespoons butter
- 1 carton (32 ounces) chicken broth
- 3/4 to 1 pound fully cooked kielbasa or Polish sausage, cut into 1/2-inch pieces
- 2 medium unpeeled Golden Delicious apples, chopped
- 1/4 teaspoon pepper
- 1/8 teaspoon salt

- In a saucepan, saute coleslaw mix, carrots, onion, celery and caraway seeds in butter for 5-8 minutes or until vegetables are crisp-tender. Stir in remaining ingredients.

- Bring the soup to a boil. Reduce the heat; simmer, uncovered, for 20-30 minutes, stirring occasionally.

Yield: 6 servings.

ham 'n' veggie soup

ham 'n' veggie soup

BARBARA THOMPSON, LANSDALE, PENNSYLVANIA

When I added some ham to this flavorful broth chock-full of vegetables, the colorful dish became a complete meal.

- 1 medium onion, thinly sliced and separated into rings
- 1 medium zucchini, cubed
- 1 tablespoon olive oil
- 1 pound sliced fresh mushrooms
- 3 cups fresh or frozen corn
- 3 cups cubed fully cooked ham
- 6 medium tomatoes, peeled, seeded and chopped
- 1/2 cup chicken broth
- 1-1/2 teaspoons salt
- 1/2 teaspoon garlic powder
- 1/2 teaspoon pepper

Shredded part-skim mozzarella cheese

- In a large saucepan, saute onion and zucchini in oil for 5 minutes or until onion is tender. Add the mushrooms, corn and ham; cook and stir for 5 minutes.

- Stir in the tomatoes, broth, salt, garlic powder and pepper. Bring to a boil. Reduce heat; cover and simmer for 5 minutes. Uncover; simmer 5-8 minutes longer. Garnish with mozzarella cheese.

Yield: 8-10 servings.

kielbasa cabbage soup

pasta sausage soup

pasta sausage soup

ALICE RABE, BEEMER, NEBRASKA

This is a good soup for our area since we have many excellent sausage makers. The soup has a rich flavor and is even tastier the next day. If you are unable to find bow tie pasta, you can use another macaroni product.

1-1/2   pounds hot or sweet Italian sausage links
1   medium onion, chopped
1   medium green pepper, cut into strips
1   garlic clove, minced
1   can (28 ounces) diced tomatoes, undrained
6   cups water
2   to 2-1/2 cups uncooked bow tie pasta
1   tablespoon sugar
1   tablespoon Worcestershire sauce
2   teaspoons chicken bouillon granules
1   teaspoon salt
1   teaspoon dried basil
1   teaspoon dried thyme

■ Remove the casings from sausage; cut into 1-in. pieces. In a Dutch oven, brown sausage over medium heat. Remove sausage with a slotted spoon; drain, reserving 2 tablespoons drippings. Saute the onion, green pepper and garlic in drippings until tender.

■ Return the sausages to the pan; stir in the remaining ingredients. Bring to a boil. Reduce heat. Simmer the soup, uncovered, for 15-20 minutes or until pasta is tender, stirring occasionally.

Yield: 12 servings.

sausage mushroom soup

TWILA MAXWELL, HERMITAGE, PENNSYLVANIA

After trying this soup in a restaurant, I went home to make it. The results were great!

1   pound bulk Italian sausage
2   cans (14-1/2 ounces each) beef broth
2   jars (4-1/2 ounces each) sliced mushrooms
1   cup finely chopped celery
1/2   cup quick-cooking barley
1/3   cup shredded carrot

■ In a large saucepan, cook sausage over medium heat until no longer pink; drain. Add the remaining ingredients. Bring to a boil. Reduce heat; cover and simmer for 10 minutes or until the vegetables and barley are tender.

Yield: 6 servings.

sausage mushroom soup

sausage tomato soup

beef and sausage soup

Darlene Dickinson, Lebec, California

Everyone enjoys this delicious soup, which is hearty and tasty. Each time I serve it, I am asked for the recipe. When that happens, I know it's appreciated!

- 1 pound beef stew meat, cut into 1/2-inch cubes
- 1 tablespoon canola oil
- 1 pound bulk Italian sausage, shaped into balls
- 1 can (28 ounces) diced tomatoes, undrained
- 3-1/2 cups water
- 1 cup chopped onion
- 1 tablespoon Worcestershire sauce
- 1 teaspoon salt
- 1/2 teaspoon Italian seasoning
- 2 cups cubed peeled potatoes
- 1 cup sliced celery

- In a Dutch oven over medium-high heat, brown beef in oil on all sides. Remove with a slotted spoon and set aside. Brown the sausage on all sides; drain. Return beef to the pan. Add the tomatoes, water, onion and seasonings.

- Bring to a boil. Reduce heat; cover and simmer for 1-1/2 hours or until beef is tender. Add the potatoes and celery. Cover and simmer for 30 minutes or until the vegetables are tender.

Yield: 6-8 servings.

beef and sausage soup

sausage tomato soup

Marilyn Lee, Manhattan, Kansas

We tasted soup a lot like this at a local restaurant. When I came across a recipe that sounded similar, I made a few changes to create this version.

- 1/2 pound bulk Italian sausage
- 1 medium onion, chopped
- 1 small green pepper, chopped
- 1 can (28 ounces) diced tomatoes, undrained
- 1 can (14-1/2 ounces) beef broth
- 1 can (8 ounces) tomato sauce
- 1/2 cup picante sauce
- 1-1/2 teaspoons sugar
- 1 teaspoon dried basil
- 1/2 teaspoon dried oregano
- 1/2 to 3/4 cup shredded part-skim mozzarella cheese

- In a saucepan, cook the sausage, onion and green pepper over medium heat until meat is no longer pink; drain. Stir in tomatoes, broth, tomato sauce, picante sauce, sugar, basil and oregano. Bring to a boil. Reduce heat; cover and simmer for 10 minutes. Sprinkle with cheese.

Yield: 6 servings.

I cut my potatoes in half before peeling. That way, if they're bad inside, I know before going through the trouble of peeling them.
—Judy B., Wall, New Jersey

MEATLESS

Good and good for you—that's a combination that you can count on when you page through this chapter filled with hearty and delicious meatless soups. With all the nutritious options, you won't be missing the meat— veggies, grains and beans will soothe and satisfy. An added bonus—they're economical, too!

mushroom barley soup

mushroom barley soup

DARLENE WEISE-APPLEBY, CRESTON, OHIO

Looking for a filling, meatless meal in a bowl? Ladle up this delicious soup. It's a treasured favorite for my family—guaranteed to warm body and soul.

- 1 medium leek (white portion only), halved and thinly sliced
- 1 cup chopped celery
- 4 garlic cloves, minced
- 2 teaspoons olive oil
- 3/4 pound sliced fresh mushrooms
- 1-1/2 cups chopped peeled turnips
- 1-1/2 cups chopped carrots
- 4 cans (14-1/2 ounces each) vegetable broth
- 1 can (14-1/2 ounces) diced tomatoes, undrained
- 1 bay leaf
- 1/2 teaspoon each salt and dried thyme
- 1/4 teaspoon each pepper and caraway seeds
- 1 cup quick-cooking barley
- 4 cups fresh baby spinach, cut into thin strips

- In a large saucepan coated with cooking spray, cook the leek, celery and garlic in oil for 2 minutes. Add the mushrooms, turnips and carrots; cook 4-5 minutes longer or until mushrooms are tender.

- Stir in the broth, tomatoes and seasonings. Bring to a boil. Reduce heat; cover and simmer for 10-15 minutes or until turnips are tender. Add barley; simmer 10 minutes longer. Stir in spinach; cook 5 minutes more or until spinach and barley are tender. Discard bay leaf.

Yield: 10 servings.

ranchero soup

LEAH LYON, ADA, OKLAHOMA

Packed with garden-fresh veggies, this "vitamin soup" goes with just about any grilled meat, fish or poultry. Carrots and fire-roasted tomatoes add great color, but the variations are almost endless.

- 1 large onion, quartered
- 3 celery ribs
- 1 medium zucchini, halved lengthwise
- 1 large sweet red pepper, quartered and seeded
- 1 poblano pepper, quartered and seeded
- 1 tablespoon olive oil
- 2 cans (14-1/2 ounces each) diced tomatoes, undrained
- 2 cans (14-1/2 ounces each) vegetable broth
- 1 cup frozen sliced carrots
- 1 cup cooked rice
- 1/2 teaspoon lemon-pepper seasoning

- Brush the onion, celery, zucchini and peppers with oil. Coat grill rack with cooking spray before starting the grill. Grill vegetables, uncovered, over medium heat for 7-8 minutes on each side or until tender (pepper skins will char).

- Immediately place peppers in a bowl; cover and let stand for 15-20 minutes. Peel off and discard charred skin. Coarsely chop grilled vegetables.

- In a large saucepan, combine the tomatoes, broth and carrots. Bring to a boil. Reduce heat. Stir in grilled vegetables, rice and lemon-pepper; heat through.

Yield: 8 servings.

Editor's Note: When cutting or seeding hot peppers, use rubber or plastic gloves to protect your hands. Avoid touching your face.

ranchero soup

portobello mushroom onion soup

portobello mushroom onion soup

MELISSA FITZGERALD, JEANETTE, PENNSYLVANIA

With a side salad, this makes a wonderful meal. Portobello mushrooms are a great addition to French onion soup.

- 5 cups thinly sliced halved onions
- 4 fresh thyme sprigs
- 3 tablespoons butter, divided
- 1-1/2 pounds sliced baby portobello mushrooms
- 3 tablespoons brandy, optional
- 3 garlic cloves, minced
- 8 cups vegetable broth
- 1 cup white wine or additional vegetable broth
- 1/4 teaspoon pepper
- 13 slices French bread
- 13 slices provolone cheese

■ In a Dutch oven or soup kettle, saute onions and thyme in 1 tablespoon butter until onions are tender, about 8 minutes. Reduce heat; cook, uncovered, over low heat for 20 minutes or until onions are golden brown, stirring occasionally. Remove the onions to a bowl.

■ In the same pan, melt remaining butter. Add mushrooms, brandy if desired and garlic; saute for 1 minute. Return onions to pan. Add broth, wine or additional broth and pepper; bring to a boil. Reduce heat; cover and simmer for 40-45 minutes or until onions are very tender.

When a recipe calls for frozen spinach, thawed and squeezed dry, I use my salad spinner. It makes it easy to get rid of the excess water without straining my fingers.— Edith L., Longwood, Florida

■ Meanwhile, place French bread slices on a baking sheet; top each slice with provolone cheese. Broil 4-6 inches from the heat for 1-2 minutes or until cheese is melted. Discard thyme sprigs from soup; top soup with cheese-topped bread.

Yield: 13 servings.

meatless tortellini soup

DONNA MORGAN, HEND, TENNESSEE

I like to top bowls of this tasty soup with a little grated Parmesan cheese and serve it with crusty bread to round out dinner.

- 2 garlic cloves, minced
- 1 tablespoon butter
- 3 cans (14-1/2 ounces each) vegetable broth
- 1 package (9 ounces) refrigerated cheese tortellini
- 1 can (14-1/2 ounces) diced tomatoes with green chilies, undrained
- 1 package (10 ounces) frozen chopped spinach, thawed and squeezed dry

■ In a saucepan, saute the garlic in butter until tender. Stir in the broth. Bring to a boil. Add tortellini; cook for 5-6 minutes or until tender. Stir in the tomatoes and spinach; heat through.

Yield: 5 servings.

meatless tortellini soup

sixteen-bean soup

to 3 hours or until beans are tender. Add tomatoes and lemon juice. Simmer, uncovered, until heated through. Discard bay leaf before serving.

Yield: 10 servings.

lentil vegetable soup

Joy Maynard, St. Ignatius, Montana

Here is one good-for-you dish that our kids really enjoy. Serve this filling soup as a meatless entree or pair it with a sandwich.

- 3 cans (14-1/2 ounces each) vegetable broth
- 1 medium onion, chopped
- 1/2 cup dried lentils, rinsed
- 1/2 cup uncooked long grain brown rice
- 1/2 cup tomato juice
- 1 can (5-1/2 ounces) spicy hot V8 juice
- 1 tablespoon reduced-sodium soy sauce
- 1 tablespoon canola oil
- 1 medium potato, peeled and cubed
- 1 medium tomato, cubed
- 1 medium carrot, sliced
- 1 celery rib, sliced

- In a large saucepan, combine the first eight ingredients. Bring to a boil. Reduce heat; cover and simmer for 30 minutes.

- Add the potato, tomato, carrot and celery; simmer 30 minutes longer or until rice and vegetables are tender.

Yield: 6 servings.

sixteen-bean soup

Laura Prokash, Algoma, Wisconsin

Count on this pleasingly seasoned, chunky soup to satisfy the whole family. My husband and kids say brimming bowls of it are flavorful and filling. I also love the fact that I can make a big pot from a handy bean mix.

- 1 package (12 ounces) 16-bean soup mix
- 1 large onion, chopped
- 2 garlic cloves, minced
- 1 teaspoon salt
- 1 teaspoon chili powder
- 1/4 teaspoon pepper
- 1/8 teaspoon hot pepper sauce
- 1 bay leaf
- 8 cups water
- 1 can (14-1/2 ounces) stewed tomatoes
- 1 tablespoon lemon juice

- Set aside seasoning packet from beans. Sort beans and rinse with cold water. Place beans in a Dutch oven; add water to cover by 2 in. Bring to a boil; boil for 2 minutes. Remove from the heat; cover and let stand for 1-4 hours or until beans are softened. Drain and rinse beans, discarding liquid.

- Return beans to the pan. Add contents of bean seasoning packet, onion, garlic, salt, chili powder, pepper, pepper sauce, bay leaf and water. Bring to a boil.

- Reduce heat; cover and simmer for 2-1/2

To make a delicious meal out of canned tomato or vegetable soup, I dilute the concentrate with V8 juice instead of water and add my homemade dumplings.
—*Esther T., Portales, New Mexico*

lentil vegetable soup

speedy vegetable soup

VERA BATHURST, ROGUE RIVER, OREGON

This fresh-tasting soup is packed with colorful, nutritious vegetables. I've recommended it to my friends for years.

2	cans (one 49 ounces, one 14-1/2 ounces) vegetable broth
2	celery ribs, thinly sliced
1	medium green pepper, chopped
1	medium onion, chopped
2	medium carrots, chopped
1	envelope onion soup mix
1	bay leaf
1/4	teaspoon garlic powder
1/4	teaspoon pepper
1	can (14-1/2 ounces) diced tomatoes, undrained

■ In a Dutch oven, combine the first nine ingredients; bring to a boil over medium heat. Reduce heat; cover and simmer for 15-20 minutes or until vegetables are tender. Add tomatoes; heat through. Discard bay leaf.

Yield: 11 servings.

vegetable soup with dumplings

KAREN MAU, JACKSBORO, TENNESSEE

Not only is this hearty soup my family's favorite meatless recipe, but it's a complete meal-in-one. It's loaded with vegetables, and the fluffy carrot dumplings are a great change of pace at dinnertime.

vegetable soup with dumplings

speedy vegetable soup

While making my vegetable soup, I accidentally opened a can of spaghetti sauce instead of tomatoes. I added it anyway, and the soup was great.
—*Ruthe P., Saskatoon, Saskatchewan*

1-1/2	cups chopped onions
4	medium carrots, sliced
3	celery ribs, sliced
2	tablespoons canola oil
3	cups vegetable broth
4	medium potatoes, peeled and sliced
4	medium tomatoes, chopped
2	garlic cloves, minced
1/2	teaspoon salt
1/2	teaspoon pepper
1/4	cup all-purpose flour
1/2	cup water
1	cup chopped cabbage
1	cup frozen peas

CARROT DUMPLINGS:

2-1/4	cups biscuit/baking mix
1	cup shredded carrots
1	tablespoon minced fresh parsley
1	cup cold water
10	tablespoons shredded cheddar cheese

■ In a Dutch oven, cook the onions, carrots and celery in oil for 6-8 minutes or until crisp-tender. Stir in the broth, potatoes, tomatoes, garlic, salt and pepper. Bring to a boil. Reduce heat; cover and simmer for 15-20 minutes or until vegetables are tender.

■ In a small bowl, combine flour and water until smooth; stir into vegetable mixture. Bring to a boil; cook and stir for 2 minutes or until thickened. Stir in cabbage and peas.

■ For dumplings, in a small bowl, combine baking mix, carrots and parsley. Stir in water until moistened. Drop in 10 mounds onto simmering soup. Cover and simmer for 15 minutes or until a toothpick inserted in a dumpling comes out clean (do not lift cover while simmering). Garnish with cheese.

Yield: 10 servings.

vegetarian split pea soup

MICHELE DOUCETTE, STEPHENVILLE, NEWFOUNDLAND AND LABRADOR

Thick and well-seasoned, this classic soup packs a healthy punch, plus plenty of fiber and protein.

- 6 cups vegetable broth
- 2 cups dried green split peas, rinsed
- 1 medium onion, chopped
- 1 cup chopped carrots
- 2 celery ribs with leaves, chopped
- 2 garlic cloves, minced
- 1/2 teaspoon dried marjoram
- 1/2 teaspoon dried basil
- 1/4 teaspoon ground cumin
- 1/2 teaspoon salt
- 1/4 teaspoon pepper
- 5 tablespoons shredded carrots
- 2 green onions, sliced

- In a large saucepan, combine the first nine ingredients; bring to a boil. Reduce heat; cover and simmer for 1 hour or until peas are tender, stirring occasionally.

vegetarian split pea soup

I add leftover grated carrot and shredded cabbage to my scalloped potatoes for extra nutrition. Even my kids love these potatoes.
—Lori M., Sheboygan, Wisconsin

sweet potato minestrone

- Add salt and pepper; simmer 10 minutes longer. Cool slightly. In small batches, puree soup in a blender; return to the pan. Heat for 5 minutes. Garnish with shredded carrots and green onions.

Yield: 7 servings.

sweet potato minestrone

HELEN VAIL, GLENSIDE, PENNSYLVANIA

Sweet potatoes add a delightful flavor to this more traditional minestrone recipe. My family can never get enough of this soup!

- 4 cans (14-1/2 ounces each) vegetable broth
- 3 cups water
- 2 medium sweet potatoes, peeled and cubed
- 1 medium onion, chopped
- 4 garlic cloves, minced
- 2 teaspoons Italian seasoning
- 6 cups shredded cabbage
- 1 package (7 ounces) small pasta shells
- 2 cups frozen peas

- In a soup kettle or Dutch oven, combine broth, water, sweet potatoes, onion, garlic and Italian seasoning; bring to a boil. Reduce heat; cover and simmer for 10 minutes. Return to a boil. Add the cabbage, pasta and peas; cook for 8-10 minutes or until the pasta and vegetables are tender.

Yield: 14 servings.

spinach vegetable soup

spinach vegetable soup

JENNIFER NEILSEN, WINTERVILLE, NORTH CAROLINA

Here's a thick soup that combines a bevy of fresh vegetables with fragrant herbs for unbeatable flavor.

- 1/2 cup chopped onion
- 1/2 cup chopped celery
- 1 tablespoon butter
- 2 cans (14-1/2 ounces each) vegetable broth
- 1-1/2 cups diced potatoes
- 1 small turnip, peeled and chopped
- 1 cup chopped carrot
- 1/2 cup chopped green pepper
- 1 teaspoon garlic powder
- 1 teaspoon each dried thyme, basil and rosemary, crushed
- 1 teaspoon rubbed sage
- 1/2 teaspoon salt
- 1/4 teaspoon pepper
- 2 packages (10 ounces each) frozen chopped spinach, thawed and well drained
- 1 can (14-3/4 ounces) cream-style corn

Dash to 1/8 teaspoon cayenne pepper

- In a Dutch oven, saute onion and celery in butter until tender. Add the broth, potatoes, turnip, carrot, green pepper and seasonings. Bring to a boil. Reduce heat; cover and simmer for 15-20 minutes or until vegetables are tender.

- Stir in the spinach and corn; cool slightly. Puree half of the soup in a blender; return to the pan and heat through.

Yield: 6 servings.

My husband does not eat green peppers, so I use fresh snow peas from my garden in any dish that calls for green pepper. They freeze well, so I have them year-round.
—Ginny B., Chase, British Columbia

marjoram mushroom soup

MICHELE ODSTRCILEK, LEMONT, ILLINOIS

This creamy soup features fresh mushrooms and the pleasant addition of marjoram.

- 1 large potato, peeled and diced
- 1 large leek (white portion only), chopped
- 1 medium onion, diced
- 2 tablespoons canola oil
- 1/2 pound fresh mushrooms, sliced
- 4 cups vegetable broth
- 1 tablespoon minced fresh marjoram or 1 teaspoon dried marjoram, divided
- 1 cup (8 ounces) sour cream
- 2 tablespoons butter

Salt and pepper to taste

- In a Dutch oven or soup kettle, saute potato, leek and onion in oil for 4 minutes. Add mushrooms and cook for 2 minutes. Stir in broth and half of the marjoram. Cover and simmer for 10 minutes or until potato is tender. Cool slightly.

- Puree in small batches in a blender; return all to pan. Whisk in sour cream and butter; season with salt and pepper. Heat through but do not boil. Just before serving, sprinkle with the remaining marjoram.

Yield: 6 servings.

marjoram mushroom soup

| roasted pepper potato soup

mixed vegetable soup

LUCILLE FRANCK, INDEPENDENCE, IOWA

This recipe is so flexible, you can use whatever veggies you have on hand. But this combination is really my favorite.

- 2 small carrots, grated
- 2 celery ribs, chopped
- 1 small onion, chopped
- 1/2 cup chopped green pepper
- 1/4 cup butter
- 2 cans (14-1/2 ounces each) vegetable broth
- 2 cans (14-1/2 ounces each) diced tomatoes, undrained
- 1 tablespoon sugar
- 1/4 teaspoon pepper
- 1/4 cup all-purpose flour

- In a large saucepan, saute carrots, celery, onion and green pepper in butter until tender. Set aside 1/2 cup broth. Add the tomatoes, sugar, pepper and remaining broth to pan; bring to a boil. Reduce heat; cover and simmer for 20 minutes.

- Combine flour and reserved broth until smooth; gradually add to soup. Bring to a boil; cook and stir for 2 minutes or until thickened.

Yield: 8 servings.

roasted pepper potato soup

HOLLIE POWELL, ST. LOUIS, MISSOURI

I really enjoy potato soup, and this rich, creamy version is different than most I've tried. I like the lemon and cilantro, but you can adjust the ingredients to best suit your family's taste buds.

- 2 medium onions, chopped
- 2 tablespoons canola oil
- 1 jar (7-1/4 ounces) roasted red peppers, undrained, chopped
- 1 can (4 ounces) chopped green chilies, drained
- 2 teaspoons ground cumin
- 1 teaspoon salt
- 1 teaspoon ground coriander
- 3 cups diced peeled potatoes
- 3 cups vegetable broth
- 2 tablespoons minced fresh cilantro
- 1 tablespoon lemon juice
- 1/2 cup cream cheese, cubed

- In a large saucepan, saute onions in oil until tender. Stir in the roasted peppers, chilies, cumin, salt and coriander. Cook and stir for 2 minutes. Stir in potatoes and broth; bring to a boil.

- Reduce heat; cover and simmer for 10-15 minutes or until potatoes are tender. Stir in cilantro and lemon juice. Cool slightly. In a blender, process the cream cheese and half of the soup until smooth. Return all to pan and heat through.

Yield: 6 servings.

Like all other fresh herbs, cilantro should be used as soon as possible. For short-term storage, immerse the freshly cut stems in water about 2 inches deep. Cover leaves loosely with a plastic bag and refrigerate for several days.

mixed vegetable soup

BEANS & LENTILS

The next time you make soup, pack it full of nutrition with beans. Kidney, great northern, pinto, lentil and even split and black-eyed pea, you'll find all the cozy bean soup recipes your heart desires right here. What's even better than pleasing your family is the money you'll save—beans are a great way to stretch your dollars.

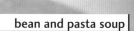

bean and pasta soup

bean and pasta soup

MARIA GOODING, ST. THOMAS, ONTARIO

We're always on the lookout for great low-fat recipes, and this soup fits the bill. Loaded with veggies and pasta, it's fast, filling and delicious. Once school starts, I make it every week.

- 1 cup uncooked small pasta
- 2 celery ribs, thinly sliced
- 2 medium carrots, thinly sliced
- 1 medium onion, chopped
- 1 garlic clove, minced
- 1 tablespoon olive oil
- 2 cups water
- 1 can (14-1/2 ounces) diced tomatoes, undrained
- 1-1/4 cups chicken broth or vegetable broth
- 1 teaspoon dried basil
- 1/2 teaspoon dried rosemary, crushed
- 1/4 teaspoon salt
- 1/8 teaspoon pepper
- 1 can (15 ounces) white kidney or cannellini beans, rinsed and drained
- 2 cups shredded fresh spinach
- 1/4 cup shredded Parmesan cheese

■ Cook pasta according to package directions. Meanwhile, in a large nonstick saucepan, saute the celery, carrots, onion and garlic in oil for 5 minutes. Stir in the water, tomatoes, broth, basil, rosemary, salt and pepper. Bring to a boil. Reduce heat; cover and simmer for 10 minutes or until carrots are tender.

■ Drain pasta; stir into vegetable mixture. Add the beans; heat through. Stir in spinach; cook until spinach is wilted, about 2 minutes. Sprinkle with Parmesan cheese.

Yield: 5 servings.

Split Pea Primer

Unlike other dried beans, split peas should not be presoaked before cooking, but they should be sorted to remove any damaged peas, pebbles or grit. After sorting, rinse split peas with cold water in a colander and cook according to recipe directions.

split pea and ham soup

LUCILLE SCHREIBER, GLEASON, WISCONSIN

Not a winter goes by that I don't fix at least one batch of this traditional pea soup. It's a hot meal that really warms up my family.

- 1 pound dried green split peas (2 cups)
- 7 cups water
- 1 teaspoon vegetable oil
- 2 cups cubed fully cooked ham
- 2 cups chopped carrots
- 1 cup chopped celery
- 1 cup chopped onion
- 1 cup diced peeled potato
- 1 teaspoon salt
- 1/2 teaspoon garlic powder
- 1/2 teaspoon pepper
- 1/4 cup chopped fresh parsley

■ In a Dutch oven or soup kettle, bring peas, water and oil to a boil. Reduce heat; cover and simmer for 2 hours, stirring occasionally. Add the next eight ingredients; cover and simmer for 30 minutes or until vegetables are tender. Stir in parsley.

Yield: 10 servings.

split pea and ham soup

pasta fagioli soup

pasta fagioli soup

BRENDA THOMAS, SPRINGFIELD, MISSOURI

My husband enjoys my version of this dish so much, he doesn't order it at restaurants anymore. With fresh spinach, pasta and seasoned sausage, this fast-to-fix soup eats like a meal.

- 1/2 **pound Italian turkey sausage links, casings removed, crumbled**
- 1 **small onion, chopped**
- 1-1/2 **teaspoons canola oil**
- 1 **garlic clove, minced**
- 2 **cups water**
- 1 **can (15-1/2 ounces) great northern beans, rinsed and drained**
- 1 **can (14-1/2 ounces) diced tomatoes, undrained**
- 1 **can (14-1/2 ounces) chicken broth**
- 3/4 **cup uncooked elbow macaroni**
- 1/4 **teaspoon pepper**
- 1 **cup fresh spinach leaves, cut into strips**
- 5 **teaspoons shredded Parmesan cheese**

- In a large saucepan, cook sausage over medium heat until no longer pink; drain and set aside. In the same pan, saute onion in oil until tender. Add garlic; saute 1 minute longer.

- Add the water, beans, tomatoes, broth, macaroni and pepper; bring to a boil. Cook for 8-10 minutes or until macaroni is tender.

- Reduce heat to low; stir in the sausage

When a recipe calls for shredded Parmesan cheese, use the cheese found in bags in the grocery store dairy section. Shredded Parmesan is often used in salads or soups where the shreds make a pretty garnish.

and spinach. Cook for 2-3 minutes or until the spinach is wilted. Garnish with the Parmesan cheese.

Yield: 5 servings.

hearty bean soup

NELDA CAMERON, CLEVELAND, TEXAS

This filling soup is a real crowd-pleaser served with fresh corn bread. No one can believe how quick and easy it is to make.

- 1 **large onion, chopped**
- 1/2 **cup chopped green pepper**
- 2 **tablespoons butter**
- 2 **garlic cloves, minced**
- 2 **cans (15-1/2 ounces each) great northern beans, rinsed and drained**
- 2 **cans (15 ounces each) pinto beans, rinsed and drained**
- 2 **cans (11-1/2 ounces each) condensed bean with bacon soup, undiluted**
- 2 **cups diced fully cooked ham**
- 2 **cups water**
- 2 **tablespoons canned diced jalapeno peppers**

- In a skillet, saute onion and green pepper in butter for 3 minutes. Add the garlic; cook 1 minute longer. Transfer to a Dutch oven. Add remaining ingredients. Cover and cook over medium-low heat for 20 minutes or until heated through, stirring occasionally.

Yield: 10 servings.

hearty bean soup

spinach lentil stew

spinach lentil stew

ALICE McEACHERN, SURREY, BRITISH COLUMBIA

When my children requested more vegetarian dishes, this chunky stew became a favorite. Red wine vinegar perks up the flavor and carrots add color. We like to ladle helpings over cooked rice.

- 1/2 **cup chopped onion**
- 2 **garlic cloves, minced**
- 1 **tablespoon vegetable oil**
- 5 **cups water**
- 1 **cup lentils, rinsed**
- 4 **teaspoons vegetable or chicken bouillon granules**
- 3 **teaspoons Worcestershire sauce**
- 1/2 **teaspoon salt**
- 1/2 **teaspoon dried thyme**
- 1/4 **teaspoon pepper**
- 1 **bay leaf**
- 1 **cup chopped carrots**
- 1 **can (14-1/2 ounces) diced tomatoes, undrained**
- 1 **package (10 ounces) frozen chopped spinach, thawed and squeezed dry**
- 1 **tablespoon red wine vinegar**

- In a large saucepan, saute onion and garlic in oil until tender. Add the water, lentils, bouillon, Worcestershire sauce, salt, thyme, pepper and bay leaf; bring to a boil. Reduce heat; cover and simmer for 20 minutes.

- Add the carrots, tomatoes and spinach; return to a boil. Reduce heat; cover and

I spice up my lentil soup by substituting salsa for half of the tomatoes.
—Myriam P., Sandwich, New Hampshire

simmer 15-20 minutes longer or until lentils are tender. Stir in vinegar. Discard bay leaf.

Yield: 6 servings.

sausage bean soup

GAIL WILKERSON, HOUSE SPRINGS, MISSOURI

This soup is so simple to assemble with ingredients that are a breeze to keep on hand, and it's delicious to boot. The filling broth with potato, sausage and vegetables makes a satisfying dish in a hurry.

- 4 **cups water**
- 1 **medium potato, peeled and chopped**
- 6 **brown-and-serve turkey sausage links (1 ounce each)**
- 2 **cans (16 ounces each) kidney beans, rinsed and drained**
- 1 **can (28 ounces) diced tomatoes, undrained**
- 1 **cup chopped onion**
- 1 **medium green pepper, chopped**
- 1 **bay leaf**
- 1/2 **teaspoon garlic salt**
- 1/2 **teaspoon seasoned salt**
- 1/2 **teaspoon pepper**
- 1/2 **teaspoon dried thyme**

- In a large saucepan, bring water and potato to a boil. Cover and cook for 10-15 minutes or until tender (do not drain). Meanwhile, crumble sausage into a skillet; cook over medium heat until browned. Drain if necessary. Add to saucepan.

- Stir in the remaining ingredients. Bring to a boil. Reduce heat; simmer, uncovered, for 8-10 minutes or until heated through, stirring occasionally. Discard bay leaf.

Yield: 10 servings.

sausage bean soup

mexican bean barley soup

ELIZABETH COLE, MAUCKPORT, INDIANA

Wonderfully warming, this soup is always on the menu for the retreats we host on our woodland farm. Everyone enjoys spooning up its yummy vegetable broth and nutritious mix of beans and barley. When I really want to bring smiles, I serve a basketful of my homemade onion-herb bread with it.

- 2 medium onions, chopped
- 3 garlic cloves, minced
- 2 tablespoons canola oil
- 1 medium turnip, peeled and diced
- 1 medium carrot, diced
- 2 tablespoons finely chopped jalapeno pepper
- 1-1/2 teaspoons ground cumin
- 1/2 teaspoon ground coriander
- 3 cans (14-1/2 ounces each) vegetable broth
- 2 cups cooked barley
- 1 can (15 ounces) pinto beans, rinsed and drained
- 2 teaspoons lemon juice

■ In a large saucepan, saute onions and garlic in oil until tender. Add the turnip, carrot and jalapeno; cook and stir until tender. Add cumin and coriander; cook and stir for 2 minutes. Add broth. Bring to a boil. Reduce heat; cover and simmer for 20 minutes.

mexican bean barley soup

Select turnips that are smooth-skinned, unblemished, heavy, firm and not spongy, and are no larger than 2 inches in diameter. Keep them in a plastic bag in your refrigerator's crisper drawer for up to 1 week.

creamy split pea soup

■ Add the barley, beans and lemon juice. Simmer, uncovered, 10-15 minutes longer or until soup thickens slightly.

Yield: 7 servings.

Editor's Note: When cutting or seeding hot peppers, use rubber or plastic gloves to protect your hands. Avoid touching your face.

creamy split pea soup

SHERRY SMITH, SALEM, MISSOURI

A friend gave me this recipe over 25 years ago. At the time, she was in her 60s and working as a cook on a riverboat barge.

- 1/2 pound sliced bacon, diced
- 1 large onion, chopped
- 2 celery ribs, sliced
- 1 pound dried green split peas
- 2 quarts water
- 2 medium potatoes, peeled and diced
- 2 cups diced fully cooked ham
- 2 teaspoons salt
- 1 bay leaf
- 1/4 teaspoon pepper
- 1 cup heavy whipping cream

■ In a Dutch oven or soup kettle, cook bacon over medium heat until crisp. Using a slotted spoon, remove bacon to paper towels; drain, reserving drippings. Add onion and celery to drippings. Saute until the vegetables are tender; drain. Add the peas, water, potatoes, ham, salt, bay leaf and pepper. Bring to a boil. Reduce heat; cover and simmer for 45 minutes or until peas are very tender, stirring occasionally. Discard bay leaf.

- Cool slightly. Process in small batches in a blender until smooth. Return to Dutch oven; stir in cream. Heat through (do not boil). Garnish with reserved bacon.

Yield: 12 servings.

black bean & salsa soup

MARY BUHL, DULUTH, GEORGIA

Salsa and cumin add just the right zip to this thick soup. I like to serve it with corn bread.

3/4 cup chopped celery
1 medium onion, chopped
3 garlic cloves, minced
1 tablespoon vegetable oil
3 cans (14-1/2 ounces each) chicken broth
2 cans (15 ounces each) black beans, rinsed and drained
1 jar (16 ounces) salsa
1 cup cubed cooked chicken breast
1 cup cooked long grain rice
1 tablespoon lime juice
1 teaspoon ground cumin

- In a large saucepan, saute celery, onion and garlic in oil until tender. Stir in the remaining ingredients; heat through.

Yield: 10 servings.

Once prepared, you can use long grain and instant rice interchangeably in a recipe that calls for cooked rice, but not when it calls for uncooked rice because they require different amounts of liquid during cooking.

pasta bean soup

pasta bean soup

BEVERLY BALLARO, LYNNFIELD, MASSACHUSETTS

My family loves this soup during our cold New England winters. It's very thick and filling.

1 large onion, chopped
1 large carrot, chopped
1 celery rib, chopped
2 tablespoons olive oil
3 garlic cloves, minced
4 cups vegetable or chicken broth
3/4 cup uncooked small pasta shells
2 teaspoons sugar
1-1/2 teaspoons Italian seasoning
1/4 teaspoon crushed red pepper flakes
2 cans (15 ounces each) white kidney or cannellini beans, rinsed and drained
1 can (28 ounces) crushed tomatoes
3 tablespoons grated Parmesan cheese

- In a Dutch oven, saute the onion, carrot and celery in oil until crisp-tender. Add garlic; saute 1 minute longer. Add the broth, pasta, sugar, Italian seasoning and pepper flakes.

- Bring to a boil. Reduce heat; simmer, uncovered, for 15 minutes or until pasta is tender. Add the beans and tomatoes; simmer, uncovered, for 5 minutes. Garnish with Parmesan cheese.

Yield: 6 servings.

black bean & salsa soup

ham & bean soup

ham & bean soup

AMANDA REED, MILFORD, DELAWARE

I learned to make this soup when we lived in Pennsylvania near several Amish families. It's a great way to use up ham and potatoes.

       1 pound dried navy beans
       2 medium onions, chopped
       2 teaspoons canola oil
       2 celery ribs, chopped
      10 cups water
       4 cups cubed fully cooked ham
       1 cup mashed potatoes (without
          added milk and butter)
     1/2 cup shredded carrot
       2 tablespoons Worcestershire sauce
       1 teaspoon salt
     1/2 teaspoon dried thyme
     1/2 teaspoon pepper
       2 bay leaves
       1 meaty ham bone or 2 smoked ham
          hocks
     1/4 cup minced fresh parsley

- Place beans in a Dutch oven or soup kettle; add water to cover by 2 in. Bring to a boil; boil for 2 minutes. Remove from the heat; cover and let stand for 1 hour.

- Drain and rinse beans, discarding liquid. In the same pan, saute the onions in oil for 2 minutes. Add celery; cook until tender. Stir

Instead of using ham hocks in soups, I buy a fully cooked ham and ask the butcher to cut it into large chunks. I freeze it until I need it. The large chunks require less trimming and provide a lot more meat than ham hocks.
—*Thela O.,*
Roscommon,
Michigan

in the beans, water, ham, potatoes, carrot, Worcestershire sauce, salt, thyme, pepper and bay leaves. Add the ham bone. Bring to a boil; reduce the heat. Cover and simmer for 1-1/4 to 1-1/2 hours or until the beans are tender.

- Remove ham bone; when cool enough to handle, remove ham from bone and cut into cubes. Return to soup. Discard bone and bay leaves. Garnish soup with parsley.

Yield: 10 servings.

too-easy tortellini soup

BETH DALEY, CHESTERFIELD, MISSOURI

For a quick soup, I combine packaged tortellini and canned goods for a minute-made dinner. Basil and Parmesan cheese round out the flavor of this easy recipe.

       4 cups chicken broth
       1 package (9 ounces) refrigerated
          cheese tortellini
       1 can (15 ounces) white kidney or
          cannellini beans, rinsed and drained
       1 can (14-1/2 ounces) Italian diced
          tomatoes, undrained
   1-1/2 teaspoons dried basil
       1 tablespoon red wine vinegar
Shredded Parmesan cheese and coarsely
          ground pepper, optional

- In a large saucepan, bring broth to a boil. Stir in tortellini. Reduce heat; simmer, uncovered, for 4 minutes, stirring occasionally. Stir in the beans, tomatoes and basil. Simmer for 4-6 minutes or until pasta is tender. Stir in the vinegar. Sprinkle with Parmesan cheese and pepper if desired.

Yield: 6 servings.

too-easy tortellini soup

spiced black-eyed pea soup

Bring to a boil. Reduce the heat; cover and simmer for 15-20 minutes. Sprinkle with cheese, parsley and bacon.

Yield: 8 servings.

macaroni bean soup

SUNDRA HAUCK, BOGALUSA, LOUISIANA

This chunky soup makes a great meatless main dish. Best of all, it's ready…set…serve in just 25 minutes. We like a lot of macaroni, so I often use more.

- 4 cups chicken broth
- 2 cups tomato juice
- 1 cup uncooked elbow macaroni
- 1 cup sliced fresh carrots
- 1 teaspoon minced garlic
- 2 medium yellow summer squash, sliced
- 1 can (16 ounces) kidney beans, rinsed and drained
- 1 teaspoon seasoned salt
- 1/8 teaspoon pepper
- 1/4 cup grated Parmesan cheese
- 1 tablespoon lemon juice

■ In a large saucepan, bring the broth, tomato juice, macaroni, carrots and garlic to a boil. Reduce heat; cover and simmer for 5 minutes or until carrots are tender. Stir in the squash, beans, seasoned salt and pepper; simmer for 10 minutes or until macaroni and vegetables are tender. Remove from the heat; stir in the Parmesan cheese and lemon juice.

Yield: 9 servings.

spiced black-eyed pea soup

DONNA AMBROSE, MT. WOLF, PENNSYLVANIA

Even people who don't care for black-eyed peas will enjoy this soup. With a crusty loaf of bread, it's a heartwarming meal for those cold winter days.

- 4 bacon strips, diced
- 1 medium green pepper, chopped
- 1 small onion, chopped
- 2 garlic cloves, minced
- 2 cans (15-1/2 ounces each) black-eyed peas, undrained
- 2 cans (14-1/2 ounces each) diced tomatoes, undrained
- 1 cup water
- 1-1/2 teaspoons salt
- 1 to 1-1/4 teaspoons ground cumin
- 1 to 1-1/4 teaspoons ground mustard
- 1 teaspoon chili powder
- 1/2 teaspoon curry powder
- 1/2 teaspoon pepper
- 1/4 to 1/2 teaspoon sugar, optional

Shredded Colby-Monterey Jack cheese and minced fresh parsley

■ In a large saucepan, cook bacon over medium heat until crisp; remove to paper towels. Drain, reserving 1 tablespoon drippings. In the drippings, saute the green pepper, onion and garlic until tender.

■ Add peas, tomatoes, water and seasonings.

Choose firm summer squash with brightly colored skin that's free from spots and bruises. Generally, the smaller the squash, the more tender it will be. Refrigerate summer squash in a plastic bag for up to 5 days.

macaroni bean soup

vegetable bean soup

BEAN EDUCATION AND AWARENESS NETWORK

Beans add extra texture and flavor to this nutritious, satisfying vegetable soup.

>   3   medium carrots, sliced
> 1-1/2   cups chopped onion
>   1   cup sliced celery
>   2   to 3 garlic cloves, minced
>   1   tablespoon canola oil
>   2   cans (14-1/2 ounces each) chicken broth
>   2   cans (15 ounces each) navy or great northern beans, rinsed and drained, divided
>   2   cups broccoli florets
>   1/2   teaspoon salt
>   1/2   teaspoon dried rosemary, crushed
>   1/4   teaspoon dried thyme
>   1/4   teaspoon pepper
>   1   cup fresh baby spinach, optional

- In a Dutch oven or soup kettle, saute the carrots, onions, celery and garlic in oil until tender. Add broth, one can of beans, broccoli and seasonings; bring to a boil. Reduce heat; simmer, uncovered, for 5-7 minutes.

- Place remaining beans in a blender or food processor; cover and process until smooth. Add to the soup with the spinach if desired; simmer for 2 minutes or until heated through.

Yield: 8 servings.

We prefer eating the tender florets of broccoli rather than the thick stems. So I slice the stems into thin rounds and freeze them. When I'm making vegetable soup, I simply pull some of them out and add to the soup.
—Persis M., Londonderry, New Hampshire

potato soup with beans

potato soup with beans

CHRISTINE ECKER, LINWOOD, NEW JERSEY

Winter winds can blow strong here on the Jersey shore. But this rich soup featuring potatoes, beans and sour cream is sure to warm your body and soul.

>   2   medium carrots, shredded
>   1   tablespoon butter
>   4   cups chicken or vegetable broth
>   3   medium potatoes, peeled and cubed
>   1   garlic clove, minced
> 1-1/2   teaspoons dill weed
>   1   can (15-1/2 ounces) great northern beans, rinsed and drained
> 4-1/2   teaspoons all-purpose flour
>   3/4   cup sour cream

Pepper to taste

- In a large saucepan, cook carrots in butter for 4 minutes or until tender. Stir in the broth, potatoes, garlic and dill. Bring to a boil. Reduce heat; cover and simmer for 25 minutes or until potatoes are tender.

- With a slotted spoon, remove half of the potatoes to a bowl; mash with a fork. Return to pan. Stir in the beans. In a small bowl, combine the flour, sour cream and pepper; add to soup. Cook over low heat for 5 minutes or until heated through (do not boil).

Yield: 6 servings.

vegetable bean soup

vegetarian white bean soup

TASTE OF HOME TEST KITCHEN

With two kinds of beans, this fresh-tasting soup makes a comforting entree. Round out the meal with warm dinner rolls.

- 2 small zucchini, quartered lengthwise and sliced
- 1 cup each chopped onion, celery and carrot
- 2 tablespoons canola oil
- 3 cans (14-1/2 ounces each) vegetable broth
- 1 can (15-1/2 ounces) great northern beans, rinsed and drained
- 1 can (15 ounces) white kidney or cannellini beans, rinsed and drained
- 1 can (14-1/2 ounces) diced tomatoes, undrained
- 1/2 teaspoon dried thyme
- 1/2 teaspoon dried oregano
- 1/4 teaspoon pepper

■ In a large saucepan or Dutch oven, saute the zucchini, onion, celery and carrot in oil for 5-7 minutes or until crisp-tender. Add the remaining ingredients. Bring to a boil. Reduce heat; cover and simmer for 15 minutes or until vegetables are tender.

Yield: 7 servings.

vegetarian white bean soup

Zucchini contains a lot of water, and freezing seems to pull the moisture to the surface, leaving a puddle upon thawing. You can add frozen zucchini directly to soup without thawing, but if you're baking, you should thaw it and blot it dry.

easy minestrone

easy minestrone

YVONNE ANDRUS, HIGHLAND, UTAH

This is a wonderful recipe to put together in the morning and forget about the rest of the day. I have three small boys who are not big fans of vegetables, but they especially enjoy this soup.

- 4 medium tomatoes, chopped
- 2 medium carrots, chopped
- 2 celery ribs, chopped
- 1 medium zucchini, halved and sliced
- 1-1/2 cups shredded cabbage
- 1 can (16 ounces) kidney beans, rinsed and drained
- 1 can (15 ounces) garbanzo beans or chickpeas, rinsed and drained
- 6 cups reduced-sodium chicken broth or vegetable broth
- 1-1/4 teaspoons Italian seasoning
- 1 teaspoon salt
- 1/4 teaspoon pepper
- 2 cups cooked elbow macaroni
- 5 tablespoons shredded Parmesan cheese

■ In a 5-qt. slow cooker, combine the first 11 ingredients. Cover and cook on low for 6-8 hours or until vegetables are tender. Just before serving, stir in macaroni and heat through. Serve with Parmesan cheese.

Yield: 10 servings.

TOMATO

There's no better savory treat than a bowl of homemade tomato soup paired with a hearty sandwich or fresh salad. Here you'll find every type of tomato soup you can imagine—with garlic, herbs, dumplings, onions or peppers—and the step-by-step instructions will make preparing a bowlful of comfort a snap, too.

tomato mushroom soup

tomato mushroom soup

BONNIE HAWKINS, WOODSTOCK, ILLINOIS

This soup recipe came about while I was experimenting with the goodies from my garden. I serve it often to my family, especially in the winter. We live in the country and raise horses, and I just love looking out my kitchen window at these fine animals as I cook!

- 1 pound sliced fresh mushrooms
- 6 tablespoons butter, divided
- 2 medium onions, finely chopped
- 1 garlic clove, minced
- 2 medium carrots, chopped
- 3 celery ribs, finely chopped
- 3 tablespoons all-purpose flour
- 8 cups beef broth
- 2 medium tomatoes, peeled, seeded and chopped
- 1 can (15 ounces) tomato sauce
- 1 teaspoon salt
- 1/2 teaspoon pepper
- 3 tablespoons minced fresh parsley

Sour cream, optional

- In a large kettle or Dutch oven, saute mushrooms in 4 tablespoons butter until tender. Remove mushrooms with a slotted spoon; set aside and keep warm.

- In the same kettle, saute the onions, garlic, carrots and celery in the remaining butter until tender. Stir in flour until blended. Add the broth, tomatoes, tomato sauce, salt, pepper and half of the reserved mushrooms. Cover and simmer for 30 minutes.

- Stir in the parsley and remaining mushrooms; simmer, uncovered, for 5 minutes or until heated through. Garnish with sour cream if desired.

Yield: 12 servings.

snowflake tomato soup

TASTE OF HOME TEST KITCHEN

Your family is bound to dig into this delectable soup! It packs lots of pleasing ingredients and is extra fun to eat when you pipe on a sour cream snowflake.

- 2 cans (28 ounces each) crushed tomatoes
- 1 can (14-1/2 ounces) chicken broth
- 2 tablespoons minced fresh oregano or 2 teaspoons dried oregano
- 1 to 2 tablespoons sugar
- 1 cup heavy whipping cream
- 1/3 cup sour cream

- In a blender, process tomatoes, one can at a time, until smooth. Transfer to a large saucepan. Stir in the broth; bring to a boil. Reduce heat; cover and simmer for 10 minutes. Stir in the oregano and sugar. Add a small amount of hot tomato mixture to whipping cream; return all to the saucepan. Cook until slightly thickened (do not boil).

- Cut a small hole in the corner of a pastry or plastic bag; fill with sour cream. Pipe a snowflake on each bowl of soup.

Yield: 8-10 servings.

snowflake tomato soup

tomato garlic soup

- Transfer 1/4 cup oil from the foil to a Dutch oven or soup kettle (discard the remaining oil). Saute onion in oil over medium heat until tender.

- Stir in the stewed tomatoes, cream, jalapenos, garlic pepper, sugar, salt, pureed tomato mixture and remaining diced tomatoes. Bring to a boil. Reduce heat; cover and simmer for 1 hour. Garnish with croutons and cheese if desired.

Yield: 18-20 servings.

quick tomato soup

JANE WARD, CHURCHVILLE, MARYLAND

My family often requests this sweet homemade tomato soup on cold winter days. It's great with a sandwich and nearly as quick to fix as the pre-packaged variety.

1/4	cup butter
1/4	cup all-purpose flour
1	teaspoon curry powder
1/4	teaspoon onion powder
1	can (46 ounces) tomato juice
1/4	cup sugar

Oyster crackers, optional

- In a large saucepan, melt butter. Stir in flour, curry powder and onion powder until smooth. Gradually add tomato juice and sugar. Cook, uncovered, until thickened and heated through, about 5 minutes. Serve with crackers if desired.

Yield: 6 servings.

tomato garlic soup

LYNN THOMPSON, RESTON, VIRGINIA

I like to make this soup when I'm expecting a lot of people for dinner. My guests always enjoy it, too.

10	whole garlic bulbs
1/2	cup olive oil
4	cans (one 14-1/2 ounces, three 28 ounces) diced tomatoes, undrained
1	medium onion, diced
3	cans (14-1/2 ounces each) stewed tomatoes
2/3	cup heavy whipping cream
1	to 3 tablespoons chopped pickled jalapeno peppers
2	teaspoons garlic-pepper blend
2	teaspoons sugar
1-1/2	teaspoons salt

Croutons and shredded Parmesan cheese, optional

- Remove papery outer skin from garlic (do not peel or separate cloves). Cut top off of garlic bulb. Drizzle with oil. Wrap each bulb in heavy-duty foil. Bake at 425° for 30-35 minutes or until softened. Cool for 10-15 minutes. Squeeze softened garlic into a blender. Add the 14-1/2-oz. can of diced tomatoes; cover and process until smooth. Set aside.

Easy ideas for soup garnishes include: finely chopped green onions or chives, minced fresh parsley, shredded cheddar cheese, grated or shredded Parmesan cheese, a dollop of sour cream and plain or seasoned croutons.

quick tomato soup

tomato basil soup

tomato basil soup

CHRIS BAKER, SOUTH LAKE TAHOE, CALIFORNIA

After just one taste of this slightly sweet tomato and herb soup, my family never went back to canned soup again! I adapted this recipe from one I saw in an old cookbook.

- 4 medium carrots, peeled and finely chopped
- 1 large onion, finely chopped
- 1/4 cup butter
- 1 can (49 ounces) chicken broth or 6 cups vegetable broth, divided
- 1 can (29 ounces) tomato puree
- 5 teaspoons dried basil
- 1-1/2 teaspoons sugar
- 1/2 teaspoon salt
- 1/2 teaspoon white pepper
- 1 can (12 ounces) evaporated milk

- In a Dutch oven, cook carrots and onion in butter over medium-low heat for 30 minutes or until the vegetables are tender, stirring occasionally. Remove from the heat and cool slightly.

- In a blender, place 1/2 of the broth and the cooled vegetables; cover and process until blended. Return to the Dutch oven. Stir in the tomato puree, basil, sugar, salt, pepper and remaining broth.

- Bring to a boil. Reduce heat; simmer, uncovered, for 30 minutes. Reduce heat to low. Gradually stir in evaporated milk; heat through (do not boil).

Yield: 6 servings.

If you'd like to lower your sodium intake, most canned tomato products have a lower-sodium version. Substitute one in your soup, and you probably won't notice the difference.

tomato soup with herb dumplings

HOLLY DUNKELBERGER, LA PORTE CITY, IOWA

Enjoy this impressive twist on an old favorite when you top each steaming bowl with herb dumplings.

- 2 cans (14-1/2 ounces each) whole tomatoes, undrained
- 4 cups tomato juice
- 1/4 cup butter
- 1 beef bouillon cube
- 1/4 teaspoon garlic powder
- 1/4 teaspoon salt
- 1/4 teaspoon pepper
- 1/4 teaspoon dried oregano

DUMPLINGS:
- 1-1/2 cups all-purpose flour
- 2 teaspoons baking powder
- 1/4 teaspoon salt
- 1/4 teaspoon poultry seasoning
- 1/4 teaspoon dried parsley flakes
- 1 egg
- 2/3 cup milk

- In a large kettle, combine the first eight ingredients; bring to a boil. Reduce the heat to simmer.

- Meanwhile, for dumplings, combine the dry ingredients in a bowl. Beat egg and milk; stir into dry ingredients until a stiff dough forms. Drop by tablespoonfuls onto simmering soup. Cover and simmer for 20 minutes or until toothpick inserted into a dumpling comes out clean (do not lift the cover while simmering). Serve immediately.

Yield: 8 servings.

tomato soup with herb dumplings

french onion tomato soup

CLARA HONEYAGER, MUKWONAGO, WISCONSIN

Tomato juice gives extra flavor to this wonderful soup that is quick and easy to prepare. I found the recipe years ago in a tomato recipe book of my mother's and have shared it with many people.

- 4 cups thinly sliced onions
- 1 garlic clove, minced
- 2 tablespoons butter
- 1 can (46 ounces) tomato juice
- 2 teaspoons beef bouillon granules
- 3 tablespoons lemon juice
- 2 teaspoons dried parsley flakes
- 2 teaspoons brown sugar
- 6 slices French bread, toasted
- 2 cups (8 ounces) shredded part-skim mozzarella cheese

- In a large saucepan, saute onions and garlic in butter until tender. Add the tomato juice, bouillon, lemon juice, parsley and brown sugar. Bring to a boil. Reduce heat; simmer, uncovered, for 10 minutes, stirring occasionally.

- Ladle soup into 10-oz. ovenproof soup bowls or ramekins. Top with French bread; sprinkle with cheese. Broil 4-6 in. from heat for 2-3 minutes or until cheese is bubbly.

Yield: 6 servings.

cream of tomato soup

french onion tomato soup

Try our own Seasoned Oyster Crackers (recipe at right) with any mild-tasting soup. They add a flavorful kick that kids and adults will savor.

cream of tomato soup

TASTE OF HOME TEST KITCHEN

A surefire chill chaser, this delightful soup really hits the spot when winter weather comes. The seasoned crackers are an addition that once you try, you can't do without!

- 1 can (14-1/2 ounces) stewed tomatoes
- 4 ounces cream cheese, cubed
- 1 medium onion, chopped
- 2 garlic cloves, minced
- 2 tablespoons butter
- 3 cans (10-3/4 ounces each) condensed tomato soup, undiluted
- 4 cans (5-1/2 ounces each) V8 juice
- 3 tablespoons tomato paste
- 1 cup half-and-half cream
- 1/2 teaspoon dried basil

SEASONED OYSTER CRACKERS:
- 3 cups oyster crackers
- 2 tablespoons canola oil
- 1 tablespoon ranch salad dressing mix
- 1/2 teaspoon garlic powder
- 1/2 teaspoon dill weed
- 9 tablespoons shredded part-skim mozzarella cheese

- In a food processor or blender, combine stewed tomatoes and cream cheese; cover and process until smooth. Set aside. In a large saucepan, saute onion and garlic in butter. Whisk in tomato soup, V8 and tomato paste until blended.

- Gradually stir in cream cheese mixture,

half-and-half and basil. Cook and stir until heated through (do not boil).

- In a large bowl, combine the oyster crackers, oil, dressing mix, garlic powder and dill; toss to coat. Ladle soup into bowls; sprinkle with crackers and mozzarella cheese.

Yield: 9 servings soup and 3 cups crackers.

onion tomato soup

LISA BLACKWELL, HENDERSON, NORTH CAROLINA

Fresh herbs really make the difference in the flavor of this low-fat vegetarian soup. It tastes delicious when it's cold outside.

      2 cups thinly sliced onions
      4 teaspoons olive oil
2-2/3 cups tomato juice
      2 cups water
      2 tablespoons minced fresh basil
      2 teaspoons minced fresh oregano
      1 teaspoon sugar
      1 teaspoon celery salt
      2 cups diced seeded plum tomatoes

- In a large saucepan, saute onion in oil until tender. Add the tomato juice, water, basil, oregano, sugar and celery salt.
- Bring to a boil. Reduce heat; simmer, uncovered, for 20 minutes, stirring occasionally. Add the tomatoes; cook 10 minutes longer.

Yield: 6 servings.

Select tomatoes that are smooth-skinned and brightly colored. Store at room temperature out of sunlight for up to 3 days.

spicy chicken tomato soup

spicy chicken tomato soup

MARGARET BAILEY, COFFEEVILLE, MISSISSIPPI

Cumin, chili powder and cayenne pepper give this slow-cooked specialty its kick. I serve bowls of it with crunchy tortilla strips that bake in no time.

    2 cans (14-1/2 ounces each) chicken broth
    3 cups cubed cooked chicken
    2 cups frozen corn
    1 can (10-3/4 ounces) tomato puree
    1 can (10 ounces) diced tomatoes and green chilies
    1 large onion, finely chopped
    2 garlic cloves, minced
    1 bay leaf
    1 to 2 teaspoons ground cumin
    1 teaspoon salt
  1/2 to 1 teaspoon chili powder
  1/8 teaspoon pepper
  1/8 teaspoon cayenne pepper
    4 white or yellow corn tortillas (6 inches), cut into 1/4-inch strips

- In a 5-qt. slow cooker, combine the first 13 ingredients. Cover and cook on low for 4 hours.
- Place the tortilla strips on an ungreased baking sheet. Bake at 375° for 5 minutes; turn. Bake 5 minutes longer. Discard bay leaf from soup. Serve with tortilla strips.

Yield: 8 servings.

onion tomato soup

tomato clam chowder

clam liquid. Stir in the water, tomato sauce, tomatoes, pepper and salt. Bring to a boil. Reduce heat; simmer, uncovered, for 30-35 minutes or until heated through. Add clams and parsley; simmer 5 minutes longer.

Yield: 11 servings.

I found that snipping green onions with a pair of kitchen shears takes only a few seconds.
—Kristy B., Kelowna, British Columbia

tomato clam chowder

WEDA MOSELLIE, PHILLIPSBURG, NEW JERSEY

Steaming bowls of this Manhattan-style clam chowder really warm our guests when they come in from the cold on Christmas Eve.

- 5 to 6 medium potatoes, peeled and diced
- 6 bacon strips, diced
- 1 small onion, finely chopped
- 2 celery ribs, chopped
- 1 garlic clove, minced
- 2 cans (6 ounces each) minced clams
- 2 cups water
- 1 can (15 ounces) tomato sauce
- 1 can (14-1/2 ounces) diced tomatoes, undrained
- 1/2 to 1 teaspoon pepper
- 1/4 teaspoon salt
- 2 teaspoons minced fresh parsley

■ Place the potatoes in a soup kettle or Dutch oven and cover with water. Bring to a boil. Reduce heat; cover and cook for 10-15 minutes or until tender.

■ Meanwhile, in a large skillet, cook bacon over medium heat until crisp. Using a slotted spoon, remove to paper towels; drain, reserving 2 tablespoons drippings. In the drippings, saute the onion, celery and garlic until tender.

■ Drain clams, reserving liquid; set clams aside. Drain potatoes and return to the pan. Add onion mixture, bacon and reserved

creamy tomato basil soup

LINDA MANUSZAK, CLINTON TOWNSHIP, MICHIGAN

My husband and I love this soup with grilled cheese sandwiches. It's so easy to make that we often have it on weeknights, and I also serve it during Lent.

- 2 tablespoons chopped green onion
- 2 garlic cloves, minced
- 1-1/2 teaspoons olive oil
- 1 can (28 ounces) crushed tomatoes
- 1 can (10-1/2 ounces) condensed chicken broth, undiluted
- 1-1/3 cups water
- 1/4 teaspoon pepper
- 3/4 cup heavy whipping cream
- 2 tablespoons sherry or additional chicken broth
- 2 tablespoons minced fresh basil
- 2 teaspoons sugar

■ In a large saucepan, saute onion and garlic in oil until tender. Add the tomatoes, broth, water and pepper. Bring to a boil. Reduce heat; simmer for 10 minutes.

■ Stir in the cream, sherry or additional broth, basil and sugar. Cook for 1 minute or until heated through (do not boil).

Yield: 6 servings.

creamy tomato basil soup

red pepper tomato soup

red pepper tomato soup

JANE SHAPTON, TUSTIN, CALIFORNIA

Vine-ripened plum tomatoes punched up with peppers, garlic and rice wine vinegar make this smooth soup a standout. Serve with cheesy garlic breadsticks and a tossed salad for supper.

- 2 medium sweet red peppers
- 2 cups water
- 10 plum tomatoes
- 1 Anaheim pepper, seeded and chopped
- 2 garlic cloves, minced
- 1 cup chicken broth
- 2 tablespoons rice wine vinegar
- 2 tablespoons minced fresh basil
- 1/2 cup shredded part-skim mozzarella cheese

- Broil red peppers 4 in. from the heat until skins blister. With tongs, rotate peppers a quarter turn. Broil and rotate until all sides are blistered and blackened. Immediately place peppers in a bowl; cover and let stand for 15-20 minutes. Peel off and discard charred skin. Remove stems and seeds. Finely chop peppers.

- In a large saucepan, bring water to a boil. Add tomatoes; cover and boil for 3 minutes. Drain and immediately place tomatoes in ice water. Drain and pat dry.

- In the same pan, combine the roasted peppers, tomatoes, Anaheim pepper and garlic; heat through. Stir in the broth and vinegar; heat through. Stir in basil. Cool slightly.

Anaheim peppers are widely available in grocery stores and have a medium-hot heat measurement.

- In small batches, puree soup in a blender. Return to the pan and heat through. Garnish with cheese.

Yield: 5 servings.

Editor's Note: When cutting or seeding hot peppers, use rubber or plastic gloves to protect your hands. Avoid touching your face.

tomato bisque

TASTE OF HOME TEST KITCHEN

A bowl brimming with this fresh, creamy soup is sure to impress. With its outstanding flavor, guests will think you fussed for hours!

- 2 garlic cloves, minced
- 2 tablespoons butter
- 2 tablespoons all-purpose flour
- 4 cups chicken broth
- 1 can (6 ounces) tomato paste
- 1/8 to 1/4 teaspoon cayenne pepper
- 1 cup half-and-half cream

Chopped fresh tomatoes, optional

- In a medium saucepan, saute garlic in butter. Stir in flour until blended; gradually add chicken broth. Stir in tomato paste and cayenne until well blended. Bring to a boil; cook and stir for 2 minutes or until thickened. Reduce heat; gradually stir in cream (do not boil). Serve immediately. Garnish with chopped tomatoes if desired.

Yield: 6 servings.

tomato bisque

CREAM SOUPS

A steaming helping of one of our cream soups is truly hearty goodness in a bowl. Indulge with one of these home-style soups the next time the mood strikes and you'll find that winter's chills will be chased away, and friends and family will request seconds, too!

broccoli & cheese soup

broccoli & cheese soup

JEAN PARE, VERMILION, ALBERTA

This is a colorful soup because the carrots contrast nicely with the broccoli. It's also quickly made in the microwave.

- 1 cup thinly sliced carrots
- 2 tablespoons plus 1 cup water, divided
- 1 package (13 ounces) frozen broccoli florets, thawed
- 2-1/2 cups milk
- 1/4 cup all-purpose flour
- 2 teaspoons chicken bouillon granules
- 1/2 teaspoon salt
- 1/4 teaspoon pepper
- 1 cup (4 ounces) shredded cheddar cheese

■ In a 2-qt. microwave-safe dish, combine carrots and 2 tablespoons water. Cover and microwave on high for 2 minutes; stir. Cover and cook 2 minutes longer or until tender. Add broccoli. Cover and microwave for 2 minutes; stir. Cover and cook 1 to 1-1/2 minutes longer or until vegetables are tender. Stir in milk.

■ In a small bowl, combine the flour, bouillon, salt and pepper; stir in remaining water until smooth. Stir into broccoli mixture. Cover and microwave on high for 6-7 minutes or until mixture is boiling and thickened, stirring every minute. Stir in the cheese until melted.

Yield: 4-5 servings.

Editor's Note: This recipe was tested in a 1,100-watt microwave.

Cream Soups and Bisques

Cream soups are pureed soups with a smooth, silky texture. The main flavor is frequently a single vegetable, such as asparagus or carrot. They may be thickened with flour or potatoes and can be made without cream. A bisque (featured in the next chapter) is a thick, rich pureed soup often made with seafood. Bisques may also be made with poultry or vegetables.

mushroom potato soup

CLARE WALLACE, LYNCHBURG, VIRGINIA

A buttery mushroom flavor blends with other veggies to make this soup robust and warming.

- 2 medium leeks, sliced
- 2 large carrots, sliced
- 6 tablespoons butter, divided
- 6 cups chicken broth
- 5 cups diced peeled potatoes
- 1 tablespoon minced fresh dill
- 1 teaspoon salt
- 1/8 teaspoon pepper
- 1 bay leaf
- 1 pound sliced fresh mushrooms
- 1/4 cup all-purpose flour
- 1 cup heavy whipping cream

■ In a Dutch oven or soup kettle, saute the leeks and carrots in 3 tablespoons butter for 5 minutes or until tender. Stir in the broth, potatoes, dill, salt, pepper and bay leaf. Bring to a boil. Reduce heat; cover and simmer for 15-20 minutes or until the potatoes are tender.

■ Meanwhile, in a large skillet, saute the mushrooms in remaining butter for 4-6 minutes or until tender. Discard bay leaf from soup. Stir in mushroom mixture. In a small bowl, combine the flour and cream until smooth; gradually stir into soup. Bring to a boil; cook and stir for 2 minutes or until thickened.

Yield: 12 servings.

mushroom potato soup

red potato soup

- In a Dutch oven or large soup kettle, saute the onion, celery and bacon until vegetables are tender; drain well. Add the milk, water, bouillon, salt and pepper; heat through (do not boil).

- In a large saucepan, melt butter; stir in flour until smooth. Cook and stir over medium heat for 1 minute. Gradually add cream. Bring to a boil; cook and stir for 1-2 minutes or until thickened. Stir into soup. Add parsley and potatoes; heat through. Sprinkle with cheese and green onions.

Yield: 18 servings.

Winter squash has hard, inedible shells and fully mature seeds. Select squash that is heavy for its size, has a hard shell and a deep color. Avoid any with cracks or soft spots.

ginger squash soup

LAUREL LESLIE, SONORA, CALIFORNIA

Everyone likes the lovely golden color and silky consistency of this soup.

- 3 cups chicken broth
- 2 packages (10 ounces each) frozen cooked winter squash, thawed
- 1 cup unsweetened applesauce
- 3 tablespoons sugar
- 1 teaspoon ground ginger
- 1/2 teaspoon salt
- 1/2 cup heavy whipping cream, whipped

- In a large saucepan, simmer broth and squash. Add the applesauce, sugar, ginger and salt. Bring to a boil. Reduce heat to low; stir in cream. Cook for 30 minutes or until soup reaches desired consistency, stirring occasionally.

Yield: 6 servings.

red potato soup

BEV BOSVELD, WAUPUN, WISCONSIN

I love to entertain, and this recipe is one of my favorites to fix for guests. Onion, celery and bacon season the thin but creamy broth in this chunky soup, which always wins raves.

2-1/2 pounds unpeeled small red potatoes, cut into 1-inch cubes
- 1 large onion, diced
- 3 celery ribs, diced
- 3 bacon strips, diced
- 8 cups milk
- 4 cups water
- 3 tablespoons chicken bouillon granules
- 1 teaspoon salt
- 1/2 teaspoon pepper
- 3/4 cup butter, cubed
- 3/4 cup all-purpose flour
- 1 cup heavy whipping cream
- 1/2 cup minced fresh parsley

Shredded cheddar cheese and chopped green onions

- Place potatoes in a saucepan and cover with water. Bring to a boil. Reduce heat; cover and cook for 10-12 minutes or until tender. Drain and set aside.

ginger squash soup

savory cheese soup

garlic soup

IOLA EGLE, BELLA VISTA, ARKANSAS

While this soup simmers, the great garlicky aroma will fill your kitchen! We love the toasted garlic bread floating on top of a rich, creamy bowlful.

>   6 garlic cloves, minced
>   1 tablespoon olive oil
>   8 cups chicken broth
>   1/2 teaspoon salt
>   1/8 teaspoon pepper
>   1/8 teaspoon dried thyme
>   1/8 teaspoon dried rosemary, crushed
>   3 egg yolks
>   1/2 cup half-and-half cream
>   8 slices frozen garlic bread, thawed and toasted
>
> **Grated Parmesan cheese**

- In a large saucepan, cook and stir the garlic in oil over low heat for 5 minutes or until lightly browned. Add the broth, salt, pepper, thyme and rosemary; simmer, uncovered, for 1 hour.

- Strain broth and return to the pan. In a small bowl, whisk egg yolks and cream. Stir in 1/2 cup hot broth. Return all to the pan, stirring constantly. Cook and stir over medium heat until soup reaches 160° (do not boil). Top each serving with a slice of garlic bread; sprinkle with Parmesan cheese.

Yield: 8 servings.

savory cheese soup

ANN HUSEBY, LAKEVILLE, MINNESOTA

This cheesy soup is great at parties. Let guests serve themselves and choose from fun garnishes such as popcorn, croutons, green onions and bacon bits.

>   3 cans (14-1/2 ounces each) chicken broth
>   1 small onion, chopped
>   1 large carrot, chopped
>   1 celery rib, chopped
>   1/4 cup chopped sweet red pepper
>   2 tablespoons butter
>   1 teaspoon salt
>   1/2 teaspoon pepper
>   1/3 cup all-purpose flour
>   1/3 cup cold water
>   1 package (8 ounces) cream cheese, cubed and softened
>   2 cups (8 ounces) shredded cheddar cheese
>   1 can (12 ounces) beer, optional
>
> **Croutons, popcorn, crumbled cooked bacon, sliced green onions, optional**

- In a 3-qt. slow cooker, combine the first eight ingredients. Cover and cook on low for 7-8 hours. Combine flour and water until smooth; stir into soup. Cover and cook on high 30 minutes longer or until soup is thickened. Stir in cream cheese and cheddar cheese until blended. Stir in beer if desired. Cover and cook on low until heated through. Serve with desired toppings.

Yield: 6-8 servings.

Place a clove of garlic on a rubber jar opener and wrap it around the garlic, then roll. It peels the garlic in a jiffy.
—*Bobbie B., Bullhead City, Arizona*

garlic soup

asparagus soup

LOIS MCATEE, OCEANSIDE, CALIFORNIA

My kids wouldn't eat asparagus when they were young. But after trying this smooth, creamy soup, they all wanted seconds. To hurry along preparation, I rely on frozen asparagus.

- 1 package (10 ounces) frozen asparagus cuts
- 1 large onion, chopped
- 1 cup water
- 1 teaspoon salt
- 1 teaspoon chicken bouillon granules
- 1/2 teaspoon dried basil
- 1/8 teaspoon white pepper
- 1-1/2 cups milk
- 1/2 cup heavy whipping cream
- Seasoned salad croutons

- In a saucepan, combine asparagus, onion, water, salt, bouillon, basil and pepper. Bring to a boil. Reduce heat; cover and simmer for 10-12 minutes or until vegetables are tender. Cool for 5 minutes; stir in milk.

- In a blender or food processor, process the soup in batches until smooth; return to the pan. Stir in cream; heat through. Garnish with croutons.

Yield: 4-6 servings.

cheesy vegetable soup

To make croutons, place bread cubes on a cookie sheet and spray with a flavored cooking spray. Season with Cajun, Italian or onion seasonings and bake until they reach the desired crispiness.
—Bob K., Germantown, Tennessee

asparagus soup

cheesy vegetable soup

DANA WORLEY, LEBANON, TENNESSEE

Shredded cheddar cheese adds flavor to this smooth-as-silk soup that's loaded with good-for-you cabbage, carrots, lima beans and potatoes. The filling dish is always a crowd-pleaser on cold winter days.

- 1 large onion, chopped
- 5 tablespoons butter, divided
- 2 cups water
- 2 cups shredded cabbage
- 1-1/2 cups frozen lima beans, thawed
- 1 cup sliced carrots
- 1 cup diced peeled potatoes
- 1 tablespoon chicken bouillon granules
- 3 tablespoons all-purpose flour
- 1/4 teaspoon paprika
- 1/4 teaspoon pepper
- 2 cups milk
- 1 cup half-and-half cream
- 1-1/2 cups (6 ounces) shredded cheddar cheese
- Minced fresh parsley

- In a large saucepan, saute onion in 2 tablespoons butter until tender. Add water, vegetables and bouillon. Bring to a boil. Reduce heat; cover and simmer for 20 minutes or until vegetables are tender.

- Meanwhile, in a small saucepan, melt remaining butter. Stir in the flour, paprika and pepper until smooth. Gradually add milk and cream. Bring to a boil; cook and stir for 2 minutes or until thickened. Reduce heat; stir in cheese until melted. Add to soup; heat through. Sprinkle with parsley.

Yield: 8 servings.

cabbage sausage soup

NANCY ALLMAN, DERRY, PENNSYLVANIA

This autumn soup that features smoked sausage is perfect for hurried cooks. My mother made it when we had an abundance of cabbage from our garden.

4	cups chicken broth
1	small cabbage, chopped (about 10 cups)
1	medium onion, chopped
1/2	pound smoked sausage, halved lengthwise and sliced
1/2	cup all-purpose flour
1-1/2	teaspoons salt
1/4	teaspoon pepper
1	cup milk

- In a Dutch oven, bring broth, cabbage and onion to a boil. Reduce heat; cover and simmer for 10-15 minutes or until cabbage is tender. Add sausage; heat through.

- In a bowl, combine the flour, salt and pepper. Gradually add milk, stirring until smooth. Gradually stir into soup. Bring to a boil; cook and stir for 2 minutes or until thickened.

Yield: 8 servings.

cabbage sausage soup

Evaporated milk is made when milk is condensed to about half of its original volume in a special heating process that removes 60% of the water in milk.

creamy chicken rice soup

creamy chicken rice soup

JANICE MITCHELL, AURORA, COLORADO

I came up with this thick, flavorful soup while making some adjustments to a favorite stovetop chicken casserole. It goes together in short order using precooked chicken chunks and a couple of pulses in a mini-processor to chop the veggies.

1/2	cup chopped onion
1	medium carrot, chopped
1	celery rib, chopped
1/2	teaspoon minced garlic
1	tablespoon canola oil
2	cans (14-1/2 ounces each) chicken broth
1/3	cup uncooked long grain rice
3/4	teaspoon dried basil
1/4	teaspoon pepper
3	tablespoons all-purpose flour
1	can (5 ounces) evaporated milk
1	package (9 ounces) frozen diced cooked chicken, thawed

- In a large saucepan, saute the onion, carrot, celery and garlic in oil until tender. Stir in the broth, rice, basil and pepper. Bring to a boil. Reduce heat; cover and simmer for 15 minutes or until rice is tender.

- In a small bowl, combine the flour and milk until smooth; stir into soup. Bring to a boil; cook and stir for 2 minutes or until thickened. Stir in the chicken; heat through.

Yield: 5 servings.

| hot dog soup

Reduce heat; cover and simmer for 25-30 minutes or until vegetables are tender, stirring occasionally.

Yield: 8 servings.

beer cheese soup

SHARON LOCK, FORMAN, NORTH DAKOTA

Onion, parsley, paprika and beer flavor this smooth, rich soup. A family friend used to invite us up for Sunday supper and served this several times. It was so simple and good!

- 2 tablespoons finely chopped onion
- 1/2 teaspoon butter
- 2 cans (10-3/4 ounces each) condensed cream of celery soup, undiluted
- 1 cup beer or nonalcoholic beer
- 1 cup milk
- 1 teaspoon Worcestershire sauce
- 1/2 teaspoon dried parsley flakes
- 1/4 teaspoon paprika
- 3/4 pound process cheese (Velveeta), cubed

■ In a large saucepan, saute onion in butter. Stir in the soup, beer, milk, Worcestershire sauce, parsley and paprika. Reduce heat; stir in cheese until melted. Heat through (do not boil).

Yield: 6 servings.

hot dog soup

KIM HOLLIDAY, BELLEFONTE, PENNSYLVANIA

We can always count on our retired pastor for good advice and recipes, like this thick and hearty soup. Full of hot dogs and vegetables, it quickly became my kids' favorite.

- 4 medium carrots, cut into thin strips
- 2 medium potatoes, peeled and cubed
- 2 medium parsnips, peeled and chopped
- 1 medium onion, chopped
- 1/4 cup butter
- 2 tablespoons all-purpose flour
- 1 package (1 pound) hot dogs, halved lengthwise and cut into bite-size pieces
- 1 can (12 ounces) evaporated milk
- 1 can (10-3/4 ounces) condensed cream of mushroom soup, undiluted
- 1 cup water
- 1 teaspoon dried basil
- 1/2 teaspoon pepper

■ In a soup kettle or large saucepan, saute the carrots, potatoes, parsnips and onion in butter for 5 minutes. Stir in flour until blended. Add the hot dogs, milk, soup, water, basil and pepper; bring to a boil.

| beer cheese soup

creamy asparagus soup

creamy corn crab soup

CAROL ROPCHAN, WILLINGDON, ALBERTA

This creamy soup is fast, easy and very tasty. Corn really stars in this delectable recipe, and crabmeat makes it a little more special. It will get high marks from both busy cooks and lovers of homemade food.

- 1 medium onion, chopped
- 2 tablespoons butter
- 3 cups chicken broth
- 3 cups frozen corn
- 3 medium potatoes, peeled and diced
- 1 can (6 ounces) crabmeat, drained, flaked and cartilage removed or 1 cup flaked imitation crabmeat
- 1 cup milk
- 1/2 teaspoon salt
- 1/4 teaspoon pepper

■ In a large saucepan, saute onion in butter until tender. Add the broth, corn and potatoes; bring to a boil. Reduce heat; cover and simmer for 15 minutes. Remove from the heat; cool slightly.

■ In a blender or food processor, puree half of the corn mixture. Return to the pan. Stir in the crab, milk, salt and pepper; cook over low heat until heated through (do not boil).

Yield: 7 servings.

creamy asparagus soup

PAT STEVENS, GRANBURY, TEXAS

After trying several different recipes for asparagus soup, I put together the best ingredients from each for my favorite version. This soup is great year-round.

- 2 medium leeks (white portion only), sliced
- 12 green onions, chopped
- 2 tablespoons olive oil
- 1 tablespoon butter
- 2-1/2 pounds fresh asparagus, cut into 1-inch pieces
- 4 cups chicken broth
- 1 cup half-and-half cream
- 1/2 teaspoon salt
- 1/8 teaspoon pepper

■ In a large saucepan, saute leeks and onions in oil and butter until tender. Add the asparagus and broth. Bring to a boil. Reduce heat; simmer, uncovered, until vegetables are tender. Remove from the heat. Set aside 1 cup of asparagus pieces.

■ In a blender, process the remaining asparagus mixture in batches until smooth; return to the pan. Stir in the cream, salt and pepper. Cook over low heat until heated through. Garnish with reserved asparagus pieces.

Yield: 6 servings.

A member of the onion family, leeks resemble oversize green onions, with wide green leaves, a fat white stalk and roots at the bulb end.

creamy corn crab soup

chicken and cheese soup

TASTE OF HOME TEST KITCHEN

This thick soup, coupled with a salad or breadsticks, makes a warming, filling meal. Chicken and cheese are a classic duo.

- 1 medium onion, chopped
- 2 to 3 garlic cloves, minced
- 1 tablespoon canola oil
- 1 tablespoon butter
- 2 tablespoons all-purpose flour
- 2 cups chicken broth
- 1 can (14-1/2 ounces) diced tomatoes, drained
- 1 cup frozen corn
- 1 can (4 ounces) chopped green chilies
- 2 cups chopped cooked chicken
- 1 can (12 ounces) evaporated milk
- 8 ounces process cheese (Velveeta), cubed
- 1/2 to 1 teaspoon ground cumin

- In a large saucepan, saute onion and garlic in oil and butter until tender. Stir in the flour until blended. Gradually add broth. Bring to a boil; cook and stir for 2 minutes or until thickened.

- Stir in the tomatoes, corn and chilies; bring to a boil. Add chicken. Reduce heat; simmer, uncovered, for 15 minutes. Add the milk, cheese and cumin. Cook and stir until cheese is melted (do not boil).

Yield: 6 servings.

Process cheese is a blend of different cheeses that is similar in flavor to the natural cheese from which it's made. Generally, it is stable at room temperature and stays smooth and creamy when it is heated. The most common brand name is Velveeta.

cheddar potato soup

cheddar potato soup

MARK TRINKLEIN, CEDARBURG, WISCONSIN

My home state is famous for cheese, which I use in many recipes such as this creamy soup. Cheddar gives it a sunny color and tantalizing taste. A good meal starter, it's also a great choice for a light lunch or supper.

- 1/3 cup chopped onion
- 1/3 cup chopped celery
- 2 tablespoons butter
- 4 cups diced peeled potatoes
- 3 cups chicken or vegetable broth
- 2 cups (8 ounces) shredded cheddar cheese
- 2 cups milk
- 1/4 teaspoon pepper
- **Dash paprika**
- **Seasoned croutons and minced fresh parsley**

- In a large saucepan, saute onion and celery in butter until tender. Add potatoes and broth; bring to a boil. Reduce heat; cover and simmer for 10-15 minutes or until potatoes are tender.

- Puree in small batches in a blender until smooth; return to the pan. Stir in the cheese, milk, pepper and paprika. Cook and stir over low heat until the cheese is melted. Garnish with croutons and parsley.

Yield: 8 servings.

chicken and cheese soup

cucumber soup

BEVERLY SPRAGUE, CATONSVILLE, MARYLAND

I dress up this soup with a colorful selection of savory garnishes. A topping of crunchy almonds contrasts nicely with this soup.

- 3 medium cucumbers
- 3 cups chicken broth
- 3 cups (24 ounces) sour cream
- 3 tablespoons cider vinegar
- 2 teaspoons salt, optional
- 1 garlic clove, minced

TOPPINGS:
- 2 medium tomatoes, chopped
- 3/4 cup sliced almonds, toasted
- 1/2 cup chopped green onions
- 1/2 cup minced fresh parsley

- Peel cucumbers; halve lengthwise and remove seeds. Cut into chunks. In a blender, cover and puree cucumbers and broth in small batches.

- Transfer to a large bowl; stir in the sour cream, vinegar, salt if desired and garlic until well blended. Cover and refrigerate for at least 4 hours. Stir before serving. Garnish with tomatoes, almonds, onions and parsley.

Yield: 12 servings.

asparagus cheese soup

cucumber soup

asparagus cheese soup

ELIZABETH MONTGOMERY, TAYLORVILLE, ILLINOIS

Thyme has a sweet, savory flavor that really enhances this creamy soup.

- 1/4 cup butter
- 1/4 cup all-purpose flour
- 2 teaspoons salt
- 1/8 teaspoon pepper
- 6 cups milk
- 4 cups cut fresh asparagus (1-inch pieces), cooked and drained or 2 packages (10 ounces each) frozen cut asparagus, thawed
- 3 cups (12 ounces) shredded cheddar cheese
- 4 teaspoons minced fresh thyme or 1-1/2 teaspoons dried thyme
- 1/8 teaspoon ground nutmeg

Croutons and additional shredded cheddar cheese, optional

- In a large saucepan, melt butter. Stir in the flour, salt and pepper until smooth. Gradually add milk; bring to a boil. Cook and stir for 2 minutes. Add asparagus and heat through. Add the cheese, thyme and nutmeg. Cook until cheese is melted, stirring frequently (do not boil). Garnish with croutons and additional cheese if desired.

Yield: 6-8 servings.

creamy carrot parsnip soup

creamy carrot parsnip soup

PHYLLIS CLINEHENS, MAPLEWOOD, OHIO

This thick concoction tastes like it's fresh from the garden. A hint of horseradish and ginger sparks every steaming spoonful.

   8   cups chopped carrots
   6   cups chopped peeled parsnips
   4   cups chicken broth
   3   cups water
   2   teaspoons sugar
   1   teaspoon salt
   1   medium onion, chopped
   4   garlic cloves, minced
   1   teaspoon peeled grated horseradish
   1   teaspoon minced fresh gingerroot
   3   tablespoons butter
   2   cups buttermilk
   2   tablespoons sour cream
Fresh dill sprigs, optional

- In a Dutch oven, combine the carrots, parsnips, broth, water, sugar and salt; bring to a boil. Reduce heat; cover and cook for 25-30 minutes or until vegetables are tender.

- In a small skillet, saute onion, garlic, horseradish and ginger in butter until tender. Add to the carrot mixture.

- Transfer soup to a blender in batches; cover and process until smooth. Return to the pan. Stir in buttermilk; heat through (do not boil).

- Garnish servings with sour cream and dill if desired.

Yield: 12 servings.

cream cheese potato soup

STACY BOCKELMAN, CALIFORNIA, MISSOURI

I came up with this soup after I had tried something similar at a restaurant. It's good with sourdough bread.

   6   cups water
   7   teaspoons chicken bouillon granules
   2   packages (8 ounces each) cream cheese, cubed
   1   package (30 ounces) frozen cubed hash brown potatoes, thawed
1-1/2 cups cubed fully cooked ham
 1/2   cup chopped onion
   1   teaspoon garlic powder
   1   teaspoon dill weed

- In a Dutch oven, combine the water and bouillon. Add cream cheese; cook and stir until cheese is melted. Stir in the remaining ingredients. Bring to a boil. Reduce heat; simmer, uncovered, for 18-20 minutes or until vegetables are tender.

Yield: 12 servings.

cream cheese potato soup

melted. Stir in the wild rice, ham, brown rice, bouillon, celery mixture and water. Return to a boil. Sprinkle with almonds if desired.

Yield: 12 servings.

creamy mushroom soup

ANNE KULICK, PHILLIPSBURG, NEW JERSEY

My daughter-in-law, a gourmet cook, served this soup as the first course for Thanksgiving dinner. She'd gotten the recipe from her mom and graciously shared it with me.

1/4	cup chopped onion
2	tablespoons butter
3	cups sliced fresh mushrooms
6	tablespoons all-purpose flour
2	cans (14-1/2 ounces each) chicken broth
1	cup half-and-half cream
1/2	teaspoon salt
1/8	teaspoon pepper

- In a large saucepan, saute onion in butter until tender. Add mushrooms and saute until tender. Combine flour and broth until smooth; stir into the mushroom mixture.

- Bring to a boil; cook and stir for 2 minutes or until thickened. Reduce heat. Stir in the cream, salt and pepper. Simmer, uncovered, for 15 minutes, stirring often.

Yield: 4-6 servings.

cheesy ham 'n' rice soup

cheesy ham 'n' rice soup

NICOLE WEIR, HAGER CITY, WISCONSIN

Here's a real gem! After tasting a similar soup at a popular restaurant in the Twin Cities, I came up with my own version. Everyone who tastes it says it's wonderful. The almonds give it a nice crunch.

4	celery ribs, chopped
1	large onion, chopped
1/4	cup butter, cubed
4	medium carrots, shredded
1/3	cup all-purpose flour
1	teaspoon salt
1/2	teaspoon pepper
2	cups half-and-half cream
8	ounces process cheese (Velveeta), cubed
4	cups cooked wild rice
3	cups cubed fully cooked ham
2-2/3	cups cooked brown rice
3	tablespoons chicken bouillon granules
8	cups water

Slivered almonds, optional

- In a large saucepan, saute celery and onion in butter until tender. Add carrots; cook and stir for 1-2 minutes. In a large kettle or Dutch oven, combine the flour, salt and pepper. Gradually stir in cream. Bring to a boil; cook and stir for 2 minutes or until thickened.

- Remove from the heat; stir in cheese until

Use an egg slicer to quickly slice fresh mushrooms. It's so easy that I don't use a knife for the task anymore. —Jennifer I., Brookhaven, Pennsylvania

creamy mushroom soup

BISQUES

Looking for the perfect warmer for crisp, cool nights? Look no further—a rich and creamy bisque is the answer. Whether it features seafood, herbs, squash or other veggies, the classic ingredients and simple preparation will please everyone, even you! They're even elegant enough to serve for special occasions.

winter squash soup

winter squash soup

ANGELA LIETTE, SIDNEY, OHIO

I enjoy trying new recipes and adding different seasonings to enhance the flavor. This is a tasty way to prepare squash.

- 2 celery ribs, chopped
- 1 medium onion, chopped
- 1 garlic clove, minced
- 3 tablespoons butter
- 3 tablespoons all-purpose flour
- 3 cups chicken broth
- 2 cups mashed cooked butternut, acorn or Hubbard squash
- 2 tablespoons minced fresh parsley
- 1/2 teaspoon salt
- 1/8 to 1/4 teaspoon ground nutmeg
- 1/4 teaspoon dried savory
- 1/4 teaspoon dried rosemary, crushed
- 1/8 teaspoon pepper
- 1 cup half-and-half cream

■ In a large saucepan, saute celery, onion and garlic in butter until tender. Stir in flour until blended. Gradually add the broth. Bring to a boil; cook and stir for 2 minutes or until thickened. Reduce heat; stir in the squash, parsley, salt, nutmeg, savory, rosemary and pepper. Simmer, uncovered, for 10 minutes or until heated through. Cool slightly.

■ In a blender or food processor, process soup in batches until smooth. Return to the pan and heat through. Gradually stir in cream. Cook 5 minutes longer, stirring occasionally.

Yield: 6 servings.

curried squash soup

EVELYN SOUTHWELL, ETTERS, PENNSYLVANIA

Cayenne pepper gives a little kick to bowls of this pretty golden soup, a first course that everyone seems to love.

- 1 butternut squash (about 1-3/4 pounds)
- 1 large onion, chopped
- 2 garlic cloves, minced
- 2 tablespoons canola oil
- 1 tablespoon all-purpose flour
- 1 teaspoon each salt and curry powder
- 1/8 teaspoon cayenne pepper
- 5 cups chicken broth

- 1 bay leaf

CILANTO CREAM TOPPING:
- 1/2 cup sour cream
- 1/4 cup heavy whipping cream
- 1/4 cup minced fresh cilantro

■ Cut squash in half lengthwise; discard seeds. Place squash cut side down in a greased or foil-lined baking pan. Bake, uncovered, at 400° for 40-50 minutes or until tender. When cool enough to handle, scoop out pulp; set aside.

■ In a large saucepan, saute onion and garlic in oil until tender. Add the flour, salt, curry powder and cayenne until blended. Stir in broth. Add bay leaf.

■ Bring to a boil; cook and stir for 2 minutes or until thickened. Reduce heat; simmer, uncovered, for 20 minutes. Discard bay leaf. Cool to room temperature.

■ In a blender, combine half of the broth mixture and squash; cover and process until smooth. Repeat with remaining broth mixture and squash. Return to the saucepan; heat through. Combine the topping ingredients; place a dollop or pipe a shape on each serving.

Yield: 6 servings.

curried squash soup

| garlic butternut bisque

broth and 2 tablespoons sage. Bring to a boil. Reduce heat; simmer, uncovered, for 25-30 minutes or until squash is tender.

- Squeeze softened garlic into a small bowl; mash with a fork. Stir into squash mixture. Cool slightly. Puree squash mixture in batches in a blender; return to pan. Stir in 1/2 cup cream, salt and pepper and remaining butter; heat through. Garnish with remaining cream and sage.

Yield: 9 servings.

zesty tomato soup

JoAnn Gunio, Franklin, North Carolina

When some friends stopped by unexpectedly, my husband came up with this fast-to-fix soup that tastes homemade. Two easy ingredients give canned soup just the right amount of zip.

   2 **cans (10-3/4 ounces each) condensed tomato soup, undiluted**
2-2/3 **cups water**
   2 **teaspoons chili powder**
Oyster crackers or shredded Monterey Jack cheese, optional

- In a saucepan, combine the first three ingredients; heat through. Garnish with crackers or cheese if desired.

Yield: 4-5 servings.

garlic butternut bisque

Della Clarke, Vista, California

With its pleasant squash and garlic flavor and golden-orange color, this rich and creamy soup is sure to be a hit whether you serve it for an everyday meal or a holiday dinner.

  2 **whole garlic bulbs**
  1 **teaspoon olive oil**
  3 **large onions, chopped**
3/4 **cup chopped carrots**
1/2 **cup chopped celery**
3/4 **cup butter, divided**
  4 **pounds butternut squash, peeled, seeded and cubed (about 8 cups)**
  6 **cups chicken broth**
  3 **tablespoons chopped fresh sage, divided**
1/2 **cup plus 1 tablespoon heavy whipping cream, divided**
1-1/2 **teaspoons salt**
1/4 **teaspoon pepper**

- Remove papery outer skin from garlic (do not peel or separate cloves). Cut tops off bulbs; brush with oil. Wrap each in heavy-duty foil. Bake at 425° for 30-35 minutes or until softened. Cool 10-15 minutes.

- Meanwhile, in a Dutch oven or soup kettle, saute the onions, carrots and celery in 1/2 cup butter until tender. Add the squash,

zesty tomato soup

harvest squash soup

harvest squash soup

MRS. H.L. SOSNOWSKI, GRAND ISLAND, NEW YORK

This soup is perfect for a group after an autumn outing. The combination of squash, applesauce and spices gives it an appealing flavor.

1-1/2 cups chopped onion
   1 tablespoon canola oil
   4 cups mashed cooked butternut squash
   3 cups chicken broth
   2 cups unsweetened applesauce
1-1/2 cups milk
   1 bay leaf
   1 tablespoon lime juice
   1 tablespoon sugar
   1 teaspoon curry powder
1/2 teaspoon ground cinnamon
1/2 teaspoon salt, optional
1/4 teaspoon pepper
1/4 teaspoon ground nutmeg

- In a Dutch oven, saute onions in oil until tender. Add the squash, broth, applesauce, milk, bay leaf, lime juice, sugar, curry powder, cinnamon, salt if desired, pepper and nutmeg. Bring to a boil. Reduce heat; simmer, uncovered, for 30 minutes. Discard bay leaf before serving.

Yield: 10 servings.

When grating zucchini, leave the stem on to give you a grip as you work.

zucchini bisque

GERMAINE STANK, POUND, WISCONSIN

Looking for a different way to serve a bounty of zucchini? Try this soup. A food processor hurries along preparation of the thick, full-flavored blend that's accented by just a hint of nutmeg.

   4 medium zucchini, shredded
   1 medium onion, chopped
1/2 cup butter, cubed
2-1/2 cups chicken broth
   1 cup heavy whipping cream
3/4 teaspoon salt
1/2 teaspoon minced fresh basil
1/2 teaspoon pepper
1/4 teaspoon ground nutmeg
Sour cream and additional nutmeg, optional

- In a large saucepan, saute zucchini and onion in butter for 5-6 minutes or until tender. Stir in broth. Bring to a boil. Reduce heat; cover and simmer for 12-15 minutes. Cool slightly.

- Transfer to a food processor or blender; cover and process on low until smooth. Return to the pan. Stir in the cream, salt, basil, pepper and nutmeg. Bring to a boil. Reduce heat; simmer, uncovered, for 1-2 minutes or until heated through. Garnish with sour cream and additional nutmeg if desired.

Yield: 6 servings.

zucchini bisque

crab bisque

CORNEY WELSH, BATON ROUGE, LOUISIANA

I decided to try my hand at making a seafood soup after tasting one while dining out. I came up with this bisque and everyone loved it. It was even featured on a local TV show recently!

  2 cups chopped onions
  1 cup chopped celery
  1 cup chopped green pepper
  4 garlic cloves, minced
1/4 cup butter
  4 cups diced peeled potatoes
  2 cups milk
  4 cups half-and-half cream
 10 ounces process cheese (Velveeta),
    cut into 1-inch cubes
  1 can (1 pound) crabmeat, drained,
    flaked and cartilage removed
3/4 teaspoon salt
1/4 teaspoon white pepper

- In a soup kettle or Dutch oven, saute the onions, celery, green pepper and garlic in butter until tender. Reduce heat to medium; add the potatoes and milk. Cook, uncovered, for 20 minutes or until potatoes are just tender, stirring occasionally.

- Remove 1-1/2 cups of the potato mixture; mash and return to the pan. Reduce heat to low. Stir in half-and-half and process cheese. Cook and stir until cheese is melted. Add the crab, salt and pepper. Cook 10 minutes longer or until heated through.

Yield: 12 servings.

crab bisque

broccoli and crab bisque

broccoli and crab bisque

DOROTHY CHILD, MALONE, NEW YORK

Since our son is a broccoli grower, our friends keep supplying us with recipes using broccoli. To this family favorite, add a tossed salad, rolls, fruit and cookies, and you have an easy but delicious supper full of nutrition.

  1 cup each sliced leeks (white part
    only), sliced fresh mushrooms and
    fresh broccoli florets
  1 garlic clove, minced
1/4 cup butter
1/4 cup all-purpose flour
1/4 teaspoon dried thyme, crushed
1/8 teaspoon pepper
  1 bay leaf
  2 cans (10-1/2 ounces each)
    condensed chicken broth, undiluted
  1 cup half-and-half cream
3/4 cup shredded Swiss cheese
  1 package (6 ounces) frozen crab-
    meat, thawed, drained and flaked

- In a large saucepan, cook the leeks, mushrooms, broccoli and garlic in butter until broccoli is crisp-tender. Stir in flour and seasonings until blended. Gradually add broth and cream.

- Bring to a boil. Cook and stir for 1-2 minutes or until thickened. Add cheese; stir until melted. Add crab; heat through but do not boil. Discard bay leaf before serving.

Yield: 5 servings.

Select firm but tender stalks of broccoli with compact, dark green or slightly purplish florets.

easy seafood bisque

CINDY ROGOWSKI, LANCASTER, NEW YORK

I've always enjoyed seafood bisque at restaurants and one day decided to try my hand at a homemade version. Everyone says this is one of the better recipes they've tasted.

1/2 cup chopped onion
1 tablespoon butter
2-1/4 cups milk
1 can (10-3/4 ounces) condensed cream of celery soup, undiluted
1 can (10-3/4 ounces) condensed cream of shrimp soup, undiluted
1 package (8 ounces) imitation crabmeat, chopped
1 teaspoon chicken bouillon granules
1/2 teaspoon dried parsley flakes
1/4 teaspoon garlic powder
1/4 teaspoon dried marjoram
1/4 teaspoon pepper

■ In a 3-qt. saucepan, saute onion in butter until tender. Stir in remaining ingredients. Cover and cook over medium-low heat for 20 minutes or until heated through, stirring occasionally.

Yield: 4-5 servings.

butternut bisque

butternut bisque

KRISTIN ARNETT, ELKHORN, WISCONSIN

I've served this wonderful soup to family as well as company. It's especially good to serve in the cooler fall months.

3-1/2 pounds butternut squash, peeled, seeded and cubed
1 cup sliced carrots
1 medium tart apple, peeled and chopped
1/2 cup chopped shallots
2 tablespoons olive oil
3 large tomatoes, seeded and chopped
4 cups chicken broth
1-1/4 cups half-and-half cream
1-1/2 teaspoons salt
1/4 teaspoon cayenne pepper
3/4 cup frozen corn, thawed
2 tablespoons minced chives
Sour cream and additional chives, optional

■ In a large bowl, toss the squash, carrots, apple, shallots and oil. Transfer to a large roasting pan. Bake, uncovered, at 400° for 1 hour or until browned and tender, stirring twice. Cool slightly. Place in a food processor or blender; cover and process until almost smooth.

■ In a Dutch oven or soup kettle, cook tomatoes over medium heat for 5 minutes. Add the pureed vegetables, broth, cream, salt and cayenne; heat through (do not boil). Stir in corn and chives. Garnish servings with sour cream and chives if desired.

Yield: 10 servings.

easy seafood bisque

CHOWDERS

Soothe and satisfy your family with a thick and chunky chowder. They can be the perfect everyday lunch or prelude to a special meal— the choice is yours. With a variety of options— from ham and rice to seafood and potatoes, you'll find empty bowls on your table when you serve any of these home-style classics.

wild rice and ham chowder

wild rice and ham chowder

ELMA FRIESEN, WINNIPEG, MANITOBA

The rich, comforting taste of this chowder appeals to everyone who tries it. I have my younger sister to thank for sharing this recipe with me years ago.

- 1/2 cup chopped onion
- 2 garlic cloves, minced
- 1/4 cup butter, cubed
- 6 tablespoons all-purpose flour
- 1/2 teaspoon salt
- 1/4 teaspoon pepper
- 4 cups chicken broth
- 1-1/2 cups cubed peeled potatoes
- 1/2 cup chopped carrot
- 1 bay leaf
- 1/2 teaspoon dried thyme
- 1/4 teaspoon ground nutmeg
- 3 cups cooked wild rice
- 2-1/2 cups cubed fully cooked ham
- 2 cups half-and-half cream
- 1 can (15-1/4 ounces) whole kernel corn, drained

Minced fresh parsley

- In a Dutch oven or soup kettle over medium heat, saute onion and garlic in butter until tender. Stir in the flour, salt and pepper until blended. Gradually add broth. Bring to a boil. Cook and stir for 2 minutes or until thickened and bubbly.

- Add the potatoes, carrot, bay leaf, thyme and nutmeg; return to a boil. Reduce heat; cover and simmer for 30 minutes or until vegetables are tender. Stir in the rice, ham, cream and corn; heat through (do not boil). Discard bay leaf. Garnish with parsley.

Yield: 8-10 servings.

harvest corn chicken chowder

JANET BOOTE, HULL, IOWA

With lots of chicken and ham, this version of corn chowder has become a favorite at my house. I like to use sweet corn I grow in my own garden.

- 1/2 cup chopped onion
- 1/2 cup chopped sweet red pepper
- 2 garlic cloves, minced
- 1 tablespoon olive oil
- 1 cup cubed fully cooked ham
- 2 cups water
- 2 cups cubed red potatoes
- 1-1/2 cups fresh or frozen corn
- 1 teaspoon chicken bouillon granules
- 3/4 teaspoon dried thyme
- 1/2 teaspoon poultry seasoning
- 1/2 teaspoon salt
- 1/4 teaspoon pepper
- 1 cup cubed cooked chicken breast
- 1 can (12 ounces) evaporated milk
- 3/4 cup milk, divided
- 1/4 cup all-purpose flour

- In a large saucepan, saute the onion, red pepper and garlic in oil until onion is tender. Add ham; cook and stir for 2 minutes. Stir in the water, potatoes, corn, bouillon, thyme, poultry seasoning, salt and pepper. Bring to a boil. Reduce heat; cover and simmer for 15 minutes or until the potatoes are tender.

- Add chicken; heat through. Stir in the evaporated milk and 1/2 cup milk; bring to a boil. Combine flour and remaining milk until smooth; gradually stir into soup. Cook and stir for 2 minutes or until thickened.

Yield: 5 servings.

harvest corn chicken chowder

salmon potato chowder

wild rice chowder

AMY CHOP, OAK GROVE, LOUISIANA

I found this years ago, and it has become a family favorite. Try adding cooked chicken or smoked sausage. There are endless possibilities for new and exciting variations.

    8 bacon strips, diced
  1/3 cup chopped onion
  1/3 cup all-purpose flour
  1/2 to 1 teaspoon salt
    4 cups water
    1 can (14-1/2 ounces) chicken broth
1-1/2 cups cooked wild rice
    1 can (12 ounces) evaporated milk
    2 cups (8 ounces) cubed process American cheese
    2 tablespoons minced fresh parsley

- In a large saucepan, cook bacon until crisp. Remove with a slotted spoon to paper towels. Drain, reserving 1 tablespoon drippings. Saute onion in drippings until tender. Stir in flour and salt. Gradually stir in water and broth. Bring to a boil; cook and stir for 2 minutes or until slightly thickened.

- Stir in the wild rice. Reduce heat; cover and simmer for 5 minutes. Add the milk, cheese, parsley and bacon; cook and stir until heated through and cheese is melted.

Yield: 6-8 servings.

salmon potato chowder

CINDY ST. MARTIN, PORTLAND, OREGON

After my husband and I caught four large salmon, my mother-in-law combined several recipes to create this delicious chowder. She served it with a salad and hot fresh bread. Now I make it regularly, too, especially for guests, who always ask for the recipe.

    2 pounds red potatoes, peeled and cubed
    1 large onion, chopped
    1 can (49-1/2 ounces) chicken broth
    1 pound salmon fillets, cut into 1-inch pieces
  1/2 pound sliced bacon, cooked and crumbled
    2 cups milk
    1 cup half-and-half cream
    1 tablespoon butter
  1/2 teaspoon salt
Pepper to taste

- In a soup kettle or Dutch oven, bring the potatoes, onion and broth to a boil. Reduce heat; cover and cook until potatoes are tender. Add salmon and bacon; cook over medium heat until fish flakes easily with a fork.

- Reduce heat; stir in the milk, cream, butter, salt and pepper; heat through (do not boil). Thicken if desired.

Yield: 14 servings.

wild rice chowder

new england seafood chowder

new england seafood chowder

KRISTINE LOWEL
SOUTHBOROUGH, MASSACHUSETTS

We find many ways to prepare the abundance of fresh seafood available in our area, and this "fish chowdy" is a hearty favorite. Featuring a flavorful combination of haddock, shrimp and scallops, the chowder is great to serve to a group.

- 4 pounds haddock fillets, cut into 3/4-inch pieces
- 1/4 pound uncooked medium shrimp, peeled and deveined
- 1/4 pound bay scallops
- 4 bacon strips, diced
- 3 medium onions, quartered and thinly sliced
- 2 tablespoons all-purpose flour
- 2 cups diced peeled potatoes
- 4 cups milk
- 2 tablespoons butter
- 1 tablespoon minced fresh parsley
- 2 teaspoons salt
- 1/2 teaspoon lemon-pepper seasoning
- 1/4 teaspoon pepper

- Place haddock in a Dutch oven; cover with water. Bring to a boil over medium heat. Reduce heat; simmer, uncovered, for 20 minutes. Add the shrimp and scallops; simmer 10 minutes longer. Drain, reserving 2 cups cooking liquid; set liquid and seafood aside.

- In a soup kettle, cook bacon over medium heat until crisp; drain on paper towels. In the drippings, saute onions until tender. Stir in

To chop carrots coarsely for soup, I peel, remove the ends and cut the carrots into quarters. Then I let the food processor do the chopping!
—Marion K., Waterloo, Iowa

flour until blended. Gradually stir in reserved cooking liquid. Bring to a boil; cook and stir for 2 minutes or until thickened. Reduce the heat. Add the potatoes; cover and cook for 15-20 minutes or until potatoes are tender.

- Add the milk, seafood, butter, parsley, salt, lemon-pepper and pepper; heat through. Sprinkle with bacon.

Yield: 15 servings.

quick corn chowder

DOROTHY FAULKNER, BENTON, ARKANSAS

My friends and family always dig in when I serve this chowder. It pairs well with a sandwich or salad.

- 1/4 cup chopped green pepper
- 2 tablespoons chopped onion
- 2 garlic cloves, minced
- 2 tablespoons butter
- 2 cans (10-3/4 ounces each) condensed cream of potato soup, undiluted
- 1 can (14-3/4 ounces) cream-style corn
- 2 cups milk
- 1 package (3 ounces) cream cheese, cubed

Pepper to taste

- In a large saucepan, saute the green pepper, onion and garlic in butter until tender. Stir in the soup, corn, milk, cream cheese and pepper. Bring to a boil, stirring frequently. Reduce heat; simmer, uncovered, for 5 minutes or until cream cheese is melted.

Yield: 4-6 servings.

quick corn chowder

clam chowder

ROSEMARY PETERSON, ARCHIE, MISSOURI

This satisfying chowder is quick to prepare and so comforting on a cold day.

- 2 cans (6-1/2 ounces each) minced clams
- 6 potatoes, peeled and diced
- 6 carrots, diced
- 1/2 cup chopped onion
- 1/2 cup butter
- 1-1/2 cups water
- 2 cans (12 ounces each) evaporated milk
- 2 cans (10-3/4 ounces each) condensed cream of mushroom soup, undiluted
- 1 teaspoon salt
- 1/2 teaspoon pepper

- Drain clams, reserving liquid; set the clams aside. In a large kettle, combine the potatoes, carrots, onion, butter, water and reserved clam juice. Cook over medium heat for 15 minutes or until the vegetables are tender. Stir in the milk, soup, salt and pepper. Simmer, uncovered, until heated through. Stir in clams.

Yield: 10-12 servings.

fresh corn chowder

fresh corn chowder

NANCY JOHNSON, CONNERSVILLE, INDIANA

On cool days, this thick, creamy chowder hits the spot as an appetizer or light lunch.

- 1 medium onion, chopped
- 6 cups fresh or frozen corn, divided
- 3 cups reduced-sodium chicken broth, divided
- 1/2 cup chopped sweet red pepper
- 1/2 teaspoon dried rosemary, crushed
- 1/2 teaspoon dried thyme
- 1/8 teaspoon pepper

Dash cayenne pepper

- Coat the bottom of a large saucepan with cooking spray. Add onion; cook and stir over medium heat for 4 minutes or until tender. Add 4 cups corn; cook and stir until corn is softened, about 5 minutes. Add 2 cups broth; bring to a boil. Reduce heat; cover and simmer for 10 minutes or until corn is tender. Cool slightly.

- In a blender or food processor, process soup in batches until smooth; return all to pan. Add the red pepper, rosemary, thyme, pepper, cayenne and remaining corn and broth; cook and stir for 10 minutes or until the corn is cooked.

Yield: 4-6 servings.

clam chowder

autumn sausage corn soup

BELINDA DESSELLE, WESTLAKE, LOUISIANA

I cook this frequently throughout the year, but my family especially loves it on chilly nights. Cayenne pepper, sausage and ham lend to its fabulous Cajun flavor.

- 3/4 **pound fully cooked smoked sausage, sliced**
- 1/4 **cup all-purpose flour**
- 1/4 **cup canola oil**
- 1/2 **cup chopped onion**
- 1/2 **cup chopped green pepper**
- 3 **green onions, chopped**
- 3-1/2 **cups water**
- 1 **package (16 ounces) frozen corn**
- 1-1/2 **cups cubed fully cooked ham**
- 1 **can (14-1/2 ounces) diced tomatoes, undrained**
- 1 **cup chopped fresh tomatoes**
- 1 **can (6 ounces) tomato paste**
- 1/4 **teaspoon salt, optional**
- 1/8 **teaspoon cayenne pepper**

Hot pepper sauce to taste

- In a large skillet, cook and stir sausage over medium-high heat until browned; drain well and set aside.

- In a Dutch oven or soup kettle, cook and stir the flour in oil over medium heat for 5 minutes or until golden brown. Add the onion, green pepper and green onions; saute until tender.

autumn sausage corn soup

creamy turkey & vegetable soup

- Stir in the water, corn, ham, tomatoes, fresh tomatoes, tomato paste, salt, if desired, cayenne, hot pepper sauce and sausage. Bring to a boil. Reduce heat; cover and simmer for 1 hour, stirring occasionally.

Yield: 11 servings.

creamy turkey & vegetable soup

LOIS HOFMEYER, SUGAR GROVE, ILLINOIS

My sisters and I made this soup with our mom when we were young. Now it's the traditional "day after Thanksgiving" soup for our own families.

- 1 **large onion, finely chopped**
- 2 **tablespoons butter**
- 3 **cups diced small red potatoes**
- 2 **cans (14-1/2 ounces each) chicken broth**
- 2 **cups cooked cubed turkey breast**
- 2 **cups frozen mixed vegetables, thawed**
- 1/2 **teaspoon salt**
- 1/2 **teaspoon white pepper**
- 1/2 **teaspoon poultry seasoning**
- 2 **cups heavy whipping cream**

- In a large saucepan, saute onion in butter until tender. Add potatoes and broth. Bring to a boil. Reduce heat; cover and simmer for 20 minutes. Stir in the turkey, vegetables, salt, pepper and poultry seasoning. Cook 10-12 minutes longer or until vegetables are tender. Stir in cream; heat through (do not boil).

Yield: 8 servings.

CHILI

You can't go wrong when you serve a crowd-pleasing chili. Whether it's your daily dinnertime crowd or a party of friends or relatives, you'll win raves if you serve one of our heartwarming chili recipes. The variety found here will please all palates, too, so if you like spicy, we have it—but if mild is your taste, it's here, too.

jalapeno pepper chili

jalapeno pepper chili

Tonya Michelle Burkhard
Port Charlotte, Florida

I like meals that are simple to prepare, yet offer maximum taste. This unforgettable chili offers extra zip with two kinds of meat, beans and jalapeno pepper.

- 1/2 pound ground beef
- 1/2 pound ground pork
- 2 cans (16 ounces each) kidney beans, rinsed and drained
- 2 cans (14-1/2 ounces each) diced tomatoes with garlic and onion, undrained
- 1 can (14-1/2 ounces) beef broth
- 1 can (8 ounces) tomato sauce
- 2 tablespoons chili powder
- 1 jalapeno pepper, seeded and chopped
- 12 hard rolls (about 4-1/2 inches), optional

Shredded cheddar cheese, sliced green onions and sour cream, optional

- In a large saucepan, cook beef and pork over medium heat until no longer pink; drain. Stir in the beans, tomatoes, broth, tomato sauce, chili powder and jalapeno. Bring to a boil. Reduce heat; cover and simmer for 20 minutes.

- Serve in soup bowls or if desired, cut the top fourth off of each roll; carefully hollow out bottom, leaving a 1/2-in. shell. Cube removed bread. Spoon chili into bread bowls. Serve with cubed bread, shredded cheddar cheese, sliced green onions and sour cream if desired.

Yield: 12 servings.

Editor's Note: When cutting or seeding hot peppers, use rubber or plastic gloves to protect your hands. Avoid touching your face.

spicy pork chili

Larry Laatsch, Saginaw, Michigan

This chili, loaded with white beans and cubes of pork, has plenty of bite. But if it's not spicy enough for you, top it with shredded jalapeno jack cheese and finely diced onions.

- 1-1/2 pounds pork tenderloin, cubed
- 2 large onions, diced
- 4 celery ribs, diced
- 2 tablespoons butter
- 6 cans (15-1/2 ounces each) great northern beans, rinsed and drained
- 4 cans (14-1/2 ounces each) chicken broth
- 2 cups water
- 2 jalapeno peppers, seeded and chopped
- 2 teaspoons chili powder
- 1/2 teaspoon each white pepper, cayenne pepper, ground cumin and pepper
- 2 garlic cloves, minced
- 1/2 teaspoon salt
- 1/4 teaspoon dried parsley flakes
- 1/4 teaspoon hot pepper sauce, optional
- 1 cup (4 ounces) shredded Monterey Jack cheese

- In a Dutch oven, cook the pork, onions and celery in butter until meat is browned. Stir in the beans, broth, water, jalapenos, spices, garlic, salt, parsley and hot pepper sauce if desired. Bring to a boil. Reduce heat; cover and simmer for 1-1/2 hours.

- Uncover; simmer 30-40 minutes longer or until chili reaches desired consistency. Sprinkle with cheese.

Yield: 15 servings.

Editor's Note: When cutting or seeding hot peppers, use rubber or plastic gloves to protect your hands. Avoid touching your face.

spicy pork chili

lime chicken chili

lime chicken chili

DIANE RANDAZZO, SINKING SPRING, PENNSYLVANIA

Lime juice gives this chili a zesty twist, while canned tomatoes and beans make preparation a snap. Try serving bowls with toasted tortilla strips.

- 1 medium onion, chopped
- 1 each medium sweet yellow, red and green pepper, chopped
- 3 garlic cloves, minced
- 2 tablespoons olive oil
- 1 pound ground chicken
- 1 tablespoon all-purpose flour
- 1 tablespoon baking cocoa
- 1 tablespoon ground cumin
- 1 tablespoon chili powder
- 2 teaspoons ground coriander
- 1/2 teaspoon salt
- 1/2 teaspoon garlic-pepper blend
- 1/4 teaspoon pepper
- 2 cans (14-1/2 ounces each) diced tomatoes, undrained
- 1/4 cup lime juice
- 1 teaspoon grated lime peel
- 1 can (15 ounces) white kidney or cannellini beans, rinsed and drained
- 2 flour tortillas (8 inches), cut into 1/4-inch strips
- 6 tablespoons sour cream

■ In a large saucepan, saute the onion, peppers and garlic in oil for 7-8 minutes or until crisp-tender. Add chicken; cook and stir over medium heat for 8-9 minutes or until no longer pink.

■ Stir in the flour, cocoa and seasonings. Add tomatoes, lime juice and lime peel. Bring to a boil. Reduce heat; simmer, uncovered, for 20-25 minutes or until thickened, stirring frequently. Stir in beans; heat through.

■ Meanwhile, place tortilla strips on a baking sheet coated with cooking spray. Bake at 400° for 8-10 minutes or until crisp. Serve chili with sour cream and tortilla strips.

Yield: 6 servings.

The spice coriander comes from the seed of the cilantro plant.

taco minestrone

CAROLE HOLDER, NORMAN, OKLAHOMA

Since my husband and I both work full-time, it's nice to have a winter pick-me-up like this zippy favorite when I need a speedy and filling entree for supper.

- 1/2 pound ground beef
- 2 cans (15 ounces each) ranch-style beans
- 2 cans (10-3/4 ounces each) condensed minestrone soup, undiluted
- 2 cans (10 ounces each) diced tomatoes and green chilies, undrained

■ In a saucepan, cook beef over medium heat until no longer pink; drain. Stir in the beans, soup and tomatoes. Bring to a boil. Reduce heat; simmer, uncovered for 15-20 minutes.

Yield: 8 servings.

taco minestrone

turkey chili

turkey chili

Celesta Zanger, Bloomfield Hills, Michigan

I've taken my mother's milder recipe for chili and made it thicker and more robust. It's a favorite, especially in fall and winter.

- 1 pound lean ground turkey
- 3/4 cup each chopped onion, celery and green pepper
- 1 can (28 ounces) diced tomatoes, undrained
- 1 jar (26 ounces) meatless spaghetti sauce
- 1 can (15-1/2 ounces) hot chili beans
- 1-1/2 cups water
- 1/2 cup frozen corn
- 2 tablespoons chili powder
- 1 teaspoon ground cumin
- 1/4 teaspoon pepper
- 1/8 to 1/4 teaspoon cayenne pepper
- 1 can (16 ounces) kidney beans, rinsed and drained
- 1 can (15 ounces) pinto beans, rinsed and drained

Sour cream, optional

- In a large nonstick skillet, cook the turkey, onion, celery and green pepper over medium heat until meat is no longer pink and the vegetables are tender; drain. Transfer to a 5-qt. slow cooker. Add the tomatoes, spaghetti sauce, chili beans, water, corn and seasonings. Cover and cook on high for 1 hour.

- Reduce heat to low; cook for 5-6 hours. Add kidney and pinto beans; cook 30 minutes longer. Garnish with sour cream if desired.

Yield: 13 servings.

slow-cooked chili

Sandra McKenzie, Braham, Minnesota

This savory chili recipe is sure to be filling, and it will warm your guests up, too.

- 2 pounds ground beef
- 1/2 cup chopped onion
- 2 garlic cloves, minced
- 2 cans (16 ounces each) dark red kidney beans, rinsed and drained
- 2 cans (16 ounces each) light red kidney beans, rinsed and drained
- 2 cans (14-1/2 ounces each) stewed tomatoes, cut up
- 1 can (15 ounces) pizza sauce
- 1 can (4 ounces) chopped green chilies
- 4 teaspoons chili powder
- 1 teaspoon dried basil
- 1/2 teaspoon salt
- 1/8 teaspoon pepper

- In a Dutch oven, cook the beef, onion and garlic over medium heat until meat is no longer pink; drain. Transfer to a 5-qt. slow cooker; stir in the remaining ingredients. Cover and cook on low for 6 hours.

Yield: 14 servings.

slow-cooked chili

white chili with hominy

TASTE OF HOME TEST KITCHEN

To make this chili a day ahead, cool, cover and chill after removing from the heat. The next day, reheat over low heat; add the sour cream, half-and-half and cilantro just before serving.

- 1 pound boneless skinless chicken breasts, cut into 1/2-inch cubes
- 1 medium onion, chopped
- 1 tablespoon canola oil
- 1 can (15-1/2 ounces) white hominy, drained
- 1 can (15 ounces) white kidney or cannellini beans, rinsed and drained
- 1 can (14-1/2 ounces) chicken broth
- 2 cans (4 ounces each) chopped green chilies
- 1 teaspoon garlic salt
- 1 teaspoon dried basil
- 1 teaspoon ground cumin
- 1/4 teaspoon white pepper
- 1/8 to 1/4 teaspoon cayenne pepper
- 1 cup (8 ounces) sour cream
- 1/3 cup half-and-half cream
- 2 tablespoons minced fresh cilantro, divided

- In a large saucepan, saute the chicken and onion in oil until chicken is no longer pink. Add the hominy, beans, broth, chilies and seasonings. Bring to a boil. Reduce heat; simmer, uncovered, for 30 minutes. Remove from the heat; stir in the sour cream, half-and-half and 1 tablespoon cilantro. Sprinkle with remaining cilantro.

Yield: 6 servings.

spicy slow-cooked chili

spicy slow-cooked chili

SABRINA CORRIGAN, WILLIAMSBURG, PENNSYLVANIA

I love that I can put the ingredients in the slow cooker and forget about it for a few hours. If you like your chili thick, you'll enjoy this version.

- 2 pounds ground beef
- 2 to 3 hot chili peppers of your choice
- 3 cans (16 ounces each) kidney beans, rinsed and drained
- 1 can (6 ounces) tomato paste
- 1 medium onion, chopped
- 1 medium green pepper, seeded and chopped
- 2 teaspoons chili powder
- 2 teaspoons cider vinegar
- 1 teaspoon garlic powder
- 1 teaspoon dried oregano
- 1/4 to 1/2 teaspoon ground cinnamon
- 1/4 teaspoon pepper
- 2 to 4 cups tomato juice

Canned beans are rinsed and drained to remove extra salt used in the canning process.

- In a large skillet, cook beef over medium heat until no longer pink; drain. Transfer to a 5-qt. slow cooker. Remove seeds from the chili peppers if desired; chop peppers. Add to the slow cooker. Stir in the beans, tomato paste, onion, green pepper, seasonings and 2 cups tomato juice.

- Cover and cook on low for 4-6 hours or until heated through, adding more tomato juice if needed to achieve desired thickness.

Yield: 8 servings.

Editor's Note: When cutting or seeding hot peppers, use rubber or plastic gloves to protect your hands. Avoid touching your face.

white chili with hominy

speedy weeknight chili

CYNTHIA HUDSON, GREENVILLE, SOUTH CAROLINA

Super-easy and great-tasting, this chili makes a big batch of great party fare. I use my food processor to chop up the veggies and cut down on prep time. It can also be low in fat if you make it with ground turkey.

- 1-1/2 pounds ground beef
- 2 small onions, chopped
- 1/2 cup chopped green pepper
- 1 teaspoon minced garlic
- 2 cans (16 ounces each) kidney beans, rinsed and drained
- 2 cans (14-1/2 ounces each) stewed tomatoes
- 1 can (28 ounces) crushed tomatoes
- 1 bottle (12 ounces) beer or nonalcoholic beer
- 1 can (6 ounces) tomato paste
- 1/4 cup chili powder
- 3/4 teaspoon dried oregano
- 1/2 teaspoon hot pepper sauce
- 1/4 teaspoon sugar
- 1/4 teaspoon salt
- 1/4 teaspoon pepper

■ In a large saucepan or Dutch oven, cook the beef, onions, green pepper and garlic over medium heat until meat is no longer pink; drain. Add remaining ingredients; bring to a boil. Reduce heat; simmer, uncovered, for 10 minutes.

Yield: 15 servings.

The term "shoepeg corn" dates back to before the American Civil War. The corn was named for its peg-like shape. Shoepeg has smaller kernels and is sweeter than yellow corn.

santa fe chili

santa fe chili

LAURA MANNING, LILBURN, GEORGIA

This colorful chili is perfect for heartwarming holiday get-togethers. My family has been enjoying it for years.

- 2 pounds ground beef
- 1 medium onion, chopped
- 2 cans (16 ounces each) kidney beans, rinsed and drained
- 2 cans (15 ounces each) black beans, rinsed and drained
- 2 cans (15 ounces each) pinto beans, rinsed and drained
- 2 cans (11 ounces each) shoepeg corn
- 1 can (14-1/2 ounces) whole tomatoes, diced
- 1 can (10 ounces) diced tomatoes and green chilies
- 1 can (11-1/2 ounces) V8 juice
- 2 envelopes ranch salad dressing mix
- 2 envelopes taco seasoning

Sour cream, shredded cheddar cheese and corn chips, optional

■ In a skillet, cook beef and onion over medium heat until meat is no longer pink; drain. Transfer to a 5-qt. slow cooker. Stir in the beans, corn, tomatoes, juice, salad dressing mix and taco seasoning.

■ Cover and cook on high for 4 hours or until heated through. Serve with sour cream, cheese and corn chips if desired.

Yield: 16 servings.

speedy weeknight chili

scarecrow chili

shrimp 'n' black bean chili

ELIZABETH HUNT, KIRBYVILLE, TEXAS

It's not spicy, but this chili is sure to warm you up during those cold winter evenings. Since this recipe calls for precooked shrimp and canned goods, it is very quick to prepare.

1/2 cup chopped onion
1/2 cup chopped green pepper
1 tablespoon canola oil
1 can (15 ounces) black beans, rinsed and drained
1 can (14-1/2 ounces) diced tomatoes, undrained
1 cup chicken broth
1/3 cup picante sauce
1 teaspoon ground cumin
1/2 teaspoon dried basil
1 pound cooked medium shrimp, peeled and deveined

Hot cooked rice, optional

■ In a large saucepan, saute onion and green pepper in oil for 4-5 minutes or until crisp-tender. Stir in the beans, tomatoes, broth, picante sauce, cumin and basil. Reduce heat; simmer, uncovered, for 10-15 minutes or until heated through.

■ Add shrimp; simmer 3-4 minutes longer or until heated through. Serve with rice if desired.

Yield: 6 servings.

There's no need to run to the store if you're out of brown sugar— you can substitute 1 cup granulated sugar or 2 cups sifted confectioners' sugar for 1 cup brown sugar.

scarecrow chili

BARB SCHLAFER, APPLETON, WISCONSIN

This chili was the star of my family's annual Pumpkin Patch Party. The hungry bunch of family and friends enthusiastically ladled up this thick chili. Even the kids loved it!

1-1/2 pounds ground beef
2 celery ribs, chopped
1 medium onion, chopped
1 can (46 ounces) tomato juice
1 can (28 ounces) diced tomatoes, undrained
1 can (16 ounces) kidney beans, rinsed and drained
1 can (10-3/4 ounces) condensed tomato soup, undiluted
1/2 cup water
2 tablespoons chili powder
1 to 2 tablespoons brown sugar
3 bay leaves

Salt and pepper to taste
2 cups elbow macaroni, cooked and drained

■ In a Dutch oven, cook the beef, celery and onion over medium heat until meat is no longer pink; drain. Add the tomato juice, tomatoes, beans, soup, water, chili powder, brown sugar, bay leaves, salt and pepper. Bring to a boil. Reduce heat; cover and simmer for 30 minutes.

■ Stir in macaroni. Cook, uncovered, 5 minutes longer or until heated through. Discard bay leaves before serving.

Yield: 16 servings.

shrimp 'n' black bean chili

zippy steak chili

mushroom salsa chili

RICHARD RUNDELS, WAVERLY, OHIO

Green, sweet red and yellow peppers give this filling chili a splash of color. I often fix it for my grandsons. Because they don't like spicy chili, I use mild salsa, but try it with a hotter variety if you prefer.

- 1 pound ground beef
- 1 pound bulk pork sausage
- 2 cans (16 ounces each) kidney beans, rinsed and drained
- 1 jar (24 ounces) chunky salsa
- 1 can (14-1/2 ounces) diced tomatoes, undrained
- 1 large onion, chopped
- 1 can (8 ounces) tomato sauce
- 1 can (4 ounces) mushroom stems and pieces, drained
- 1/2 cup each chopped green pepper, sweet red and yellow pepper
- 1/2 teaspoon dried oregano
- 1/4 teaspoon garlic powder
- 1/8 teaspoon dried thyme
- 1/8 teaspoon dried marjoram

■ In a large skillet, cook beef and sausage over medium heat until meat is no longer pink; drain. Transfer meat to a 5-qt. slow cooker. Stir in the remaining ingredients. Cover and cook on low for 8-9 hours or until vegetables are tender.

Yield: 8 servings.

zippy steak chili

DENISE HABIB, POOLESVILLE, MARYLAND

Looking for a chunky chili with a little extra-special kick for Super Bowl Sunday? Try this recipe. It was given to me by a co-worker originally from Texas. I've made it on numerous occasions and always get rave reviews.

- 1 pound boneless beef sirloin steak, cut into 1/2-inch cubes
- 1/2 cup chopped onion
- 2 tablespoons canola oil
- 2 tablespoons chili powder
- 1 teaspoon garlic powder
- 1 teaspoon ground cumin
- 1 teaspoon dried oregano
- 1 teaspoon pepper
- 2 cans (10 ounces each) diced tomatoes and green chilies, undrained
- 1 can (15-1/2 ounces) chili starter

Shredded cheddar cheese, chopped onion and sour cream, optional

Drain, rinse and pat cooked pork sausage dry with paper towels before using in a recipe to cut calories and fat.

■ In a large skillet, cook steak and onion in oil over medium heat until meat is no longer pink. Sprinkle with seasonings.

■ In a 5-qt. slow cooker, combine the tomatoes and chili starter. Stir in beef mixture. Cover and cook on low for 6-8 hours or until meat is tender. Serve with cheese, onion and sour cream if desired.

Yield: 5 servings.

mushroom salsa chili

spicy hearty chili

MELISSA NEWMAN, DANVILLE, PENNSYLVANIA

My husband, Jeff, makes THE BEST chili. This recipe is chock-full of healthy vegetables and just enough heat to warm you to your toes!

- 1 **pound lean ground beef**
- 1 **cup chopped onion**
- 10 **garlic cloves, minced**
- 2 **cups chopped green peppers**
- 1-1/2 **cups chopped sweet red peppers**
- 1-1/2 **cups chopped celery**
- 3 **jalapeno peppers, seeded and chopped**
- 3 **cans (14-1/2 ounces each) petite diced tomatoes, undrained**
- 2 **cans (16 ounces each) kidney beans, rinsed and drained**
- 1 **can (28 ounces) tomato sauce**
- 1 **can (12 ounces) tomato paste**
- 1 **cup water**
- 1/2 **cup light beer or nonalcoholic beer**
- 3 **tablespoons chili powder**
- 1 **teaspoon crushed red pepper flakes**

- In a large saucepan or Dutch oven coated with cooking spray, cook the beef, onion and garlic over medium heat until meat is no longer pink; drain. Stir in the peppers, celery and jalapenos. Cook and stir for 8 minutes or until vegetables are crisp-tender.

- Stir in the remaining ingredients. Bring to a boil. Reduce heat; simmer, uncovered, for 1 hour, stirring occasionally.

Yield: 10 servings.

Editor's Note: When cutting or seeding hot peppers, use rubber or plastic gloves to protect your hands. Avoid touching your face.

green chili stew

green chili stew

TASTE OF HOME TEST KITCHEN

Your family will love the zesty flavor of this hefty stew. You'll appreciate the change-of-pace—and the extra change you'll pocket using less expensive pork cuts! Serve it over rice, noodles or mashed potatoes.

- 1/4 **cup all-purpose flour**
- 1/2 **teaspoon salt**
- 1/4 **teaspoon pepper**
- 2 **pounds boneless pork, cut into 1-1/2-inch cubes**
- 2 **tablespoons canola oil**
- 1 **large onion, chopped**
- 2 **garlic cloves, minced**
- 1 **can (14-1/2 ounces) diced tomatoes, undrained**
- 1 **cup water**
- 2 **cans (4 ounces each) chopped green chilies**

Minced fresh cilantro, optional

- In a large resealable plastic bag, combine the flour, salt and pepper. Add pork, a few pieces at a time, and shake to coat. In a pressure cooker over medium heat, brown pork in oil. Add onion and garlic; cook and stir for 3 minutes. Add the tomatoes, water and chilies.

- Close cover securely; place pressure regulator on vent pipe. Bring cooker to full pressure over high heat. Reduce heat to medium-high and cook for 8 minutes. (Pressure regulator should maintain a slow steady rocking motion; adjust heat if needed.)

- Remove from the heat. Immediately cool

spicy hearty chili

according to manufacturer's directions until pressure is completely reduced. Sprinkle with cilantro if desired.

Yield: 6 servings.

firehouse chili

RICHARD CLEMENTS, SAN DIMAS, CALIFORNIA

As one of the cooks at the firehouse, I used to prepare meals for 10 men. This chili was among their favorites.

- 4 **pounds ground beef**
- 2 **medium onions, chopped**
- 1 **medium green pepper, chopped**
- 3 **cans (14-1/2 ounces each) stewed tomatoes, cut up**
- 4 **cans (16 ounces each) kidney beans, rinsed and drained**
- 1 **can (14-1/2 ounces) beef broth**
- 3 **tablespoons chili powder**
- 2 **tablespoons ground coriander**
- 2 **tablespoons ground cumin**
- 4 **garlic cloves, minced**
- 1 **teaspoon dried oregano**

■ In a Dutch oven or soup kettle, cook the beef, onions and green pepper over medium heat until meat is no longer pink; drain. Stir in the remaining ingredients. Bring to a boil. Reduce the heat; cover and simmer for 1-1/2 hours or until flavors are blended.

Yield: 11 servings.

I chop sweet red peppers, green peppers and onions separately, place them in glass jars, then keep them in the fridge. When any recipe calls for peppers or onions, I have them handy.— Charley G., Tucson, Arizona

zippy three-bean chili

zippy three-bean chili

AGNES HAMILTON, SCOTT DEPOT, WEST VIRGINIA

I use convenient canned pinto, black and great northern beans to speed up preparation of this special chili. The one-dish meal has a stew-like consistency and a peppy Tex-Mex flavor.

- 1 **pound lean ground beef**
- 1/2 **cup chopped onion**
- 1 **cup chopped fresh mushrooms**
- 1/2 **cup chopped green pepper**
- 1/2 **cup chopped sweet red pepper**
- 1 **garlic clove, minced**
- 2 **cups water**
- 1 **can (14-1/2 ounces) diced tomatoes and green chilies, undrained**
- 1 **envelope taco seasoning**
- 1 **can (15-1/2 ounces) great northern beans, rinsed and drained**
- 1 **can (15 ounces) black beans, rinsed and drained**
- 1 **can (15 ounces) pinto beans, rinsed and drained**
- 8 **tablespoons shredded cheddar cheese, divided**

■ In a large saucepan, cook beef and onion over medium heat until meat is no longer pink; drain. Add the mushrooms, peppers and garlic; cook and stir 3 minutes longer or until vegetables are almost tender. Stir in the water, tomatoes and taco seasoning.

■ Bring to boil. Reduce heat; simmer, uncovered, for 30 minutes. Add beans; simmer 30 minutes longer. Sprinkle each serving with 1 tablespoon cheese.

Yield: 8 servings.

firehouse chili

italian chili

italian chili

TASTE OF HOME TEST KITCHEN

By adding Italian seasoning and fresh veggies, we put an Italian spin on traditional Southwestern-style chili and created this slow-simmered dish.

> 1 **pound ground beef**
> 1/2 **pound bulk Italian sausage**
> 1 **can (28 ounces) diced tomatoes**
> 1 **can (8 ounces) tomato sauce**
> 1 **cup chopped onion**
> 1 **cup chopped sweet red pepper**
> 1 **cup water**
> 1/2 **cup chopped celery**
> 1/4 **cup beef broth**
> 1 **tablespoon each chili powder and Italian seasoning**
> 1 **teaspoon sugar**
> 1 **teaspoon minced garlic**
> 1/2 **teaspoon salt**
> 1 **can (16 ounces) kidney beans, rinsed and drained**
> 1 **cup sliced fresh mushrooms**
> 1 **cup diced zucchini**
> 3 **tablespoons minced fresh parsley**
> **Shredded part-skim mozzarella cheese, optional**

- In a large skillet, cook the beef and the sausage over medium heat until no longer pink. Meanwhile, in a 3-qt. slow cooker, combine the tomatoes, tomato sauce, onion, red pepper, water, celery, broth, chili powder, Italian seasoning, sugar, garlic and salt.

- Drain beef mixture; add to the slow cooker. Cover and cook on low for 6 hours or until vegetables are tender.

Barley and beans absorb a lot of soup broth. If you like barley in your soup but the leftovers are too thick, add extra broth to leftovers while reheating to achieve the desired consistency.

- Add the beans, mushrooms, zucchini and parsley. Cover and cook on high for 30 minutes or until vegetables are tender. Serve with cheese if desired.

Yield: 6 servings.

chili with barley

SHIRLEY MCCLANAHAN, FALMOUTH, KENTUCKY

This is one of those quick but delicious, one-dish dinner recipes you can never have too many of. It's a perfect, stick-to-the-ribs meal on those cold winter days when you need to be warmed from the inside out. My family loves it and even our minister raved about it at a potluck supper.

> 1 **pound ground beef**
> 1 **medium onion, chopped**
> 2 **garlic cloves, minced**
> 4 **cups water**
> 1 **cup quick-cooking barley**
> 1 **can (15-1/2 ounces) chili beans, undrained**
> 1 **can (14-1/2 ounces) diced tomatoes, undrained**
> 1 **can (6 ounces) tomato paste**
> 1 **envelope chili seasoning**

- In a large saucepan, cook the beef, onion and garlic over medium heat until meat is no longer pink; drain. Add water; bring to a boil. Stir in the barley. Reduce heat; cover and simmer for 10 minutes or until barley is tender. Stir in the beans, tomatoes, tomato paste and chili seasoning; heat through.

Yield: 6-8 servings.

chili with barley

chipotle turkey chili

chipotle turkey chili

CHRISTIE LADD, MECHANICSBURG, PENNSYLVANIA

I combined a few chili recipes I had and came up with this spicy, low-fat variety. It's great served with crusty rolls or baked tortilla chips.

- 1 can (7 ounces) chipotle peppers in adobo sauce
- 1-1/4 pounds lean ground turkey
- 3 medium carrots, chopped
- 1 medium green pepper, chopped
- 1/2 cup chopped onion
- 4 garlic cloves, minced
- 1 can (28 ounces) crushed tomatoes
- 1 can (14-1/2 ounces) reduced-sodium chicken broth
- 1 can (8 ounces) tomato sauce
- 1-1/2 teaspoons dried oregano
- 1-1/2 teaspoons dried basil
- 1 teaspoon chili powder
- 1/2 teaspoon ground cumin
- 1 can (16 ounces) kidney beans, rinsed and drained
- 1 can (15 ounces) garbanzo beans or chickpeas, rinsed and drained

■ Drain chipotle peppers; set aside 2 tablespoons adobo sauce. Seed and chop three peppers; set aside. (Save remaining peppers and sauce for another use.)

■ In a large Dutch oven or soup kettle coated with cooking spray, cook the turkey, carrots, green pepper, onion, garlic and reserved peppers over medium heat until meat is no longer pink; drain if necessary. Stir in the tomatoes, broth, tomato sauce, oregano, basil, chili powder, cumin and reserved adobo sauce. Bring to a boil. Reduce heat; cover and simmer for 1 hour.

■ Stir in the beans. Cover and simmer for 15-20 minutes or until heated through.

Yield: 8 servings.

Editor's Note: When cutting or seeding hot peppers, use rubber or plastic gloves to protect your hands. Avoid touching your face.

barbecued turkey chili

MELISSA WEBB
ELLSWORTH AIR FORCE BASE, SOUTH DAKOTA

The first time I made this, it won first prize at a chili cook-off. It takes just minutes to stir up, and the slow cooker does the rest. It's often requested by friends and family when we all get together.

- 1 can (16 ounces) kidney beans, rinsed and drained
- 1 can (15-1/2 ounces) hot chili beans
- 1 can (15 ounces) turkey chili with beans
- 1 can (14-1/2 ounces) diced tomatoes, undrained
- 1/3 cup barbecue sauce

■ In a 3-qt. slow cooker, combine all of the ingredients. Cover and cook on high for 4 hours or until heated through and flavors are blended.

Yield: 4-6 servings.

barbecued turkey chili

chicken chili

TASTE OF HOME TEST KITCHEN

Assemble this midday and your dinner will be ready and waiting for you when you get home. What a treat.

- 1-1/2 **pounds boneless skinless chicken breasts, cut into 1/2-inch cubes**
- 1 **cup chopped onion**
- 3 **tablespoons canola oil**
- 1 **can (15 ounces) cannellini or white kidney beans, rinsed and drained**
- 1 **can (14-1/2 ounces) diced tomatoes, undrained**
- 1 **can (14-1/2 ounces) diced tomatoes with mild green chilies, undrained**
- 1 **cup frozen corn**
- 1 **teaspoon salt**
- 1 **teaspoon ground cumin**
- 1 **teaspoon minced garlic**
- 1/2 **teaspoon celery salt**
- 1/2 **teaspoon ground coriander**
- 1/2 **teaspoon pepper**

Sour cream and shredded cheddar cheese, optional

- In a large skillet, saute chicken and onion in oil for 5 minutes or until chicken is browned. Transfer to a 5-qt. slow cooker. Stir in the beans, tomatoes, corn and seasonings. Cover and cook on low for 5 hours or until chicken is no longer pink. Garnish with sour cream and cheese if desired.

Yield: 6 servings.

chicken chili

Worcestershire sauce contains salt, vinegar, spirit vinegar, molasses, sugar, salt, anchovies, tamarinds, shallots or onions, garlic, and secret spices and flavoring.

heartwarming chili

heartwarming chili

AUDREY BYRNE, LILLIAN, TEXAS

A touch of baking cocoa gives this chili a rich flavor without adding sweetness. When I was growing up in the North, we served chili over rice. But after I married a Texan, I began serving it with chopped onions, shredded cheese and, of course, corn bread!

- 1 **pound ground beef**
- 1 **large onion, chopped**
- 2 **cans (16 ounces each) kidney beans, rinsed and drained**
- 2 **cans (14-1/2 ounces each) diced tomatoes**
- 1 **can (8 ounces) tomato sauce**
- 1 **medium green pepper**
- 3 **tablespoons chili powder**
- 1 **tablespoon ground cumin**
- 2 **garlic cloves, minced**
- 1 **teaspoon baking cocoa**
- 1 **teaspoon dried oregano**
- 1 **teaspoon Worcestershire sauce, optional**

Salt and pepper to taste

- In a large saucepan, cook beef and onion over medium heat until the meat is no longer pink; drain. Add the remaining ingredients; bring to a boil. Reduce heat; cover and simmer for 3 hours, stirring occasionally.

Yield: 4 servings.

chunky chili

JOLENE BRITTEN, GIG HARBOR, WASHINGTON

My family (especially my dad) loves chili. After experimenting with several recipes, I came up with my own version that uses ground turkey and is conveniently prepared in a slow cooker.

  1 **pound ground turkey or beef**
  1 **medium onion, chopped**
  2 **medium tomatoes, cut up**
  1 **can (16 ounces) kidney beans, rinsed and drained**
  1 **can (15 ounces) chili beans, undrained**
  1 **can (15 ounces) tomato sauce**
  1 **cup water**
  1 **can (4 ounces) chopped green chilies**
  1 **tablespoon chili powder**
  2 **teaspoons salt**
  1 **teaspoon ground cumin**
3/4 **teaspoon pepper**
Sour cream and sliced jalapenos, optional

- In a large skillet, cook turkey and onion over medium heat until meat is no longer pink; drain. Transfer to a 3-1/2-qt. slow cooker.

- Stir in the tomatoes, beans, tomato sauce, water, chilies, chili powder, salt, cumin and pepper. Cover and cook on low for 5-6 hours or until heated through. Garnish with sour cream and jalapenos if desired.

Yield: 6-8 servings.

anytime turkey chili

anytime turkey chili

BRAD BAILEY, CARY, NORTH CAROLINA

I created this dish to grab the voters' attention at a chili contest we held in our backyard. With pumpkin, brown sugar and cooked turkey, it's like an entire Thanksgiving dinner in one bowl.

2/3 **cup chopped sweet onion**
1/2 **cup chopped green pepper**
1-1/2 **teaspoons dried oregano**
  2 **garlic cloves, minced**
  1 **teaspoon ground cumin**
  1 **teaspoon olive oil**
  1 **can (16 ounces) kidney beans, rinsed and drained**
  1 **can (15-1/2 ounces) great northern beans, rinsed and drained**
  1 **can (15 ounces) solid-pack pumpkin**
  1 **can (15 ounces) crushed tomatoes**
  1 **can (14-1/2 ounces) chicken broth**
1/2 **cup water**
  2 **tablespoons brown sugar**
  2 **tablespoons chili powder**
1/2 **teaspoon pepper**
  3 **cups cubed cooked turkey breast**

- In a large saucepan, saute the onion, green pepper, oregano, garlic and cumin in oil until vegetables are tender. Stir in the beans, pumpkin, tomatoes, broth, water, brown sugar, chili powder and pepper; bring to a boil. Reduce heat; cover and simmer for 1 hour. Add turkey; heat through.

Yield: 8 servings.

Don't be misled by the label "extra light" on your olive oil. It refers to the mild flavor and very pale color of the oil, not its nutritional content.

chunky chili

CHILLED FRUIT & VEGGIE SOUPS

When we hear the term soup, cold concoctions usually don't come to mind, but a cool fruit or veggie soup is not only a great refresher, it can be nutritious, too! As a starter for a special meal or a cooler on a warm summer day, try these soups and they'll soon become favorites around your house, too.

smooth strawberry soup

smooth strawberry soup

JANICE MITCHELL, AURORA, COLORADO

Each year, we wait impatiently for the strawberries to start producing so we can make this great soup. The berry flavor is complemented by a sprinkling of sweetly spiced croutons.

- 1 quart strawberries, halved
- 2 cups apple juice
- 1 cup (8 ounces) sour cream
- 1/2 cup packed brown sugar
- 1/2 cup honey
- 2 tablespoons lemon juice
- 1-1/2 cups half-and-half cream
- 3 tablespoons orange juice, optional

CINNAMON-SUGAR CROUTONS:

- 3 slices white bread, crusts removed and cubed
- 2 tablespoons butter
- 1 teaspoon cinnamon-sugar

- In a large bowl, combine the first six ingredients. Place half of the mixture in a blender; cover and process until pureed. Transfer to a large bowl. Repeat with the remaining strawberry mixture.

- Stir in cream and orange juice if desired. Cover and refrigerate for 2 hours.

- Meanwhile, in a small skillet over medium heat, saute bread cubes in butter until golden brown. Remove from the heat. Sprinkle with cinnamon-sugar; toss to coat. Cool. Stir soup before serving; garnish with croutons.

Yield: 6 servings.

Rhubarb Basics

The stalks of rhubarb vary in color from pale pink to cherry red. Fresh rhubarb is available April through June. Select stalks that are firm and crisp, avoid any limp ones. Store unwashed rhubarb in the refrigerator for up to 1 week. Sliced rhubarb can be frozen for 9 months. Always trim and discard any leaves because they contain oxalic acid and are toxic.

spiced rhubarb soup

RENEE PARKER, CHESTER, SOUTH CAROLINA

This very pretty soup is perfect for spring. My whole family loves the fresh flavor of rhubarb, so they all really enjoy this chilled soup.

- 8 cups diced fresh or frozen rhubarb, thawed
- 3-1/2 cups water, divided
- 1 cup sugar
- 4 cinnamon sticks (3 inches)
- 1/4 teaspoon salt
- 3 tablespoons plus 1-1/2 teaspoons cornstarch
- 1 lemon slice
- 4 tablespoons sour cream

- In a large saucepan, bring rhubarb, 3-1/4 cups water, sugar, cinnamon sticks and salt to a boil. Reduce heat; simmer, uncovered, for 20 minutes or until rhubarb is tender. Discard cinnamon sticks. Strain rhubarb mixture; discard pulp. Return liquid to the pan; bring to a boil.

- Combine cornstarch and remaining water until smooth; stir into saucepan. Cook and stir for 2 minutes or until thickened. Remove from the heat; add lemon slice. Cover and refrigerate until chilled. Discard lemon slice. Ladle soup into bowls. Garnish each serving with 1 tablespoon sour cream.

Yield: 4 servings.

spiced rhubarb soup

chilled mixed berry soup

TASTE OF HOME TEST KITCHEN

As a lovely addition to a luncheon menu, our home economists recommend this cool, fruity soup featuring three kinds of berries.

> 1 cup sliced fresh strawberries
> 1/2 cup fresh raspberries
> 1/2 cup fresh blackberries
> 1 cup unsweetened apple juice
> 1/2 cup water
> 1/4 cup sugar
> 2 tablespoons lemon juice
>
> Dash ground nutmeg
>
> 2 cartons (6 ounces each) raspberry yogurt

- In a heavy saucepan, combine the berries, apple juice, water, sugar, lemon juice and nutmeg. Cook, uncovered, over low heat for 20 minutes or until berries are softened. Strain, reserving juice. Press berry mixture through a fine meshed sieve; discard seeds. Add pulp to reserved juice; cover and refrigerate until chilled.

- Place berry mixture in a food processor or blender; add yogurt. Cover and process until smooth. Pour into bowls.

Yield: 4 servings.

tart cherry soup

tart cherry soup

NEVA ARTHUR, NEW BERLIN, WISCONSIN

Serve this refreshing chilled concoction as a light first course or for dessert, topped with a dollop of yogurt or whipped topping.

> 2 cans (14-1/2 ounces each) water-packed pitted tart cherries
> 1/2 cup orange juice
> 1/2 cup sugar
> 2 tablespoons lime juice
> 1 teaspoon grated lime peel
> 1/2 teaspoon ground cinnamon
> 4 lime slices

- Place the cherries in a blender or food processor; cover and process until finely chopped. Transfer to a saucepan; add the orange juice, sugar, lime juice, peel and cinnamon. Bring to a boil. Reduce heat; cover and simmer for 10 minutes. Refrigerate until chilled. Garnish with lime slices.

Yield: 4 servings.

chilled mixed berry soup

strawberry soup

PHYLLIS HAMMES, ROCHESTER, MINNESOTA

I enjoyed a berry soup at a restaurant several years ago. The manager gave me some of the ingredients and none of the amounts, so I tinkered with what I had to get this perfect rendition.

>   1   pound fresh strawberries
>   1-1/4   cups vanilla yogurt, divided
>   3   tablespoons confectioners' sugar
>   2   tablespoons orange juice concentrate
>   1/8   teaspoon almond extract or 1/2 teaspoon lemon juice

- In a food processor or blender, combine the strawberries, 1 cup yogurt, confectioners' sugar, orange juice concentrate and extract; cover and process until smooth. Garnish each serving with a dollop of remaining yogurt.

Yield: 3 servings.

| chilled blueberry soup

chilled blueberry soup

EDITH RICHARDSON, JASPER, ALABAMA

With 100 blueberry bushes in my garden, I'm always looking for recipes calling for this sweet-tart fruit. So I was delighted when my granddaughter shared this one with me.

>   1/2   cup sugar
>   2   tablespoons cornstarch
>   2-3/4   cups water
>   2   cups fresh or frozen blueberries
>   1   cinnamon stick (3 inches)
>   1   can (6 ounces) frozen orange juice concentrate
>   Sour cream, optional

- In a large saucepan, combine sugar and cornstarch. Gradually stir in water until smooth. Bring to a boil over medium heat; cook and stir for 2 minutes or until thickened.

- Add blueberries and cinnamon stick; return to a boil. Remove from the heat. Stir in orange juice concentrate until thawed. Cover and refrigerate for at least 1 hour. Discard cinnamon stick. Garnish with sour cream if desired.

Yield: 4 servings.

strawberry soup

easy gazpacho

CHRIS BROOKS, PRESCOTT, ARIZONA

"Simple as can be" best describes this hearty cold soup. You just chop and combine the ingredients, then chill for a few hours. It tastes great with crunchy croutons or breadsticks.

- 1 **can (46 ounces) vegetable juice**
- 1 **can (10-1/2 ounces) condensed beef consomme, undiluted**
- 2 **cups chopped cucumber**
- 2 **cups chopped tomatoes**
- 1 **cup chopped green pepper**
- 1/2 **cup chopped onion**
- 1/2 **cup chopped celery**
- 1/3 **cup red wine vinegar**
- 2 **tablespoons fresh lemon juice**
- 2 **garlic cloves, minced**
- 3 **to 4 drops hot pepper sauce**

- In a large bowl, combine all ingredients. Cover and chill for 2-3 hours before serving. Serve cold.

Yield: 12 servings.

shrimp blitz

shrimp blitz

JEANNETTE AIELLO, PLACERVILLE, CALIFORNIA

On a hot summer day, this refreshing soup really hits the spot. I've made it for special-occasion luncheons as well as for casual dinners with friends.

- 1 **bottle (8 ounces) clam juice**
- 1 **package (8 ounces) cream cheese, softened**
- 1 **bottle (32 ounces) tomato juice**
- 1 **package (5 ounces) frozen cooked salad shrimp, thawed**
- 1 **medium ripe avocado, peeled and diced**
- 1/2 **cup chopped cucumber**
- 1/3 **cup chopped green onions**
- 2 **tablespoons red wine vinegar**
- 2 **teaspoons sugar**
- 1 **teaspoon dill weed**
- 1 **garlic clove, minced**
- 1/2 **teaspoon salt**
- 1/4 **teaspoon hot pepper sauce**
- 1/8 **teaspoon pepper**

- In a blender, combine clam juice and cream cheese; cover and process until smooth. Pour into a large serving bowl. Stir in the remaining ingredients. Cover and chill for at least 4 hours.

Yield: 8 servings.

easy gazpacho

spanish gazpacho

DAVE SCHMITT, HARTLAND, WISCONSIN

There's a bounty of vegetables in this tantalizing chilled soup. Its fresh flavor makes it an ideal addition to summer luncheons or light suppers.

- 5 pounds tomatoes, peeled and quartered
- 3 medium carrots, quartered
- 1 large cucumber, peeled and quartered
- 1 large sweet red pepper, quartered
- 1 large green pepper, quartered
- 1 sweet onion, quartered
- 2 garlic cloves, minced
- 1/3 cup olive oil
- 3 tablespoons balsamic vinegar
- 1-1/2 teaspoons salt
- 1/2 teaspoon pepper

- In batches, place the ingredients in a blender; cover and process until soup reaches desired texture. Pour into a large bowl. Cover and refrigerate for 1-2 hours before serving.

Yield: 12 servings.

summer soup

spanish gazpacho

Balsamic vinegar is made from sweet white grapes and aged in wooden barrels for at least 10 years (that explains the hefty price). You can substitute cider vinegar or a mild red wine vinegar.

summer soup

LIZ FICK, LITCHVILLE, NORTH DAKOTA

Unlike many chilled soups, this one isn't pureed, so you'll find plenty of chunky vegetable bits in each savory spoonful.

- 1 bottle (46 ounces) reduced-sodium V8 juice
- 2 cans (14-1/2 ounces each) Italian diced tomatoes, undrained
- 2 cans (5-1/2 ounces each) spicy hot V8 juice
- 1 medium green pepper, chopped
- 1 cup shredded carrots
- 1/2 cup chopped green onions
- 1/2 cup reduced-fat zesty Italian salad dressing
- 2 tablespoons lemon juice
- 1 tablespoon sugar
- 2 teaspoons Worcestershire sauce
- 1 garlic clove, minced
- 3/4 teaspoon celery salt
- 1/2 teaspoon salt

- In a large bowl, combine all of the ingredients. Cover and refrigerate for at least 2 hours before serving.

Yield: 12 servings.

garbanzo gazpacho

MARY ANN GOMEZ, LOMBARD, ILLINOIS

This chunky chilled soup is terrific in warm weather, but our family loves it so much I often prepare it in winter, too. I made some slight changes to suit our tastes, and the fresh, flavorful combination has been a favorite ever since.

1	can (15 ounces) garbanzo beans or chickpeas, rinsed and drained
1	can (14-1/2 ounces) Italian diced tomatoes, undrained
1-1/4	cups V8 juice
1	cup beef broth
1	cup quartered cherry tomatoes
1/2	cup chopped seeded cucumber
1/4	cup chopped red onion
1/4	cup minced fresh cilantro
3	tablespoons lime juice
1	garlic clove, minced
1/2	teaspoon salt
1/4	teaspoon hot pepper sauce

- In a large bowl, combine all the ingredients; cover and refrigerate until serving.

Yield: 6 servings.

garbanzo gazpacho

icy olive soup

icy olive soup

THERESA GOBLE, MUSCATINE, IOWA

When summer turns up the heat, I reach for this cool soup. The color of the olives contrasts nicely with the creamy yogurt base.

2	cups (16 ounces) plain yogurt
2	cans (10-1/2 ounces each) condensed chicken broth, undiluted
2	cans (2-1/4 ounces each) sliced ripe olives, drained
1	cup coarsely chopped cucumber
1/2	cup chopped green onions
1/2	cup chopped green pepper
1/2	cup sliced pimiento-stuffed olives
1/8	teaspoon white pepper

Seasoned croutons, optional

- In a large bowl, stir yogurt until smooth. Whisk in broth. Add the next six ingredients; mix well. Cover and chill for 4 hours. Stir before serving. Garnish with croutons if desired.

Yield: 6 servings.

chunky gazpacho

shrimp gazpacho

TASTE OF HOME TEST KITCHEN

This spicy tomato-based soup from our very own home economists features shrimp, cucumber and avocados.

- 6 cups spicy hot V8 juice
- 2 cups cold water
- 1 pound cooked medium shrimp, peeled and deveined
- 2 medium tomatoes, seeded and diced
- 1 medium cucumber, seeded and diced
- 2 medium ripe avocados, diced
- 1/2 cup lime juice
- 1/2 cup minced fresh cilantro
- 1/2 teaspoon salt
- 1/4 to 1/2 teaspoon hot pepper sauce

■ In a large bowl, combine all ingredients. Cover and refrigerate for 1 hour. Serve cold.

Yield: 12 servings.

chunky gazpacho

TASTE OF HOME TEST KITCHEN

Healthy vegetables are the basis of this cold, tasty soup. For a spicier version, use spicy V8 juice.

- 6 medium tomatoes, seeded and chopped
- 1 medium green pepper, chopped
- 1 cup chopped peeled cucumber
- 1 cup chopped red onion
- 4 cups tomato juice
- 1 teaspoon dried oregano
- 1 teaspoon dried basil
- 1/2 teaspoon salt
- 1/2 teaspoon minced garlic
- 1/4 teaspoon pepper
- Dash hot pepper sauce
- 3 tablespoons snipped chives
- Chopped sweet yellow pepper, optional

■ In a large bowl, combine the tomatoes, green pepper, cucumber and onion. In another large bowl, combine the tomato juice, oregano, basil, salt, garlic, pepper and hot pepper sauce; pour over vegetables. Cover and refrigerate for at least 4 hours or overnight. Sprinkle with chives and yellow pepper if desired.

Yield: 6 servings.

shrimp gazpacho

COOKING FOR 2

Looking to make a home-cooked, hearty meal without any leftovers? Try one of these never-fail, two- or three-serving soups designed just for a cozy couple's table. And since all of the soups in this chapter have been pared down to serve just a few, you won't waste food, either. So make a soup for two and enjoy a great lunch or light dinner that you won't have to eat all week!

oriental shrimp soup |

oriental shrimp soup

MICHELLE SMITH, SYKESVILLE, MARYLAND

I love this soup so much, I sometimes double the recipe. If I have leftover chicken or pork, I sometimes substitute it for the shrimp.

- 1 ounce uncooked thin spaghetti, broken into 1-inch pieces
- 3 cups plus 1 tablespoon water, divided
- 3 packets chicken bouillon and seasoning mix
- 1/2 teaspoon salt
- 1/2 cup sliced fresh mushrooms
- 1/2 cup fresh or frozen corn
- 1 teaspoon cornstarch
- 1-1/2 teaspoons reduced-sodium teriyaki sauce
- 1 cup thinly sliced romaine lettuce
- 1 can (6 ounces) small shrimp, rinsed and drained
- 2 tablespoons sliced green onion

- Cook pasta according to package directions.

- In a large saucepan, combine 3 cups water, bouillon and salt; bring to a boil. Stir in mushrooms and corn. Reduce heat; cook, uncovered, until vegetables are tender.

- Combine the cornstarch, teriyaki sauce and remaining water until smooth; stir into soup. Bring to a boil; cook and stir for 1-2 minutes or until slightly thickened. Reduce heat. Drain pasta; add the pasta, lettuce, shrimp and green onion to the soup; heat through.

Yield: 4 servings.

bacon clam chowder

BETTY LINEAWEAVER, PARADISE, CALIFORNIA

Chopping the clams into tiny pieces adds big flavor to this full-bodied chowder. Everyone says it's the best they've ever tasted. I like to serve it with garlic bread or a side salad.

- 1 can (6-1/2 ounces) minced clams
- 1 cup reduced-sodium chicken broth
- 1 medium potato, peeled and cubed
- 1/2 cup chopped celery
- 1/4 cup chopped onion
- 1/2 teaspoon chicken bouillon granules
- 1/4 teaspoon dried thyme
- 1 tablespoon cornstarch
- 1/2 cup half-and-half cream
- 1-1/2 teaspoons butter
- Dash cayenne pepper
- 2 bacon strips, cooked and crumbled

- Drain clams, reserving juice; set aside. Place the clams in a food processor; cover and process until finely chopped. Set aside.

- In a large saucepan, combine the broth, potato, celery, onion, bouillon and thyme. Bring to a boil. Reduce heat; simmer, uncovered, for 10-12 minutes or until vegetables are tender. Stir in the reserved clam juice.

- Combine the cornstarch and cream until smooth; gradually stir into soup. Bring to a boil; cook and stir for 2 minutes or until thickened. Stir in the butter, cayenne and clams. Cook and stir over medium heat for 3-4 minutes or until heated through. Garnish with bacon.

Yield: 3 servings.

bacon clam chowder

white bean soup

white bean soup

LINDA MIRANDA, WAKEFIELD, RHODE ISLAND

Cute Parmesan crisps make a zippy topping for this rich, full-flavored soup. We love the Italian sausage garnish.

- 1/4 cup shredded Parmesan cheese
- Cayenne pepper
- 1/4 pound bulk Italian sausage
- 2 tablespoons chopped onion
- 1 teaspoon olive oil
- 1 garlic clove, minced
- 1 can (15 ounces) white kidney or cannellini beans, rinsed and drained
- 1 cup chicken broth
- 1/4 cup heavy whipping cream
- 2 teaspoons sherry, optional
- 1 teaspoon minced fresh parsley
- 1/8 teaspoon salt
- 1/8 teaspoon dried thyme

- Spoon the Parmesan cheese into six mounds 3 in. apart on a parchment paper-lined baking sheet. Spread into 1-1/2-in. circles. Sprinkle with a dash of cayenne. Bake at 400° for 5-6 minutes or until light golden brown. Cool.

- In a saucepan, cook sausage and onion in oil over medium heat until meat is no longer pink; drain. Remove and keep warm.

- In the same pan, saute garlic for 1-2 minutes or until tender. Stir in the beans, broth, cream, sherry if desired, parsley, salt, thyme and a dash of cayenne. Bring to a boil. Reduce heat; simmer, uncovered, for 12-15 minutes or until heated through. Cool slightly.

When I have leftover elbow macaroni, I put it in a greased baking dish, season it with oregano, salt and pepper, top it with chopped tomatoes and shredded mozzarella cheese and bake it until it's heated through.— Carol F., Richard, Saskatchewan

- Transfer to a blender; cover and process on high until almost blended. Pour into soup bowls; sprinkle with sausage mixture and Parmesan crisps.

Yield: 2 servings.

soup for two

MARGERY BRYAN, ROYAL CITY, WASHINGTON

The flavorful broth is chock-full of veggies, chicken and macaroni. By changing the vegetables, you can make it different every time.

- 1/2 cup chopped onion
- 1/2 cup chopped carrot
- 1 tablespoon butter
- 1 can (14-1/2 ounces) chicken broth
- 2/3 cup cubed cooked chicken
- 1/2 cup cauliflowerets
- 1/2 cup canned kidney beans, rinsed and drained
- 1/4 cup uncooked elbow macaroni
- 1 cup torn fresh spinach
- 1/8 teaspoon pepper
- Seasoned salad croutons, optional

- In a saucepan, saute onion and carrot in butter for 4 minutes. Stir in the broth, chicken, cauliflower, beans and macaroni. Bring to a boil. Reduce heat; cover and simmer for 15-20 minutes or until macaroni and vegetables are tender. Add spinach and pepper; cook and stir until spinach is wilted. Garnish with croutons if desired.

Yield: 2 servings.

soup for two

potato vegetable soup

potato vegetable soup

JAN HANCOCK, EVANSVILLE, WISCONSIN

Thick as a chowder and packed with colorful veggies, this comforting soup makes cozy fare on blustery early spring evenings.

- 1 bacon strip, diced
- 1 medium potato, peeled and cubed
- 1/2 medium carrot, sliced
- 1/2 cup water
- 2 tablespoons chopped celery
- 2 tablespoons chopped onion
- 1/4 teaspoon salt
- 1/8 teaspoon pepper
- 1 tablespoon all-purpose flour
- 1 cup 2% milk
- 1/4 cup shredded cheddar cheese
- 2 teaspoons butter

- In a small saucepan, cook bacon over medium heat until crisp. Using a slotted spoon, remove to paper towels; drain. In the same pan, combine the potato, carrot, water, celery, onion, salt and pepper. Bring to a boil. Reduce heat; cover and simmer for 15 minutes or until vegetables are tender.

- In a small bowl, combine flour and milk until smooth; stir into vegetable mixture. Bring to a boil; cook and stir for 2 minutes or until thickened. Reduce heat. Add cheese and

Cut leftover beef into cubes and combine sliced red potatoes and chopped onion in a skillet with a little olive oil, salt and pepper. Fry until potatoes are tender.
—Robyn S., Ronald, Washington

butter; stir until cheese is melted. Garnish with bacon.

Yield: 2 servings.

anniversary chowder

BARBARA HARRISON, RINGOES, NEW JERSEY

I wanted to duplicate the soup we had for our wedding anniversary dinner, so I put this recipe together, using salmon we had purchased in Alaska.

- 2 small red potatoes, cubed
- 1/2 medium carrot, finely chopped
- 1/4 cup finely chopped onion
- 2 tablespoons butter
- 2 cups half-and-half cream
- 1 can (6 ounces) boneless skinless salmon, drained and flaked
- 1/2 cup fresh or frozen corn
- 1/4 teaspoon dried rosemary, crushed
- 1/4 teaspoon dried parsley flakes
- 1/4 teaspoon salt
- 1/8 teaspoon pepper
- 1/8 teaspoon rubbed sage
- 1/8 teaspoon dried thyme

- In a large saucepan, saute the potatoes, carrot and onion in butter until tender. Reduce heat; stir in remaining ingredients. Cook and stir for 10 minutes or until heated through.

Yield: 2 servings.

anniversary chowder

beefy mushroom soup

GINGER ELLSWORTH, CALDWELL, IDAHO

This is a tasty way to use leftover roast or steak and get a delicious supper on the table in about a half hour. The warm, rich taste of this mushroom soup is sure to please.

- 1 medium onion, chopped
- 1/2 cup sliced fresh mushrooms
- 2 tablespoons butter
- 2 tablespoons all-purpose flour
- 2 cups reduced-sodium beef broth
- 2/3 cup cubed cooked lean roast beef
- 1/2 teaspoon garlic powder
- 1/4 teaspoon paprika
- 1/8 teaspoon salt
- 1/4 teaspoon pepper

Dash hot pepper sauce
- 1/4 cup shredded part-skim mozzarella cheese, optional

- In a large saucepan, saute the onion and mushrooms in butter until onion is tender; remove with a slotted spoon and set aside. In a bowl, whisk the flour and broth until smooth; add to the pan. Bring to a boil; cook and stir for 1-2 minutes or until thickened.

- Add the roast beef, garlic powder, paprika, salt, pepper, hot pepper sauce and onion mixture; cook and stir until heated through. Garnish with cheese if desired.

Yield: 3 cups.

spiced shrimp bisque

beefy mushroom soup

To ripen an avocado, place it in a paper bag with an apple. Poke the bag with a toothpick in several spots and leave at room temperature. The avocado should be ripe in 1 to 3 days.

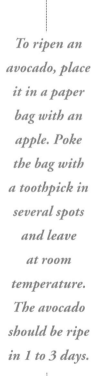

spiced shrimp bisque

KAREN HARRIS, CASTLE ROCK, COLORADO

I enjoy both Cajun and Mexican cuisine, and this elegant soup combines the best of both. I serve it with a crispy green salad and glass of white wine for a simple but very special meal.

- 1/2 cup chopped onion
- 2 garlic cloves, minced
- 1 tablespoon olive oil
- 1 tablespoon all-purpose flour
- 1 cup water
- 1/2 cup heavy whipping cream
- 1 tablespoon chili powder
- 2 teaspoons chicken bouillon granules
- 1/2 teaspoon ground cumin
- 1/2 teaspoon ground coriander
- 1/2 pound uncooked medium shrimp, peeled and deveined
- 1/2 cup sour cream

Fresh cilantro and cubed avocado, optional

- In a large saucepan, saute onion and garlic in oil until tender. Stir in flour until blended. Stir in the water, cream, chili powder, bouillon, cumin and coriander; bring to a boil. Reduce heat; cover and simmer for 5 minutes.

- Cut shrimp into bite-size pieces; add to soup. Simmer 5 minutes longer or until shrimp turn pink. Gradually stir 1/2 cup hot soup into sour cream; return all to the pan, stirring constantly. Heat through (do not boil). Garnish with cilantro and avocado if desired.

Yield: 3 servings.

golden carrot soup

ALINE WINJE, SLOCAN, BRITISH COLUMBIA

This is a great-tasting soup to make on a chilly day. It's easy to fix, too. The rich-colored soup has a mild flavor with just a hint of garlic.

- 1/2 **cup chopped onion**
- 1/4 **teaspoon minced garlic**
-   2 **tablespoons butter**
-   2 **cups water**
-   1 **cup sliced carrots**
-   2 **tablespoons uncooked long grain rice**
-   2 **teaspoons chicken bouillon granules**
-   2 **tablespoons minced fresh parsley**

■ In a small saucepan, saute onion and garlic in butter until tender. Add the water, carrots, rice and bouillon; bring to a boil. Reduce heat; cover and simmer for 20-25 minutes or until carrots and rice are very tender.

■ Remove from the heat; cool slightly. Transfer to a blender or food processor; cover and process until pureed. Return to the saucepan; heat through. Sprinkle with parsley.

Yield: 2 servings.

*I always have leftover chicken broth, so I pour the extra broth into an ice cube tray and freeze for future use.
—Maralyn B., Sebastian, Florida*

hominy sausage soup

hominy sausage soup

JESSIE GUNN STEPHENS, SHERMAN, TEXAS

I developed this subtle soup as a starter for a Southwest-style lunch. I serve it with cheese nachos and follow up with chicken or beef taco salad.

- 1/4 **pound bulk pork sausage**
-   1 **teaspoon cumin seeds**
- 1/8 **teaspoon ground coriander**
- 1/8 **teaspoon cayenne pepper**
-   2 **cups chicken broth**
- 3/4 **cup hominy, rinsed and drained**
-   1 **to 2 tablespoons chopped jalapeno pepper**
- 1/4 **teaspoon pepper**
-   1 **tablespoon minced fresh cilantro**

■ Crumble sausage into a small skillet. Cook over medium heat for 3-4 minutes or until no longer pink; drain. In a saucepan, toast cumin seeds over medium heat for 2-3 minutes or until browned. Stir in coriander and cayenne; cook and stir for 30 seconds.

■ Add the broth, hominy, jalapeno, pepper and sausage. Bring to a boil. Reduce heat; simmer, uncovered, for 12-15 minutes or until heated through. Stir in cilantro.

Yield: 2 servings.

Editor's Note: When cutting or seeding hot peppers, use rubber or plastic gloves to protect your hands. Avoid touching your face.

golden carrot soup

broccoli-cauliflower cheese soup

cream of wild rice soup

MARILYN AUSLAND, COLUMBUS, GEORGIA

My husband and I call this our favorite soup. It's so comforting when summer ends and the weather turns cool.

- 1/4 cup chopped onion
- 1/4 cup thinly sliced celery
- 1/4 cup sliced fresh mushrooms
- 1 green onion, thinly sliced
- 1/4 cup butter
- 1/4 cup all-purpose flour
- 1/8 teaspoon pepper
- 1 can (14-1/2 ounces) chicken broth
- 1 cup cooked wild rice
- 1/4 cup diced fully cooked lean ham
- 1-1/2 teaspoons diced pimientos
- 1/2 cup half-and-half
- 1 tablespoon sliced almonds, toasted, optional

- In a saucepan, saute the onion, celery, mushrooms and green onion in butter until tender. Stir in the flour and pepper until blended. Gradually stir in broth. Bring to a boil; cook and stir for 1-2 minutes or until thickened. Reduce heat. Stir in the rice, ham and pimientos; heat through. Stir in half-and-half; heat through (do not boil). Sprinkle with almonds if desired.

Yield: 3 servings.

broccoli-cauliflower cheese soup

BETTY CORLISS, STRATTON, COLORADO

Even my husband, who's never been a fan of broccoli, likes this creamy soup. It's a great way to use vegetables from our garden.

- 3/4 cup small cauliflowerets
- 3/4 cup small broccoli florets
- 1/4 cup chopped onion
- 1/4 cup halved thinly sliced carrot
- 1 to 2 tablespoons butter
- 1-1/2 cups 2% milk, divided
- 1/2 teaspoon chicken bouillon granules
- 1/4 teaspoon salt

Dash pepper

- 2 tablespoons all-purpose flour
- 1/3 cup cubed process cheese (Velveeta)

- In a large saucepan, cook the cauliflower, broccoli, onion and carrot in butter for 5 minutes or until vegetables are crisp-tender. Stir in 1-1/4 cups milk, bouillon, salt and pepper. Bring to a boil. Reduce heat; simmer, uncovered, for 5 minutes or until vegetables are tender, stirring occasionally.

- Combine the flour and remaining milk until smooth; add to saucepan. Bring to a boil; cook and stir for 1-2 minutes or until thickened. Reduce heat; add cheese and stir until melted. Serve immediately.

Yield: 2 servings.

Add leftover cooked wild rice to pancake batter. These hearty breakfast cakes, topped with butter and syrup, are a hit with my grandchildren.
—Carroll W., Foxboro, Wisconsin

cream of wild rice soup

stuffed green pepper soup

flavorful italian soup

SHIRLEY TAYLOR, RUSSIAVILLE, INDIANA

I first tasted a soup similar to this at a restaurant. They wouldn't give me the recipe, so I went home and created my own. I like to serve this spicy soup with biscuits, breadsticks or corn bread.

- 1 Italian sausage link, casing removed
- 1 can (14-1/2 ounces) chicken broth
- 1/2 cup water
- 1/2 cup cubed peeled potatoes
- 1/4 cup chopped carrot
- 1/4 cup chopped onion
- 1/4 cup canned sliced mushrooms
- 1/4 teaspoon dried basil
- 1/8 teaspoon Italian seasoning
- 1/8 to 1/4 teaspoon hot pepper sauce

Dash celery seed

Dash garlic salt

- 1/3 cup broken uncooked spaghetti (2-inch pieces)

- Crumble sausage into a large saucepan; cook over medium heat until no longer pink. Drain. Add the broth, water, vegetables and seasonings; bring to a boil. Reduce heat; cover and simmer for 30 minutes.

- Add spaghetti. Cover and simmer 8-10 minutes longer or until spaghetti and vegetables are tender.

Yield: 2 servings.

When one of our recipes calls for Italian sausage, it is referring to sweet Italian sausage. Recipes using hot Italian sausage specifically call for that type of sausage.

stuffed green pepper soup

KAYLYN VANDERVEEN, GRAND RAPIDS, MICHIGAN

My husband and I first tasted this soup in a restaurant and just loved it. Because I'm diabetic, I came up with this healthier—but just as tasty—version!

- 6 uncooked breakfast turkey sausage links, casings removed
- 1/2 cup diced green pepper
- 1/4 cup finely chopped onion
- 1/4 cup water
- 3/4 cup chicken broth
- 1 can (10-3/4 ounces) condensed tomato soup, undiluted
- 1/8 teaspoon garlic powder

Dash pepper

- 3/4 cup cooked rice

- Crumble sausage into a saucepan; cook over medium heat until no longer pink. Drain. Add green pepper, onion and water. Cover and cook for 5 minutes.

- Stir in broth; bring to a boil. Reduce heat; cover and simmer until vegetables are tender. Stir in the tomato soup, garlic powder and pepper; cover and simmer for 30 minutes. Add rice; heat through.

Yield: 3 servings.

flavorful italian soup

veggie soup for 2

LUCILLE FRANCK, INDEPENDENCE, IOWA

My sister, who worked as a dietitian for years, gave me this recipe. I sometimes double or triple this soup when my family gathers for the holidays.

- 1/2 small carrot, grated
- 1/2 celery rib, chopped
-   2 tablespoons chopped green pepper
-   1 tablespoon chopped onion
-   1 tablespoon butter
-   1 cup reduced-sodium chicken broth
-   1 can (14-1/2 ounces) diced tomatoes, undrained
- 3/4 teaspoon sugar

Dash pepper

1-1/2 teaspoons cornstarch

- In a small saucepan, saute the carrot, celery, green pepper and onion in butter until tender. Set aside 2 tablespoons broth. Add the tomatoes, sugar, pepper and remaining broth to vegetable mixture; bring to a boil. Reduce heat; cover and simmer for 10 minutes.

- Combine cornstarch and reserved broth until smooth; gradually add to the soup. Bring to a boil; cook and stir for 2 minutes or until slightly thickened.

Yield: 2 servings.

For a fast meal, saute 1/4 cup each chopped onion and green pepper. Stir in 1 cup of chopped leftover chicken, steak or pork and 1/2 cup salsa. Serve with sour cream and tortilla chips.
—Jennifer B., Fishs Eddy, New York

creamy broccoli soup

creamy broccoli soup

DIANE VENTIMIGLIA, ATLANTA, MICHIGAN

My husband and I find this great soup a tasty way to add nutritious broccoli to our diet. It's so thick and filling that all you need to complete the meal is a salad and bread.

- 3/4 cup cubed peeled potatoes
-   1 medium carrot, sliced
-   2 cups frozen chopped broccoli
-   2 tablespoons butter
-   2 tablespoons all-purpose flour

1-1/2 cups 2% milk, divided

- 1/4 to 1/2 teaspoon salt
- 1/4 teaspoon dried thyme

Dash ground nutmeg

Dash pepper

- Place potatoes and carrot in a small saucepan; cover with water. Bring to a boil. Reduce heat; cover and simmer for 15-20 minutes or until tender. Meanwhile, cook broccoli according to package directions; drain and set aside.

- In a small saucepan, melt the butter. Stir in flour until smooth; gradually add 1/2 cup milk. Bring to a boil; cook and stir for 1 minute or until thickened. Add the salt, thyme, nutmeg and pepper.

- Drain potato mixture; cool slightly. In a blender, combine the potato mixture,

veggie soup for 2

broccoli and remaining milk; cover and process until smooth. Add to the thickened milk mixture. Return to a boil. Reduce heat; simmer, uncovered, for 10 minutes or until heated through, stirring occasionally.

Yield: 2 servings.

creamy spring soup

DORA HANDY, ALLIANCE, OHIO

At the end of a tiring cold day, I wanted something quick and warm. I whipped up this hearty soup in a flash.

      1   **can (14-1/2 ounces) chicken broth**
      4   **fresh asparagus spears, trimmed and cut into 2-inch pieces**
      4   **baby carrots, julienned**
  1/2   **celery rib, chopped**
      1   **green onion, chopped**
Dash garlic powder
Dash pepper
  3/4   **cup cooked elbow macaroni**
      1   **can (5-1/2 ounces) evaporated milk**
  3/4   **cup fresh baby spinach**

■ In a saucepan, combine the first seven ingredients. Bring to a boil. Reduce heat; cover and simmer for 5 minutes or until vegetables are tender. Stir in the macaroni, milk and spinach; heat through.

Yield: 2 servings.

creamy spring soup

spicy turkey chili

Don't throw away those tough ends when trimming fresh asparagus. Cook and drain the ends, then puree them with a bit of water or chicken broth in a blender until smooth. Freeze for future use in soups.
—Pauline S., Mt. Morris, Michigan

spicy turkey chili

MARLENE GRAVAT, ST. LOUIS, MISSOURI

This chili is a scrumptious change of pace, thanks to ground turkey and the addition of cinnamon and allspice. It was an instant hit with my husband, who tends to favor traditional beef chili.

  1/4   **pound lean ground turkey**
      1   **small onion, chopped**
      1   **cup canned Italian diced tomatoes with juice**
      1   **can (8 ounces) tomato sauce**
  1/2   **cup canned kidney beans, rinsed and drained**
1-1/2   **teaspoons chili powder**
  3/4   **teaspoon white wine vinegar**
  1/2   **teaspoon Worcestershire sauce**
      1   **bay leaf**
  1/8   **teaspoon salt, optional**
  1/8   **teaspoon garlic powder**
  1/8   **teaspoon crushed red pepper flakes**
Dash ground cinnamon
Dash ground allspice
      2   **tablespoons shredded cheddar cheese, optional**

■ Crumble turkey into a saucepan; add onion. Cook over medium heat until meat is no longer pink; drain. Add the tomatoes, tomato sauce, beans, chili powder, vinegar, Worcestershire sauce and seasonings. Bring to a boil. Reduce heat; simmer, uncovered, for 15 minutes or until thickened. Discard bay leaf. Garnish with cheese if desired.

Yield: 2 servings.

BREADS & ROLLS

We all know it—homemade bread is the perfect companion to a hearty soup. This special bonus section offers a hand-selected variety of special breads from Taste of Home that complement the texture and flavors of the soups in this book. You'll find a bevy of options here.

tomato focaccia

tomato focaccia

MARY LOU WAYMAN, SALT LAKE CITY, UTAH

I top these savory appetizers with tomatoes, onion and Parmesan cheese.

2-1/2 to 3 cups all-purpose flour
1 teaspoon salt
1 teaspoon sugar
3 teaspoons active dry yeast
1 cup warm water (110° to 115°)
1 tablespoon olive oil

TOPPING:
1 tablespoon olive oil
2 tablespoons grated Parmesan cheese
1 tablespoon minced fresh rosemary
2 garlic cloves, minced
1/4 teaspoon salt
1 small red onion, thinly sliced and separated into rings
3 to 4 medium plum tomatoes, thinly sliced

- In a large mixing bowl, combine 2-1/2 cups flour, salt and sugar. Dissolve yeast in water; stir in oil. Add to dry ingredients; beat until smooth. Stir in enough remaining flour to form a soft dough.

- Turn onto a floured surface; knead until smooth and elastic, about 6-8 minutes. Place in a greased bowl, turning once to grease top. Cover; let rise in a warm place until doubled, about 30 minutes.

- Punch the dough down. On a lightly floured surface, roll dough into a 12-in. circle. Place on a greased 12-in. pizza pan. Brush with oil. Combine the Parmesan cheese, rosemary, garlic and salt; sprinkle over dough. Arrange onion rings and tomatoes over top, pressing down lightly.

- Bake at 400° for 15-20 minutes or until crust is golden brown. Cut into wedges.

Yield: 10 servings.

parmesan breadsticks

GAYLENE ANDERSON, SANDY, UTAH

These tender breadsticks fill the kitchen with a tempting aroma when they are baking, and they're wonderful served warm. My family tells me I can't make them too often.

2 packages (1/4 ounce each) active dry yeast
1-1/2 cups warm water (110° to 115°)
1/2 cup warm milk (110° to 115°)
3 tablespoons sugar
3 tablespoons plus 1/4 cup butter, softened, divided
1 teaspoon salt
4-1/2 to 5-1/2 cups all-purpose flour
1/4 cup grated Parmesan cheese
1/2 teaspoon garlic salt

- In a large mixing bowl, dissolve yeast in warm water. Add the milk, sugar, 3 tablespoons butter, salt and 2 cups flour. Beat until smooth. Stir in enough remaining flour to form a soft dough.

- Turn onto a floured surface; knead until smooth and elastic, about 6-8 minutes. Place in a greased bowl, turning once to grease top. Cover and let rise in a warm place until doubled, about 45 minutes.

- Punch the dough down. Turn onto a floured surface; divide into 36 pieces. Shape each piece into a 6-in. rope. Place 2 in. apart on greased baking sheets. Cover and let rise until doubled, about 25 minutes.

- Melt remaining butter; brush over dough. Sprinkle with Parmesan cheese and garlic salt. Bake at 400° for 8-10 minutes or until golden brown. Remove from pans to wire racks.

Yield: 3 dozen.

parmesan breadsticks

braided onion loaf

braided onion loaf

LINDA KNOLL, JACKSON, MICHIGAN

This recipe won the blue ribbon for "Best Loaf of Bread" at our county fair a few years ago. One bite and you'll see why the tender, savory slices appealed to the judges.

1	package (1/4 ounce) active dry yeast
3/4	cup warm water (110° to 115°)
1/2	cup warm milk (110° to 115°)
1/4	cup butter, softened
1	egg
1/4	cup sugar
1-1/2	teaspoons salt
4	to 4-1/2 cups all-purpose flour

FILLING:

1/4	cup butter, softened
3/4	cup dried minced onion
1	tablespoon grated Parmesan cheese
1	teaspoon paprika
1	teaspoon garlic salt, optional

Melted butter

- In a large mixing bowl, dissolve yeast in warm water. Add the milk, butter, egg, sugar, salt and 2 cups flour; beat until smooth. Add enough of the remaining flour to form a soft dough. Turn onto a floured surface; knead until smooth and elastic, about 6-8 minutes. Place in a greased bowl, turning once to grease top. Cover and let rise in a warm place until doubled, about 1 hour.

- For filling, in a bowl, combine the butter, onion, Parmesan cheese, paprika and garlic salt if desired; set aside. Punch dough down; turn onto a lightly floured surface. Divide into thirds. Roll each portion into a 20-in. x 4-in. rectangle. Spread filling over rectangles. Roll up jelly-roll style, starting from a long side.

Most bread recipes call for varying amounts of flour because it depends on the humidity when the bread is made. The range is usually 1/2 cup. Start with the least amount and add only enough extra flour to form a dough that's not sticky.

- Place ropes on an ungreased baking sheet; braid. Pinch ends to seal and tuck under. Cover and let rise until doubled, about 45 minutes. Bake at 350° for 30-35 minutes or until golden brown. Brush with melted butter. Remove from pan to a wire rack.

Yield: 1 loaf.

cracked pepper bread

JOY McMILLAN, THE WOODLANDS, TEXAS

Basil, garlic, chives and Parmesan cheese give this tall, tender loaf a real Italian flavor. When it's baking, the whole kitchen smells wonderful.

1-1/2	cups water (70° to 80°)
3	tablespoons olive oil
3	tablespoons sugar
2	teaspoons salt
3	tablespoons minced chives
2	garlic cloves, minced
1	teaspoon garlic powder
1	teaspoon dried basil
1	teaspoon cracked black pepper
1/4	cup grated Parmesan cheese
4	cups bread flour
2-1/2	teaspoons active dry yeast

- In bread machine pan, place all ingredients in order suggested by manufacturer. Select basic bread setting. Choose crust color and loaf size if available. Bake according to bread machine directions (check the dough after 5 minutes of mixing; add 1 to 2 tablespoons of water or flour if needed).

Yield: 1 loaf.

cracked pepper bread

breadsticks with parmesan butter

breadsticks with parmesan butter

ELAINE ANDERSON, ALIQUIPPA, PENNSYLVANIA

My kids love these tender breadsticks, and so does everyone else who tastes them. Any leftovers are great with butter and honey for breakfast the next day.

- 2 packages (1/4 ounce each) active dry yeast
- 1/2 cup sugar, divided
- 2 cups warm water (110° to 115°), divided
- 3 tablespoons vegetable oil
- 1 egg
- 1 teaspoon salt
- 4-1/2 to 5 cups all-purpose flour
- 1/2 cup butter, softened
- 2 tablespoons grated Parmesan cheese
- 1/4 to 1/2 teaspoon garlic powder

- In a large mixing bowl, dissolve yeast and 1 tablespoon sugar in 1 cup warm water. Add the oil, egg, salt, 2 cups flour and remaining sugar and water. Beat until smooth. Stir in enough remaining flour to form a soft dough.

- Turn onto a floured surface; knead until smooth and elastic, about 6-8 minutes. Place in a greased bowl, turning once to grease top. Cover and let rise in a warm place until doubled, about 40 minutes.

- Punch the dough down. Turn onto a floured surface; divide into 36 pieces. Shape each piece into a 6-in. rope. Place 2 in. apart on greased baking sheets. Cover and let rise until doubled, about 25 minutes.

- Bake at 400° for 10-12 minutes or until golden brown. Meanwhile, in a small mixing bowl, cream the butter, Parmesan cheese and garlic powder. Serve with breadsticks.

Yield: 3 dozen breadsticks and about 2/3 cup butter.

Don't store homemade yeast breads in the refrigerator— they'll quickly go stale. Instead, store in an airtight container at room temperature.

basil garlic bread

CHRISTINE BURGER, GRAFTON, WISCONSIN

My family members have always been big on bread. And when I created this simple loaf, they asked for it time and again. If there is any left over, I like it for toast in the morning.

- 2/3 cup warm milk (70° to 80°)
- 1/4 cup warm water (70° to 80°)
- 1/4 cup warm sour cream (70° to 80°)
- 1-1/2 teaspoons sugar
- 1 tablespoon butter, softened
- 1 tablespoon grated Parmesan cheese
- 1 teaspoon salt
- 1/2 teaspoon each minced garlic, dried basil and garlic powder
- 3 cups bread flour
- 2-1/4 teaspoons active dry yeast

- In bread machine pan, place all ingredients in order suggested by manufacturer. Select basic bread setting. Choose crust color and loaf size if available.

- Bake according to bread machine directions (check dough after 5 minutes of mixing; add 1 to 2 tablespoons of water or flour if needed).

Yield: 1 loaf.

Editor's Note: If your bread machine has a time-delay feature, we recommend you do not use it for this recipe.

basil garlic bread

mexican corn bread

SANDY GAULITZ, SPRING, TEXAS

I work at an elementary school, and a couple times a year we have a gathering where everyone brings a favorite dish to pass. A friend shared this delicious corn bread and it was a big hit.

- 2 packages (8-1/2 ounces each) corn bread/muffin mix
- 1 medium onion, chopped
- 2 cups (8 ounces) shredded cheddar cheese
- 1 can (14-3/4 ounces) cream-style corn
- 1-1/2 cups (12 ounces) sour cream
- 4 eggs, beaten
- 1 can (4 ounces) chopped green chilies
- 1/3 cup canola oil
- 1 tablespoon finely chopped jalapeno pepper

- In a bowl, combine corn bread mix and onion. Combine the remaining ingredients; add to the corn bread mixture just until moistened. Pour into a greased 13-in. x 9-in. x 2-in. baking dish.

- Bake at 350° for 50-55 minutes or until lightly browned and the edges pull away from sides of pan. Serve warm. Refrigerate leftovers.

Yield: 18-24 servings.

Editor's Note: When cutting or seeding hot peppers, use rubber or plastic gloves to protect your hands. Avoid touching your face.

bacon onion turnovers

bacon onion turnovers

CARI MILLER, PHILADELPHIA, PENNSYLVANIA

Potluck-goers will enjoy these cute pastry packets, whether they eat them by hand or by fork. The bacon-onion filling is tasty, and the turnover shell is crispy on the outside, tender on the inside.

- 3 packages (1/4 ounce each) active dry yeast
- 1/2 cup warm water (110° to 115°)
- 1 cup warm milk (110° to 115°)
- 1/2 cup butter, melted
- 2 teaspoons salt
- 3-1/2 to 4 cups all-purpose flour
- 1/2 pound sliced bacon, cooked and crumbled
- 1 large onion, diced
- 1 egg, lightly beaten

- In a large mixing bowl, dissolve yeast in warm water. Add the milk, butter and salt; beat until smooth. Stir in enough flour to form a soft dough.

- Turn onto a floured surface; knead until smooth and elastic, about 6-8 minutes. Place in a greased bowl, turning once to grease top. Cover and let rise in a warm place until doubled, about 30 minutes.

- Punch dough down. Turn onto a lightly floured surface; divide into 30 pieces. Roll each into a 4-in. circle. Combine bacon and onion; place about 2 teaspoons on one side of each circle. Fold dough over filling; press edges with a fork to seal. Place 3 in. apart on greased baking sheets. Cover and let rise in a warm place until doubled, about 20 minutes.

- Brush with egg. Bake at 425° for 10-15 minutes or until golden brown. Remove to wire racks. Serve warm.

Yield: 2-1/2 dozen.

Use a plastic bowl rather than a glass one when mixing bread dough or pie crust. The dough won't stick to the bowl and is much easier to handle.
—Gill M., Methuen, Massachusetts

mexican corn bread

a guide to herbs & spices

- Store dried herbs and spices in tightly closed glass or heavy-duty plastic containers. It's best to keep them in a cool, dry place; avoid storing them in direct sunlight, over the stove or near other heat sources.

- For best flavor, keep dried herbs and ground spices for up to 6 months. They can be used if they are older, but the flavors might not be as intense. Whole spices can be stored for 1 to 2 years.

- Select fresh herbs that are fragrant with bright, fresh-looking leaves. Avoid those with wilted, yellowing or browning leaves. Wrap fresh herbs in a slightly damp paper towel and place in a resealable plastic bag. Press as much air as possible out of the bag and seal. Store in the refrigerator for 5 to 7 days.

- To substitute dried herbs for fresh, use one-third less. For example, if a recipe calls for 1 tablespoon fresh, use 1 teaspoon dried.

ALLSPICE
Available as whole, dried berries or ground. Blend of cinnamon, clove and nutmeg. Use for baked goods, jerked meats, sauces, sausage, preserves, roasts, root vegetables.

ANISEED
Available as oval, greenish-brown seeds. Licorice-like flavor similar to fennel. Use for cookies, cakes, breads, pickles, stews, seafood, beets, cauliflower, pasta sauces.

BASIL
Available as fresh green or purple leaves or dried and crushed. Sweet flavor with hints of mint, pepper and cloves. Use for tomato sauce, pestos, chicken, meat, zucchini, summer squashes.

BAY LEAF
Available as whole, fresh or dried, dull green leaves. Savory, spicy and aromatic. Use for soups, stews, casseroles, pickles, meat.

BLACK/WHITE PEPPER
Available whole, cracked, coarse or ground (black); whole or ground (white). Black has a sharp, hot, piney flavor; white is milder. Use for all types of cooking; white adds pepper flavor without flecks.

CARAWAY SEEDS
Available as light to dark brown seeds. Sweet blend of dill and anise flavors. Use for breads, cakes, biscuits, pork, cheese, potatoes, sauerkraut.

CARDAMOM
Available as green pods, brownish-black seeds or ground. Sweet, spicy flavor and slightly pungent. Use for baked goods, chicken, curries, meat.

CAYENNE PEPPER
Available ground, also known as ground red pepper. Pungent, hot flavor. Use for chili, soups, sauces, beans, poultry, meat, seafood.

CELERY SEED
Available as light-brown or tan seeds. Strong and bitter flavor. Use for fish, eggs, cheese, salad dressings.

CUMIN
Available as seeds and ground. Pungent, earthy, slightly bitter flavor. Use for beans, chili, pork, chicken, stews.

CHERVIL
Available as fresh leaves or dried and crushed. Fresh has a hint of anise; dry has a hint of parsley flavor. Use for fish, eggs, poultry, salads.

DILL
Available as fresh leaves, dried and crushed or seeds. Fresh, sweet, grassy flavor. Use for pickles, fish, cucumbers, breads, tomatoes.

CHIVES
Available as fresh or freeze-dried hollow stems. Delicate and peppery, mild onion flavor. Use for potatoes, eggs, sauces, seafood, salads.

FENNEL
Available as seeds. Sweet and mildly licorice-like flavor. Use for baked goods, seafood, sausage, pork.

CILANTRO
Available as fresh leaves. When dried, it's known as coriander. Pungent, strong flavor. Use for ethnic dishes (such as Mexican or Asian), salsa, tomatoes, chicken, pork, seafood.

GINGER
Available as fresh root, crystallized or ground. Pungent, sweet, spicy, hot flavor. Use for baked goods, pumpkin, pork, chicken.

CINNAMON
Available as sticks or ground. Sweet and pungent flavor. Use for baked goods, fruit desserts, warm beverages.

MACE
Available ground. Nutmeg-like flavor. Use for baked goods, poultry, fish.

CLOVES
Available whole or ground. Pungent, medicinal, sweet flavor. Use for baked goods, fruit desserts, ham, lamb, warm beverages.

MARJORAM
Available as fresh leaves, dried and crushed. Oregano-like flavor. Use for tomato dishes, meat, poultry, seafood, vegetables.

CORIANDER
Available as dried and crushed leaves, seeds or ground seeds. Mildly sweet, spicy flavor. Use for ethnic dishes (North African, Mediterranean, Asian), stews, curries, pork, lentils.

MINT
Available as fresh leaves or dried and crushed. Fresh, strong, cool flavor. Use for lamb, salsas, vegetables, meats.

MUSTARD

Available ground or as seeds. Pungent, sharp, hot flavor. Use for meats, vinaigrettes, seafood, sauces.

NUTMEG

Available whole or ground. Sweet, spicy flavor. Use for baked goods, custards, vegetables, poultry, meat.

OREGANO

Available as fresh leaves, dried and crushed or ground. Pungent, slightly bitter flavor. Use for tomato dishes, chicken, pork, lamb, vegetables.

PAPRIKA

Available ground. Mild to hot, sweet flavor. Use for poultry, shellfish, meat, vegetables.

PARSLEY

Available as fresh leaves, curly or Italian (flat-leaf), or dried and flaked. Fresh, slightly peppery flavor. Use for poultry, seafood, tomatoes, pasta, vegetables.

POPPY SEEDS

Available as seeds. Nut-like flavor. Use for baked goods, fruits, pasta.

ROSEMARY

Available as fresh leaves on stems or dried. Pungent flavor with a hint of pine. Use for lamb, poultry, pork, vegetables.

SAFFRON

Available as threads (whole stigmas) or powder. Pungent, bitter flavor. Use for bouillabaisse, curries, fish, poultry, rice.

SAGE

Available as fresh leaves, dried and crushed or rubbed. Pungent, slightly bitter, musty mint flavor. Use for pork, poultry, stuffing.

SAVORY

Available as fresh leaves, dried and crushed or ground. Piquant blend of mint and thyme. Use for beans, lentils, lamb, poultry.

SESAME SEEDS

Available as seeds. Nut-like flavor. Use for breads, chicken, seafood, noodles, chickpeas.

TARRAGON

Available as fresh leaves or dried and crushed. Strong, spicy, anise-like flavors. Use for poultry, seafood, meats, vegetables.

THYME

Available as fresh leaves or dried and crushed. Pungent, earthy, spicy flavor. Use for meat, poultry, lentils, soups, stews.

TURMERIC

Available ground. Pungent, bitter, earthy flavor. Use for curries, lamb, chicken, meat, beans, lentils.

GENERAL RECIPE INDEX

POTATOES & SWEET POTATOES

PUMPKIN

RICE

SAUSAGE & HOT DOGS

SOUP MIXES

SPINACH

SQUASH & ZUCCHINI

TOMATOES

ALPHABETICAL INDEX